CHILDREN with FRAGILE X SYNDROME

A Parents' Guide

Edited by Jayne Dixon Weber

All rights reserved under International and Pan-American copyright conventions. Published in the United States of America by Woodbine House, Inc., 6510 Bells Mill Road, Bethesda, MD 20817-1636. 800-843-7323.
http://www.woodbinehouse.com

Cover Illustration: Elizabeth Wolfe

Fig. 1, Chapter 1 and Fig. 1, Chapter 3 courtesy of Genetics and IVF Institute, Fairfax, Virginia
Figs. 2 and 3, Chapter 3 courtesy of Genzyme Genetics, Scottsdale, Arizona

Library of Congress Cataloging-in-Publication Data

Children with fragile X syndrome: a parents' guide / edited by Jayne Dixon Weber
    p.   cm
   Includes bibliographical references and index
   ISBN 0-933149-77-8 (pbk.)
   1. Fragile X syndrome. 2. Fragile X syndrome—Patients—Rehabilitation.
   I. Weber, Jayne Dixon.

RJ506.F73C482000
616.85'88042—dc21

00-026932
CIP

Manufactured in the United States of America

10 9 8 7 6 5 4 3 2 1

TABLE

OF

CONTENTS

ACKNOWLEDGEMENTS

First, I wish to extend my warmest appreciation to Amy Cronister. She is the one who approached the publisher with the idea and the *need* for this book. She provided invaluable input and editorial comments to the manuscript. Thanks to her, this book is a reality!

Thanks to Mary Jane Clark who begins the book with a Foreword that is both touching and encouraging.

I am especially indebted to the individual authors of the chapters, for giving their time and sharing their knowledge all in the hope it will benefit children with fragile X syndrome and their families.

Special thanks to Dr. Randi Hagerman for sharing her vast knowledge of fragile X syndrome in the two chapters she authored.

I am grateful to all of the families who provided Parent Statements and photographs of their wonderful children. They brought *life* to this book.

Thanks to everyone at Woodbine House. I feel very fortunate to have had a chance to work with people who are so dedicated to improving the lives of children with disabilities.

My family gave me a tremendous amount of support. Special thanks go to my children, who inspire me by their simple, uncomplicated views of life, and to my husband whose love and encouragement (and meals) are never-ending.

FOREWORD

Mary Jane Clark

I remember so very clearly the day that we heard the diagnosis. David, our seven month old son, the baby who had earned a 10 Apgar score in the delivery room, had something called fragile X syndrome. Something that I never knew existed. Something that has gone on to shape David's life and everyone around him in very profound ways.

But that early spring afternoon, as a doctor and a wonderful geneticist tried to explain to two stunned parents why their baby was not progressing as he should, I could not see down the road to any positive things that could come from such a shattering diagnosis. Instead, I struggled to understand what medical professionals were saying and as the magnitude of their words sank in, I was devastated and confused.

There had been no mental retardation that I knew of in my family, yet I was a carrier. If fragile X was the most common form of genetically transferred mental retardation, why had I never heard of it? And the possible scenarios painted for David's progress terrified me.

We went for another consultation with another doctor, one who reportedly had more experience with fragile X. His outlook was grimmer still and he brought up institutionalization.

How could this all be happening?

But it was happening, and I struggled to understand my new, uncertain world with no guidebook to help me navigate this unknown and scary journey.

Fortunately for me, my geneticist told me of a professional conference on fragile X syndrome scheduled in Princeton, New Jersey. There I met Dr. Randi Hagerman who provided the first real rays of hope in that dark time. I will be forever grateful for that.

As the years have passed, I've been privileged to meet other parents with children with fragile X. Most have their own heartbreaking stories of misdiagnosis and medical ignorance. Some have done their own research in trying to figure out what is wrong with their children and have had to instruct their unknowing physicians to test for fragile X. I have been so impressed by the valiant efforts of these parents. No one wants to face that something isn't right with his or her child. It's easier to hear that "Boys are slower than girls" or "He'll outgrow it." It takes guts not to give up and to fight on for a diagnosis, when every fiber in one's being wants to deny that something is wrong.

For, in the beginning, I wished I didn't know. The diagnosis was so defining, so devastating. The future looked so bleak.

But now, 11 years later, David has done so much better than those first, dreadful predictions and I am certain it is better to know. There are so many things that can be done to maximize the outcome for our children and to make things manageable for ourselves. But, first, you have to know what you are dealing with.

For those of you who are just finding out about fragile X, take heart. This book, *Children with Fragile X Syndrome: A Parents' Guide,* is the handbook that I wished had been there a decade ago when I was struggling to understand our new world. For those of us who are further along on our fragile X journey, this wonderful compilation of topics by the top professionals in the fragile X field is a first-rate resource for understanding and dealing with our unique, challenging, loving, and oh-so-loveable children.

No one said it was going to be easy, but we are not alone. This book is a gigantic help, for our children, for their siblings, for their relatives, for their doctors, for their teachers, and for us, their parents, who love them most of all.

INTRODUCTION

Jayne Dixon Weber

When Ian was young, "Hey!" is what my sociable little fellow would say to get people to talk to him. He learned very quickly how to get someone's attention. "Hey what?" or "Hey yourself" were the responses he most often received, usually resulting in some kind of conversation, however short. We soon progressed to "What are you doing?" a question that *everyone* can answer. Ian liked to ask people that question when we were in the grocery store. "I'm shopping" or "I'm just standing here" was usually followed up with "What are *you* doing?" He would just smile, look down at the ground and say "Nothing." We are now on a first name basis with most of the people at the grocery store, the trash collectors, the firefighters, and all of our "neighbors." He talks to people when we go hiking in the mountains and anyone who has a dog. He takes a genuine interest in what other people are doing. Mister Social.

Welcome to the world of fragile X syndrome. Congratulations just for reaching this point. I am sure it wasn't easy. Getting a correct diagnosis can be a challenge. As you know it can take years, searching for a doctor who listens and understands, undergoing endless tests, and finally finding the answer to so many questions. While I cannot promise you that you won't have more struggles, my goal is to provide you with information, ideas, guidance, and inspiration. I hope to show you that you are not alone and to help you see, if you haven't already, that you have a child who's "pretty cool."

One of my greatest incentives for getting this book published was the lack of information available on fragile X syndrome, particularly information for parents. The contributing authors, a talented team of parents and professionals, have provided you with what is currently known about fragile X syndrome. Certainly new information will develop over the years, but this book will give you a great beginning, not only medically, but in your daily and family life as well.

There is a lot of information in this book and it may seem overwhelming at first. Some concepts may be applicable to you now, while other information may be relevant later. If the exact ideas don't work for you, I hope they can provide a springboard for your own innovations.

Throughout the book I have included statements made by parents who have a child or children with fragile X syndrome. They offer glimpses into real lives, and the challenges that we all face at one time or another. Through these statements, you will see that while all of our children have fragile X syndrome, they are also unique individuals.

While it might sometimes be easier if someone told you what to do, the authors have tried to provide you with the tools and resources that will help you figure out what is best for you and your child. Included at the end of the book are resources for your use. There is a *Reading List* that recommends books for additional reading. There is a *Resource Guide* that lists state and national organizations that can provide you with helpful information specific to your state. There is also a *Glossary* that explains some of the terms used in the text, as well as terms you may hear in the medical and educational communities.

Finally, a note about the use of "he" and "she" in the book. Most people who are "affected" with fragile X syndrome are boys. Girls are usually, *but not always*, affected to a lesser degree than boys are. As a result, we use "he" throughout the book and when appropriate address girls in separate sections. We do not intend to ignore anyone so if you have daughters who are affected, please know that "he" can also mean "she."

I hope the knowledge you gain from reading this book will empower you to grow as a parent, and also enable you to help your child grow. It takes courage and occasional bursts of persistence to fulfill your role. So "Hey," now that I've got *your* attention, I wish you the best of luck and hope you have many successes with your child and family.

1

WHAT IS

FRAGILE X

SYNDROME?

Randi Jenssen Hagerman, M.D.

This is the Meyer family story as told by Claire, the mother:

> *"It's a boy!" I can still remember the wonderful feelings that rushed over me when I heard those words. Although I'm not sure why, I had really wanted my first child to be a boy. All of the months of waiting, anticipating, and wondering had finally ended with a birth that, for us, was awe inspiring. We named our son Jackson.*
>
> *I was allowed three months off from my job. When I went back to work, I was permitted to work at home two days a week for my first six months back on the job. I figured I would eventually go back to work in the office full time and that it would be no big deal. But . . . .*
>
> *I had been on bed rest the last two months of my pregnancy because my blood pressure had gone up. That meant I had to quit working earlier than expected. In those two months I did a lot of thinking about my life and the new direction it was heading. I began to realize how fragile life is when my labor had to be induced because of my high*

blood pressure. Then Jackson had to be helped out because his heart rate started to drop.

He was jaundiced at birth and we watched him closely for the first couple of weeks. We laid him in the sun regularly during the day. The jaundice soon passed. The other issue we noticed at birth was that Jackson had crossed eyes. We found out that "a lot of children have crossed eyes at birth and they outgrow it."

What amazed me most during this time was the overwhelming feelings of love that I immediately developed for this child. Before I had children, a friend had tried to describe to me the feelings a child can bring out in you. I hadn't understood the kind of love he had talked about until now. I quickly realized that going back to work would be difficult. I wanted to stay home full time with this tiny, helpless baby.

Over the next month, I did not see any improvement in his crossed eyes. I took him to an ophthalmologist when he was two months old even though Jackson's pediatrician kept telling me he would outgrow it. I was concerned when the ophthalmologist, too, wanted to watch and wait for awhile. There was something else about Jackson's eyes that did not look quite right to me, but I could not figure it out. They looked a little like he had Down syndrome, but I knew he did not have Down syndrome.

Another concern we had at this time was that Jackson's cries often included periods of ear-piercing screams. I was nursing, and he seemed very sensitive to what I ate. If I ate anything spicy or any green vegetables, he would cry for one to three hours after nursing. Sometimes, though, he would have crying spells for no apparent reason at all.

At Jackson's four-month checkup, his pediatrician said everything was fine and to come back in two months. I almost shouted, "He's not tracking objects, doctor."

Making it clear that he thought I was just an overanxious new mom, he passed an object in front of Jackson's face. He looked at me quickly and said with urgency, "You have got to get this child to an ophthalmologist right away."

"Well, I just happen to have an appointment tomorrow," I said, letting him know that at least I was doing something about this issue.

"Good, I'll give your ophthalmologist a call today," was all he could mumble.

I walked into the ophthalmologist's office with mixed emotions the next day. He took a quick look at Jackson and then told me, "Your pediatrician doesn't think your child can see." I felt a huge lump forming in my throat.

"Can he?" was all I could whisper.

"I think he can, but his eyes are so crossed that he does not know what to look at. I think it's time to patch his eyes so only one eye works at a time. We're going to get him some glasses too." I was left with a glimmer of hope.

I never confronted our pediatrician about Jackson's vision difficulties. Looking back, I can't believe how naive and passive I was. I would like to think it was because Jackson was my first child and I didn't know any better. I also think that I suspected that there was something more going on than just crossed eyes and I didn't know what to do. I don't know why I didn't go out and find a new doctor right away. I wanted to believe that he was truly interested in finding out what was going on with Jackson.

The hope that Jackson could see continued when we started patching his eyes. Each day we covered one of his eyes for a couple of hours. Every day we alternated eyes. Finally, he started tracking objects. He could see. He could really see.

After a while, Jackson couldn't stand the feeling of the patch on his face. He started to tear it off. I knew the patches were really helping him, though, so I did everything I could to keep them on his face. One day we resorted to using duct tape to keep the patch on. I sat down and cried when I saw what he looked like. I went into the ophthalmologist's office and told him I couldn't do this anymore. Instead, he suggested putting a patch on a glass lens rather than on his face. Thank goodness I had found a doctor who was willing to listen.

At Jackson's six-month checkup, I told the pediatrician that Jackson was not sitting up. I added that Jackson's back had always seemed to curve whenever I held him up. I agreed with the doctor (probably the only time I ever agreed with him) that Jackson did not have curvature of the spine. He told me that as Jackson learned to crawl, his back would get stronger, and he would be able to sit up. "He'll outgrow it!" So my husband, Tony, and I got down on the floor with Jackson and actually moved his arms and legs for him in an attempt to teach him to crawl. Within the next week, Jackson started crawling more.

We went to visit my family when Jackson was just past six months of age. He had some unusual crying spells during the next few days. We attributed it to the plane flight and the change of environment. Then, the night before we were supposed to come home, Tony, who was changing Jackson's diaper, called for me. Jackson's entire groin area was swollen and hard as a rock. My mother, a surgical nurse, said quite calmly, "We need to get him to the emergency room, right away." It was that "right away" that hung in my ears as I held him in my arms in the car. The emergency room doctor took one look at him and said he had to bring in a pediatrician. The pediatrician took one look at him and said he had to bring in a urologist. The urologist recommended immediate surgery. During that surgery a fourth doctor had to be called in— a general surgeon—to repair an incarcerated hernia, caused when part of the intestine fell through the membrane, forming a "kink" in the bowel. We spent the next week in the hospital.

I had a lot of time to think in the week after Jackson's surgery. It was a week of unexpected "vacation" and even with all of the anxiety surrounding the surgery, I remember the week being a calm, reflective time. When anyone close to you has unexpected surgery, it stops you in your tracks emotionally. Fifty years ago this type of hernia would have killed a child. I began to wonder about my son and his many challenges.

When Jackson was ten months old, we went back to the pediatrician for a checkup. Jackson's back was still curving when I held him. I don't think I will ever forget my pediatrician's words, which seemed laced with disgust at my overprotectiveness. "Well, if you are so concerned about *it, go have him evaluated by a physical therapist." Well, I did and he was immediately diagnosed with hypotonia— low (floppy) muscle tone in the upper body. Physical therapy was started immediately.*

After a couple of physical therapy sessions, the social worker who worked in the pediatric unit asked to speak with me. She said something like, "We think your son may have more issues than just hypotonia. We recommend further testing." I think I was partially devastated and partially relieved that these issues weren't all in my head. We had him tested further. We started Jackson in speech and occupational therapy right away.

When Jackson was 16 months of age, the pediatrician suggested we look into having tubes implanted into Jackson's ears to reduce the number of ear infections he got. By this time he had had 15 ear infections. The Ear, Nose, and Throat (ENT) Specialist could not believe we had waited so long to consider tubes. I blamed it on the pediatrician.

Unfortunately, the tubes did not make much of a difference. Jackson's ear infections continued. After another year, the ENT recommended taking out Jackson's adenoids and putting in new tubes. Jackson was not quite two years of age when he had this third surgery. His recovery took a week. The good part? I held him eight hours a day for that week and loved every minute of it.

Around this time, we finally switched pediatricians. I cannot believe I did not make the switch earlier. Our new pediatrician looked at Jackson's history and immediately tested for fragile X syndrome. And guess what? I came home from swimming one night and Tony put his arm around me and said, "You are looking at a little boy with fragile X syndrome." "Noooo," I fell into a chair crying. Deep in my heart I was not surprised. Tony started crying. Jackson started crying. I looked up at Tony and whispered, "I think I'm pregnant."

Our new pediatrician's nurse had mistakenly given me the go-ahead to get pregnant. I had called the doctor's office to ask about getting pregnant because the testing for fragile X syndrome was taking so long (over two months). We had not researched information on fragile X syndrome because we didn't want to get ourselves worked up over something we didn't know for sure. So we did not know about the hereditary aspects of the syndrome. The pediatrician realized the nurse's mistake, but forgot to call me back.

When the pregnancy diagnosis was confirmed, I just stared at the nurse in my OB's office. Her smile turned to concern. "Is this good news?" she asked. I paused, probably a little too long and replied quietly, "Yeah, I think so." She had no idea what had happened in my life during the past two weeks. I was still in shock. It angers me that this joyous time was stolen. Instead of surprising my husband with some happy news, I looked at him with tears in my eyes and nodded my head up and down.

There is good news. If I had waited to get the test results before getting pregnant, I probably would never have had another child. As it was, my new baby was the daughter I had always wanted. Elizabeth was tested in utero and found to not even be a carrier of an altered fragile X gene.

My son's diagnosis was the end of a time of uncertainty and the beginning of a new journey. We knew we needed to muster up the drive and courage to raise a child like Jackson. We wanted and needed to understand more about fragile X syndrome.

▪▪ Introduction

Many, many parents have struggled with the mystifying behaviors and developmental differences the Meyer family wrestled with for so long. Despite their hardships, however, the Meyers were lucky. In the past, there were no answers. Instead, parents were often told that their child had hyperactivity, a short attention span, learning difficulties, or developmental delays, but no one could explain the whole puzzling picture. Now we can. We know that what is behind these behaviors and differences is something called fragile X syndrome, and that it is a lot more common than anyone ever realized.

Although much still remains to be learned about fragile X syndrome, awareness of the condition is increasing, and effective medical intervention and educational strategies are being developed.

Today, children with fragile X syndrome no longer face lifetimes of low expectations and limited opportunities. Your role as parents is critical and, to be effective, you need to understand fragile X syndrome, what it is, what causes it, and how it affects your child. This chapter starts you off with the basics of fragile X syndrome.

∷ What Is Fragile X Syndrome?

Fragile X syndrome is a genetic (inherited) condition. It is caused by a change, or mutation, in the genetic information on the X chromosome. This change leads to a broad range of symptoms. The early signs of fragile X syndrome usually include language delays and hyperactivity. There is often intellectual impairment, which can range from mild learning disabilities to severe mental retardation. The intellectual, physical, and behavioral difficulties tend to be greater in boys than in girls.

Current estimates are that 1 in 1000 to 4000 people worldwide have developmental delays due to fragile X syndrome. Additionally, about 1 in 250 females and 1 in 700 males is a "carrier" for fragile X syndrome, but do not have any symptoms. A carrier is a person who is unaffected intellectually, but who is at risk to have children or grandchildren with fragile X syndrome.

The following section gives a brief overview of the genetic changes that cause fragile X syndrome. Chapter 3 provides more details on genetics.

∷ Why Is the Condition Called Fragile X Syndrome?

The human body is made up of billions of tiny cells. Every part of our bodies, from our brain to our muscles to our toenails, is made of cells. Cells perform the essential jobs of life. Our muscle cells move our bodies, the cells that make up our heart pump blood, and our brain cells enable us to think. In almost each and every cell throughout our bodies there are genes.

Genes control our heredity. They determine the makeup and characteristics of every person. Physical characteristics such as eye, hair, and skin color are fixed by genes. Other characteristics such as intelligence and personality are also strongly influenced by genes.

DNA, deoxyribonucleic acid, is the chemical basis of genes. It has a structure resembling a twisted ladder; the rungs of this ladder carry the genetic code involving four nucleotide bases: adenine, thymine, guanine, and cytosine. Every three nucleotides in the DNA ladder form the code for an amino acid; these amino acids are the building blocks of proteins which are the main structures in our bodies.

Genes are grouped into clusters called chromosomes. These chromosomes are in turn grouped into pairs. One chromosome in each pair comes from the mother's egg and one from the father's sperm at conception. That is what causes the almost infinite variety among people; everyone has their own unique genetic makeup.

Ordinarily, human cells contain 23 pairs of chromosomes, for a total of 46. One of these pairs is the sex chromosomes. This set of chromosomes determines whether an embryo develops as a boy or a girl. If the sex chromosomes consist of two X chromosomes, the baby is a girl. If there is one X and one Y chromosome, the baby is a boy. The mother always gives an X chromosome. The father can provide either an X or a Y chromosome, which determines the sex of the child.

Fragile X syndrome gets its name from an unusual feature that can be seen on the X chromosome in people with the condition and in some carriers. When the chromosomes of someone with fragile X syndrome are prepared in a laboratory and viewed under a microscope, a percentage of the cells appear to have an X chromosome that has a dangling piece or that is broken off at the bottom end. See Figure 1. This chromosome is called the "fragile X chromosome," and the location on the chromosome where the break appears is called the "fragile X site."

▪ What Causes Fragile X Syndrome?

For many years the connection between the fragile X chromosome and the characteristics seen in people with fragile X syndrome was poorly understood. In 1991, however, the gene that causes the condition was identified by an international group of researchers. This gene, called "FMR1," which stands for "Fragile X Mental Retardation 1," is located in the region of the fragile X site.

Fragile X syndrome occurs when the FMR1 gene becomes altered. The alteration, or mutation, in the FMR1 gene is an expansion of a sequence of Cytosine-Guanine-Guanine (CGG) repeats. Although everyone has an FMR1 gene with approximately 5 to 50 CGG repeats, the number of CGG repeats in people with fragile X syndrome is far greater, 200 or more. This is called a "full mutation," and it causes the FMR1 gene to turn off or not work properly. An FMR1 gene that is turned off does not produce enough or any of the protein coded for by the FMR1 gene. Although the exact function of this protein is not yet fully understood, it is known to be critical to intellectual development and functioning. People who are carriers of fragile X have between 50 and 200 *CGG* repeats; this is termed a "premutation." Most carriers are unaffected intellectually because they have normal levels of the FMR1 protein. However, carriers are at very high risk to have children with the full mutation and fragile X syndrome.

∷ FIGURE 1. FRAGILE X CHROMOSOME

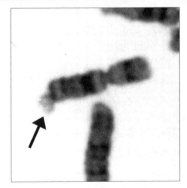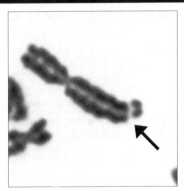

Two ways fragile X chromosomes may appear: an X chromosome with a dangling piece (left) and one that is broken (right).

If your child has fragile X syndrome, it is because he inherited an altered or mutated FMR1 gene from one of his parents. As far as anyone knows, the altered gene for fragile X syndrome is always passed down from one affected family member to another.

▪▪ Why Does Fragile X Syndrome Vary in Severity?

Why are some children with the fragile X chromosome affected only mildly or not at all and others seriously affected? Recent research seems to point to an answer. Studies show that how seriously a fragile X chromosome affects a child depends on the number of generations through which it has been passed. This is because each time the altered gene is passed on, the excessive genetic material at the fragile site usually expands. Once a person has 200 or more CGG repeats, they have a full mutation and are usually affected by fragile X syndrome. It is therefore possible that children who show no symptoms of fragile X syndrome could just be carriers of the mutation (or premutation) that has not passed through enough generations to create symptoms. Studies also show that, for unknown reasons, the expansion to a full mutation occurs only when the mother passes on the gene, not the father.

Girls with a full mutation usually have milder symptoms than boys. Remember, girls have two X chromosomes, so the undamaged X chromosome can usually compensate for the one with the fragile X mutation. In girls, fragile X syndrome most commonly causes math difficulties, a short attention span, and sometimes language delays. In boys, on the other hand, there is only one X chromosome, so there is no way to compensate if a full mutation is present and no FMR1 protein is produced. Thus, males are usually more significantly affected by fragile X syndrome than females.

Of course, a child's fragile X gene is not the only factor that affects his or her development. Other genes that the child has and the family environment in which he is raised can also have a great impact on development. This is another reason there is so much variability in how fragile X syndrome affects people.

▪▪ What Are Children with Fragile X Syndrome Like?

Children with fragile X syndrome are basically like every other child. They are human beings who happen to have some differences. As you read about the characteristics of fragile X syndrome, try not to lose sight of your child and what makes him like every other child.

In explaining how fragile X syndrome can affect children, it helps to look at boys and girls separately. This is because some effects of fragile X syndrome often differ significantly between the sexes. However, even if your child is a girl, you should read the sections on males. Girls can have the same types of symptoms as boys.

Physical Characteristics

Some children with fragile X syndrome, especially girls, are physically just like any child. Others have obvious or subtle physical differences. The most common differences are described below.

Boys

Most boys with fragile X syndrome show some or all of a group of physical differences. In fact, it is this group of differences that often enables doctors and scientists to identify children who might have fragile X syndrome.

There are three specific differences in appearance that tend to occur most often in boys with fragile X syndrome. Called the "triad" by doctors and researchers, these differences are:

1. a long face;
2. prominent or long ears; and
3. large testicles (macroorchidism).

These differences are cosmetic; they do not affect how boys function in life. Their longer face is usually noticeable only by someone trained to spot this feature.

As with all the symptoms of fragile X syndrome, researchers do not yet know how they are caused by the specific genetic mutation except that it is related to a lack of FMR1 protein. We do know, however, that 80 to 90 percent of males with fragile X syndrome have one or more of the characteristics listed above by the time they reach adulthood. Some features, such as a long face and macroorchidism, are more common in males who have reached puberty. Many other physical features are associated with fragile X syndrome. The list below includes the characteristics that doctors may look for in diagnosing fragile X syndrome. Bear in mind, however, that not every boy with fragile X syndrome will have all of the following characteristics. Sometimes there are no obvious physical symptoms at all. Remember, too, that some features are more noticeable as people get older. Medical concerns and treatment are discussed in Chapter 4.

Loose Connective Tissue. The material that holds our bodies together (for example, ligaments, tendons, and skin) tends to be looser or more relaxed in males with fragile X syndrome. This results in some very common physical differences, including unusually flexible or hyperextensible finger joints and double-jointed thumbs and fingers. The loose connective tissue may also affect your child's feet. Boys with fragile X syndrome can also have pronated ankles (ankles that turn in) and flat feet (no arch in the foot). The use of orthotics or other shoe inserts may remedy these characteristics.

On rare occasions, loose connective tissue can cause joints to be easily dislocated. That is, the bones can become displaced from their sockets or joints. The joints usually affected are the elbows, knees, and hips. Joint dislocations must be treated by a medical doctor.

Loose connective tissue is also thought to be associated with recurrent ear infections, perhaps because the eustachian tube, the small tube that connects the middle ear with the back of the throat, is floppy or collapsible. Loose connective tissue may also explain the increased frequency of hernias seen in people with fragile X syndrome.

Heart Murmurs. According to one study, about 50 percent of men with fragile X syndrome were found to have "mitral valve prolapse." In this condition, the mitral valve, which usually prevents the blood from reentering the upper chamber of the heart after it has been pumped out, is floppy. As a result, it may swing back during contraction of the ventricles, causing a clicking sound or a murmur that can be heard during an examination. This characteristic may be related to the loose connective tissue which has been associated with fragile X syndrome. If a click or murmur is heard by your doctor, a further evaluation by a cardiologist is advised. The study that found this condition in men with fragile X syndrome also found that mitral valve prolapse is less common in young children with fragile X syndrome and suggests that this problem develops in adolescence and adulthood.

Low Muscle Tone (Hypotonia). Some young children with fragile X syndrome have muscle tone that is decreased in the torso area. As a result, they may not be able to sit alone by six months of age and may not learn to walk until later than usual. Hypotonia usually improves with age and with treatment such as physical therapy and occupational therapy.

Large or Cupped Ears. Perhaps related to the loose connective tissue, many individuals with fragile X syndrome have ears that are larger and wider than usual. Often they have a cupping or bowing at the top because the fold near the top of the ear is often not well-developed. When this fold is not present, the ear will cup back and then forward causing the ears to be more prominent.

Simian Crease, Sydney Line, or Single Palmar Crease. About 40 percent of males with fragile X syndrome have a single crease instead of a double crease on the upper part of the palm. Often the crease will be continuous from one side of the palm to the other.

Vision Impairments. Males with fragile X syndrome can have a wide variety of vision impairments, including nearsightedness, farsightedness, amblyopia (vision loss from a lazy eye), strabismus (crossed eyes), astigmatism (blurred vision caused by irregularities in the shape of the cornea), and nystagmus (jerking of the eyes back and forth). These conditions usually respond to treatment.

Palate. Another characteristic seen in many people with fragile X syndrome is a palate (roof of the mouth) that is often high and somewhat narrow. People with fragile X syndrome are also slightly more likely to have cleft palate (a split in the roof of the mouth) than usual. The high, narrow palate can be associated with dental malocclusion ("bite" problems) and sometimes orthodontia is necessary for treatment.

Scoliosis. Preliminary studies have shown that about 10 to 20 percent of males with fragile X syndrome have scoliosis, or an abnormal curvature of the spine. This may be related to hypotonia or loose connective tissue. Your doctor should periodically check to see if a curve is developing. If found, this condition should be treated and monitored by an orthopedic doctor.

Motor Tics. Approximately 10 to 20 percent of children with fragile X syndrome have motor tics, jerky movements, that generally affect the face, arms, or legs. For example, repetitive eye blinking or facial grimacing may occur. This problem is also seen in 10 percent of the population without fragile X syndrome. If motor tics are excessive, they can be treated with medication. In general, motor tics improve with age.

Head Size and Shape. The head of a child with fragile X syndrome tends to be a little larger in circumference than other children's and the forehead may be broad. This increased size is related to the fact that children with fragile X syndrome have a larger brain than other children. There appears to be a tendency for overgrowth in children with fragile X syndrome. That is, height and weight, as well as head size, may be larger than other children. This should not be of concern because the tendency for overgrowth tends to disappear by puberty. Young adults with fragile X syndrome usually have the same head size as other people. Some reports suggest that males with fragile X syndrome often have a large chin.

Height. Some boys with fragile X syndrome are taller than average in early childhood. By adulthood, however, about 20 to 25 percent of males with the condition are significantly shorter than the general population.

Skin. The skin, particularly the skin on the hands of people with fragile X syndrome, often has a very soft or velvet-like quality. This characteristic may be associated with loose connective tissue, discussed above.

Club Foot. Club foot is the result of underdevelopment in the lower leg and malformation of the foot which makes it shorter and more compact. Its cause is not known. Boys with fragile X syndrome are more likely to have club foot, although this occurs in fewer than 5 percent of individuals with fragile X syndrome.

Hallucal Crease. Many boys with fragile X syndrome have a hallucal crease; that is, they have a single crease in the middle of the ball of their feet.

Pectus Excavatum of the Chest. Many boys with fragile X syndrome have an indentation in the center of the chest. The indentation is a result of the way the bones come together and it is usually minimal in people with fragile X syndrome. It is not associated with medical complications.

Attractive Appearance. Children with fragile X syndrome, in general, are very attractive physically. The feature of soft skin seems to play a role in this attribute.

Girls

Girls are much less likely than boys to have the physical characteristics typical of fragile X syndrome. Many girls have no noticeable physical differences at all, but some girls may have several of the features described above. The physical differences that girls are most likely to have are: 1) slightly prominent ears; 2) a long face; 3) flexible finger joints; and 4) flat feet.

Intelligence and Learning

Just as fragile X syndrome can cause a spectrum of physical features, it can also affect mental abilities in several different ways. The clinical terms used to describe intellectual impairment are learning disability and mental retardation. Each of these terms covers a wide range of abilities. Fragile X syndrome is the most common cause of what doctors refer to as "inherited mental retardation." But not all children with fragile X syndrome have mental retardation. Some score in the low average, average, or above average range on tests of general intelligence, but have mild cognitive difficulties or learning disabilities in one or more specific areas. To get an idea of how fragile X syndrome will affect your child's cognitive abilities, it may help to learn a little about the differences between mental retardation and learning disabilities.

Learning Disabilities

A learning disability is a neurological condition that interferes with a child's ability to learn information or skills in one or more specific areas. For example, a child might have a learning disability that makes it difficult for him to learn to read or to understand math concepts. Or a child might have a learning disability that interferes with his ability to form letters on paper with a pencil or pen. In other areas of learning, however, the child would have average or above average abilities.

Depending on their severity, learning disabilities can have a slight to significant impact on a child's ability to learn. A child with a mild learning disability may get by so well in the classroom that his learning disability is never diagnosed. A child with moderate or severe learning disabilities may need to receive special educational help in order to make progress in the areas in which he has difficulties.

Mental Retardation

Mental retardation is defined as a lifelong condition that causes significantly below average abilities in all areas of learning and development. As a result of these lower than average abilities, children who are diagnosed with mental retardation learn skills more slowly than other children, and may never learn some skills as well as other children. Areas of learning that are impaired include cognitive (reasoning, problem-solving) skills, as well as social, communication, movement, and self-help skills.

Two factors are taken into account in determining whether a child has mental retardation. First, how does he function on a day-to-day basis compared to other children his age? Is he learning to walk, talk, and identify colors at about the same age as most children, or is he lagging behind? Second, how does he perform on tests of general intelligence (IQ tests) compared to other children his age? The average range of scores of the general population on these tests is generally considered to be between about 80 and 110. More than two-thirds of all people taking IQ tests score in this range. Scores between 70 and 79 are regarded as being in the borderline range between average intelligence and mental retardation. If your child's IQ score falls below 70, he will usually be diagnosed with mental retardation.

There is a wide range of intelligence among all children, including those diagnosed with mental retardation. Each person has learning strengths and learning weaknesses whether they score in the "normal" range or in the range of mental retardation. Children with an IQ roughly between 50 and 69 are described as having mild mental retardation. Children who are somewhat more affected are said to have moderate mental retardation, with IQ scores between 35 and 50. Children with IQ scores lower than 35 are said to have severe mental retardation. The degree of a child's mental retardation may also be described by how much support the child needs to function independently. That is, an individual with mental retardation may need intermittent, limited, or extensive support, and may need different levels of support at different stages in his life. The impact of fragile X syndrome and mental retardation on development is explained in Chapter 7.

Cognitive Abilities of Individuals with Fragile X Syndrome

Males

To date, researchers have discovered that males who are carriers with a premutation usually have normal intelligence. Approximately 1 in 700 males in the general population has the premutation. Males with the full mutation have cognitive deficits ranging from mild to severe. In the past, most of these males scored in the 40s on IQ tests, and therefore had moderate mental retardation. More recently, less affected individuals have been identified who produce a significant level of the FMR1 protein. Approximately 10 to 15 percent of males with fragile X syndrome may actually have a borderline to low normal IQ with learning disabilities. These children usually have difficulty with their attention span, impulsivity, auditory processing, math skills, abstract reasoning, and distractibility.

Females

Females with fragile X syndrome can have the same range of intelligence as boys with fragile X syndrome. In general, however, girls are less likely than boys to have cognitive difficulties. And when they do have cognitive difficulties, they are usually milder. Approximately 70 percent of girls with the full fragile X mutation score below 85 on IQ tests. Some of these girls have borderline normal intelligence, and others have mild mental retardation. The other 30 percent of girls with the full mutation have an IQ greater than 85, although the majority have learning disabilities.

The most common learning disability for girls is in math. This is thought to be because fragile X syndrome impairs abstract reasoning skills, and math involves a great deal of abstract reasoning. Many girls also have language learning disabilities. They may be slow in their language development, they may have difficulty in expressing themselves well, and may have trouble understanding complex information. Sometimes a short attention span interferes with processing auditory information.

Cognitive Strengths

Although many boys with fragile X syndrome have cognitive delays, they often share certain cognitive strengths as well. About 30 percent of boys with fragile X syndrome read far better than would be expected based on their overall IQ score. They may also have good memories for information they pick up on their own from the environment. This may include sports trivia, information about television programs, and information from signs in their environment. Most are good at remembering information about subjects in which they have a special interest such as cars, trucks, dinosaurs, dogs, and sports. Young children with fragile X syndrome often score particularly well on measures that evaluate vocabulary development and visual matching tasks. Many young children with fragile X syndrome may score higher on intelligence tests when they are under the age of seven than they do later in childhood or after puberty. This is because, in many instances, children with fragile X syndrome learn at about 50 to 70 percent of the rate of their peers. Consequently, a 7 year old may function at about a 4 to 4½ year level (a 2½-year difference), whereas a 17 year old may be developmentally between 10 to 12 years of age (at least a 5 year difference).

Sensory Integration Characteristics

Sensory integration refers to our ability to take in, sort out, and make use of information received from our senses of sight, hearing, taste, smell, touch, and movement. Sensory integration is how we organize sensory input to make sense of the information we receive, and how we organize our movements or verbal responses. For example, it enables us to recognize that a car speeding rapidly toward us honking its horn means danger, and that we should jump out of the way.

Sensory integration is essential for almost every human activity. For example, writing with a pencil requires that you hold the pencil firmly, but not too firmly, press against the paper with the right amount of pressure, and use your sense of sight to guide your muscles to make the proper movements.

Many children with fragile X syndrome have some type of difficulty with sensory integration, or difficulty processing, organizing, and responding to information relayed to the brain from their senses. These sensory difficulties may include over- or under-sensitivities to particular sensations or the inability to screen out important sensations from unimportant ones. Some researchers think that the reason for these difficulties is that people with fragile X syndrome have a cerebellum that is somewhat smaller than usual. The cerebellum is a part of the brain that plays a key role in processing sensory information.

The sensations that children with fragile X syndrome most often have trouble integrating are touch, sound, sight, and movement.

Touch. Many children with fragile X syndrome are extra sensitive to input from their sense of touch. They may dislike the way certain kinds of fabric feel against their skin, or find the touch of labels in their clothing extremely irritating. They may be very sensitive to or dislike people touching them. They may also dislike the feeling of certain foods in their mouth and they may gag easily. When a child actively resists or becomes upset at certain kinds of touch, he is said to be tactile defensive. About 60 to 90 percent of boys with fragile X syndrome have some tactile defensiveness and girls who are significantly affected may also have the condition.

Sound. Children with fragile X syndrome often have trouble with auditory processing—dealing with sounds in their environment. They may not be able to comprehend complex information or filter out unimportant noises like the humming of a light fixture. Loud sounds or high pitched noises may also be very bothersome especially if they are unexpected.

Sight. Children with fragile X syndrome are easily overwhelmed by the visual information they take in through their eyes. As with sounds, they often appear unable to filter out the important sights from the unimportant. For example, they may be confused or upset by flashing lights or feel uncomfortable at parties or in a grocery store where a lot of different activities are going on at once. Because of their confusion or irritation, they may have a behavior outburst such as yelling or a tantrum in these circumstances. Children with fragile X syndrome are also very sensitive to eye contact and may avoid it.

Movement and Balance. There are several other sensations that children with fragile X syndrome can have trouble integrating. One type of sensation is processed through the vestibular system, which helps control posture, balance, and muscle tone. Another type is processed through the proprioceptive system, which provides input about the position of the body in space. Difficulty processing this sensory input can lead to complications such as toe walking. A child may have dyspraxia, difficulty planning a sequence of movements such as touching each finger in sequence or writing.

Behavioral Characteristics

A variety of behaviors are also associated with fragile X syndrome. These behaviors include hand flapping, hand biting, poor eye contact, and frequent tantrums. Many researchers believe that these behaviors are the result of the sensory integration difficulties described above. Remember, children with fragile X syndrome are unable to block out or organize incoming sensations in the usual way. So they may use behavior such as hand flapping in an attempt to calm themselves, to make sense of their world, or to give themselves consistent stimuli or input. When too much information floods the brain, a tantrum may be their body's response to the overstimulation. Because many children with fragile X syndrome have speech delays, behavior is one way they may "speak."

The most common behaviors of children with fragile X syndrome are explained below. About 60 to 90 percent of boys with fragile X syndrome have at least one of these behaviors. Girls who are significantly affected by fragile X syndrome may also have one or more of these behaviors.

Hand Flapping or Hand Biting. Some children with fragile X syndrome flap or bite their hands when they are excited or angry. They may do this to try to calm themselves or to give their brain one clear stimulus to focus on when they are overwhelmed. Sometimes children bite their hands so often that calluses form. Some children give these behaviors up on their own or can be taught not to bite or flap their hands, but children who are significantly affected may continue to do them as adults.

Stiffening. When a child with fragile X syndrome is upset, frustrated, or angry, his whole body or just his hands may tense up or become rigid in a fisting movement. Young children who do not have fragile X syndrome may have this movement up until approximately two years of age. I used to call this behavior a "power salute" when I saw it in my own children when they were angry. In children with fragile X syndrome, this power salute can be seen periodically even into adulthood when they are angry.

Tantrums. Although children with fragile X syndrome have more tantrums than other children, they are not "bad" children. They simply tend to be more confused or overwhelmed by sights and sounds in their environment. Often their reaction to this overstimulation may be to cry, yell, hit, or flail about. These tantrums may be worse in children who do not have adequate language to communicate their feelings or needs. Violent or aggressive behavior occurs in 30 percent of boys, although this is not usually noticed until puberty. It may be important to modify your child's environment to avoid overstimulation or tantrum behavior.

Poor Eye Contact. Many children with fragile X syndrome have great difficulty making direct eye contact with anybody for more than a few seconds. This may be because gazing directly into someone else's eyes gives them more visual information than they can process. They look away to avoid being overwhelmed.

Difficulty Relating to Others. Most children with fragile X syndrome are quite interested in relating socially to other people. The sensory integration issues, however, often cause them to avoid eye contact or to turn away physically from other children who are interested in interacting. In addition, their hyperactivity, impulsivity, and short attention span may cause others to turn away from them.

Perseveration. Perseveration, or repeating the same actions, words, or behavior over and over, is very common among children with fragile X syndrome. For example, they may ask a question many times, even after the answer is given, or may play a videotape over and over again. Your child is not trying to be obstinate. Instead, this perseveration is believed to be related to the lack of FMR1 protein. It is important to recognize this behavior and help your child shift to another activity. This type of behavior may bother people who do not understand the circumstances. It is also habit forming, but by changing it, you are helping your child get off the "treadmill." In dealing with this type of behavior, it may also be helpful to turn the tables on your child. For example, if your child keeps asking you, "Why is the sky blue? Why is the sky blue?" Try asking *him* the same question. It could be that he knows the answer and just wants to demonstrate that to you.

Hyperactivity and a Short Attention Span. All boys who are affected by fragile X syndrome have some difficulty with a short attention span and approximately 80 percent are also hyperactive. Approximately 30 percent of girls who have the full mutation also have a short attention span and difficulty with concentration, although hyperactivity is less frequent. Hyperactive behavior includes moving around from one activity to another, having difficulty in sitting in a seat, having trouble listening to information, or focusing on a task for more than a few moments or minutes. These difficulties can interfere with learning because it is difficult for the child to concentrate on the information that the teacher is giving him.

Anxiety. Anxiety is common in both boys and girls affected by fragile X syndrome. The majority of girls with fragile X syndrome are shy and socially anxious, particularly in situations involving many people. They may also become anxious in new or unfamiliar situations. Girls who have hyperactivity may have less social anxiety because impulsivity may make them more likely to jump into social interactions. In boys with fragile X syndrome, anxiety can combine with the sensory integration issues and lead to a feeling of being overwhelmed or overstimulated in new situations.

Hypervigilance. Many children with fragile X syndrome have hypervigilance, or have an intense interest in events that are occurring around them. This may be related to anxiety and may be a significant issue in new situations. Your child may learn the names of all of the children in his class in the first week of school or he may be the first to know who is absent from school on a particular day. Hypervigilance may increase anxiety, which in turn may increase hypervigilance, and this can become a vicious cycle. You can help this by watching for the physical signs, such as increased perseveration, hand flapping, or hand biting. You may need to break this cycle. Talk about the activity with your child in very matter-of-fact terms. Keep it very simple. If the anxiety continues or escalates, redirect your child to a calmer activity.

Depression. Girls who are carriers of fragile X syndrome often have difficulties with depression or mood changes. This may be related to a tendency to worry about details. If they have a child who has fragile X syndrome, their depression may also be related to taking care of a child who has challenging behavior.

Autism and Autistic-like Behaviors. About 15 percent of children with fragile X syndrome have severe difficulty in relating to others, which can be associated with autism. This is more common in children who have moderate or severe mental retardation. These children may meet the diagnostic criteria for autism in addition to having fragile X syndrome. The majority of children with fragile X syndrome, however, do not have autism, although they may have many autistic-like features such as hand flapping and poor eye contact as discussed above. When a child has difficulty relating to others—also known as "pervasive lack of relatedness"—he may not try to communicate or interact with other people. He may avoid contact with others almost completely and withdraw into his own world.

Behavioral Strengths

Children with fragile X syndrome are generally very social and friendly with other people. Their excellent imitation skills are very obvious when it comes to behavior. Children with fragile X syndrome model many of the behaviors they observe—and you know that means both the good and the not-so-good behaviors. Therefore it is important whenever possible to integrate your child into educational or recreational settings with typical peer models.

Speech and Language Characteristics

Children with fragile X syndrome are often slower to learn to speak. Although there is a wide variability among males, females are generally not as affected. Some boys reach speech milestones at the same age as other children. Others are significantly delayed and may use sign language for several years.

Once children with fragile X syndrome do learn to speak, many tend to perseverate. That is, they repeat words, phrases, and sentences over and over. They also tend to talk fast and loud. There is a cluttered quality to their speech—words are not pronounced very clearly, and may sound mumbled. Your child may also have trouble focusing on a topic, wandering from subject to subject (called tangential speech). For example, your child may all of a sudden start talking about something he saw on a movie from the night before. Children with fragile X syndrome may also have echolalia, a tendency to repeat what they hear word-for-word, again both the good and the bad, sometimes to excess.

Speech and Language Strengths

The quality of speech generally improves tremendously with age. Although there can be drawbacks associated with their ability to mimic, such as learning inappropriate words, this is more than outweighed by the strength of their ability to repeat what they hear. Just be aware what your child might hear in a particular situation. Children with fragile X syndrome usually have receptive language skills that are *much* better than their expressive skills. That is, they understand a lot more than they can verbally tell you. Although this is true for many children, it is particularly so with children who have fragile X syndrome.

Your Child's Health

In general, children with fragile X syndrome are just as healthy as other children. The characteristic of loose connective tissue, however, may predispose your child to have more frequent middle ear infections (otitis media) or sinus infections. Because recurrent ear infections can interfere with speech and language development, it is

important that they be
treated properly. Also, about
15 to 20 percent of children
with fragile X syndrome
have seizures. Seizures are
involuntary movements, behaviors, or changes in consciousness triggered by abnormal electrical discharges
in the brain. Chapter 4 explains the medical concerns
and treatments associated
with fragile X syndrome.

▪▪ The Diagnosis of Fragile X Syndrome

It is important to make the diagnosis of fragile X syndrome as
early as possible so that appropriate treatment can be started for
your child. Early diagnosis is also important so that genetic counseling can be available for both you and your relatives. Genetic counseling is described in detail in Chapter 3.

If every child with fragile X syndrome had all or most of the
symptoms described in this chapter, it would be easier to diagnose
the condition. Some children with fragile X syndrome, however,
have only a few of the symptoms described. For example, a girl
with fragile X syndrome might have ears that are slightly larger or
more prominent than usual and appear rather shy or socially anxious, but otherwise seem like any other girl. In addition, young
children often do not have the typical physical features associated
with fragile X syndrome. In these children, it is usually their behavior, such as language delays, hyperactivity, or tantrums, that suggests the diagnosis.

The checklist in Figure 2 was developed to help physicians and
other health care providers identify children who *might* have fragile
X syndrome. This checklist can be scored with zero points if the feature is not present, one point if the feature is present to a mild or
borderline degree or has been present in the past, and two points if
the feature is definitely present. Children with an overall score of 16
or higher have a 45 percent chance or greater of having fragile X

syndrome. If there is a family history of mental retardation, the chance of having fragile X syndrome is at least 30 percent.

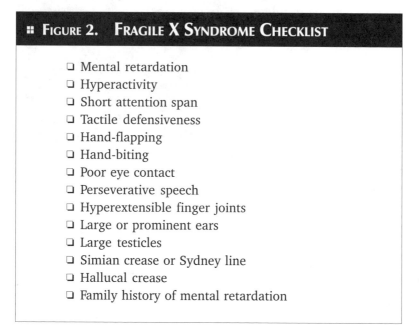

■■ FIGURE 2. FRAGILE X SYNDROME CHECKLIST

❑ Mental retardation
❑ Hyperactivity
❑ Short attention span
❑ Tactile defensiveness
❑ Hand-flapping
❑ Hand-biting
❑ Poor eye contact
❑ Perseverative speech
❑ Hyperextensible finger joints
❑ Large or prominent ears
❑ Large testicles
❑ Simian crease or Sydney line
❑ Hallucal crease
❑ Family history of mental retardation

If your child seems to fit the physical and behavioral profile for fragile X syndrome, your doctor should order a blood test to confirm the diagnosis. Since 1991, the test of choice for diagnosing fragile X syndrome is a DNA test that looks specifically at the FMR1 gene and any alteration in its size. This test can identify both carriers who are unaffected and individuals who have the condition, as well as be used for prenatal diagnosis.

■■ Treatment of Fragile X Syndrome

As yet there is no cure for fragile X syndrome, but there are effective ways of treating many of its symptoms. With the right kinds of help, all children with fragile X syndrome can increase their independence, improve their ability to get along in the world, and maximize their development and learning. The precise form your child's treatment will take depends on his unique strengths and needs. Most likely, however, he will benefit from a combination of special education, individual therapy, and medication.

If your child has any cognitive difficulties, he can benefit from an educational program tailor-made to help him learn. At school, teachers will work with him using strategies known to be helpful with children who have fragile X syndrome, learning disabilities, hyperactivity, or attentional difficulties. For example, because children with fragile X syndrome often have trouble with abstract learning, teachers will try to make learning experiences as concrete as possible. The use of good role models can also be used in school. See Chapter 8 for more information on educational programs for children with fragile X syndrome.

Your child might also benefit from a wide variety of therapies. Speech and language therapy, for example, can help your child learn to communicate more fluently and understandably. Occupational therapy can help him overcome his sensory integration problems, or teach him to calm himself when he is feeling overwhelmed. Physical therapy can improve your child's muscle tone, as well as help him get over gravitational insecurities or movement planning difficulties. Vision therapy can help his eyes move in a coordinated fashion.

Some symptoms of fragile X syndrome can be improved through medication. As mentioned above, seizures can frequently be reduced or eliminated with medication. There are also medications that can improve hyperactivity or distractibility.

Finally, you as a parent will play a critical role in your child's treatment. Teachers and therapists will show you ways that you can help your child reach his potential. For example, they might help you learn to structure the events in your child's day so that he will be less likely to get overloaded.

▪▪ Fragile X Syndrome—Past, Present, and Future

Fragile X syndrome has probably been around as long as man has existed. It occurs in all ethnic and racial groups around the world. But until recently, it was not recognized as a syndrome at all. Instead, people with fragile X syndrome were diagnosed as having mental retardation, autism, Tourette syndrome, Sotos syndrome, Prader-Willi syndrome, or X-linked mental retardation. And because they were misdiagnosed, they did not receive the education and support that would have allowed them to fit into society. Consequently, many people with fragile X syndrome were consigned to unfulfilling lives, or even ended up in institutions. Even today, it is likely that a significant number of residents in state institutions (approximately 3 to 7 percent) are people with undiagnosed fragile X syndrome. In 1943 two physicians from England, Martin and Bell, first reported a family tree that included several males who had mental retardation. They did not recognize the physical features of fragile X syndrome, nor were they able to make the diagnosis. However, they reported that there are hereditary causes of mental retardation most likely associated with the X chromosome, which affects males more severely than females. In 1969 Herbert Lubs published a paper describing fragile X syndrome in two boys with mental retardation. He first identified the fragile site on the bottom end of the X chromosome, which was subsequently used for diagnosis until DNA testing became available.

In the late 1970s Grant Sutherland from Australia recognized the importance of using folic acid deficient tissue culture media to identify the fragile site on the bottom end of the X chromosome. This allowed many people worldwide to make the diagnosis of fragile X syndrome during the 1980s. Finally, in May of 1991, a collaborative, international effort, including Stephen Warren from Atlanta, Georgia, David Nelson from Baylor Medical School in Houston, Texas, and Ben Oostra from Rotterdam in the Netherlands, jointly described the *CGG* expansion in addition to sequencing and naming the FMR1 gene. Internationally, other groups, including Jean-Louie Mandel and Isabel Oberle in France, Grant Sutherland in Australia, and Kay Davies in England, also recognized the *CGG* expansion in those with a full mutation. The identification of the FMR1 mutation led to widespread use of DNA testing to more exactly identify fragile X syndrome in individuals who are affected and in carriers who are unaffected.

Although past generations of children with fragile X syndrome were shortchanged in opportunity and understanding, today's generation is more fortunate. Recent advances such as improvement in medications, therapies, and educational intervention, coupled with almost certain future breakthroughs, should ensure that children with fragile X syndrome will have more meaningful, fulfilling lives.

One reason things are looking up for children with fragile X syndrome is that society is gradually becoming educated about the condition. Although fragile X syndrome is still far from being a household word, newspaper and journal articles, television programs, and parent advocates are all helping to increase public awareness. Obviously the more people who know about fragile X syndrome, the less likely children with the condition will be misdiagnosed, mistreated, and misunderstood.

Direct DNA testing has led to the identification of more mildly affected individuals with fragile X syndrome, particularly individuals who just have learning delays or emotional difficulties. Direct DNA testing has also improved prenatal diagnosis. Research is now underway concerning the function of the FMR1 protein. This protein has important functions in the brain and in the connective tissue, and understanding these functions will lead to better treatment. Protein replacement may be possible in the future.

Gene therapy is on the horizon and may be a reality within the next 10 years. Gene therapy includes replacing or altering the mutated gene so that it works normally. This may provide a more specific therapy or perhaps a cure for fragile X syndrome.

∷ Conclusion

Before your child was diagnosed with fragile X syndrome, you probably had many questions. Why does he act the way he does? Why is his learning so slow? Why does he have so many outbursts?

Getting the diagnosis and reading this chapter probably gave you the answers to just some of your questions. Although you likely have a better understanding of why your child is the way he is today, you may still have many questions about what to expect tomorrow. This is as it should be. There are an infinite variety of factors affecting your child's future, only one of which is fragile X syndrome. For example, the quality and amount of education and therapy your child receives can have a significant influence on his development, and so can the types of support you give him at home. Furthermore, the FMR1 gene is not the only gene that influences your child's intellectual, language, and attentional abilities, and is, therefore, not the sole determinant of his potential.

True, if your child is affected by fragile X syndrome, his future will be different from what it would be otherwise. Your involvement in your child's life may also be different than you had planned, but different does not necessarily mean worse. Chances are the more you get to know your child, the more you will lose sight of the differences. Instead you will come to see him for who he is—your child, who just happens to have fragile X syndrome. Having knowledge of fragile X syndrome will help you understand and interact with your child more effectively. Sharing this knowledge will also help others give him the best treatment available.

■■ Parent Statements

We had no clue what fragile X syndrome was—never heard of it.

I knew something was wrong because our son cried constantly.

Before we got the diagnosis, we just wanted our son to stop vomiting.

We investigated numerous other possible reasons for his delays before the fragile X testing was done.

When Alex was 18 months and not talking we knew something was wrong. So, first we had a hearing test and then an MRI, then an ABR to look at the signals from the ear to the brain, then an EEG (the worst), then lastly the bloodwork (cytogenetic), which came back positive.

A developmental pediatrician ordered a chromosome test and we were told the results were negative for any genetic illnesses, including fragile X. The results were actually "inconclusive" and one year later, at the urging of our school staff, our son had the FMR1 test and he was diagnosed with fragile X.

We went through eleven months of crying for five to six hours at a time. Nine hospitalizations for crying and reflux. Four neurologists prescribing every medicine from aspirin to phenobarbital.

Our son's first pediatrician didn't have a clue. He made me feel bad when I questioned him or raised concerns.

I had concerns from the time he was about a year old. So many toys and activities didn't interest him, including playing with other children. His motor skills were delayed as was his speech, and he was very clingy—however, our pediatrician felt he was developing appropriately.

When we finally received a diagnosis, my first reaction was, "I've been expecting so much of the boys—and they are retarded! Perhaps I should expect less of them." Of course, that reaction lasted only a few minutes—as I realized that they would have to negotiate life in the world, regardless of their specific diagnosis.

Will he live a normal life span or will physical limitations (mitral valve prolapse, seizures) cut it short? I wanted to know if we had to prepare ourselves not only for his learning struggles but also for an early death.

I was very anxious to hear success stories about fragile X individuals and their careers, because I wanted to know our son still had a lot of opportunities for success as an adult.

After we got the diagnosis, we felt so grateful and blessed that so many researchers, doctors, and geneticists had been studying fragile X syndrome for the benefit of people they didn't even know.

There's a whole world of disability that I never knew existed.

I am very grateful that my son is a gorgeous, handsome boy, but because his "condition" is not visibly apparent, people are sometimes quick to judge his behavior…and our parenting.

Living with fragile X syndrome has also shown us how many caring and concerned people there are in the world and that's been one of the silver linings.

I want him to feel his life is full and happy and not dictated by a diagnosis.

I wonder how people will treat him when I'm not there or another advocate is not there to explain his strengths and his needs.

My highest hope is he will fit into school and society without anyone hurting his feelings or making him feel inadequate.

I worry about what will happen to our son after we die. I don't spend a lot of time thinking about it, but that's scary to me.

I just want my son to have some friends as he grows up and when he is older.

2

YOUR EMOTIONS

Jayne Dixon Weber

▪▪ Introduction

So now, you have finally gotten the diagnosis. Fragile X syndrome. Whether your child was diagnosed yesterday or two months ago or two years ago, the variety and intensity of emotions this diagnosis brings out can be overwhelming. Although each of us will experience our own unique blend of emotions in our own unique sequence, you will feel, to one degree or another, many of the emotions this chapter discusses.

The emotions you will feel are very personal. Remember always, however, that they are nothing to feel ashamed of. Almost every parent of a child with fragile X syndrome—not to mention parents of other children with and without disabilities—feels a wide range of both positive and negative emotions. It is completely natural for this to happen. So please don't burden yourself with guilt or shame.

You will experience one set of feelings when your child is young, and another set when he is older. The challenges that come with growing up will set off some of these emotions and your past experiences will influence how you respond. Some of the emotions will recur throughout your life. For example, you may feel shock for a while when you get the diagnosis of fragile X syndrome for your child. But you may feel sadness off and on for the rest of your life. Then again, you may discover an abundance of love inside you.

This chapter discusses the range of emotions you may have felt from before your child was diagnosed to what you may be feeling now. And it offers suggestions on ways to deal with these emotions.

■■ What Is the Matter with My Child?

Remember this from before you got the diagnosis? "My child is not meeting developmental milestones." "My son is not sitting up and he is ten months old." "My child does not talk." "Why is my child so aggressive?"

The questions went on and on.

Guilt

As if there's not enough things in life that can bring on this emotion. "Maybe it was something I did when I was pregnant." "Maybe it is my parenting style." "Maybe I should have nursed (or nursed a little longer)." "Maybe I did not provide enough stimulation for my child when he was a baby."

Frustration

Feel free to scream at the following sentence. "Your child will outgrow it."

And then there's, "Don't worry so much. Boys are always slower."

It is hard enough dealing with a child who is challenging in so many ways. Add in a pediatrician who pats you on the head and tells you not to worry. It is always a good idea to talk to more than one doctor, if you question what your doctor is saying. It can take a tremendous amount of strength and courage, not to mention time, to find someone willing to really listen to you about your child and his challenges. But do what it takes to find a good doctor. And when you hear a medical doctor give his *opinion*, find the courage to speak up if you don't agree. The first time is the hardest. It becomes easy very quickly—automatic before you know it. And the doctor will listen.

Ambivalence

You know something is going on with your child, but you really do not want to hear it. "Your child appears to have developmental delays in some areas." What does that mean? You may ask, "Don't you know what the problem is? How many things do you want to test for?" At this point, without a diagnosis, emotions often cycle back to guilt. It can be a lonely time.

The rest of this chapter focuses on the feelings you may experience when you receive the diagnosis of fragile X syndrome for your child. The information presented below may confirm what you have already been feeling inside and will hopefully help you through a rough time.

■■ "Your Child Has Fragile X Syndrome"

When you finally hear those words, a lot of different emotions can follow.

Relief

"There is a reason for all these challenges I have been facing. It was not something I did or did not do when I was pregnant. It has nothing to do with my discipline style. It is so good to finally stop wondering and guessing."

This emotion will be the only short-lived one. Other emotions will arrive shortly, and they will stay for a while.

■■ After the Diagnosis

After receiving the diagnosis of fragile syndrome, you may feel a flood of emotions. At first it will feel like riding a roller coaster while wearing a blindfold. You know there are going to be ups and downs, you know there will be some twists and turns, but you do not know when any of these things will happen. In the next stage, which could last between six months and two years, you are still on the roller coaster, but you don't have the blindfold on anymore. You are able to see what is coming. With time, you will get off the roller coaster, and you will design your own ride. You will be in control again.

Shock

"I can't believe this is happening to me. What is this going to do to the rest of my life? To my family? To my marriage? To me?"

Confusion

"I have never heard of this. What does genetic disorder mean? What does this mean for my child? Can it be fixed? Will he outgrow it? This kind of thing only happens to somebody else. What do I do now? Where do I begin? Should I tell other people in my family? Should I keep it a secret?"

"What will I do when someone makes fun of my child? Will I attempt to talk to the person, scream, or crawl inside a shell?"

Anger

"This is not fair. I have worked too hard in my life to end up with this. I do not want to deal with this. I do not have time to deal with this."

Denial

"Maybe my child will grow out of this. What if the blood samples taken were mixed up with somebody else's? What if the testing was not done correctly? My child seems to be doing better already."

Fear and Apprehension

"I'm scared now...of everything about my child."

Sadness and Sorrow

"I want to stay in my house and not come out. I do not have anything to look forward to. It has been a struggle since he was born and now I know it won't ever end. Will I ever laugh again? Will I even smile? I will remember the day we got the diagnosis for the rest of my life."

"Birthdays are so difficult because they are a reminder of how delayed my child is. I can't imagine what it would be like to have a child who doesn't have fragile X syndrome."

"My child does not have any friends. Other children his age all have friends. They invite each other over to play. Our phone never rings."

"Sometimes I just cry all day."

"I am so tired."

Helplessness

"I can't do this. I don't even know where to begin. Will somebody get me started in the 'right' direction? Will somebody tell me what to do? Will somebody do this for me? I am so overwhelmed."

Frustration

"I can't figure out why my child ... cries so much, does not like to be touched, is so aggressive, can't overcome this?"

"Why can't other people be more understanding and have more patience with my child? Why can't I?"

"My doctor does't even seem to understand what I'm going through."

Uncertainty

"What does this mean for the future—both my child's and my family? I need to know what is going to happen. I can't stand all of the unknowns."

Resentment

"No one I know has this problem. Their children seem to learn so easily and quickly. Their children get dressed on their own. Everything I do with my son seems to take so much time and effort. I just want something to be easy like it is for them."

Grief

"I have so much sorrow . . . for me and my child. I am so depressed. I am exhausted. There go all my dreams. Why bother even dreaming anymore?"

Betrayal

"Why do *I* have a child like this? What did I do to deserve this? Why did my doctor go on and on about how he was going to outgrow this? Why didn't anyone prepare me for this?"

Shame and Embarrassment

"I do not share stories about my child. I do not compare 'notes' with my friends. I am even uncomfortable with my good friends, much less with friends I see infrequently."

"I do not like to go out in public. I love my son to death but when he starts flapping his arms, I either want to hug him to hold his arms down or act like I don't know him."

"I constantly make excuses for my child—about his still wearing diapers, about his speech, about his lack of fine motor skills, about his lack of gross motor skills, about ...."

Hopelessness

"There is no solution to this problem. What do I have to look forward to?"

Loneliness

"Nobody can relate to what I am going through. I do not even want to attempt to describe or discuss it because other people just don't get it.'"

Guilt

"This is all my fault."

"I found myself apologizing to my husband for doing this to him."

"My daughter who is unaffected is a carrier."

Self-Pity

"My life is so tough. You think you've got problems. Nobody's problems are as bad as mine. I don't want this life!"

Anxiety

"I need to know everything *today* about fragile X syndrome."

"I feel I have to take my child to as many therapists as I can. I don't even want to be late; if anything I arrive early. I would never miss an appointment unless my child is really sick."

▪▪ Take a Deep Breath

Whatever you are feeling is okay. You are not the only one who has felt this variety of emotions. They are *all* acceptable in your situation.

One mother told me that it took her awhile to feel comfortable telling her neighbors about her son and the diagnosis of fragile X

syndrome. Then when she did, some of the neighbors told her that they suspected all along that something was not right, but that it was the doctor's job to say something, not theirs. When she questioned her daycare providers, they said the same thing, "Oh yeah, he should be making a lot more types of sounds." The mother told me, "People I trusted made me feel stupid. It made me angry and I resented them. Those feelings were piled on top of the emotions involved in dealing with the diagnosis."

Another mom told me that she felt so guilty about having a child with fragile X syndrome that she found herself apologizing to her husband. After the first time her husband slowly shook his head and said, "You don't need to apologize now or ever. It was something that *we* did not know about. It's no one's fault." After a hug he added, "It was just meant to be."

One dad was relieved to get the diagnosis. "My wife and I knew there was something different about our son. We've met lots of other parents where we take our son to therapy who don't have a diagnosis. They run test after test, and then they rerun some tests. I feel we can now focus our work. And the diagnosis has helped us understand some of our son's behavior." But there was another emotion the dad still felt: "While I was relieved to get the diagnosis, I can still remember the *sting* I felt when I heard, 'Your son has fragile X syndrome.'"

Love

"I cannot believe how much I love my son. I cannot believe how much I have learned from him. I have a newfound respect for life. And my son loves me so unconditionally. I make mistakes and he is so forgiving."

Acceptance

"I am proud of my son. So what if he can't do things as well as others—I know he is working hard."

Happiness

"My son is so happy . . . it makes *me* happy. Sometimes I even consider myself fortunate."

Confidence

"I can do this!"

Excitement

"I have a wonderful child who I love and who loves me. I'm going to see things in life I have never seen before!"

Hopeful

"I've got challenges ahead of me, but things always seem to work out...."

■■ Dealing with Your Emotions

You

Emotions are a big part of you. Look at how much your daily actions, thoughts, and words are responses to how you feel. Think about the days when you feel happy and carefree. The roof could cave in and you would laugh it off. Think about those days when you feel angry and resentful. You may as well wear a sign on you that says "Stay Out Of My Way!"

Some people go up and down emotionally all the time. Others are up a lot. And there are those who are down most of the time. Become aware of who you are emotionally. It will give you a sense of being in charge.

One way to gain some awareness is to write a list of (major) events that have happened to you or thoughts you have had since the time you found out you were pregnant through to today. Think back to those events and right next to them write down at least one emotion you remember feeling. Here's an example:

I found out I was pregnant.	*Happiness*
We delivered a healthy baby boy.	*Love*
Our son was sick a lot.	*Concern*
I got the runaround from my pediatrician.	*Frustration*
We got the diagnosis.	*Shock, betrayal, guilt*
I told another child that my son did not have a disability	*Denial, embarrassment*
Our son turned two years old.	*Sadness, grief, happiness*

We tried to find a babysitter.	*Resentment, hopelessness*
Our son started to put words together.	*Happiness, love*
Another child made fun of our child.	*Anger, loneliness*
I found myself yelling at my son all day (or what seemed like all day).	*Guilt, self pity, frustration*
We started our son on medication.	*Fear, guilt, embarrassment, relief*
Our son started kindergarten.	*Fear, happiness, sadness, relief*
My son said, "I love you" for the first time	*Love, happiness*
One day the guys who drive the garbage truck let our son throw trash into the back of the truck and work the levers that push and compact the trash.	*Shock, happiness, love*
Our son turned eight years old.	*Shock, grief, happiness, love*
As our son walked out the door one day, he announced he was going over to a neighbor's house to play. He never heard my, "Have a good time!"	*Happiness*

Everyone experiences and deals with emotions in their own way. One way of dealing with the avalanche of emotions that may descend upon you is to become aware of the emotion you feel. Acknowledge the feeling, whether it is good or bad. Give it a name. Accept it. It is a part of you. I wrote this one day:

I feel so sad. Sad for my child, sad for me. This is what it feels like to be sad. Now, why am I sad? This

*morning at the park two children made fun of the way
my son looks. They mimicked his speech and his facial
expressions. This was the first time this had ever happened to me. When I told a friend, she wanted to know
what I had said to the other children. "Nothing," I said,
"I was so shocked I didn't know what to say. I was
scared. What should I say?" My friend told me that I
have to educate others and she gave me some examples
of what I could say when it happened again ... because
she said it would happen again. I'm still sad, but I've
learned something from being sad. Next time this
happens, it will be different.*

If you are particularly troubled by your emotions, try to figure
out what brought them on. There is not always a specific event. The
cause could be something that someone said. It could be physiologi-
cal, environmental, or just where you are in your life. Birthdays may
be hard. Maybe some friends tell you about their wonderful vacation
to a theme park and you wonder if your child will ever be able to
tolerate a place like that, much less enjoy it.

I always seem to have a difficult time when my son, Ian, has his
birthday. His Individualized Education Program or IEP (discussed in
Chapter 8) usually occurs around the same period. It is at that time
every year when we are apprised of Ian's current status, and we have
to help determine goals for the coming year. It is the time of year
when some people see my child's disability before they see him. They
view my child as a list of characteristics, and not always the positive
ones. My difficulty around this time seems to be passing quicker
every year. I seek to continually surround myself with positive people,
and the numbers are growing.

Times around big transitions can be difficult as well. My emotions started swirling when Ian started preschool. They went hay-
wire when he started kindergarten. Although I found Ian's preschool
situation to be ideal, elementary school has been much more of a
challenge. There are more *systems* to deal with. Ian's needs continue
to change and become more complicated. This has sparked frequent
emotional adjustments for me.

As you struggle through some of the more trying emotions,
remember they will pass. There will be hard times. If you work

through them, you get stronger. Learn from the tough
times. Grow from them. And
get ready for the next one.

Underneath some of the
rotten feelings are some hidden gems. With time and
work, you can have a lot of
good times. Occasionally you
will have a dip during a hard
time. It is like flying in an airplane on a lifelong trip. You
will go through a few storms.
Some will be worse and last
longer than others. But they

will always pass. And because you are flying at a different altitude
than many of your friends, you will get to see and do things that they
don't. Strive to make your altitude (or should it be attitude) higher
than everyone else's. For example, ever since Ian was diagnosed I
feel in some ways that I have become an observer in life. When I
think back to his learning to sit, to crawl, and to walk, I actually got
to see a child learn in slow motion. I saw all of the steps it takes to
actually sit up. I got to see what many parents don't see. It wasn't a
blur for me. I have learned how to treasure the smallest of steps.

Gaining awareness of the emotion you are feeling can actually
help you deal with it in a positive way. Is there any aspect of a situation that you can do something about? Avoid the situation? Educate
someone? Try to resolve how you will handle similar situations in
the future and move on.

Work through each feeling as much as you can. "I am angry
because…. I am sad because…." It does not matter what brought it
on. Just try not to wallow in it.

Your personality and your life experiences will influence your
emotions and guide how you deal with them. There are so many variables in everyone's life; it is impossible to predict how you are going
to feel. Everything in your life— from your childhood experiences, to
the kind of parents you had and how they treated you and each other,
to how differences were viewed or discussed, to the types of people to
whom you were exposed, to your own awareness of yourself, to your

own personality—will affect how you respond to different situations. For example, growing up with a sibling or a cousin who has special needs will give you an awareness that few people have. You will find that many emotions will be dealt with early in your child's life. Denial, anger, guilt, and sadness are part of the "grieving" cycle. Believe it or not, they will help you move on. These emotions may seem to engulf you in the early months and years. But as time goes on, they will appear less often, and love and acceptance will dominate most of the time. You may even reach a point when you can feel a particular emotion coming on.

This type of awareness will enable you to meet your challenges head on, because you will have an idea of what to expect and hopefully have your supports in place. Just because you can feel an emotion coming on, though, does not always make it easier to deal with. When emotions tend to recycle, there is usually a similar, but new, issue to deal with.

> When Ian started preschool at the age of two, he had only recently been diagnosed. I was still dealing with the shock and guilt that came with the diagnosis. Ian had separation anxiety. I had to educate the whole school community about fragile X syndrome. And throughout the school year we had behavioral issues to deal with. I struggled with everything.
>
> At age three, I had to educate a new preschool staff. The sadness came back because the behavioral issues continued; they wore me down. It seemed like I was continually educating people.
>
> When Ian was four, I thought I would be able to start a year with the same teacher. She quit. I had to educate a new teacher. The behavior issues continued.
>
> Each fall I started noticing the discrepancy in development between Ian and his peers. Hindsight showed that I was in the midst of all this before I realized how unhappy I was. The sadness seemed to come back every year. Some of the reasons were the same, some were not. We started Ian on medication when he was four and a half years old. Many of the behavioral issues stopped immediately. I felt anxious a lot of the time.

Ian started kindergarten the next year, at age five. I can't ever remember feeling so miserable, about every-thing. The task of setting up an inclusive environment in a public school seemed overwhelming. Every one of the "rotten" emotions descended. I took it a day at a time. First grade dawned just as difficult for me. I finally figured out that school was just not going to get easy. The issues get more difficult and complicated each year.

The transition to second grade was more challenging, physically and emotionally, than ever. I spent more time at school than I ever had. Ian wouldn't go to the bathroom with anyone but me. I went up to the school two to three times a day until he was comfortable going with an aide.

When Ian started third grade, I cleared my calendar for the month of September. I prepared myself emotionally for the worse. I figured that if it doesn't take as much time and energy as I expect then I'm one step ahead. There were more familiar people at the start of the year than there had ever been. The only new person was the aide who was to be in the classroom. The first week was rough. Things actually started to smooth out in the second week. I was pleasantly surprised. Toileting is still an issue. My fingers are crossed.

Every fall a transition has to be made—a transition for my son and a transition for me. There is always someone to educate. I now know that educating others will be a lifelong process. But there are always new twists. Every year there are new issues to deal with. But the emotions recycle around these times. I expect them now. Wish I could say I look forward to them, but the predict-ability alone helps.

Sadness and grief may cycle in and out for your whole life. Initially you may feel sad because of the diagnosis. Later you may feel sad because your child cannot do what other children his age are doing. Sadness may come on when other children make fun of your child. It may make you sad to think of your child's future.

Among the most challenging emotional aspects is the resurfac-ing of feelings you thought you had already dealt with successfully. I thought I dealt with getting Ian's diagnosis pretty successfully. I thought I had accepted my "new" life. I was up and down during the first year, but many of the difficult emotions seemed to pass pretty quickly. My most intense emotions arrived a year after we got the diagnosis. Ian's third birthday was approaching. It was time for his first IEP. We had been struggling with some aggression by Ian at his preschool. An avalanche of emotions hit. I thought I had already dealt with all of the issues; I thought that once I accepted my new direction, life would go on like it had before. I thought I was doing pretty well. Then all of a sudden, every one of the emotions described earlier descended upon me, *again*. They came on fast and furious. I got very angry again. I was devastatingly sad. I cried all of the time. I didn't know these emotions would cycle back; I didn't want them back. The emotions had only gone dormant for a year.

They hadn't gone away. They were just waiting for the right moment to resurface. I really began to realize that Ian and his fragile X syndrome were going to be with us for the rest of our lives. Every year there were going to be new issues that had to be dealt with. Some issues would be easy to handle. Other issues would bring out emotions that had been waiting patiently inside me for just the right time to resurface.

The difficult times still slow me down, which I try to look at as something we can all use more of. I look at my life to see if there is something I want to try to change. My husband and I talk a lot during these times, and they soon pass. I feel more and more acceptance every year.

■■ Your Spouse

Your spouse may not respond to the news about your child in the same way that you do. Each of us deals with our emotions in our own way. It can sometimes be hard to respect how others respond. Some spouses may not seem that bothered by having a child with fragile X syndrome; they may be very accepting. Others may have a lot of anger, or they may withdraw. It can be a source of conflict in a marriage.

Strive to communicate with each other and to support each other. This may mean giving each other some time to sort out feelings. Give each other all the time needed. Let your spouse know you're willing to talk at anytime. Also let your spouse know you're there to listen at anytime. Don't forget that unspoken support such as a hug or a smile is just as valuable as spoken words.

I will never forget the time I looked up at Larry and told him that I did not want Ian's diagnosis to tear us apart. "I want this whole situation to drive us closer together."

Do not let your situation tear you apart. Talk about your feelings. Realize each of you will react differently—to the situation and to your emotions. Be accepting. Help each other. Make the decision that you will take turns being up. The "up" person can help the "down" person smile. Find something to joke about. Compare notes on who changed the most diapers, who was up the most during the night, who spent the most time driving around in the car, going to work, or going to the doctor and therapy appointments, who has the most patience, who wants to have the most patience, who's the grumpiest, who can make the funniest face....

Learn to become comfortable enough with each other to say, "I'm grumpy today. I *want* to be grumpy today. I'm enjoying being grumpy. So don't try to make me laugh." Once you have said it, it is almost impossible to actually stay grumpy. Learning to vocalize your feelings will help you deal with the emotion and move on.

Find time to be alone. Don't forget to get a babysitter occasionally so you and your spouse can get out alone together. Taking time to talk with your spouse alone is one of the best ways to strike a healthy balance in your lives. Often these talks will bring you closer when you discover your spouse is feeling the same way you feel or is worried about the same thing you are. Or maybe you can share ideas on dealing with your emotions. You can both work on acceptance, and you can both work on laughing again.

Moms vs. Dads

Compared to my husband, my emotions have gone up and down more intensely. But then again, "they" say that women who carry the fragile X gene may tend to be more depressed than other women. Larry and I talked a lot about our feelings in the months after we got the diagnosis. It was nice because Larry had never been the kind to talk much about his feelings. But over the next year, I noticed that I was the one who seemed to be having difficulty with the diagnosis. I was the one who wanted to talk about things. I have to say, though, that Larry was always there when I needed to talk.

I remember asking Larry about a year after the diagnosis, "Don't you ever get sad or depressed? You never mention that you're having any difficulties with this diagnosis." Larry told me that he felt he had dealt with the issues in the months after the diagnosis, and acceptance had come quickly. Six months later, though, we were out on a date. He looked at me and said, "I'm having a difficult time."

"About Ian?" I asked.

He nodded his head. "Do you want to talk? I'm feeling pretty good about the situation right now." I thought it was about time for me to be "up." I assumed the "up" role and helped Larry talk through a tough time for him.

We got the diagnosis that Ian had fragile X syndrome almost six years ago. (I am somewhat embarrassed to admit that I know the exact date.) I asked Larry in retrospect to talk about the emotions he has experienced over these years. Here's what he told me:

> The diagnosis immediately turned a short term "he'll-grow-out-of-it" situation into a long-term issue. That made me sad. Guilt and denial were never much of an issue with me. Over the years, one of the big concerns for me was Ian's aggressive behavior. It's been frustrating because we didn't know where it was coming from and it's made me a little more fearful of the future.

> Ian takes a lot of time. We have to look at every situation and consider how Ian will react or be affected. You do get used to the daily issues. They become part of your life. You really don't know any different.

> I never hesitate to talk to other people about Ian. The only time I don't is when I don't have the time. I hate to just say, "He has fragile X syndrome" and leave.

> It is the 20 years from now that's always at the back of my mind. How dependent will he be on us? I never dwell on it though; I can't.

I have noticed that the main difference in how Larry and I deal with our emotions stems from my need to analyze the emotion from every angle, particularly if it is a more difficult one. What brought it on? How does this make me feel? Do I like it? Could I have changed the situation? What should I do next time? Larry looks at an issue, attempts to change what he can, tries to accept what he can't, looks at the positive, and moves on. We learn a lot from each other.

▪▪ Find Support

There are several ways to find emotional support. Some of these include:

- Seeking out information, both about emotions and about fragile X syndrome;
- Talking to people with whom you have an emotional attachment, such as family and friends;
- Talking to people in the medical field.

When working through an emotion, seek out information on emotions—from what can bring on an emotion to the actual emotion itself. Go through the exercise outlined earlier to gain awareness of your own emotions. There are books dedicated solely to feelings. These books go into great detail about feelings and provide wonderful insight in how to deal with them. There are also books written by people who describe their experiences of having a child with a disability. The Reading List at the end of the book lists some. Doing both of these things—looking internally at your own emotions and also reading about them—gives you insight into yourself and what makes you tick.

Information about fragile X syndrome may also allow you to put aside some of your feelings of confusion and uncertainty. There is a fair amount of information available; however, I must caution you that a lot of the information is very technical and medical in nature. Also, be careful about bombarding yourself with too much information at first. This can magnify your feeling of being overwhelmed.

My husband and I sought out information on fragile X syndrome in a pretty methodical way. First we wanted general information about fragile X syndrome. Then we needed to know more about the genetic aspects. Medical issues also became critical for us. Then we focused on development, therapy, and schooling. We really had to consciously balance our information seeking with the day-to-day running of our family. It took us a while to get comfortable with the notion that we don't have to read and know everything today. A lot of our learning came from just living with our child.

The second source of support is your family and friends. I started small; my emotions were kept between my husband and me. I talked to my husband a lot initially. Who else could better understand what I was going through? Who else had the investment in our family? I wanted to work through the shock, denial, and guilt—some of the emotions that can seem scary—by myself and with my husband. I was not ready to share this new information with a large group of people. At the same time I found that I had feelings that I wanted to work through by myself. I didn't know what it was going to take to get me past my initial sadness. I spent many hours just sitting by myself, almost daydreaming; I spent some restless nights too.

I slowly added other people into my new life. I was quite selfish with who I let into the emotional side of my life, the side of my life that included a disability. I was *fragile* at different times and I didn't want to risk being rejected or judged by anyone. I was afraid to see how people would respond when I told them about Ian. I was still figuring out how to respond and emotionally I couldn't afford to have someone respond negatively. Over time, my support system changed and expanded. It will change as you and your family's emotional needs change and as your whole family grows both physically and emotionally.

We soon sought support from both our extended family and close friends. We went to them at about the same time because, although we wanted and needed the support of our extended family, they live 1000 miles away. Our friends were just down the street. Although each was only a phone call way, it was different knowing that a friend could be there in five minutes.

Our support network expanded from there. Our son started in preschool right after he was diagnosed. The preschool was inclusive: there were ten children, five had identified needs and five5 did not. The preschool was based at a university; the classroom had one teacher and usually three to four helpers who were graduate students in speech pathology. There was also an Early Childhood Specialist who was a consultant to the preschool classroom.

These people were the nicest people I had ever met in my life. They were understanding and nurturing in every respect. They were as curious to learn about fragile X syndrome as I was. There was a continual information exchange. Here I worked through some of the initial stages of receiving the diagnosis for our son. With them I cried, I laughed, I watched Ian grow, and I had help in dealing with Ian's challenging behavior. Looking back, I was really sheltered at the university. Everyone at the preschool accepted my son for who he was. They cheered all of his successes. They valued my input as much as I valued theirs. I also became empowered—empowered to advocate for my son. After three years in this setting, Ian had to move on to kindergarten. I wasn't ready, but it was time.

Although Ian (and I) moved on to kindergarten, the support I found at that preschool was too much for me to leave behind completely. My daughter soon went through the same program as a peer role model. And the university hired me to be a Family Resource Consultant for the preschool. And while I have enjoyed helping families, the support that drew me there and allowed me to grow continues to this very day.

Another source of support while Ian was in preschool was an organized playgroup we joined. This situation had its difficult moments because none of the other children in the group had a disability, and I kept comparing my child to the other children. But what I found was a group of mothers who were all very supportive of each other. Everyone in the group had an issue to deal with at one time or another, and we would all rally around each other in an empathetic and sympathetic way

At about the same time, I started developing relationships in our neighborhood. We are fortunate to live in a neighborhood filled with children of all ages. We have lived in our neighborhood longer than any other family, so Ian was already here when the other families moved in. The other children got to know Ian pretty quickly, often at his initiation. Ian is very friendly and was always the first one out to watch the moving truck deliver furniture.

Ian has pushed Larry and me to get to know the other children in our neighborhood. There's a group of about 14 children ranging in age from preschool to high school who play together and look out for each other. And while we know the playing together won't last forever, it has brought our neighborhood together.

Every year Ian's range of wandering has increased, along with my comfort level. We live in an area where the streets are arranged to look kind of like the letter *B*. Our house is situated right in the center of the straight line. Because the children play together so much, many of the families have also gotten to know each other well. And as Ian has gotten to know the children, he has also gotten to know the adults. He'll go over and talk to them about the work they are doing on their house, or he will help them in their gardens, and he often helps them mow their lawns. We have annual parties on many of the big holidays, and all of the neighbors chip in. In a sense, we have created the support of an extended family right in our own neighborhood. The convenience of neighborhood support has really spoiled us; I think it has spoiled everyone in the neighborhood.

School friends and families can be another good source of support. This may take a little more work because telephoning and driving are usually involved. I think this will become more important to us as the children in the neighborhood grow and develop their own friendships outside the neighborhood.

Next we got involved with a fragile X syndrome support group. It was interesting and comforting to be with other families who had children or relatives with fragile X syndrome. We found that: 1) families of children with fragile X syndrome share a bond—their children, their challenges, and their shared experiences; 2) this bond can lead to support and understanding and friendships; 3) these groups are a good way to seek support; and 4) they do not have to be formal with set meetings and agendas, but can even be online.

Support groups and parent networks are always forming across the country for families with fragile X syndrome. The Resource Guide at the end of the book contains listings and information about how to find a group in your area. If there is not an organized fragile X syndrome support group in your area, the National Fragile X Foundation will be able to provide you with a local parent contact, or you may be interested in a group for parents of children with all kinds of disabilities. This can be just as valuable. Contact your local school district, social services agency, or check with your local office of The Arc or Association for Community Living (ACL).

One other area of support that can help both you and your child is talking to and working with people in the medical field. Share the "challenge" with a physical or occupational or speech therapist. Exchange ideas on working with your child. They have an objective viewpoint about your child, and sometimes just talking to them about your child's issues will give you ideas to try at home. Also use your child's pediatrician as a source of information and support. While you may need to educate the doctor on fragile X syndrome, use it as an opportunity to build a relationship based on sharing information and ideas on raising your child.

Another option for getting the support you need is professional counseling. There are many reasons why people utilize this resource. For example, it may be helpful if you are feeling consumed by emotions. Counseling is an option if you prefer to work through your feelings in a more private and confidential manner. You do not have to wait for things to be "in shambles" to seek out professional help either. Some people seek out therapy to help them deal with their feelings or life problems in general. Doing that may help you deal with your child. In counseling, remember that when it comes to living with a child with fragile X syndrome, there are many *right* ways. Seek understanding of yourself.

▪▪ Take a Break

The all-important break. Take a break from your child, your house, your spouse, your work, all of your responsibilities. Guilt free. Do something you really enjoy doing. Arrange your schedule so you can treat yourself on a regular basis. Take a yoga class, learn to paint, stay up late and read a book, go to a movie, or just go on a walk.

The kinds of breaks you need will change as your child grows. When Ian was young, going to the grocery store for one hour by myself was enough of a break for me (I must have really been desperate). As he got older, I added a regular monthly outing with friends. Soon I started looking for three to four hours out by myself. Now I like to have three to four hours in my house by myself.

The kinds of breaks you take are really a product of the goal you set for yourself, whether you realize it or not, whether you write it down or not. When your child is young, your goal may be to just get away from your house, to forget about being a parent, to think about something else. Another goal may be to keep up with old friends. So schedule a monthly outing to meet with friends and talk about whatever you want to talk about. Whatever the goal, it is very important to set them for yourself. They give you direction. *Go ahead and write them down; you are more likely to achieve them if you do.* I find that when I schedule an activity, it almost always happens. I never get around to finding the time if I don't actually plan something. Setting a date, making a schedule seems to make the commitment real for me.

Sometimes I feel guilty about leaving. But I am always happier when I get home. It didn't take me long to realize that the children need time alone with dad too.

Goal setting is important for every parent, but especially for parents of children with disabilities. It is easy to stop dreaming. It is easy to let your child consume your life. Granted, there will be periods of time when you need to be consumed by your child. But try to make those periods short. And never stop dreaming *your* dreams.

I have always been a morning person so I generally get up one hour before anyone else. Ian is often up by 6 a.m., so that means I'm usually up by 5 a.m. I usually go for a walk—rain or snow—unless it's below ten degrees. I rarely miss this chance to get out because it can be the only break I get all day. The days I do not get up and Ian gets up early can be the longest days. My schedule also means that I am usually in bed by 9:30 p.m.

Activities involving other people can also be helpful and they provide a schedule of their own. I joined a book group; we meet once a month. I find I really enjoy discussing a book I have read. I don't always get the book read in time, but my goal is to read one book per month. It's that scheduled nightly reading that doesn't always get done. I have also developed a passion for antiques. I don't buy much, but I love to see "what used to be."

I tend to combine activities that I do alone with ones I do with other people. Sometimes it is nice to feel unencumbered by having to communicate with someone else. Other times, conversation with friends is just what I need.

What happens when you get a goal written down and it is not met? Is it the goal or the timing that's not right? You always have the luxury of changing one or the other or both if you choose.

∷ Your Emotions and Your Child

Your relationship with your child will change as you and he grow up together. You have a child who has a wonderful personality, likes to joke and laugh, and knows how to love. This person just happens to also have a disability.

You have a child who has fragile X syndrome. How do you feel about the cause of your emotional upheaval? Think about this: You are not always going to be happy having a child with a disability. But nobody is happy all of the time—even people who have typically developing children. Sometimes you may find yourself frustrated by the disability, but just as often you may be frustrated by the arrival of a new skill, such as "No!" The disability will always be there. Cheer *all* developmental gains. Focus on what your child *can* do.

One area that is hard for many families is avoiding being over-protective of their child. You know your child better than anyone else and you know how much easier it is to keep your child at home in a predictable, safe environment. You do not have to face any stares or hear any comments and you do not have to worry about your child losing it in an overstimulating place.

But you both have to take risks too. So he lost it at the mall the last time you were there. It doesn't mean it is going to happen again. Use judgment in determining when and where you go with your child. He is always growing and changing, and he will surprise you. He needs to explore the world out there, even if it is at a different pace from what you are used to. Slow down to your child's pace as often as you can. You might be surprised at how much you have been missing.

We went to a restaurant when Ian was about two years old. He started crying before we even had our food. I walked back and forth with him in the parking lot until eventually we had to have our food packaged to take with us. Larry looked at me and angrily stated,

"We're never eating out again!" We soon learned to pick the places that serve the right food at the right pace.

▪▪ Dealing with Others

Your Immediate Family

If your child with fragile X syndrome has siblings, recognize that they also have their own emotions to work through. Be aware that their emotions will be very similar to what you are experiencing or have experienced, only at a different level of maturity:

- "Why do I have to have a brother like this?"
- "I get embarrassed by some of the things he does when we go out in public."
- "It's not fair, you never have time for me!"
- "Does he have to do *that?*"

Go back through the list of emotions and apply them to your children. As you gain an awareness of your own emotions, you may be able to help them handle theirs. Talk to your children about what they are feeling. If it seems appropriate, let them know you have felt the same way too:

"We'll never know why you have a brother like this. I have sometimes wondered why I have a son with fragile X syndrome. I get sad. I get angry. It's okay for you to be sad and angry too. I won't get mad at you for feeling that way. Tell me more about how you are feeling."

* * * *

"I got embarrassed a couple of times by your brother too. He started jumping up and down and flapping his arms one time when we were watching a tractor work. One guy said that he must have had too much sugar. Another commented on how excited your brother was. There was also another child watching who had a look of shock on his face. I went up and put my arms around Ian to try to get him to stop flapping his arms. He stopped for a second, and then he pushed me away so he could start again. I just let him go. I worried about what others

would think. Now I realize that is how his body reacts when he is excited about something. There is nothing you or I can do to stop it. He might outgrow it someday. But I have accepted it now. Instead of worrying about what others are thinking, it tickles me to watch their reactions, and I get excited right along with Ian. I only intervene when something inappropriate is said."

* * * *

"Thanks for telling me that you feel I do not have enough time for you. Ian has extra needs, but you have needs too and I cannot forget about those. I will work on it, okay? Any ideas on how we can spend more time together?"

Your children's curiosity will lead to some tough questions, but will enable you to give them information they seek. For example, my daughter asked one day, "Mom, if Ian is older than me, why does he still wear diapers?" I told her that Ian has a harder time learning to use the bathroom than she had. I point out that he is making progress; it's just a little slower. That seemed to satisfy her then.

I am also watching my daughter's skills advance past Ian's. "I color better than Ian, don't I?" I have always tried to be very careful about comparing my two children. "I like both of your pictures. Look how you use color differently than Ian. I like to see you both work so hard on your pictures."

When my daughter turned five, I started talking to her about fragile X syndrome and pointed out some of the characteristics. I wanted to educate her as much as I could before she started kindergarten. I wanted her to be ready when other children asked about her brother.

Grandparents and Aunts and Uncles

Your extended family may or may not have a difficult time having a grandchild with a disability. Be prepared for them to have their own emotions to work through at the start, including shock, denial, anger, and guilt. Put yourself in their position. They will have many of the same emotions as you do; only theirs will be from a *distance*, even if they live close. Some of their emotions may be stronger than yours; some may also be more muted. They will probably have very little knowledge of fragile X syndrome. Maybe after they have worked through some of their own issues, they will grow into the support you want and need. When it comes to your extended family, there are so many variables it is hard to predict the response. Keep some of these variables in mind when dealing with your response to their emotions.

- Where they live—This will affect how often they see your child and how well they get to know your child.
- Their upbringing—Many children with disabilities used to be institutionalized, so your extended family may not have ever been around these "special" people. They may lack experience and information.
- Their personality.
- Whether they are a carrier of the altered gene.

Concern about being a carrier can add a complicated dimension to your extended family's adjustment. There can be a tremendous negative impact felt throughout the family because of the hereditary nature of fragile X syndrome; it can also bring a family closer together.

Grandparents may experience the list of emotions described above just as uncomfortably as you do. They may become extremely depressed when they learn they may have passed the gene to their daughter. There can be terrible guilt associated with this. As a parent yourself now, you can begin to understand this. Think how you feel when your

child gets sick or hurt. You want to "make it better." It's hard to watch your child struggle in any way. Well, your parents are going to watch you struggle for a while, and it won't be easy for them. And how they respond to watching you struggle may vary from one extreme to another, from withdrawing to trying to "make it better." Give them some time, and give them some information too. It's going to take more than a Band-Aid to fix this "owie."

Sometimes approaching the issue in a matter-of-fact way can make it easier to talk to your parents. If you can trace it back to a grandparent, then you can trace it back to a great-grandparent. Show that it has been in the family long before the grandparents were even born. Research is underway to figure out why and when the gene changes. No one controls what the gene does or when it does it. You know your family. Approach them in a way that you think is best. Just be prepared for any and every thing when you let them in on the news.

I have heard of one family with a boy with fragile X syndrome whose parents have told only one extended family member and it was not their parents. Some people place a real stigma on anyone who has a disability. Some people live in communities where acceptance of people who are different is very low. There are other families who have broadcast it across the country so siblings can be tested for carrier status and make informed decisions about having children.

Hope that it will bring your family closer. You can share the successes. You can share the setbacks. You can share your strategies. You can share your dreams.

Friends

Whether you surround yourself with lots of friends or you prefer the friendship of one or two people, they add a joy to our lives that's unlike any other. You may have friends who knew you before you had children or maybe you have developed friendships since you had children. Hopefully you have both. Different kinds of friends can provide you with different kinds of support. You may have friends who you prefer to spend time with alone. Other friends may be seen in family gatherings. There's joy, and support, to be found in both situations.

How did your friends react when you told them your son had fragile X syndrome? Did they respond *correctly*? I hope they did, in whatever way was important to you. But if they didn't, don't judge them too harshly. Think how shocked you were to find out about your child. I can't imagine your friends won't react very similarly. That shock may come out in inappropriate ways. It may be "I'm sorry" to silence to "I kind of suspected something."

Your friends, like your family, will experience emotions very similar to what you felt. Their emotions may take a little different twist to them. Relief that you finally got a diagnosis. Sorrow to see you so sad. Relief that it is not them. Guilt that they feel this latter type of relief. Your friends, like you, will have to work through some of these negative emotions to be able to move on. They will move on to finding love and acceptance in your child and admiration in you. Be patient.

Strangers

Think how you acted around strangers before your child was diagnosed with fragile X syndrome. Excited about a new baby? Were you proud parents? Maybe you suspected something was not right, but most likely it didn't stop you from showing that baby off! I hope you reveled in hearing all of the *oohs* and *aahs*. Most children with fragile X syndrome don't *look* any different from other children when they are very young. It's part of what makes fragile X syndrome tricky to diagnose at an early age.

So what happens after your child is diagnosed with fragile X syndrome? It may or may not change how you act around strangers initially. Most people will probably still not notice anything different about your child. Only you will know. You can go on like you've been—being an excited, proud parent. But since strangers can't tell, they won't know that you may be swirling with emotions. It can be a hard time. Take your time and do what feels right to you. If you don't feel like getting out in public, stay home for a while. The public's not going anywhere.

Also in the early years, you can *hide* the disability for a while. You can hide it by saying that boys are always a little slower. Is that okay to do? This is a comfort issue. You have to accept the disability to a certain extent yourself before you can talk to others about it. Because the disability may not be immediately obvious to others when your child is young, it gives you time to get to know your child. Some children with fragile X syndrome function at about half their actual age, the delay at one year is only six months, so it's not that big of a deal. As your child grows, you begin to notice the difference and so will others. But as your child grows so does your comfort zone. Sometimes you may even forget that your child has a disability. You will laugh right along with your child even if it is something very silly—and you won't care who sees you or what they think.

I remember feeling so happy after our son was born. Our first child, wow. Right after my son was diagnosed, all of a sudden I felt different about being around strangers. In some ways I was scared. I thought people were going to start looking at my son and then look away real fast, like you do when you're trying not to stare at someone. Initially I was a little worried about what others were going to think. And I was really worried about how they were going to respond. My worries stemmed from my own self-imposed insecurities about having a child with a disability. I was so fragile at the beginning that if someone had responded in the least bit negatively, I would have probably burst into tears right on the spot. So until I was stronger, I went about my business with blinders on. I made very little eye contact and I hardly talked to anyone I didn't know well.

As my son grew, my confidence grew. I became acutely aware of how strangers responded to my son. Sometimes I would actually look at them to see how they were going to respond. I went through a phase when I let my emotions get all tied up into what others were thinking. Thank goodness that didn't last for long. I rarely think about it now.

You will develop your own response to strangers—from explaining the disability, to staring back, to ignoring. These encounters can bring out strong emotions. It is okay to feel whatever you feel. I used to get embarrassed when Ian would perseverate in front of strangers. I don't anymore. There will be a lot of ignorant people who don't place a value on or accept diversity. There will also be strangers who will reinforce your belief that there are good people in this world.

There is an outdoor mall close to our house where a lot of musicians congregate on the weekends. Ian is particularly drawn to people who play the guitar. One day Ian was listening to three women play folk music. They would alternate their own music with requests from Ian. They called him by name. We sat and listened to them for close to 30 minutes. As we got up to go home one of the women looked at me and said, "Ian's a beautiful person."

I smiled and nodded my head, "Yeah, he is."

■■ Conclusion

Having a child with fragile X syndrome can bring out your emotional side. It is healthy to feel and express those emotions. Gaining an awareness of your feelings will help you deal with them. Take as much time as you need to work through each emotion. The hard times *will* pass. You *will* be stronger. Just knowing that some of the difficult emotions will recur can make it easier on you. You will start to feel them coming on. And know that those, too, will pass.

I don't know whether or not it is because I carry a premutation of the fragile X gene, or whether it is just a function of having children, but my emotions now come on stronger than ever. The highs are real high and the lows are real low. I have been both happier and sadder than I have ever been in my life. These intense emotions have surprised me, they make me feel alive, and they make me feel human.

Take care of yourself. There will be times when you will have to emotionally support your spouse and your other children. There will be times when they will support you.

See your child before you see the disability. This is a child who has more to offer than you ever imagined. This is a child who will teach you more than you ever learned in school. This is a child who will bring out the kind of love in you that you never knew you had.

❚❚ Parent Statements

Right after my child was diagnosed, all I heard about was all of the "problems" he was going to have. I deleted the word from my vocabulary.

❧

I just cried and cried.

❧

I kept thinking I had done something wrong when I was pregnant.

❧

I felt like I was losing my mind—I saw things no one else saw.

❧

I wondered, "Does this mean that he's retarded?" Prior to the diagnosis, we had believed and hoped that the struggles our son was facing would someday be alleviated. This diagnosis seemed like such a limiting reality.

We were searching for the person or the teaching method or just enough repetition of a skill or task that would "flip the switch" and get our son beyond his struggles. We still are!

Sometimes I am grateful that we had so many years without a diagnosis, because it forced us to get to know our children and set expectations according to their individual abilities, rather than some pre-set standard. On the other hand, we put a lot of energy into seeking reasons for our sons' slow development, energy which could have been better directed to planning programs for our sons, enjoying their company, and even taking time for ourselves.

I went to live with my parents in Florida.

The actual diagnosis was delivered to us over the phone by a genetics counselor who seemed unaware of or unmoved by the tremendous emotional impact of her news. It would have been so much more helpful if she had just made a simple comment like, "I know this must be very difficult news to hear"—anything that indicated she understood this was more than a simple piece of information.

When we found out William had fragile X syndrome, we were shocked! So I went to the medical school in Dallas and got on line with MED-LINE and pulled up every abstract and document that "fragile X" pulled up. There wasn't much, but it did have The National Fragile X Foundation's name and address.

It drastically altered the dreams that we had for him and the dreams we had for ourselves.

I cried, I prayed, I talked to family and friends who listened and were loving and let me say how I really felt (not the chipper stuff) and I remembered that in many ways nothing had changed—we were still a family, we still had our beautiful children, we still had to make dinner and go to work and school. Life goes on.

Both of our first instincts were to think, "How can I get out of this?" Well, we decided that we couldn't.

All I could think about was all of the times I had called someone "retarded" when I was a child.

I reacted to my son the same way after the diagnosis as I did before the diagnosis—with unconditional love.

I think I responded with a little more empathy after my son was diagnosed.

In some ways I was more relaxed with my child after we got the diagnosis—I could stop looking.

My parents were a little defensive. "All that testing will do is point the finger at someone." It took some educating to realize it was much more than that.

My Dad was very embarrassed that he "passed this thing on." He still apologizes every so often and says, "If I could take it away from you I would."

We live in a family of "intellectuals," meaning that we tend to deal with difficult issues by learning more about them. Luckily we have also found our sons so engaging that they have been able to show us the way to deal with our emotional stresses. The fun of being involved in their lives has been a great stress reliever.

❧

My husband and I separated.

❧

My parents were totally supportive and so were the medical people.

❧

I was glad to find out so I could learn everything about fragile X syndrome so I could help my son.

❧

There are many unknowns and so we generally don't talk too much about them. It will be easier to deal with each issue as it arises. In the meantime, we are enjoying our kids as they learn new things and discover their world.

❧

We didn't tell our friends at first.

❧

We were particularly devastated by the diagnosis of our younger son, Samuel, since he was only two months old and didn't seem to have any indications of fragile X syndrome, and of course, we were hoping for a negative test result. With Patrick, we already anticipated something to explain the delays we'd observed for about a year.

❧

Since it's been nearly a year since the diagnoses, I'd say we're still grieving the loss of the little boys we thought we had, but have adjusted our expectations for them gradually over time.

We are very aware of the fact that we don't have a regular family life because of behavioral issues, delayed communication, and physical limitations.

We get pretty excited with every new accomplishment and milestone reached, such as Patrick leaving his much-loved bottle for the cup at 30 months, and Sam standing up supported by the sofa. Yet there's often a twinge of sadness knowing how much further ahead they could be if it wasn't for their genetic make-up.

The easy people to tell were the ones who were eager to learn about fragile X syndrome with us. With others we minimized the diagnosis, as if by us accepting his diagnosis we were denying his accomplishments and his positive characteristics.

We truly believe that honesty is the most productive way to deal with strangers—which does not mean that we tell all immediately upon meeting people, but rather that we try to answer any questions very matter-of-factly.

There were many times when we preferred to forego an office picnic or social event rather than subject ourselves to having our children compared to those of co-workers. We're not proud of this.

It is hard for me to watch my son want to join in play time with other children and not be able to.

My emotions are "in check" now due to Prozac and a healthy attitude.

3

THE GENETIC ASPECTS OF FRAGILE X SYNDROME AND GENETIC COUNSELING

Brenda Finucane, M.S. and
Amy Cronister, M.S.

▦ Introduction

Many parents who find out the cause of their child's learning difficulties are relieved to at last have a diagnosis. Finally there are some answers to the many questions they have had. But learning about a child's diagnosis can also be a painful process. Most parents feel an acute sense of loss for the child they had expected.

With time, support, and understanding, most families do adjust. Because fragile X syndrome is an inherited condition, however, the diagnosis brings with it additional concerns. You need to understand how fragile X syndrome may affect not only your child but others in your family. If you have no other known relative with learning difficulties, this may be information you were unprepared to hear. If you have dealt with learning difficulties in your family before, the diagnosis may finally give a name to a condition that has been passed from one generation to another.

This chapter explains what is currently known about the genetics of fragile X syndrome and its transmission from generation to generation. By learning the basics you will understand how the diagnosis affects your immediate family as well as your relatives. The chapter reviews the laboratory testing that was used to confirm the fragile X diagnosis in your child and outlines other testing options you or your relatives may wish to consider when planning a family. Finally, the chapter describes what genetic counseling involves and explains how it can help you and other family members.

■■ The Basics of Heredity

Genetics affects everyone's lives enormously. We are all very much the products of what we inherit from our parents. Think about your own family tree and how you resemble each other. Physical features, such as height and bone structure and even some aspects of your personality, may seem to come from one or both of your parents. Some features are common throughout your entire family. Perhaps some family members share the same hair texture. The color of your child's eyes or the shape of her chin is proof that genetics is a fundamental part of life. With this in mind, let's start with some of the basics.

When a father's sperm and a mother's egg join, a cell, called a zygote, is formed. All the rest of the cells that eventually develop into a child start from that zygote. During pregnancy this one cell divides into two, the two cells divide into four, and so on until there are thousands and thousands of cells. All these cells share the same genetic characteristics as that first zygote.

Each cell in the body contains the genetic material known as DNA (deoxyribonucleic acid). DNA is a very long and complex molecule containing different substances. Specific regions of the DNA, called genes, contain instructions for making chemicals called proteins. Proteins, which are produced from conception onward, play an important role in how a person develops mentally and physically.

Genes are packaged into structures called chromosomes. Although you cannot see genes, with the aid of a microscope you can see chromosomes. Figure 1 at right shows chromosomes as they actually appear under a microscope. Most people have 46 chromosomes which come in pairs that scientists have numbered 1 through 23. One chromosome from each pair is inherited from the mother and one from the father. The 23rd pair consists of the sex chromosomes, X and Y, and they de-

:: **FIGURE 1.** **CHROMOSOMES UNDER MICROSCOPE**

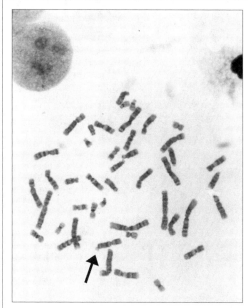

Chromosomes as they appear under a microscope. The arrow points to the fragile X site.

termine whether a person is male or female. Figures 2 & 3 (pages 70 and 71) show karyotypes, pictures of chromosomes, for a male and a female. A girl has two X chromosomes, a boy has two different chromosomes, one X and one Y. Each parent provides one of the chromosomes; however, the mother always provides an X. In other words, it is the father and the sex chromosome he passes to his child that determines whether a baby is a boy or a girl. Figure 4 (page 72) shows how the sex chromosomes are inherited.

The gene that is responsible for fragile X syndrome is the FMR1 gene, which is located on the X chromosome. During the formation of egg and sperm and throughout life, genes can change. Changes within genes, known as mutations, happen as part of a naturally occurring process that helps human beings adapt and survive as a species. Some mutations are beneficial while others are not. Fragile X syndrome is caused by mutations in the FMR1 gene that occur over several and perhaps many generations.

▪▪ FIGURE 2. MALE KARYOTYPE

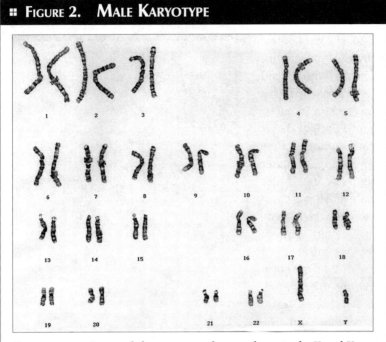

Karyotype, or picture of chromosomes, for a male; note the X and Y chromosomes.

▪▪ Changes in the FMR1 Gene and Fragile X Syndrome

The FMR1 gene is found among all people in the general population. With very sophisticated laboratory techniques, scientists have been able to closely examine the structure of the normal FMR1 gene and compare it to the changed, or mutated, FMR1 gene seen in fragile X syndrome.

The FMR1 gene normally consists of a repeated sequence of DNA, specifically CGG...CGG...CGG, and so on. The C stands for cytosine and the G stands for guanine, two different substances known as nucleotide bases, which can make up DNA. The number of times the CGG sequence is repeated in the FMR1 gene varies in size from one person to another. Usually the FMR1 region contains less than 50 CGG repeats, but can also contain as few as 5 CGG repeats. Some people in the general population have a higher number of repeats in their FMR1 region, between 50 and 200 CGG repeats. This number of repeats is

■■ FIGURE 3. FEMALE KARYOTYPE

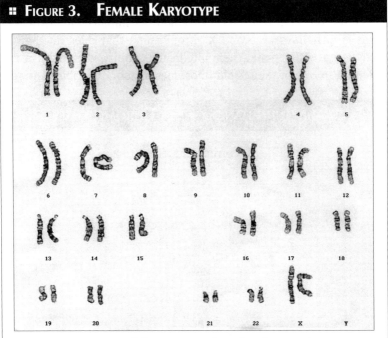

Karyotype, or picture of chromosomes, for a female; note the two X chromosomes.

termed a premutation. Studies show that a premutation in the FMR1 gene region does not interfere with intellectual development. The FMR1 premutation is special, however, because it can expand in size when it is passed from parent to child. The specific mechanism that causes this expansion, however, is not yet understood.

For unknown reasons, when women with a premutation pass the altered gene to a child, sometimes it expands in size to more than 200 CGG repeats. An FMR1 gene of this length is usually methylated; this means that the FMR1 gene is turned off and cannot perform its function. We refer to this methylated and expanded FMR1 gene as a full mutation.

The FMR1 gene is responsible for producing a chemical, called the FMR1 protein, that is critical for intellectual development. When this chemical is reduced in amount or absent altogether, intellectual development is altered. We do not currently understand how the FMR1 protein affects intellectual development, but we do know that most children and adults with a full mutation do not produce enough

FMR1 protein. As a result, as many as 99% of boys and men with the full mutation have some level of cognitive impairment. However, because girls have a second X chromosome that does not have a methylated FMR1 gene, their intellectual ability, even with a full mutation in one of their X chromosomes, is more variable. The rea-

∎ FIGURE 4.   INHERITANCE OF SEX CHROMOSOMES

Female Carrier

Woman who has a fragile X mutation on one of her two X chromosomes

Her egg cells

Egg cell without a fragile X mutation

Egg cell with a fragile X mutation

Plus a father's X

Plus a father's Y

Plus a father's X

Plus a father's Y

Girl without a fragile X mutation

Girl with a fragile X mutation

Boy without a fragile X mutation

Boy with a fragile X mutation

son why one girl has learning problems and another does not is still only partly understood.

There are some people with fragile X syndrome who have an altered gene that varies in size from cell to cell. People with a full mutation in some cells and a premutation in others are termed mo-

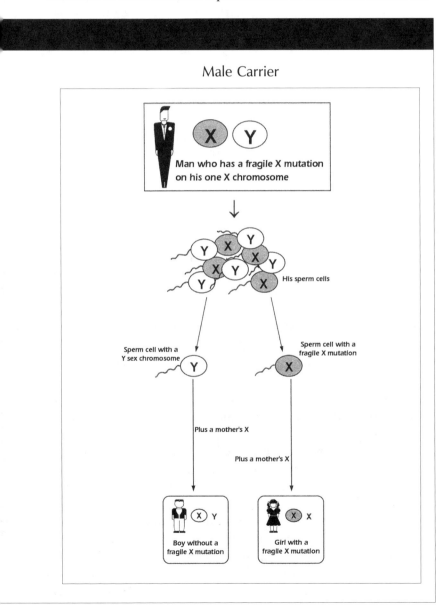

Male Carrier

Man who has a fragile X mutation on his one X chromosome

His sperm cells

Sperm cell with a Y sex chromosome

Sperm cell with a fragile X mutation

Plus a mother's X

Plus a mother's X

Boy without a fragile X mutation

Girl with a fragile X mutation

saics. Mosaicism is not uncommon. About 15 percent of males and about 7 percent of females affected by fragile X syndrome have mosaicism. Mosaicism has also been observed in carrier females (discussed below) with no apparent intellectual difficulties.

Even though the vast majority of people with fragile X syndrome have the CGG type of mutation, there are a few individuals who have been found to have different changes in the FMR1 gene, such as deletions (missing sections of the gene). People with these rarer types of changes are physically, behaviorally, and intellectually indistinguishable from people who have fragile X syndrome with a large CGG repeat pattern. The type of FMR1 mutation found in an individual, however, becomes important when other members of the family are considering testing. This is because the laboratory test used to detect an unusual CGG pattern cannot always detect other rare mutations.

❚❚ Fragile X Inheritance

Figure 5 (page 75) shows a family tree in which fragile X syndrome has caused learning difficulties in a number of family members. It demonstrates the way fragile X syndrome can be inherited. John inherited the fragile X syndrome from his mother, who has no intellectual difficulties but has a premutation. She inherited her premutation from her father. He shows no effects of fragile X syndrome whatsoever. John's first cousin, Jim, also has fragile X syndrome. He too inherited the condition from his mother who also inherited the altered gene from her father who also shows no symptoms of fragile X syndrome. And finally, Jim's sister, Mary, has a full mutation, but has no intellectual difficulties. She has, however, both a son and daughter with fragile X syndrome.

From this example you can see that fragile X syndrome can be passed from generation to generation in a variety of ways. A premutation in a woman can change to a full mutation when passed to her son. Also for unknown reasons, a premutation will not change to a full mutation when passed from father to daughter. We also see from this family tree that a premutation can pass from mother to daughter and from father to daughter without becoming a full mutation, but when passed from mother to child in the next generation, suddenly cause cognitive impairment in several family members. The

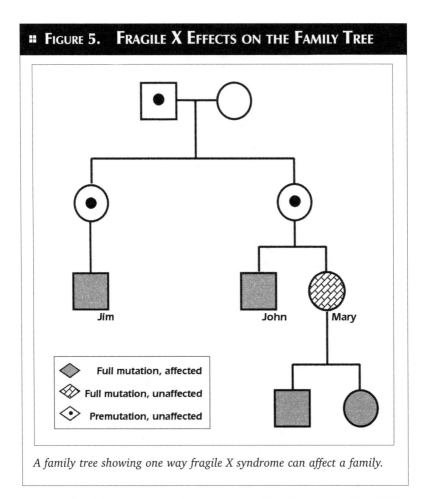

▪▪ FIGURE 5. FRAGILE X EFFECTS ON THE FAMILY TREE

Jim

John   Mary

Full mutation, affected
Full mutation, unaffected
Premutation, unaffected

A family tree showing one way fragile X syndrome can affect a family.

reason why this occurs remains a mystery. The discovery of the FMR1 gene and the mutation that leads to fragile X syndrome, however, have provided some pieces to the puzzle which are explained below.

Carriers

The term "fragile X carrier" is used to describe both males and females who do not show any symptoms of fragile X syndrome but have one FMR1 gene that has been changed. Carrier males have a premutation whereas carrier females can have either a premutation or a full mutation (see below). One concern of people who are carriers is their risk to pass a changed gene to their children.

Carrier Males. Two medical terms you may have heard used to describe men or boys who are carriers of a changed FMR1 gene are "nonpenetrant males" and "transmitting males." If you are a man who has been shown to be a carrier, all of your daughters will inherit the fragile X mutation from you. And for unknown reasons, your daughters will tend to inherit a CGG repeat pattern similar in size to yours. Therefore, your risk to have a daughter who is affected by fragile X syndrome from your side of the family is virtually zero. Because your daughters inherited a premutation, however, your grandchildren are at risk for intellectual impairment.

As a male carrier, you cannot pass the FMR1 premutation to your sons. This is because any son you have inherits his Y sex chromosome from you, with his X chromosome coming from his mother.

Carrier Females. If you are a woman who is a carrier of a changed FMR1 gene, your chance to pass the altered FMR1 gene to your children is 50 percent. See Figure 4 (page 72). If you do pass the changed FMR1 gene to either your daughters or sons, the chance that he or she will be affected by fragile X syndrome is related, in part, to the size of your CGG repeat pattern.

If you have a full mutation, you have a 50 percent chance with every pregnancy that your child will inherit that full mutation. A son who inherits a full mutation has a 99 percent chance of having a cognitive impairment, with a daughter having approximately a 50 percent chance.

If you have a premutation, and pass that X chromosome to your child, the chance that he or she might have a child with mental impairment will vary. A premutation in the range of 60-69 repeats, for example, has approximately a 20 percent chance of expanding to a full mutation, while an FMR1 premutation of greater than 90 CGG repeats is more unstable and will almost always expand in the next generation.

Information Is Changing

Specific information about a person's risk regarding fragile X syndrome may change as our understanding of the fragile X mutation increases. To receive the most accurate and current information, speak with your doctor or a genetic counselor to see if additional testing or counseling is indicated.

▪ Testing for Fragile X Syndrome

The diagnosis of fragile X syndrome may have first been mentioned by your family doctor or one of your child's teachers or therapists. Or a developmental pediatrician, neurologist, or geneticist evaluating your child may have suspected fragile X syndrome based on your child's behavior, speech and language, or physical appearance. But to be certain that the diagnosis is actually fragile X syndrome, a genetic blood test is required.

Chromosome Testing

If your child was tested in the early 1990's or before, it is possible that the blood test used was a chromosome test, also known as cytogenetic analysis. A chromosome test for fragile X syndrome is a very specialized study that looks to see if a person has any fragile X chromosomes. As described in Chapter 1, people with fragile X syndrome have an X chromosome with a little piece dangling or broken off its bottom end.

Cytogenetic analysis was the standard test for fragile X syndrome until the early 1990's. This test was very useful for diagnosing people who have fragile X syndrome, because it was 90 percent accurate for detecting children and adults with the condition. In the early to mid 1980's, this chromosome test was also the only one available for detecting people who were fragile X carriers. However, for carrier testing, the chromosome test was not ideal, because it could only detect about 1 percent of carrier males and only about half of carrier females.

DNA Linkage Testing

In the mid 1980's a blood test was developed that can actually look at a person's DNA, and through very sophisticated testing, was sometimes able to predict whether or not a person was a fragile X carrier. This was accomplished by comparing the DNA patterns of relatives at risk for being carriers with the DNA from one or more members who were *known* to have fragile X syndrome. This comprehensive testing was known as fragile X linkage analysis. Although fragile X linkage analysis was helpful in identifying carriers, it was not useful for diagnosing people with fragile X syndrome. Consequently, chromosome testing remained the standard test for just confirming fragile X syndrome.

Linkage testing, though useful for carrier testing, also had its limitations. Of greatest concern was the small chance a person might be falsely predicted to be a carrier, or a carrier may not be detected. Overall, linkage analysis was about 95 percent accurate for those families in which comparison testing could be done.

Because of the superiority and greater accuracy of direct DNA analysis (described below), families who had chromosome testing or DNA linkage studies in the past should consider being retested to confirm earlier results. To discuss whether retesting is appropriate, you should contact the genetics center that performed the original study. In addition, if anyone in your family had a chromosome or linkage study and received inconclusive results, FMR1 DNA testing may confirm or rule out the fragile X diagnosis.

FMR1 DNA Analysis

Fragile X FMR1 DNA analysis, also known as direct DNA analysis, is now considered the "standard" for fragile X testing. It is 99 percent accurate. It is by far the most accurate diagnostic test for determining whether or not a person is a carrier, for confirming that a person has fragile X syndrome, and for studying developing babies before birth. The cost of testing is less expensive than fragile X chromosome or DNA linkage studies and ranges from approximately $250.00 to $350.00. Results are usually available in two to three weeks.

The FMR1 DNA test examines a person's FMR1 gene by using specialized laboratory techniques called southern blot analysis and PCR (polymerase chain reaction). Southern blot analysis is used to measure the size of the CGG repeat and in most cases will also determine whether the FMR1 gene is turned on or off (methylated). PCR may be performed in combination with Southern blot, or, in some circumstances, used alone. PCR is more precise than Southern blot for measuring CGG repeat patterns of less than 200 CGG repeats.

‡‡ Family Planning

Family planning is a common concern for many people with a family history of fragile X syndrome. Finding out that one is at risk for having a child with a disability can have a profound effect on a person's life plans. If your family tree shows that you may be a carrier of the altered fragile X gene, you should consider speaking with a genetic counselor before you or your spouse become pregnant to discuss all your reproductive options and testing. If testing has shown that you have either a premutation or a full mutation, it is especially crucial that you meet with a genetic counselor to learn about your family planning options.

Prenatal Diagnosis

Prenatal diagnosis—testing for fragile X syndrome in a baby before it is born—is one option you may wish to consider when planning a family. Some parents choose to have prenatal diagnosis and some do not. It is a very personal choice and usually depends on your specific risks, your family situation, background, religious views, past experiences, and personal feelings.

Prenatal diagnosis using direct DNA analysis can detect whether or not a fetus has fragile X syndrome. For some parents, the results will not show fragile X syndrome, and they can stop worrying. Unfortunately, if the fetus has fragile X syndrome, there is currently nothing a doctor can do to prevent the developing baby from having this condition. Consequently, parents who learn that their developing baby has fragile X syndrome must make the difficult choice between continuing and ending the pregnancy. For some parents, knowing beforehand that their child will have fragile X syndrome helps them prepare for the challenges that lie ahead.

Testing during pregnancy can be done by either chorionic villus sampling (CVS) or amniocentesis. The fetal cells obtained from either of these procedures are tested by direct DNA analysis which can measure the size of the CGG repeat pattern within the FMR1 gene. Both CVS and amniocentesis can be done in a doctor's office or at a hospital clinic.

Chorionic Villus Sampling. CVS is performed at 10 to 12 weeks of pregnancy. During the procedure a small amount of chorionic villus tissue is withdrawn from the placenta through a tube inserted through the vagina into the uterus. This tissue develops from the same fertilized egg cell as the fetus and goes on to form part of the placenta, which is attached to the uterus. To obtain the chorionic villus tissue, the doctor first performs an ultrasound scan (sonogram) which shows a picture of the fetus. Once the fetus and the position of the placenta are located, the doctor gently inserts either a thin catheter (tube) through the woman's cervix or inserts a thin needle into the woman's stomach skin to enter the womb. For either approach, the doctor watches the fetus on ultrasound throughout the procedure. Using gentle suction, a small amount of chorionic villus tissue is removed through the tube or needle and used for the genetic testing.

Amniocentesis. Amniocentesis is the withdrawal, through a needle inserted into the uterus, of a small amount of the fluid that surrounds the developing baby. The procedure is usually done when a woman is about 16 weeks pregnant. To perform an amniocentesis, a doctor inserts a very thin needle through a woman's stomach skin into her womb, using an ultrasound scan of the fetus. About an ounce or less of fluid is removed. The fluid, called amniotic fluid, contains cells which have been naturally shed by the developing baby. These cells can then be used for genetic testing. Results are usually available within three to four weeks.

All aspects of both CVS and amniocentesis should be discussed with a genetic counselor or other trained professional. Because each procedure poses a small risk to the pregnancy for infection, bleeding and miscarriage, the risks, benefits, and limitations should be clearly understood.

Preimplantation Diagnosis

Preimplantation diagnosis is a highly technical procedure that involves DNA testing of in vitro fertilized embryos (eggs which are fertilized outside a woman's body) and is performed before pregnancy begins. Only embryos that are shown to be free of the fragile X mutation are implanted into the mother's uterus. However, because of its extremely low success rate, this option is not currently available. Nevertheless, your genetic counselor will be able to provide you with more information should this procedure become available.

Adoption

Some couples, when faced with the risk of having a child with a disability, choose not to have any biological children or to limit the size of their existing family. For families who still have a strong desire to raise children, adoption may be an appropriate choice. Although fewer healthy babies are available for adoption now than in years past, the fact remains that thousands of couples still successfully adopt children every year. To find out more about adoption choices, contact: The National Adoption Center, 1500 Walnut Street, Suite 701, Philadelphia, PA 19102; (215) 735-9988.

■■ Genetic Counseling

What Is A Genetic Counselor?

Fragile X syndrome has a particularly complex and confusing inheritance pattern because of the many different ways males and females can be affected. If you are having difficulty keeping all your facts straight, you are not alone. Many physicians and genetics professionals also have trouble keeping up with the explosion of information about fragile X syndrome. With a condition this complicated, it is best not to rely solely on information given to you by family members or by other parents of children with fragile X syndrome. What is true for one family with fragile X syndrome may not be true at all for your family, depending on the repeat size of the mutation and how it has been passed down. It is, therefore, very important that you seek genetic counseling from an appropriately trained professional once the diagnosis of fragile X syndrome has been confirmed. For families affected or potentially affected by fragile X syndrome, it is time extremely well spent.

In the United States most professionals referred to as "genetic counselors" have a

Master's degree in human genetics or genetic counseling. Some Master's level genetic counselors are called "genetics associates." The term "geneticist" usually refers to physicians or doctoral level scientists, many of whom are also involved in the counseling process. Counselors are certified by the American Board of Genetic Counseling, while physicians and lab researchers achieve certification through the American Board of Medical Genetics.

Families seek or are referred for genetic counseling for many different reasons. Frequently, a child with a developmental delay is referred for a genetic evaluation to see if a cause can be found. In the course of this work-up, he may be diagnosed as having fragile X syndrome, and the parents then meet with a genetic counselor to understand the meaning of the diagnosis for their child and for future generations of their family. A genetic counselor can also help them to understand and cope with the many painful and distressing emotions that go along with finding out about the diagnosis. In addition, couples may meet with a genetic counselor when they undergo prenatal testing for fragile X syndrome.

Often, the relatives of people with fragile X syndrome seek genetic counseling to find out if they themselves are carriers. And even when there is no known diagnosis of fragile X syndrome, people may be referred for genetic counseling and fragile X syndrome testing if there is a history of mental retardation or learning disabilities in the family. All of these are valid reasons to see a genetic counselor, and they underscore the many different roles that genetic counselors can play.

If your child was diagnosed with fragile X syndrome through a genetics center, you have probably already met with a genetic counselor. Sometimes a child may be diagnosed with fragile X syndrome by someone other than a genetics professional. For example, more and more pediatricians are ordering fragile X blood tests through their private offices, rather than going through a genetics center, and you may not get a comprehensive genetics evaluation. The blood test for fragile X syndrome is only part of the genetic counseling process, however, and it is crucial that you meet with a genetic counselor to discuss the many implications of your child's diagnosis. Your family doctor or pediatrician may be able to refer you to a local genetics center. You can also contact the National Fragile X Foundation or your local fragile X resource center, for a list of geneticists in your area. Other national organizations, such as the March of Dimes Birth Defects Foundation [(914) 428-7100], publish state-by-state directories of centers that provide genetic counseling. The Resource Guide at the back of this book provides a list of organizations you can contact for information and support.

The Family Work-Up

No matter what your particular family history reveals, if you have a child or relative with fragile X syndrome, other members of your family could also be at risk for having children with fragile X syndrome. One of the primary tools of the genetic counselor is the family tree, or pedigree, as it is called. By asking you very specific questions about your extended family, the counselor can construct a diagram that allows him or her to better see how the fragile X mutation has been passed down in your family and to specifically identify relatives at risk. A pedigree can also alert the counselor to the existence of other conditions or factors unrelated to fragile X syndrome, such as hereditary cancers, which could have implications for your family.

In preparation for your meeting with a genetic counselor, you should find out as much as you can about the health of relatives in your immediate and extended families. The ages, causes of death, general health, and intellectual functioning of your parents and their siblings are useful facts. If you don't already know, find out where your family originated (for example: Europe, Africa, Asia), because this information can help a counselor pinpoint hereditary risk factors for conditions other than fragile X syndrome which might be related to your ethnic ancestry. If possible find out which relatives may have required special tutoring, or who perhaps had evidence of learning difficulties (as inferred, for example, from dropping out of school), even if they were not specifically diagnosed. Steer clear of vague or rumored information that seems questionable. It is better to know a small amount of accurate information than to know large amounts of unreliable family information that cannot be confirmed.

Staying In Touch

One of the most important roles of the genetic counselor is to translate complex genetic information into understandable terms and to help families understand how this applies specifically to them. Counselors recognize that much of the information they give to parents at the time of a child's diagnosis will not be remembered, or may be misunderstood in the midst of all the emotions that surface during this trying time. It is, therefore, very appropriate for parents to stay in contact with a counselor by phone and to schedule follow-up meetings. Counselors expect that they may need to repeat information, to answer questions, and to meet with families several times to make sure that all their questions and concerns are being addressed. So never hesitate to ask your genetic counselor to repeat information or explain information more simply. It is their job to make sure you understand fragile X syndrome and its impact on your family.

Sharing Information about the Diagnosis

In addition to coming to terms with the diagnosis of fragile X syndrome in your child, you will need to face the implications of the diagnosis which will likely extend far beyond your own immediate family. Many parents, when first learning about fragile X syndrome, naturally want to keep this information private for a time until they can better understand and accept it themselves. Unfortunately, from the outset, there are usually other relatives in the immediate and extended family who need to be informed about the fragile X diagnosis. In reality there are few truly urgent situations that would require you to immediately tell extended family members about the fragile X diagnosis, so work through your own emotions for a short time before informing the rest of your family. One important exception is if there are other couples in your extended family who are actively planning pregnancies or are already pregnant, in which case the information should be given to them as soon as possible so they can seek genetic counseling.

If your child is the first one in the family to be diagnosed with fragile X syndrome, you may have the difficult responsibility of informing other relatives. As the bearer of important genetic information, you can expect to be met with a variety of reactions, not all of them sympathetic. Some family members may be very defensive, feeling that this is your problem, not theirs. Some may become very upset and anxious, while others may deny the presence of obvious fragile X symptoms in their undiagnosed children. Also troubling are the reac-

tions of family members who simply make light of the information as if it could never happen to them, even though they may be at high risk for having children with fragile X syndrome. These are all normal and typical responses to learning about a potential genetic risk in a family. When the news comes from a relative, all the emotions involved may be heightened. Chapter 2 explains some of the many emotions triggered by the diagnosis of fragile X syndrome in your child.

For reasons of privacy and confidentiality, you cannot simply give the phone numbers of your relatives to a genetic counselor and expect her to inform them about the fragile X syndrome diagnosis. Difficult as it is, the initial discussion about fragile X syndrome must come from you. It is often helpful to work out a specific plan before you start contacting other family members, in order to minimize misunderstandings. First, a genetic counselor can help you to identify which relatives are potentially at risk for carrying the fragile X mutation. Next you should decide how much information you wish to tell your relatives. It is important to remember that, while you have a responsibility to inform other family members, you are not expected to provide them with detailed genetic counseling. You need to give them enough information so that they realize that the diagnosis has direct implications for them, but it is best not to get into a detailed discussion of actual risk numbers and types of testing.

One approach is to contact your relative by phone or in person, and to explain as simply as possible that your child was diagnosed with a hereditary condition called fragile X syndrome. Briefly say that the syndrome can cause a variety of learning difficulties, ranging from mild learning disabilities to severe mental retardation. Explain that you were very shocked to find this out and a genetic counselor advised you that the gene for this syndrome could run in the extended family. State that you met with a genetic counselor, and want to share the information you have learned about your child's diagnosis because of the possibility that extended family members might be fragile X carriers. Reassure your relative that highly accurate testing is available for fragile X syndrome.

If your relative presses you for specific answers to technical and hypothetical questions which make you uncomfortable, or for which you do not know the answers, you can explain that fragile X syndrome is very complicated and, although you are learning to understand how it relates to your own child, you do not know enough about it to answer his or her questions. Give your relative the phone number of the genetic counselor you work with, and tell him or her that the counselor suggested that he or she call. If you have not already done so, tell your genetic counselor about any aspects of your child's personal history that you do not want discussed with other relatives.

An important final step is to follow up your verbal conversations with relatives with written information about fragile X syndrome. Your genetic counselor can provide you with a letter that discusses how the diagnosis was made in your child and outlines the reasons why other family members should seek genetic counseling. Because the letter is written by someone other than you,

your relative is less likely to view this as a personal attack. The counselor can also include a list of medical genetics centers in your relative's region where he or she can go for genetic counseling.

There is no way around it; no one likes to be the bearer of bad news. Yet many parents feel a strong obligation to inform their extended family, because in a sense it was their child who caused this diagnosis to be uncovered. It is sometimes difficult to know where your responsibility for this information ends. Once you have provided adequate and appropriate information to your relatives, including a detailed letter and the specific name and phone number of a genetic counselor, then the decision to pursue or ignore this information is up to them. A relative may decide not to seek carrier testing or to have any of her children tested. This relative may not agree with performing a prenatal diagnosis or may not be interested in learning any more about fragile X syndrome. These may not be the decisions you would make, but every person has the right to make his or her individual choice regarding matters related to a genetic diagnosis. Once you have given your relative accurate information and the names and telephone numbers of professionals who can provide further help, it is not your responsibility to change the person's mind or to make sure that he or she follows through with testing.

Sometimes the situation is more complex, however. Your relative may refuse to relay the information you give her to members of her own family. For example, a woman whose son was diagnosed with fragile X syndrome told her sister about the diagnosis. The sister, who had three daughters in their twenties, refused to tell her daughters because she felt they were not carriers and did not want to worry them needlessly. The first woman was faced with a terrible dilemma: Should she tell her adult nieces about fragile X syndrome and risk destroying her relationship with her sister, or should she stay silent? The woman chose not to discuss it with her nieces, but a few years later, when one of them became engaged, she could no longer maintain her silence. At a family gathering, she told her niece about her son's diagnosis and suggested that she seek genetic counseling. As expected, the woman's sister was initially furious. But all three of her daughters supported their aunt and said that they were glad to find out before planning their families. The experience has left some scars on the relationship between the woman and her sister, but she feels confident that she did the right thing, particularly since one of her nieces was ultimately found to carry a fragile X premutation.

Whatever reaction you receive to the information you share with your extended family, always remember that you did nothing to cause fragile X syndrome to appear in your family. Fragile X mutations are no one's fault, and you have nothing to be ashamed of in conveying the news of your child's diagnosis to your family. The information you offer is critical for your family to plan their lives and make important decisions, even if they do not exactly appreciate receiving it.

These types of situations are particularly difficult and there is no simple solution that works in all cases. A genetic counselor can help you to identify different options and strategies that may make it easier to deal with these sensitive family issues. He or she can put you in touch with local support groups and other parents in your area. He or she can also refer you to a family therapist if you wish.

■■ Conclusion

The birth of a child with fragile X syndrome forever changes the course of a family. The life plans of a couple just starting out may be dramatically altered when there are genetic factors involved. Yet most families adapt in many creative and positive ways. Important to the adjustment process is fully understanding your child's developmental outlook and the reproductive implications for your family. Genetic counseling is an opportunity to carefully examine your family tree, review how the condition is inherited, and discuss available testing and family planning options. By combining education with emotional support, genetic counseling can help you make informed decisions, help you with the adjustment process, and, ideally, help you keep hope for the future.

■■ Parent Statements

It's just a simple blood test, but thinking about the family repercussions made it overwhelming.

My parents (my son's grandparents) were hesitant at first, but only until we explained the bigger picture to them. We were sure it was from my Dad since he has a brother with difficulties, but it turned out it was my Mom. We had been diagnosed for six to eight years before she got the diagnosis, but it seems like yesterday.

I am pretty sure my brother is affected, but I have not seen him since I was 13 years old. My folks don't really want to tell him. Where does personal obligation begin and end?

Whew—what a relief! Finally, somebody who took the time to explain things to us! Once we felt like we got a handle on what fragile X syndrome was, we began to try to figure out how this was going to affect us and what Alex needed.

I learned about the genetics of fragile X syndrome through journal articles and a genetics counselor. Although the information was complicated, it was explained very well.

I was told I might feel guilty about being a carrier and passing this on to my son, but I never have felt that. It was 100 percent out of my control.

I think that fragile X syndrome has bonded certain members of our family together because we now have another common denominator. It's something we learn about together.

I felt such an urgency after the diagnosis to get my questions answered regarding the genetics of fragile X and where our son was in terms of degree of involvement. It was very helpful to meet with a geneticist and a developmental pediatrician very soon after getting diagnosed.

Information about fragile X syndrome should come with the diagnosis, on the same day. It would be a lot to absorb, but you wouldn't be left wondering.

When I found out fragile X syndrome was inherited, I felt guilt ridden.

It did not affect my relationship with anyone except my husband.

I was relieved to understand why I had to be tutored in math and my obsession about being organized and keeping my house clean.

I feel sad for my sister. Granted, I'm the one with the child with fragile X syndrome, but, now, she will probably never have children of her own.

In one sense, the genetic aspect of fragile X syndrome is quite fascinating. In our family tree it shows up here and there. We'd all like to know why it is showing up so much now.

We decided to tell our extended family about our children's diagnosis by letter, since they were all scattered across the continent and some overseas. We wrote the letter over several weeks' time, so we could add to and edit it as we made our own adjustment.

It took several months from the time we got the diagnosis to the time we were ready to share the news with our families. In the meantime, we sought out the support of close friends, some our age and some older, who acted almost like surrogate family members, unconditionally supportive, and emotionally involved in our lives, but without the other baggage families tend to bring. By the time we responded to our families, we were strong enough to offer them the support and understanding we had received.

Genetic testing allowed me to see that it wasn't my fault.

It didn't really bother me that much—it was more of a relief because I'd been analyzing what I had done when I was pregnant.

We had no idea what we were being tested for, therefore had no qualms about consenting to it.

I think we were somewhat relieved to have our suspicions confirmed. We knew something was going on, but thought perhaps we were just paranoid first-time parents.

MEDICAL CONCERNS AND TREATMENT FOR CHILDREN WITH FRAGILE X SYNDROME

Randi Jenssen Hagerman, M.D.

■ Introduction

Parents of children with fragile X syndrome want the same good health and wellness for their children that all parents want. Thanks to increased knowledge about fragile X syndrome and improved medical care, children with fragile X syndrome live healthier lives today than ever before. Although it is more likely children with fragile X syndrome will encounter some of the conditions and problems discussed in this chapter, you can expect your child to live a full and healthy life. Current studies show that most people with fragile X syndrome have an average life span, just like everyone else.

Although medical science cannot change the gene that caused your child's fragile X syndrome, it can improve many of the symptoms and complications that are often associated with the condition. These treatments can help remove some of the obstacles that would otherwise impede your child's growth, learning, and health. For example, medications for attention deficit disorder can increase your child's ability to concentrate on school work; eyeglasses can bring your child's world into focus; speech therapy can help your child be understood by others; and physical or occupational therapy can help improve your child's movement and coordination.

This chapter describes the most common medical concerns that children with fragile X syndrome may have and their treatments. Although the list of possible complications may seem foreboding, the intention is not to scare you. Few children with fragile X syndrome have all, or even most, of these complications. Often when one of these conditions is present, it is in a mild or treatable form. However, being aware of possible problems and their treatments will help you to be an informed consumer of medical services. This is especially important if your child's physician is not well acquainted with fragile X syndrome. What works best for treating children with fragile X syndrome is often the same thing that works for children who do not have this condition. And because establishing a good working relationship with your child's health care providers is important for success, this chapter provides information on finding a physician for your child and offers hints on working with medical professionals.

Chapter 1 describes the physical characteristics of children with fragile X syndrome. Some of these characteristics can lead to medical conditions and complications. Talk to your child's physician if you have concerns in any of the following areas.

▪▪ Conditions Associated with Loose Connective Tissue

Ear Infections

Children with fragile X syndrome often have recurrent middle ear infections, called otitis media. Middle ear infections can cause ear pain; your child may pull at his ear because of the discomfort. He may also run a fever. Be forewarned, however, that some children with fragile X syndrome have a high tolerance for pain and may not show symptoms of pain in their ear. Others may "act out" if they lack the speech skills to describe their ear pain or discomfort. Otitis media can start in the first year of life and reappear many times up until a child is five years old.

One explanation for the frequency of ear infections is that some children with fragile X syndrome have collapsible eustachian tubes. These tubes run from the middle ear to the back of the throat and are supposed to drain fluid that can accumulate in the middle ear. Collapsible is the term used to describe a "floppy" or "flexible" tube. These tubes can collapse, thereby making a child prone to middle ear infection because the fluid does not drain properly, allowing bacteria to grow. Researchers think that the collapsible tubes result from another common fragile X syndrome characteristic, loose connective tissue.

The characteristic facial features of fragile X syndrome—long face and high, arched palate—can also make ear infections more likely. These features can change the angle of the slope of the eustachian tube, reducing drainage from the middle ear. Because the angle of the tube is flat, fluid can remain in the middle ear for extended periods, making it susceptible to infection.

Ear infections are frequently accompanied by a fluid buildup in the middle ear behind the eardrum. When this happens, your child's hearing can be reduced for prolonged periods. Whatever hearing he has can also be distorted by ear infections, making it harder for him to develop speech and language. Because children with fragile X syndrome often experience language delays anyway, it is crucial that ear infections be promptly treated.

Most ear infections are effectively treated with antibiotics. Antibiotics are often either in liquid or pill form. The antibiotics usually have a flavor that is agreeable to children and must be taken for ten days. It takes that long to rid the body of the infection completely. Be sure to follow the prescribed doses.

There are a variety of antibiotics that can be used to fight infections. You may have to try a couple of different types to find the one that works best for your child. Your doctor will keep track of what he prescribes, but it is important for you to provide feedback. Your pharmacy can provide information on the possible side effects of any medication. For example, antibiotics can cause your child's stool to loosen for the ten days he is on the medication.

If infections keep recurring your child may need to have P.E. (pressure equalizing) tubes inserted through his eardrums. These

tubes look like tiny plastic rivets and are usually inserted under anesthesia by an ear, nose, and throat (ENT) doctor. There is little pain from inserting the tubes and recovery is usually very short, generally no more than a few hours. Having this ventilation hole allows fluid to drain out the eustachian tube more effectively under most circumstances; the P.E. tubes also allow fluid to drain from the ear when it becomes infected. The tubes may remain in the ears for months and sometimes for years. It is uncertain why they stay in some children's ears longer than others. Sometimes the tubes have to be reinserted if they fall out. Rarely they have to be surgically removed. P.E. tubes are most helpful in the first three to five years of life when recurrent ear infections are common. They will help to ensure normal hearing even in times of infection.

For some children, P.E. tubes alone do not stop the ear infections. For them, parents report good results when the adenoids, glands in the back of the throat that can block drainage from the eustachian tubes, are also removed. This procedure is also done by an ENT, usually on an outpatient basis; recovery generally takes two to three days.

If you are concerned about your child's hearing, talk to his physician or an ENT. An audiological exam, a sophisticated test that measures your child's hearing, may be recommended. Your child's regular physician should be able to refer you to a competent ENT; you can also contact your local medical center or university affiliated hospital for a referral.

Hernias

Hernias occur in approximately 15 percent of children and adults with fragile X syndrome. This is thought to be caused by loose connective tissue. They occur when all or part of an organ protrudes through a tear in the surrounding tissue. In children with fragile X syndrome, hernias occur most often in the groin, and on occasion in the umbilical area. Frequently, hernias are first diagnosed in early infancy. All hernias should be evaluated by your physician because they often require surgery for repair.

When a hernia occurs in the groin, part of the intestine squeezes through a hole or tear in the tissue between the intestine area and the groin area. The intestine that squeezes through causes the groin area to swell. The intestine can become "kinked," causing a loss of the ability to have a bowel movement. This condition is quite painful and requires immediate surgery to retrieve the intestine and repair the tear in the tissue. Your child is then watched closely the next few days until regular bowel movements return. In rare cases there are complications with regaining regular bowel movements. Surgery is then required to remove the damaged part of the intestine that was "kinked" when it fell into the groin area. The long-term prognosis is good if surgery occurs in a timely fashion.

Reflux

About 20 percent of young children with fragile X syndrome have gastroesophageal reflux. Reflux is associated with recurrent vomiting, particularly in infancy. It occurs when the ring-like muscle, called the sphincter, at the top of the stomach relaxes, allowing stomach contents to flow back up through the esophagus and sometimes into the mouth. This sphincter is supposed to close so food does not move into the esophagus. Relaxation of this sphincter usually allows air to be burped out of the stomach, but if it relaxes too much, stomach contents escape into the esophagus. It is believed that loose connective tissue may cause the sphincter to be more relaxed than it is supposed to be. Reflux can irritate the esophagus, causing pain and irritability. On rare occasions, refluxed stomach contents can be aspirated or breathed into the lungs and lead to pneumonia.

Special feeding techniques can usually minimize reflux in infants. For example, give your child more frequent but smaller portions of food or formula. Thicken his formula with cereal. It may also help to place your child in a semi-upright position for 45 minutes to an hour after meals to give your child's stomach a chance to empty. Consult your child's doctor if reflux symptoms occur regularly. A variety of medications can decrease reflux. If the condition is severe, surgery may be needed.

Cleft Palate

Rarely babies with fragile X syndrome are born with cleft palate. Perhaps this is related to loose connective tissue problems. A cleft palate is a fissure in the roof of the mouth which happens very early in development if the roof of the mouth does not close properly. It is usually seen at the time of birth. Cleft palate causes difficulty with feeding; milk often regurgitates into the throat behind the nose (nasopharynx). Special nipples can be used until your child undergoes corrective surgery, usually during the first year of life, by an oral surgeon. The long-term prognosis is good.

▪▪ Orthopedic Concerns

Fragile X syndrome often causes a variety of orthopedic conditions. Children with fragile X syndrome often have joints that may be overly flexible (hyperflexible). Loose connective tissue and low muscle tone, called hypotonia, are also common and may affect how your child's joints work. Occasionally, these orthopedic conditions can require medical treatment. This section describes the most common orthopedic characteristics in children who have fragile X syndrome and explains how they are treated.

Flat Feet and Pronated Ankles

The majority of children with fragile X syndrome, especially boys, have flat feet and ankles that turn inward (pronated ankles). Scientists think that loose connective tissue plays a large role in this characteristic. This can cause uneven wearing of the shoes, but usually this does not cause pain. High-top shoes with proper arch supports are generally all the treatment needed. If your child's feet and ankles become painful, however, or if his ankles keep turning further and further in, you should consult an orthopedist, a doctor who specializes in bone and joint difficulties. This doctor may prescribe orthotics, plastic shoe inserts designed to provide additional support for your child's feet. In very rare cases, surgery may be required.

Scoliosis

About 20 percent of children with fragile X syndrome develop curvature of the spine, called scoliosis. The cause of this is unknown.

If your child's physician detects scoliosis, your child will need X-rays and follow-up by an orthopedist. In cases to date, the scoliosis seen in patients has been mild and has stabilized on its own. No bracing or surgery has been required. Scoliosis can affect your child's posture, stature, sitting balance, walking ability, and heart and lungs. The orthopedist will carefully monitor the curvature of your child's spine over the years. Your child will also be examined for any back or rib deformities caused by the scoliosis.

Joint Dislocation

Rarely in children with fragile X syndrome, their ligaments are so loose that joints are easily dislocated. This is thought to be caused by loose connective tissue around the joints. That is, the joint may actually come apart or slip out of appropriate alignment because the ligaments and tendons holding the bones together are too flexible. The hip joint can also be dislocated at the time of birth. Sometimes the kneecap and the elbow dislocate during childhood. These dislocations can be quite painful and require immediate medical attention. The joint may not look any different to you when it is dislocated, but your child will probably not use the affected joint.

You should never attempt to put your child's joint back in its place. Your child will probably be most comfortable with the least movement possible until you can see a doctor. The joint will be sore for a few days after the doctor puts it back into place.

If your child has joints that tend to dislocate, consult an orthopedist as soon as possible. The doctor may recommend physical therapy to strengthen the joint. The child's activities may also need to be limited depending on how easy his joint tends to dislocate. Surgery may be needed to tighten the ligaments.

∷ Heart Conditions

Approximately 50 percent of adult males with fragile X syndrome have a type of heart condition known as mitral valve prolapse. The mitral valve separates two chambers of the heart, the left atrium from the left ventricle. If a person has mitral valve prolapse, the mitral valve bows up when the left ventricle contracts. This causes a clicking sound or murmur that is audible through a stethoscope, the instrument doctors use to listen to your heart.

Usually mitral valve prolapse does not cause any medical complications, and your child's activities will likely not need to be restricted. Rarely, however, it can lead to mitral regurgitation in which the mitral valve allows blood to flow back into the left atrium when the heart muscle contracts. This can lead to excess stress on the left ventricle.

If your child's physician hears a murmur or clicking sound, request a referral to a cardiologist, a medical doctor who specializes in the functioning of the heart and heart disorders. The cardiologist can determine whether your child has mitral regurgitation or simply mitral valve prolapse. The cardiologist can also recommend precautions to reduce the risk of your child developing a heart infection, called endocarditis. Endocarditis can occur with any abnormality of the heart because bacteria, which rarely get into the blood stream, tend to settle on an abnormal area in the heart. Precautions generally include giving your child antibiotics such as penicillin before he has surgical or dental procedures which are likely to be associated with bacteria. These antibiotics can clear the bloodstream of bacteria that might otherwise settle in the affected area of the heart, such as a prolapsing mitral valve, and cause an infection. This type of antibiotic treatment is called subacute bacterial endocarditis (SBE) prophylaxis.

▪▪ Vision Concerns

Children with fragile X syndrome often have vision difficulties that can interfere with early learning if not properly treated. The cause of these problems is not known. This makes it essential that your child see an ophthalmologist within the first four years of life. An ophthalmologist is a medical doctor who specializes in the treatment of eye disorders. This doctor can examine your child's eyes for conditions that might be impeding vision. Eyeglasses may be prescribed, medications may be needed, vision therapy may be recommended, or surgery may be necessary to correct vision.

In addition to ophthalmologists, there are optometrists, who are non-M.D. professionals who specialize in eye disorders. Optometrists can examine the eyes, prescribe lenses, and provide vision therapy. But they cannot perform surgery or prescribe medication. It is prudent to seek more than one doctor's opinion on your child's eyes and what should be done to correct the vision.

The sections below describe the most common eye conditions children with fragile X syndrome have.

Strabismus

Approximately 10 to 30 percent of children with fragile X syndrome have strabismus. In this condition, one or both eyes may have weak eye muscles, making it difficult or impossible to focus both eyes on an object. One or both eyes may turn out (exotropia), or they may turn in (esotropia). If not treated, strabismus can lead to a lack of development in the optic cortex of the brain, the area of the brain that perceives visual stimuli and allows the development of depth perception. This in turn can lead to amblyopia, a condition in which the brain turns off or suppresses the vision from the weak eye to prevent blurred or double vision. The result is that the visual processing center of the brain does not fully develop and the eye will have poor vision that cannot be corrected with glasses. By later childhood, this suppression may become irreversible, resulting in a permanent loss of vision in the weak eye. It is for this reason that early and regular eye examinations are important.

Treatment for strabismus involves strengthening the weaker eye muscle. A patch or a blurred lens may be placed over the "good" eye to force the weaker eye to work in order to stimulate the optic cortex and help it develop. Corrective lenses may be prescribed. Eye exercises that strengthen the eye muscles are also being used with success, particularly in combination with corrective lenses. Surgery on the eye muscles may also be recommended. Surgery is often successful, but on rare occasions a second surgery is needed.

Nearsightedness and Farsightedness

Children with fragile X syndrome often have decreased visual acuity, which means they either cannot see objects well close up or cannot see well at a distance. Farsightedness occurs when they see distant objects clearly, but nearby objects are blurred. Nearsightedness is just the opposite: nearby objects are clear, but distant objects are blurred. Corrective lenses are used to treat both of these conditions. If your child complains of blurred vision, eye strain, eye pain, or if there is concern during routine vision screening at your school, your child should be examined by an ophthalmologist.

On rare occasions, nystagmus, or constant jerking of the eyes from side to side, may be seen in a child with fragile X syndrome. Also ptosis, a condition where the eyelid droops, may occur in children with fragile X syndrome. It may be especially noticeable when your child is tired. Nystagmus and ptosis both require an ophthalmologic evaluation.

Assessing visual acuity in young children with fragile X syndrome can be challenging. Ophthalmologists dilate the eyes and then shine a light into the eye to examine the retina to determine if corrective lenses are needed. This shows the doctor the shape of the eye, and enables him or her to determine the lens required to correct the vision. Ophthalmologists also use observation skills in determining the corrective lens required. They observe how your child uses his eyes when objects are moved in various directions and when different kinds of eye activities are performed. The accuracy of these vision assessments increases as your child becomes verbal.

■■ Reproductive Issues

As Chapter 1 discusses, large testicles (macroorchidism) are one of the features of fragile X syndrome in males. Often, testicular size changes dramatically at puberty. In approximately 80 percent of males with fragile X syndrome, testicles eventually grow to two or three times typical size. Usually, this increased testicle size does not lead to any medical complications.

Although they rarely father children, men who have fragile X syndrome are usually fertile. In a male with a full mutation, the sperm carries the premutation only. All daughters of a male with a full mutation will be carriers only and unaffected intellectually by fragile X syndrome. All sons of a father with fragile X syndrome will be unaffected by the condition, because they receive the Y chromosome—not the X chromosome—from their fathers. Occasionally females with symptoms of fragile X syndrome have enlarged ovaries. Again this seldom leads to any medical concerns. Interestingly, in approximately 15 to 20 percent of carrier females who do not show symptoms of fragile X syndrome, premature ovarian failure occurs. This means that their estrogen levels drop at an earlier age than usual and menopause may begin before the age of 40. On rare occasions, menopause may occur as early as the twenties. Although this phenomenon has not been fully studied, preliminary evidence suggests that premature menopause is related to being a carrier of the fragile X mutation. There is currently no treatment for ovarian failure, except estrogen replacement.

No one yet knows how or why the altered fragile X gene causes these changes in the male and female reproductive systems. The fragile X mutation, however, may interfere with the production and regulation of hormones in the body.

∷ Seizures

About 20 percent of boys and a smaller percentage of girls with fragile X syndrome have seizures. Seizures are caused by periodic bursts of unusual electrical activity in the brain that lead in some cases to unconsciousness and abnormal movements. The lack of the FMR1 protein is associated with seizures, but the exact mechanism is unknown.

There are several different types of seizures, classified according to the symptoms they produce. The most common types of seizures in children with fragile X syndrome are:

- **Tonic-clonic** *(formerly known as grand mal)*—usually involves jerking and stiffening of the arms and legs.
- **Absence** *(formerly known as petit mal)*—involves staring and eye blinking.
- **Simple partial** *(formerly known as focal motor)*—only one part of the body shows stiffening or jerking; the child is usually awake and alert during this seizure.
- **Complex partial** *(formerly known as temporal lobe)*—there is a change in consciousness and sometimes unusual behaviors; automaton-like movement may occur.

Seizures often start during the first six years of life. You should have your child evaluated for seizures if you notice staring spells, spacey episodes, unusual jerking, or unexplained falls. The abnormal electrical activity in the brain can be detected with an EEG (electroencephalogram). During this test, your child will be hooked up to a machine that measures and records the electrical activity in his brain. The test is painless, although the electrodes attached to your child's skull may look frightening to him or bother him if he is tactilely defensive. Because electrical discharges are more likely to occur when your child is asleep, you may be asked to bring him in for testing when he is sleepy. If you and your doctor agree, the technician who performs the EEG may give your child some medication to help him sleep during the study.

Although a seizure can be alarming to watch, your child will not hurt himself if you take appropriate action. Here are some steps to follow:

1. Keep calm, loosen your child's clothing, and put something soft under his head. Turn your child to one side, but do not try to restrain him. Do not put anything into his mouth; he *cannot* swallow his tongue.

2. Remove hard, sharp objects from the area so that he won't hurt himself if he moves around.

3. After the seizure is over, keep your child lying on his side and allow him to rest. He may be confused, and you may need to help him get his bearings. Tell him specifically where he is and suggest a quiet activity until he is reoriented.

4. If the seizure lasts more than five minutes, or if your child appears to pass from one seizure to another without regaining consciousness, call the doctor or an ambulance. Be sure that your physician gives you specific written instructions beforehand about when to have your child taken directly to the hospital.

In many children with fragile X syndrome, seizures may decrease or disappear with age. Sometimes, however, people need to take medications to control their seizures for their entire lives. A range of medications, called anticonvulsants, is available, and usually a drug or combination of drugs can be used to reduce the frequency or severity of your child's seizures. It may take time to find the right medication for your child. Your child's doctor, usually a neurologist, will start by giving your child one medication, then ask you to observe your child for signs of improvement or side effects such as sedation, rash, irritability, or stomach aches.

Periodically your doctor will do blood tests to check the level of medication in your child's bloodstream. The physician may then increase or decrease the dosage, or recommend trying a different medication, depending on the test results and your feedback. The goal is to find the medication that will give your child the maximum benefit with a minimum of undesirable side effects.

The medication most often used for controlling seizures in children with fragile X syndrome is carbamazepine (Tegretol™). It is often helpful in reducing simple partial, complex partial, and tonic-clonic seizures. Carbamazepine can also help reduce inappropriate behavior such as aggression and hyperactivity (discussed later in this chapter). Side effects can include sleepiness (in about a third of patients), as well as lowered white cell count and liver toxicity or irritation of the liver (which is rare). Your doctor will test your child's blood regularly for these side effects. If they are found, the medication will be reduced or discontinued.

If carbamazepine is not effective in controlling your child's seizures, other anticonvulsant medication may be prescribed, such as valproic acid (Depakote™). Although this medication produces good results in many children who have seizures, few researchers have studied its effectiveness in children with fragile X syndrome. It can produce side effects that include appetite changes, hair thinning, stomach aches, and liver and pancreas irritation. Because of these potential side effects, your child should be closely monitored if he is prescribed any anticonvulsant medication.

▪▪ Behavior

Children with fragile X syndrome sometimes behave in ways that are considered unusual or troublesome. For example, they may be overly active or impulsive, behave aggressively, have frequent tantrums, or become anxious or depressed for no apparent reason. Over time children can learn to control these behaviors through their educational and therapeutic programs. For example, if overstimulation triggers your child's tantrums, an occupational therapist can teach him calming techniques, physical relaxation techniques, self-hypnosis, or other methods of handling the stresses that upset him. And as Chapters 5 and 8 discuss, there are also a variety of behavior management techniques that parents and teachers can use to help children learn to behave more appropriately.

Sometimes if a child's behavior interferes significantly with his ability to socialize or to pay attention and learn, medications may also be helpful. The sections below discuss the medications currently used to affect the behaviors associated with fragile X syndrome.

Attention Deficit Hyperactivity Disorder (ADHD)

Attention deficit hyperactivity disorder (ADHD) is a condition that disrupts the ability to focus and maintain attention, make choices, and benefit from teaching. Symptoms include:

1. The inability to sit still or to control the urge to be physically active;
2. Impulsivity, or acting without thinking—for example, constantly interrupting others or being bossy;
3. Difficulty paying attention, together with rapid loss of interest in the topic of conversation or in activities; and
4. Aggressive behavior in some—examples include hitting, kicking, or throwing tantrums.

In the past, ADHD was known as "hyperactivity."

About three to five percent of all typically developing children have ADHD. It is diagnosed about six times as often in boys as in girls. Typical children with ADHD may blurt out answers before a question is completed, talk excessively, have trouble following directions, seem very restless, or be unable to focus their attention regularly. If they are very "impulsive," they may behave dangerously or recklessly—running into the street or grabbing a pot on the stove even though they know about "danger" and "hot." Parents of children with ADHD are likely to describe them as "climbing the walls" or "driven."

Actually hyperactivity is not always the primary symptom of ADHD. In some children, the only major symptom is the inability to pay attention. They may simply be unable to focus their attention and effort or may give up when an activity becomes slightly difficult. They may often miss much of what is said or shown to them. Most of these children, however, are able to focus their attention for longer periods of time if they find an activity especially engrossing.

All boys who have fragile X syndrome have some difficulty paying attention, and at least 80 percent meet the detailed diagnostic criteria for ADHD. Approximately 30 percent of girls who have fragile X syndrome have ADHD. Special educational help and an appropriate classroom environment can often help children with ADHD learn. Sometimes medication is used along with educational approaches to treat ADHD. Your child's physician can tell you whether your child might benefit from medication. Alternately, you may wish to consult a psychologist if your child's behavior is your main concern.

Whatever type of professional you consult, you can expect the diagnostic process for your child to include a thorough medical evaluation. It is often through medical evaluation of hyperactivity or ADHD that fragile X syndrome is diagnosed. Usually medications used to treat hyperactivity without fragile X syndrome can also be helpful for children with fragile X syndrome. Medication should be considered only one part of a treatment program which should also include behavioral interventions, therapies, and special education support.

Research has shown that specific medications can dramatically improve many children's behavior. In fact, medication for ADHD was first used successfully in 1937 in a residential facility for children with behavioral issues in Providence, Rhode Island. These medications can greatly improve many children's ability to attend and focus their attention on learning tasks. Although parents are sometimes apprehensive about using any medications with their children on a long-term basis, most physicians consider medications the primary treatment for a child who has a clear diagnosis of ADHD.

The medications most often used to control symptoms of ADHD are stimulant medications. They are so called because they stimulate certain neurotransmitter systems—nerve pathways that relay messages—in the brain. The neurotransmitters stimulated by these medications help to inhibit or curb inappropriate behavior, mood, and action. Improved inhibition—the ability of a child to stop himself from doing something—leads to decreased impulsivity and hyperactivity and increased attention span. Auditory processing, reaction time, sensory integration, and motor coordination may also be aided by these medications.

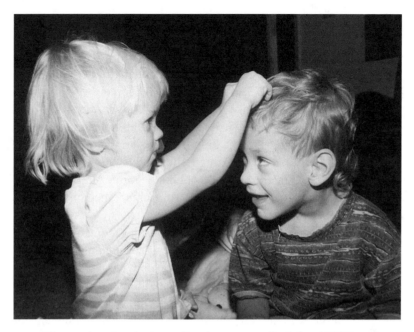

The main stimulant medications prescribed for ADHD are me-thylphenidate (Ritalin™), dextroamphetamine (Dexedrine™ and Adderall ™), and pemoline (Cylert™). In addition to decreasing ADHD symptoms, all four medications can produce a range of side effects. One of the major side effects is reduced appetite. This side effect can lead to weight loss. Height growth is only affected if weight loss is significant. Usually the higher the dose, the more likely it is that appetite will be reduced. One solution is to time the dosage so that it is taken at or during a meal and not in between meals. Appetite usually improves as one dose is wearing off and the next dose is going into effect. Stimulant medications can also cause an increase in the heart rate and blood pressure. And in rare cases, pemoline causes a skin rash or liver irritation or liver failure.

Because of the possible side effects, children on stimulant medi-cation should visit their physician every three to six months. During these visits, the physician should look at changes in weight and height, as well as check blood pressure and heart rate. The doctor can then adjust the dosage or change medications if the side effects outweigh the benefits.

As discussed in Chapter 1, approximately 10 to 20 percent of children with fragile X syndrome have motor tics. Motor tics are quick movements of the muscles that generally affect the face, arms, or legs. Stimulant medication can worsen tics in approximately 30 percent of children who have tics before stimulants are given. In general, children with fragile X syndrome are quite sensitive to stimulant medication. Stimulants often make them more irritable, particularly when they are under five years of age or when given a higher dose. For these reasons, stimulant medication is usually started at the lowest dose possible. For methylphenidate, the lowest dose is a 5 mg tablet. Even this dose may be too large for a child with fragile X syndrome who is under five years old. The tablet may need to be halved and given in two 2.5 mg doses per day. Methylphenidate is usually given two or three times a day in the short acting form, but it also comes in a long acting 20 mg SR (slow release) tablet. Dextro-amphetamine comes in a 5 mg spansule form which is long acting and is usually given once in the morning. Adderall™, a mixture of four amphetamine salts, comes in a long acting 5 mg tablet that can be given once or twice a day. The lowest dose of pemoline is 18.75 mg, which is also long acting; however, pemoline is rarely used because of the risk of liver failure in approximately 1 in 100,000.

If stimulant medications are not effective in controlling your child's ADHD symptoms, a "tricyclic" medication such as imipramine (Tofranil™) may be tried. Usually tricyclic medications are not as effective as stimulants in improving impulsivity, distractibility, and attention span. Imipramine can also cause a variety of side effects; so its use must be closely monitored. In at least half of children with fragile X syndrome, imipramine seems to increase outburst behavior (either verbal or physical). If outbursts are already a concern for your child, imipramine would not be a good choice. Imipramine can also increase heart rate and prolong the electrical conduction time in the heart. This means that if your child is prescribed this drug, he should be monitored with periodic electrocardiograms (EKG), including a baseline EKG and EKGs following an increase in dosage. Imipramine usually does not decrease the appetite as much as stimulant medications, nor does it make motor tics worse. In addition, it can improve bed wetting by changing sleep patterns if your child happens to have difficulty in this area.

A relatively new medication in the treatment of ADHD is clonidine (Catapres™). Clonidine was originally developed to treat high blood pressure; it is considered to be an antihypertensive drug.

This medication is more commonly used to control tics in children with Tourette syndrome. It improves attention span and concentration in some children with hyperactivity. Clonidine may be most beneficial in children who are extremely hyperactive, easily overwhelmed or hyperaroused by stimuli, or have tantrum behavior. This describes many children with fragile X syndrome.

A recent survey of families with fragile X syndrome has shown that clonidine was helpful for approximately 80 percent of children in which it was tried. The main side effect of clonidine is sleepiness, which increases with the dose. Consequently, clonidine should be started at a very low dose such as 0.05 mg (1/2 of a tablet) twice a day. In addition, if your child is prescribed this medication, he should have periodic follow-up visits with his doctor. An EKG is also recommended in follow-up since rare cases of cardiac arrhythmias or unusual heart rhythms have been reported with clonidine.

A controversial treatment for ADHD you may hear about is folic acid. Different researchers have written conflicting reports about its effectiveness, but some studies suggest that it improves attention span and concentration in some children with fragile X syndrome. In our experience at the Fragile X Treatment and Research Center in Denver, Colorado, folic acid has helped about 50 percent of young children with fragile X syndrome. There have also been reports from parents and professionals that folic acid may improve speech, particularly articulation and motor coordination. If folic acid is suggested for your child, a trial of two to three months should be long enough to see if attention span, concentration, and speech or motor coordination improve. If there is no improvement, the folic acid should be discontinued. A child is usually treated with a dose of 10 mg per day, which can be taken in liquid or tablet form. Because folic acid may cause deficiencies in vitamin B6 and occasionally zinc, multivitamins should be taken at the same time, and periodic checkups and blood testing are required. It may also cause your child's stool to be a little looser.

Studies are currently underway to evaluate the effectiveness of a medication similar to folic acid, leucovorin. Preliminary results suggest that it helps some young children with fragile X syndrome. However, its effectiveness was not significant for the group as a whole. Its response rate appears to be similar to what is seen with folic acid. A significant drawback of treating children with leucovorin is that it is an extremely expensive medication.

Aggression or Violent Outbursts

Aggressive behavior or violent outbursts are seen in approximately 30 percent of adolescents and adults (mostly male) who have fragile X syndrome. A typical outburst may involve hitting someone nearby when upset or frustrated. Medication is used to inhibit this behavior if it occurs frequently because of the potential for the child to hurt himself or other people.

To date no controlled studies have been done to determine the most effective medication for managing these behaviors. But doctors who specialize in treating people with fragile X syndrome have learned from experience that some medications may be more useful than others. Fluoxetine (Prozac™) or other medications, such as sertraline (Zoloft™) and fluvoxamine (Luvox™), have been used commonly to treat aggressive behaviors because they reduce anxiety and improve mood. They are also helpful in improving depression and decreasing obsessive-compulsive behavior. Side effects can include agitation, insomnia, and nausea. If agitation leads to more aggressive behavior, then fluoxetine should not be used or it should be discontinued. Counseling is also recommended to decrease aggression and to monitor the benefits and side effects of medication. Behavioral therapies are also used.

Other medications that can be helpful for decreasing aggression include carbamazepine, valproic acid , and clonidine described above. In addition, thioridazine (Mellaril™) or risperidone (Risperdal™), which are antipsychotic medications, can be used to control aggressive behavior in children and adults with fragile X syndrome when other medications have not been helpful. They can also decrease delusions, paranoia, and hallucinations which can also be associated with aggression. Psychotic thinking such as this can occur on occasion in people with fragile X syndrome. The downsides of any antipsychotic medication include a number of unwanted side effects, all of which occur more often at higher doses. The most common side effects are sleepiness and increased appetite, leading to obesity. They can also cause a dry mouth and low blood pressure. With high dose, long-term use, antipsychotics can lead to even more disturbing side effects. These include akathisia, involuntary restless movements, and tardive dyskinesia, a condition that causes facial movements such as sucking or lip smacking, grimacing, a fixed upward gaze, or unusual body movements. Risperidone is the least likely to cause these problems; if they occur the dose should be lowered. An additional medication that can help reduce violent aggressive behavior is lithium carbonate (Eskalith™). It acts as a mood stabilizer. Its main side effect is disturbance of kidney function, which can lead to an increase in urination and electrolyte abnormalities (imbalances of sodium and potassium in the blood). At higher doses it may cause sleepiness and an unstable walk. Patients taking this medication need to see their physician regularly for tests to measure the blood level of lithium and electrolytes, as well as for kidney function studies.

Anxiety and Depression

In general, challenging behavioral symptoms are much less of a concern for females with fragile X syndrome than for males. For example, only about 30 percent of females have symptoms of ADHD, and aggressive behavior and violent outbursts are rare. But as Chapter 1 discusses, females with fragile X syndrome have a tendency to be anxious or depressed. Emotional difficulties are particularly a challenge for adolescent and adult females with fragile X syndrome. Mild difficulties can often be treated successfully with counseling, but medications can also be helpful, particularly if the anxiety or depression becomes severe or interferes with everyday social activities.

Unfortunately no controlled studies have been carried out to determine the most effective medications for females with fragile X syndrome affected by anxiety or depression. Some specialists have found certain medications work better than others. To treat anxiety or obsessive behavior, the most commonly used medications are the serotonin agents such as Prozac™, Zoloft™, or Paxil™. They are not addictive and they are safer than benzodiazepines such as Valium™.

Depression has been treated with a variety of medications, including the tricyclic medications discussed in the section on ADHD. In addition, fluoxetine (Prozac™) or other serotonin agents are effective for depression. Prozac can also improve mood swings, obsessive-compulsive behavior, and outburst behavior in females with fragile X syndrome. Controlled studies are needed so that the effectiveness of these medications can be carefully assessed. Some individuals do fine long term with just a short course of medication such as six months. Others find the medication helpful for a long period of time such as two to three years.

▪▪ Finding the Right Pediatrician and Physician

As parents, it is important you find a primary doctor for your child who meets both your needs and your child's. Your child needs a doctor who is familiar with or at least willing to learn about fragile X syndrome and its various characteristics. It is important to find a doctor who tries to put your child at ease, or at least listens to your suggestions about how to put him at ease. This can involve everything from his or her tone of voice to the way he or she touches your child. You need someone who is willing to take the time to explain things to you in terms you can understand. Seek a pediatrician who does not talk down to you. In your child's life, the pediatrician will be an important member of your child's team of medical professionals. Other general areas to consider in seeking and working with medical professionals are found in the following section.

Depending on where you live, you may have a choice of pediatricians. Feel fortunate if you are in that position. Many will not have that luxury. Take the time then to find the one that works well with you, your child, and your family. If you do not have a choice, work to build a relationship with your doctor.

Remember in either case, it takes time to build relationships. Initially you may find doctors intimidating because you think that they know everything. But there is an information exchange that needs to occur continually. Many parents seek out medical information about fragile X syndrome and share this with their physician. Parents need to monitor side effects of drugs, and can often provide doctors important information about their child's behavior or symptoms they see at home.

Be prepared for appointments with your child's doctor. Write down all your questions beforehand so you do not forget any of them. Bring them up one by one. If the doctor does not volunteer the information you want to know, *ask*. Seek a relationship of mutual respect. Respect the doctor for the knowledge he or she has and the work he or she does. Expect the doctor to respect you for the knowledge you have and the work that you do.

Many physicians may not be experienced in treating children with fragile X syndrome. However, all general physicians can educate themselves regarding this common condition. If your regular physi-

cian is not experienced or comfortable with the medications discussed in this chapter, ask him or her to consult with a developmental pediatrician, a psychiatrist, or a neurologist who is. Consultations once or twice a year can provide guidance to your physician concerning your child's medical needs and give you the information you need to best help your child. The National Fragile X Foundation has a directory of knowledgeable professionals experienced with fragile X syndrome around the country.

Finding caring, competent medical professionals is the key to helping your child make the most of his abilities. Here are some additional hints:

1. Ask other parents of children with fragile X syndrome about medical professionals their child has seen. Although not always accurate, the grapevine may be useful in narrowing down the field.

2. Try contacting a university-affiliated medical school in your area. They often have top-notch professionals with years of experience in their field of expertise. Make sure when you make an appointment, though, that your child will actually see the physician you request.

3. If your area has a children's hospital or regional child development clinic, check into the services they provide. These facilities offer a wide range of professional services, with a fee based upon family income. Check in the "Public Health Clinic" or "Physicians/Pediatricians: Developmental Pediatricians" sections in your phone book.

4. Your physician or your child's pediatrician can be a good source of names for specialists such as neurologists and ophthalmologists. So too can the local branch of The Arc (formerly known as the Association for Retarded Citizens) in the USA or the Association for Community Living (ACL) in Canada.

Once you have set up an initial appointment, your search is not necessarily over. You will want to determine as quickly as possible whether the professional will be responsive to your needs, or whether you should keep looking. In general, it may help if you think about what you value in *your* physician—whether it is technical skills, personality, demeanor, or availability—and then use these values as your guides.

You may want to begin by asking the professional what kind of training and experience he or she has had with children who have fragile X syndrome. Next try to get a feel for his or her attitude toward you and your child. Does he or she show respect for your child as a person, spending time talking with her, explaining or demonstrating what will take place before doing a medical procedure? Can your child communicate with him or her and vice versa? Does he or she treat you as an expert with knowledge about your child that only you could have? Does he or she value your opinion?

While you are trying to gauge the doctor's suitability, pay attention to the kinds of explanations he or she offers you. It is very important that he or she speak in a language you can understand, and not withhold any information vital to the well-being of your child. Whenever a test is to be performed, he or she should carefully explain the procedure and any risks involved, and let you know if there may be side effects of medications. He or she should welcome your questions and make sure you understand the answers. Just as importantly, he or she should show respect for your feelings and those of your child, no matter what news he or she has to tell you. He or she should be able to explain information humanely, never in an off-hand or cruel manner. In short, the doctor should treat you like a real person with real feelings.

Of course you may not be able to make a judgment about all these factors on your first visit. And there are other questions that it may take several weeks or months to find the answers to. For example, there may be some times when it is more critical for your child to receive immediate medical care than others. How responsive is the professional in emergency situations? Does he or she make room in his or her schedule to see you and your child right away? Remember that no two physicians, psychiatrists, neurologists, or other specialists are alike. If you have had a difficult or bad experience before, tell the professional who will see your child. Also explain what you expect from this evaluation or visit. Tell the doctor when you are pleased and thankful for the services you have received, and also tell him or her when you are not pleased. Above all be honest with yourself and the professional. Be honest about things that are happening at home, any relevant aspects of your lifestyle, and practical limitations on your time and energy. For example, let the doctor know if you cannot afford a particular test for your child, or if you would like help breaking your child of the habit of sleeping in your bed. Be honest about how much time you can devote to your child's education and treatment. Also try to be honest with yourself about your child's skills and needs so you can have realistic expectations about how much the physician or specialist can do for your child. And if in all honesty you do not think the physician or specialist is doing a good enough job, go elsewhere. After all, it is your child and your money!

Even if you are basically satisfied with your physician, you should never hesitate to ask for a second opinion. Feel free to consult another doctor whenever you have any questions about other treatment options, or are unsure that your child's progress or improvement is as it should be. Trust your instincts. You should also seek another opinion when your current physician is unwilling to change your child's treatment or try another approach when the current approach is not successful.

As you begin to assemble a team of competent, compassionate professionals to care for your child, you may find that you need to take on the role of a service coordinator or case manager. That is, it may be up to you to make sure that all the various medical professionals involved with your child are kept informed and coordinated. You may also need to juggle the many logistical and scheduling issues associated with coordinating medical and other professional consultations. You will need to keep track of when your child needs to be seen again by a given specialist, and also follow any recommendations he or she may make for you and your child's regular pediatrician to carry out. Be sure to keep a file with copies of reports from each evaluation performed on your child. That way you will always have this information at your fingertips whenever educational or medical professionals are making plans for your child. Finally, every time professionals meet to discuss your child and his treatment, you should see that they use the opportunity to make sure that your child receives all the evaluations and professional consultations he needs.

Besides acting as your child's service coordinator, you should also do what you can to make sure doctor visits or hospitalizations are as pleasant as possible for your child. If your child is to have a potentially traumatic test or procedure, such as drawing blood, it often helps to visit the doctor's office in advance to let your child get accustomed to the surroundings and the people. You can also prepare him by telling him a simple story with a happy ending about the upcoming visit or procedure. To minimize waiting time, try to schedule appointments for periods when the doctor is less busy. And before you leave the house, always

call ahead to find out if the doctor is behind schedule. Finally, be prepared to explain your child's special needs not only to the doctor, but to his or her staff. For example, if your child becomes very uneasy in a crowded, noisy waiting room, ask the receptionist if you can wait in an examination room instead. If your child is very sensitive to touch around his face, tell the audiologist *before* she tries to put earphones on your child's head.

▪▪ Conclusion

One of the most important things parents do for their children is make sure they grow up healthy. As the parent of a child with fragile X syndrome, you may find this job a little more complicated because of the range of medical and behavioral issues your child may have. But you can succeed in enabling your child to live a full and healthy life.

In general you can follow the same steps as any parent to ensure your child's optimum health. You can familiarize yourself with possible conditions that might impair your child's health and development. You can promptly notify your child's physician at the first hint of a medical concern. And you can help your child follow through on any treatment prescribed. With proper diagnosis and treatment of the conditions described in this chapter, there is no reason your son or daughter should not enjoy a healthy childhood and a healthy life.

∷ Parent Statements

It's too much work! My whole life is ear infections, doctor appointments, therapy sessions, hospitalizations, and reading up on fragile X syndrome. There's no time to play. I just want to quit.

Our son had a major sleep disorder. He didn't sleep through the night or take a nap until he was three and a half years old.

Tony had life threatening reflux. After almost choking to death, we called 911. He was already limp and blue. He had surgery for the reflux at three months.

Our son can't entertain himself and he won't stay with anyone other than a grandparent or me.

Alex was on antibiotics for about eight months straight once he started school. Every respiratory infection caused bad earaches. So over time we have had two sets of tubes put in his ears and at the last surgery had his adenoids shaved. The tubes have helped tremendously, not only with infections, but with his hearing, too.

He had recurrent ear infections and one set of ear tubes. He also coincidentally has asthma.

My son's reflux is mainly controlled with medicine now. He has no resistance and catches every little thing.

Our son used to have crying spells that would go on for hours at a time.

❧

The first time I gave my son some Ritalin, I cried.

❧

Medication was a lifesaver for us.

❧

I was too embarrassed to tell any of my friends I was putting my son on medication. When they noticed a change in Tony (for the better) I was able to tell them.

❧

If it is the right medication, you will know within a couple of days.

❧

It is hard for me to think he might have to be on some kind of medication for the rest of his life.

❧

I have just had to come to terms with the fact that William's chemistry is different than my husband's or mine.

❧

Whenever we have to make a medication change, I prepare myself for a couple of months of chaos.

❧

I wish the medication aspect wasn't such a trial and error, that it was more scientific and precise. I guess I want it to be easier.

❧

Our son could not go to school if he wasn't on some kind of medication for his hyperactivity and short attention span.

❧

Finding a pediatrician who was willing to fight for Tony and us with the insurance company, and willing to help us to try new things that might come out, was a difficult process. We finally found one who was at the top of his class at medical school and was interested in learning about fragile X syndrome, but he had not had any other patients like Tony. Here again I, as his mother, was put in the position of being the expert on something that I had not been educated to handle.

We are in the process of "molding" our pediatrician into what we want him to be! It takes mutual trust, respect, and a willingness on both parts to learn.

Pediatricians frequently have had little to no experience with developmentally delayed kids and we as parents shouldn't expect them or trust them with all the decision-making authority. It should be a collaboration between home, school, and specialists in development.

I have a wonderful pediatrician, but it took a lot of searching to find her.

I had a terribly hard time switching pediatricians. It was almost overwhelming. But am I glad I did! He's the greatest.

Your relationship with teachers, doctors, and therapists should follow some of the basic rules for social interaction—courtesy, understanding, and mutual concern (not just concern for your child). Remember to thank them often and ask how you can help. It should be a joint effort between professionals and families, not an adversarial relationship. It really does "take a whole village to raise a child."

The medical issues can take up so much time and money. My goodness, just the issues around the eyes and the ears are enough to keep you in the doctor's office once a week. Add therapy on top of that and you end up broke.

5

DAILY CARE

David York Moor, MRCGP (UK)
Family Physician

■ Introduction

Looking after the daily care of a child with fragile X syndrome can be challenging. It can be very challenging to look after *any* child. Although it is natural to make it more difficult for ourselves by concentrating on the negative aspects of our child's performance, if we look at the positive aspects of what they can do, life becomes easier. The task we are given, however, is not an easy one, and it is important that we do not neglect ourselves or the other members of our family while trying to do what is best for our child with fragile X syndrome.

All parents are their child's first teachers. Because you know your child best, you will always be the most understanding and most sensitive teacher for your child. For example, your child's speech may be unintelligible to strangers, but as a parent you may know instantly what he is trying to say. You are the critical link between your child and the outside world.

In taking care of your child, you may sometimes think that everything is twice as hard for you, but turn it around and think about it from your child's point of view. Certainly his life is harder than it would be if he did not have fragile X syndrome. He has difficulty receiving and processing incoming information; on top of that he is only a child, not familiar with the ways of the world. You, the adult with experience, must be his guide.

The basis for the daily care of a child with fragile X syndrome is in almost every way the same as that for all children. True, there are differences; and this chapter aims to explain those differences. But for your child's sake and for yours, don't forget how much like other children your child really is.

:: Daily Routine

Sooner or later all children develop a daily routine of eating, sleeping, activity, and rest. Your child will too. This section of the chapter explains some of the routine daily events in your child's life and offers suggestions on how to make them go smoothly for you and your child.

Structure and Reliability. Because it may likely be harder for your child to sort the mass of information and sensations coming his way, predictability and routine in his daily life are critical. Your child needs familiar landmarks, routines, and structures that he can identify. Although each child is unique in how well he can tolerate variation or change in routine, it is best to introduce change gradually. By establishing and maintaining regular routines each day, you can make life easier for your child and consequently for you and your family.

Schedules. If you have put in the effort to create a predictable routine, it is important to find ways to show and tell him what it is. There are many easy ways to communicate your child's schedule to him. Show your child what is going to happen in advance by drawing simple pictures or signing. For example, you can draw a picture of a dish, knife, fork, and spoon to indicate a mealtime. A picture of a bath can be used later in the day. If you draw your pictures on small squares of paper, these can be sequenced in a row to indicate what will be done first. This way you can map out your child's day. Also, talk to your child about what is going to happen in advance and then remind him every so often. This is especially helpful if his routine will be different. All of us manage easier in steady routines. This is even more true for a child with fragile X syndrome; your child may show great displeasure at a change in routine. However, if your child knows about the change in advance he is less likely to react negatively.

Fit Your Child's Activities into the Context of a Regular Day. None of us have identical days throughout the week. Our children with fragile X have to learn this. So try to maintain regular routines each day, but make sure that your child knows that each day is different. For example, "Today is Wednesday; we go to the swimming pool on Wednesdays, but today we are also going to go to the Post Office because we have a package to mail." Try explaining the change in routine a few days before it actually occurs so your child can get used to the idea. Talk about what to expect during the new part of the routine or maybe read a picture book about the Post Office.

Handling Transitions. Major transitions such as moving into a new house or changing schools can be managed by incorporating the daily techniques that are explained above. Try to keep your child's routine as stable as possible. For example, ask your child's previous teacher to give you a list of his daily school schedule so that this can be passed on to the new school. See the new classroom and care staff before your child attends the school. Discuss with the new staff the difficulties that your child has with change to ensure as smooth an integration as possible. Again, talk about and read books about the elements of the change such as a new route to school, new teachers, or new buildings.

∷ Daily Activities

In establishing a daily routine, there are many separate activities each day that your child will encounter, and you with him. In approaching daily life with him, try to strike a balance between your controlling and guiding him and allowing him to exercise control. One way to do this is to give your child choices. This permits expansion of expression. You may have to offer limited choices in some situations rather than free choice, because it may be too much for your child to make a decision if there are a lot of options. For example, "What would you like to drink— milk or juice?" Some restriction of choice is also reasonable because children with fragile X may have favorites to the exclusion of all else. If my son could have his own way, he would only ever wear one pair of blue pajamas. This obviously is not practical.

Dressing

When young, care has to be taken with dressing children with fragile X syndrome because they are often hypotonic; that is, their muscles have less tone or resistance. Consequently, their arms and legs may not always go down sleeves and trouser legs as you might expect. Dressing is often easier with your child on your lap. This method combines pulling

the clothes on while your child resists, by pushing his arms and legs out. The result is that he actually helps you slip him into his clothes.

Children with fragile X syndrome can also be very sensitive to sensations. This is sometimes called tactile defensiveness, when the child is hypersensitive to touch, and it may affect your choice of clothes for your child. For example, your child may not like the idea of short sleeves and short trousers in the summer because they expose his skin to the wind. He may also not like to have his clothes tucked in. The accommodations for these preferences are usually quite simple. Involve your child in choosing what he will wear each day. At first limit his choice, and gradually move toward letting him choose what he wants to wear.

There are many ways to make dressing easier for your child to do himself. For example, shoes with Velcro fastenings are great because your child can fasten them himself. There are also pullover shirts and pants with elastic waists. Initially these just take little reminders that "tags go in the back."

Meals

With a few exceptions, there are no significant differences in what children with fragile X syndrome eat compared to other children. They eat the same type of food and usually eat the same quantities. There are, however, two special considerations in planning your child's nutrition.

The first thing to remember is that some children with fragile X syndrome may require greater amounts of food than you might expect. This is because they may be hyperactive and because boys with fragile X syndrome tend to be larger than their age peers when they are young. As a result, the time interval between our standard three meals per day may be too long for them. Mid-morning and mid-afternoon snacks may be needed to keep your child going. One complication is that your child may not be able to clearly communicate when he is hungry. He may signal you in various ways that he is hungry. You may notice changes in his behavior: he may become less cooperative and less happy and he may go to the cupboard or refrigerator to seek food. He may just be signalling his hunger and trying to help himself. My son points to his mouth to indicate that he is hungry or thirsty.

Nutrition for children with fragile X syndrome, like other children, should include a balanced diet. For children with fragile X syndrome with ADHD, avoid foods that contain known additives and colorants which provoke hyperactivity, such as caffeine in coffee, tea, and cola drinks.

Food Texture and Temperature. Some parents notice that they have difficulty feeding their child unless the food is of a particular consistency or temperature. You may have to experiment to find what is right for your child. This may be a particular problem for babies with fragile X syndrome who may not suckle well and often have difficulties in the transition to semi-solid and solid foods.

Mealtime. You probably do not need this book to know that mealtimes with children—any children—can be both enjoyable and challenging. The same rules, manners, and routine that work for all families will work for you, with a couple of twists. First involve your child as mush as possible in the preparation of the meal. Depending upon age, it may be possible for him to help prepare the table. You can use this to help with counting as well. It can be helpful for him to have his own special placemat which, if large enough, will help you get over the problem of spillages. As your child learns, he may be able to choose and prepare his own breakfast. Supervision may be needed as far as correct amounts of ingredients; otherwise you may find him with a little cereal, lots of sugar, and the bowl overflowing with milk. Also what he may want to eat may not be the most healthy diet for him, so you may need to guide his choices. Also, if you do not permit him to get too full on snacks before meals, he will probably eat better.

When eating out at restaurants or with other people, here are some suggestions. During these meals, people usually sit opposite each other. This arrangement may not always suit your child. He may eat better with no one sitting opposite him. Many families' meals are social occasions where friends and relatives are brought together. This may be a situation that your child does not like because he has to be near or opposite someone unfamiliar to him or because of the increased noise of the group. Similarly, party occasions such as birthdays may not be as wonderful for a child with fragile X syndrome.

As much as possible, try to stick to rules you would use for any other child. Anger and exasperation on your part will do little to improve your child's table manners. Sometimes your child may try attention seeking behavior. Just ask the other people at the table to ignore this performance. Occasionally your child may have to be asked to leave the table if his behavior is too extreme, just as you would with any other child. One final suggestion, keep your mealtimes as regular for your child as you can. He may not be able to be as flexible as others and may even need to be fed before others.

Toilet Training

Although children with fragile X syndrome often experience delays in toilet training, most will achieve satisfactory toilet training. Toilet training is often related to a child's level of understanding. Some parents are able to toilet train their children from a very early age, just by repeatedly putting the child on the potty. Most children, however, need to be able to feel when they need to go to the potty and know what to do when they feel that way.

Because children with fragile X syndrome have problems with sensory integration, it may not be until they are bursting to go to the toilet that they realize what this urgent sensation is. Then they have to communicate this need to those around them, and by the time the message gets through, it may be too late. This will, therefore, require some anticipation on your part, so that your child can be helped to recognize these sensations. There may be some frustrating times, but remember that, like mealtimes, anger and exasperation will do little to move things along. A reliable washing machine and lots of pairs of pants are the best options.

At night you can help your child by not giving him too much to drink, or, more importantly, drinks that have a diuretic effect on the kidneys (which cause more urine to be produced). These include tea, coffee, cola, and carbonated drinks. A special mattress cover that protects the mattress and allows a quick change of sheets is a great advantage. Again, a good washing machine is a great help here.

Because children with fragile X syndrome like to copy others, you can use their imitation skills to teach them to sit on a toilet from about two to three years of age. Many children have bowel movements 20 to

30 minutes after eating. Try to develop a routine to sit on the toilet at these times. Some children with fragile X syndrome, however, have very active bowels and may go to the toilet four or more times per day with little warning. You may need to consult your physician on this matter to gain better control. He or she may suggest a medication that reduces bowel motility and bowel movements.

Toilet training requires patience for any child. In time children do learn to use the toilet, surrender their beloved diapers, and stop having accidents. But it can be a long road; there is no use getting upset with your child if he does not succeed or has an accident. It will only aggravate both of you. Try not to set your sights too high, and work patiently and consistently.

If your child is not toilet trained by school age, this may have to become part of his learning package at school, and you should be upfront about this. It is fair for your child's teachers to know about this issue beforehand; they should not have to find out for themselves on the first day of school.

Dental Care

Toothbrushing. Good attention to dental care is important for all children. Regular assisted brushing of your child's teeth is essential to avoid repeated dental treatment for cavities. How well your child with fragile X syndrome will learn to clean his teeth will depend on his level of comprehension. In most children and adults, it is often the fear of long sessions in the dentist's chair that induces good dental hygiene, but it may be more difficult to communicate this to your child. You may therefore need to be vigilant about your child's toothbrushing. Sometimes an electric toothbrush may be the quickest way of cleaning teeth, but your child may not like this because of tactile hypersensitivity.

Visits to the Dentist. Start regular checkups with your dentist at an early age. If you have other children, get your child to go along with them. Let him sit in the waiting room and then in the dentist's chair, just to gain the experience. It will show him that going to the dentist is not a fearful experience. Nevertheless, you may find that your child will not want to spend much time in the dentist's chair, but will want to get away before the dentist has had a good look at his teeth. Some gentle calming and coaxing may help on this front.

Children with fragile X syndrome are prone to dental crowding. Your dentist may refer you to an orthodontic doctor in this situation.

As discussed in Chapter 4, children with fragile X syndrome may have a heart condition called mitral valve prolapse. This condition can slightly change how blood is pumped through the heart. As a result, there may be pockets of blood inside the heart that may pool in which bacteria may collect. Because some dental procedures can introduce bacteria from the mouth into the blood, it may be necessary for your child to take antibiotics beforehand, called subacute bacterial endocarditis (SBE) prophylaxis. The antibiotics can be given just before and after the procedure to ensure that no bacteria take hold in your child's heart. Your pediatrician or physician should be able to advise you on this matter.

Personal Hygiene

Washing. Like everyone, children with fragile X syndrome need to learn good washing routines and techniques. Unfortunately there is nothing about fragile X syndrome that will relieve you of the eternal parental task of keeping your children clean! There is also nothing special about fragile X syndrome that requires keeping your child cleaner than other children. The same standards and techniques will work for your child that work for other children.

Washing is a good activity to teach by example. For example, when you brush your teeth in the morning, have your child do the same alongside you. Have your child wash his face when you wash yours. If you use a soft face cloth and water at a moderate temperature, you are more likely to get good cooperation. Similarly, if your child sees you wash your hands after you use the toilet, it will be easier to get him to do the same. This is an example of using your child's good imitative skills to his advantage.

Haircuts. Haircuts may be difficult for your child. He may be hypersensitive to touch so that someone touching his head and hair may provoke quite a reaction, not to mention tickly bits of hair falling down his neck. You may need to find a sympathetic hairdresser who knows your plight and can tolerate a little disruption in the salon. It may help to have your child sit on your lap to have it done. It also may help to take your son's favorite toy along for him to hold or use some other means of distraction.

Bathtime. Bathtime should be part of a pleasurable, regular prebedtime routine. First, allow your child to help get the bath ready. Be sure to check the water temperature as it may be too hot or cold for comfort, and your child may not be easily able to communicate this to you. Show your child how to wash, but allow him time to relax in the water, play, and enjoy himself. Afterwards, dry him all over with a soft towel and encourage him to help get himself dressed. Follow this directly with toothbrushing to encourage routine.

Understanding temperature control is one of the problems that your child may have with sensory integration. Do not assume that because he turns the hot tap on that the bath water is too cold for him; he may not realize that the water is already hot enough. Showers can be an option for children with fragile X syndrome, but again be careful with temperature control. Make sure the temperature is correct before allowing him into the shower, and teach him not to fiddle with the temperature controls.

Bedtime

Bedtime routine is an extension of the bathtime routine. It is a time to encourage your child to become quiet and ready for sleep. Darken the room by using a dimmer switch or curtains or blinds. Try playing a tape of soothing music that your child particularly likes and comes to associate with bedtime. Regular patterns of behavior on your part help with this. Reading a favorite story or two always helps. Encourage your child to take part in this activity by pointing out pictures or words. Often children with fragile X syndrome will know whole stories by heart, but still delight in hearing the same one over and over again. You may want to choose one particular book to signify that it is time for sleep. Similarly your child may have one particular cuddly toy that he likes to snuggle down with. It is also time for a hug and a kiss, even if your child's tactile defensiveness causes some resistance. Children with fragile X syndrome need love and affection too!

Play and Exercise

Play and exercise are just as important for your child as for any other child. Your child may not want to participate in activities where there are a lot of other children around because of the noise and overstimulation. If your child has some autistic-like behaviors, he may prefer his own company, but he should still be given opportunities to take part in group activities.

Both play and exercise may require a lot of one-on-one attention by you. Going for a walk may seem pointless, but it provides subjects for conversation. Walking provides good exercise and gives an opportu-

nity to learn traffic awareness and road safety. From your child's point of view, there may be a special objective or incentive: my son is motivated to go for walks because we walk past the train station near our house where he can see trains come and go. Try all the usual activities that any young child likes to do.

Computers and Videos

Some children with fragile X syndrome have autistic-like characteristics such as social avoidance and aversion to eye contact. As a consequence, they may not relate well to other people. They may, however, work and play very well with computers because there is no one's face confronting them and they can work at their own pace. Also, computers never lose their patience or get tired of repetitive actions, a positive delight for children with fragile X syndrome. There are many types of special needs software available today in addition to the off-the-shelf software most children enjoy. Children with fragile X syndrome also learn much from appropriate videos. However, because of their excellent imitative skills, it is wise to avoid videos with violence and inappropriate behavior and language.

:: Outside the Home

Shopping

Be aware that your child may not like shopping situations, especially when he is young. There is often too much stimulation in a crowded supermarket, department store, or mall. Not only are there lots of strange people, but there are bright lights and loud noises. If you want to get your child used to shopping, start small. Try going to a small store near your house at a time when it is uncrowded. Then try to increase his tolerance from there.

When you shop with your child, aim to buy just a few things. Keep the shopping trip short. Ask your child to help with the basket and to help put the objects into the basket. This keeps him focused and involved. At the checkout ask him to help get the items out and to then give the clerk the money. Complete the activity by asking your child to collect and load up your purchases.

Restaurants

Restaurants pose similar challenges as shopping to children with fragile X syndrome. They can be crowded and noisy. Like shopping, start slowly. Choose a quiet restaurant for the first time. Don't go to the fanciest place in town. Go to a place where they have food your child is sure to like and they can bring it quickly. If you keep things simple, it will be more successful.

Libraries

Thank heavens these days libraries are still fairly quiet places. The children's section, however, is often busy with children selecting books, listening to stories, and talking. There is no reason not to take your child along. You may be pleasantly surprised by the books he chooses. If the library is a relatively quiet and calm environment, it may actually be appealing for your child. The challenge, of course, is to teach him the appropriate behavior, but do not let your image of the libraries of your childhood discourage you from trying.

Movies and Concerts

Be prepared to get the same response from your child in a movie theater that you get in a supermarket. The entire situation with all of the noise, rapid changes of light and dark, and a big screen may be too much for your child. On the other hand, he may be able to handle this environment. Again start slowly with quiet, more tranquil movies, and go from there. You may have to teach your child that this is a "no-talking" place, and practice that skill a little.

Fireworks

Most all young children are initially afraid of fireworks. To young children with fragile X syndrome, however, the unpredictability of the situation can be overwhelming—near total darkness followed by sudden explosions of light and sound. Children with fragile X syndrome can get used to fireworks, but they need to be introduced to them initially from the safety of indoors, where the possibility of totally escaping exists. Try a video or TV broadcast of fireworks on the Fourth of July to get him started.

Travel and Vacations

Travel with a child with fragile X syndrome can be both a delight and a challenge. Some children like routine so much that even a change in the route to school upsets them. Nevertheless, life does not run along such straight and rigid lines that you can be expected to always go the same way, and as a parent you should not always be dominated by your child's needs in this manner. Your child does need to experience other forms of travel, and you may be pleasantly surprised how much he enjoys bus or train rides. My son would go on a train ride every day of the week if he could.

Airplane travel may not be so easy. Airports in themselves may cause hyperstimulation. There are crowds, lights, and lots of noise. Not all airports are cozy or have direct connecting links from plane to plane without leaving the building. At some there is a bus trip or a walk to a plane that may even have its engines running. Once inside the plane, there is a claustrophobic seat and no means of getting off for a while. Can you imagine a situation more likely to overload your child? You may find that your long anticipated vacation has turned into a nightmare before you have even reached your destination.

You may come to the conclusion that once in a while you deserve a vacation without your child. This can be especially beneficial to you as parents to recharge, but also to other children who can get squeezed out by the needs of your child with fragile X syndrome.

Friend's and Relative's Houses and Other Excursions

Your child will benefit from trips to relatives' and friends' houses. If going to stay, ensure that your child has one place in the house where he can retreat to if necessary for some peace and quiet. If possible on repeat visits, try to ensure that this place is the same so he knows which is his room. Take some of your child's possessions, such as books, a cassette player, and toys, so they can be placed in this room to give it a familiar feel.

There is no reason why you should not take your child to places like zoos or animal parks. However, you may find that some of the more exciting theme parks may not be to your child's liking, especially if there is too much visual and auditory stimulation, nor may you all cope with the inevitable lines and waiting. This really is a "try-it-and-see" situation; you may have to beat a hasty retreat from some places, but you may be pleasantly surprised at others.

Know How Much Your Child Can Handle

No child with fragile X syndrome can be cocooned from the outside world; new experiences and change are a part of growth and development. Initially he may rebel against a new or different situation and may need coaxing to come along. Sometimes he will dig in his heels; and you might as well bang your head against a brick wall. Your job as his parent is to learn to spot the situations, such as supermarkets, that may be overwhelming for your child. This is difficult initially, but soon you will see them coming a long way off. In these situations you may have to bite your lip and keep your cool, giving in gracefully to your child. As your child grows, his ability to handle different situations will also grow. As with most children, if the experience can be positive, a better long term result will be achieved.

Dealing with Strangers

Every day of your lives, you and your child will encounter people who do not know you. There is no way to avoid this, and trying to avoid it hurts your child. But remember always that you and your child have the same right as everyone else to be out in public and to do what everyone else does. Most people you encounter will not notice or care about you or your child. Others will notice your child briefly and then move on. Some will show some reaction, some negative and some positive. Try to remember the times when you met a nice person who showed interest in your child or offered you some support.

Not every social contact, however, is pleasant. There are still many people who are uncomfortable around people with disabilities or who are just grumpy. For example, you may come up against strangers who, seeing your child on the supermarket floor in a tantrum, will think that you are a terrible parent who has no control over your child. Be ready to respond in one of two ways: 1) tell him or her that your child has fragile X syndrome and give a quick explanation of it if needed or 2) tell them to "Mind your own business." You are not responsible for making the world accept your child in the same way you do; however, you should demand simple courtesy. Just try your best to help your child learn appropriate behavior in public. But never be pushed around by what you think other people are thinking.

Educating Others. Use as many opportunities as you can to educate others about your child and about fragile X syndrome. Fragile X syndrome is not well known yet in the general public, but awareness is growing slowly. The more you can tell people about it the better. You do not need to be out for sympathy, but some understanding of your situation will come with it. Most people are genuinely interested when told about the condition. Keep your explanations short and simple, and be open to answering some questions. This will help make your child a real person in your community and help pave his way in the future.

■■ Other Daytime Challenges

Outbursts

All children act out when they are overwhelmed by a situation. However, for children with fragile X syndrome, it often takes less to overwhelm them. As discussed above, loud noise, crowds, or bright lights may spark an outburst that is really your child expressing the stress he feels. Remember your child cannot easily shut out or process these stimuli; his sensory system becomes overloaded. When this happens, your child will appear to be out of control. He may shout, hit, cry, put the brakes on so that you cannot make him go farther, or he may even throw himself to the ground. In these situations, find an escape route for you both.

When your child has an outburst or tantrum, move your child to a place that is quiet and calm. Do not escalate the problem by raising your voice or trying to restrain him. Let him calm himself gradually. Use soothing techniques such as quietly talking to your child, stroking rhythmically, and rocking. After the tantrum has passed, deal with what caused it. When he is calm, talk about it with him. Occasionally you may have to continue with your child kicking and screaming. This too shall pass, but it can be exceedingly exhausting for both of you.

Crying

Finding the cause of your child's crying may be difficult, especially if he has difficulty communicating. There are a few things you can do, however. Try to assess whether your child is sick or in pain. Look at clues from the preceding few days or hours. Does your child seem feverish or has his appetite been diminished lately? If your child is prone to ear infections, the basis of the crying may be pain, in which case giving him an appropriate painkiller for his age may be suitable. If no physical reason can be found, try the calming techniques mentioned above. Allow your child to be in a soothing and safe environment at home in his room with his favorite toys and comforts.

When You Cannot Understand What Your Child Is Saying

If your child has speech difficulties, his speech may become even less distinct when he is upset. He can talk so fast that it is impossible even for you to understand. This can only add to his stress. At these times try to listen for a key word that may guide you to the cause. Reflect the word back to him in a questioning tone. You may then unlock the mystery with a torrent of other words from which you can make sense. Also try to piece his words together with his actions to find clues. You may have to ask a series of questions such as "Are you hungry?" "Do you want a drink?" "Do you want to go to the toilet?" You may have to use signs or symbols if you think this will help. For example, my son will often communicate by pointing, so that if we ask him to show us, he will often lead us to what he is after. Sometimes your child may not be able to explain what he wants. In these situations "Show me" may provide the key. You may be led to the heart of the matter by this approach.

Perseveration

Children with fragile X syndrome sometimes become obsessed with particular activities or behaviors such as videos or computer games. This is called perseveration. Sometimes the obsession can be used creatively as a means of learning something thoroughly. Some educational computer games are helpful with reading and numbers. However, it can also become a seemingly mindless routine; your child may become stuck or obsessed by one particular part of a program which he especially enjoys, and he may need help moving on from this. Your child may feel more comfortable in this situation, but it is okay to interrupt him and get him to try something new. To do this, provide a substitute activity, perhaps with you involved, possibly one that is related in some

way to what he was doing. To persuade your child to change from the preferred behavior, the alternative behavior must be at least as pleasant. If it is less pleasant than the original, you might find him objecting strongly. There is also nothing wrong in putting your foot down and saying "You have done that for long enough now, come and do this instead." You can prevent a tantrum by using a kitchen timer to permit a certain length of time for a particular activity. When the timer sounds for the end of the allotted time, you may initially have to be firm with your child, but he will soon learn that when the timer goes off, his time is up.

Impulsive Behavior

As discussed in Chapter 4, children with fragile X syndrome can sometimes be impulsive; it may be part of attention deficit hyperactivity disorder (ADHD). But, there may also be reasons for your child's impulsive behavior. It may be a misunderstanding between your child and yourself, maybe a misinterpreted name. For example, "I'm going to get Rachael from Sarah's house," causes excitement to my son, as another Sarah has a house with a pool where we go sometimes. Usually clear explanation is the key. However, the old saying "actions speak louder than words" often applies with children with fragile X syndrome. It may be easier for your child to communicate what he wants by doing it rather than just talking about it.

Infant and Toddler Behavior

You may have quite a challenge with an infant or toddler. It is a time when developmental changes are rapidly occurring. Your child may suddenly seem to be left behind by other children his age. With his imperfect ability to make order of all sensations, it may all seem too much for him. You may feel your child is floundering. For this reason, he may stay in a dependent, infant mode longer than might be expected. Progress does occur and you must take heart at all the changes—big and small—when they do happen. Many parents look ahead blankly thinking, "My child will never achieve what other kids achieve." Perhaps you need to adjust your goals so they are right for your child. This can be a harsh learning time for parents.

This period of time often coincides with the diagnosis of fragile X syndrome. There are often emotional reactions, such as grief and anger, that can obscure a parent's view of his or her child's needs. It may for a while seem to be just a day-to-day existence; however, your child's needs are greater than other children at this critical time. This is when you need the most help and support from family and professionals. Ask for help, seek counseling, and get your bearings. The individual developmental needs of your child can be assessed through the agency responsible for providing early intervention or special education in your area, and your infant or toddler can begin to receive the services to which he is entitled. Your pediatrician, geneticist, and local school can help guide you toward evaluation and services.

▪▪ Discipline and Behavior Management

General Rules

Although your child has some differences from other children, this does not mean that he deserves or should be allowed to avoid following family rules. Yes, allowances must and should be made for him. No, it is not acceptable for inappropriate behavior to be excused just because he has fragile X syndrome. It is not fair to any of your children for rules to differ among siblings. Although some allowances may be made for age and ability, the rules should stay the same.

Your child needs to understand that he is responsible for his actions. He needs to learn this for now and for his later life. At home he should be allowed to make mistakes without harm or too great a penalty. Be nurturing and supportive, not negative. For example, every day your child may want to pour milk into his cereal bowl. Children with fragile X syndrome often do things too fast, and he may spill milk. Your approach should be: "You poured that a little too fast, please get a cloth," rather than "I've told you over and over pour the milk *slowly.*" Any parent will tell you that this advice is far easier said than done, especially when it is the hundredth time the same thing has happened, but it is very unlikely you will successfully change behavior by being negative.

Your child needs to see that inappropriate behavior will not lead to positive gains. He may use inappropriate behavior to get something he wants: attention or avoidance of an unwanted chore. For example, he may have been watching a favorite TV program just before a meal. He may deliberately misbehave at the meal table so that he can be sent away and get back to the TV. Watch for this kind of behavior. Never assume your child is impaired in his ability to manipulate you. Your challenge is to try to understand the cause of his behavior, and then figure out how to redirect or channel him.

To understand your child's behavior you may need to first understand the aim of his behavior. Most behavior can be broken down into:

- **Antecedent**—what goes on before the behavior;
- **Behavior**—what happens as a result of A;
- **Consequence**—what happens as a result.

An example of this may be:

- **Antecedent**—your child is hungry;
- **Behavior**—he starts crying because he cannot express that he is hungry verbally;
- **Consequence**—you give him something to eat, and this quiets him.

Quite rapidly your child learns that each time he wants something to eat, he cries. He is duly rewarded and reinforced by getting the food. This behavior is basic, even in newborns, but can be changed by anticipating that your child is hungry and offering food before the crying starts. In this way your child gets what he wants without the reinforcement of unwanted behavior (crying). In order to understand your child, you may have to become a mini-psychologist. Look for the Antecedent, the Behavior, and the Consequence, and try not to reward the Behavior with the Consequence. Think of your job as breaking the chain. My son likes to sit in the middle of the back seat of our car so that he has a good view ahead. If we put him in a different position, this just provokes unpleasant behavior toward whoever is sitting in "his place." The Antecedent is who sits where in the car, the Behavior is my son creating a fuss in the back of the car, and the Consequence is distraction for all others in the car.

Behavior is one way that your child "talks." In children who have learning disabilities or language delays, there may be immense frustration in communication. By watching your child's behaviors you can often understand what he is trying to say. We found with our child that often he would sneak to the refrigerator and take a yogurt or two. We soon learned that he needed food more often than at standard mealtimes.

Inappropriate behaviors may also reflect your child's difficulties with sensory integration. As discussed above, situations we can easily manage may overwhelm your child. A classic example may be the school assembly where the whole school crowds into a hall and sings. The behavior may be some type of disruption or an attempt to get away from the situation. The consequence is that your child may be labelled as troublesome in assemblies.

Behavior Management Techniques

If I can give you one piece of advice about enforcing appropriate behavior it would be to say "no" and mean it. Often it is much harder to say "no" than to say "yes." All children at every stage of development are adept at expanding and exploiting situations. This is part of learning to understand boundaries in life, and most learn quite quickly how to take advantage of openings. However, boundaries and limits need to be set and stuck to. You should be firm and consistent. Similarly, both parents need to take the same line. Otherwise you will find your child playing one parent against the other. It helps for both parents to become aware of each other's parenting style and to make changes so that they are more uniform.

Remember the "ABC" of Behavior Management. Do not reward negative behavior. You may have to use distraction techniques to move your child's attention on to something else until you can address the antecedent issue. Otherwise it may appear you are rewarding the negative behavior. For example, if your child is acting up because he cannot watch television, and you give in immediately in order for peace and quiet, this reinforces the behavior for the future. You may have to suggest an alternative activity which you know he likes to head him off. Later you may choose to agree to his request.

Do not make your child's issue your issue. Let's say you need to go to the grocery store. If you ask your child to put on his shoes and he says "No!" what do you do? Try to be flexible enough to say, "Well, let me know when you are ready, but if we don't leave in five minutes, we won't have time to get a treat (or go visit your friend) like you wanted." Or, "I'll be outside waiting for you," and then leave him in the house alone if you can do so safely. If it is important that you get to the store right away, then of course you will have to push the issue.

Another useful technique is to catch the behavior before it occurs. Watch for the antecedent, and try to anticipate from your experience what the behavior and the consequence may be. Often you can intercept the inappropriate behavior before it develops. For example, if you know your child is going to create a fuss about putting on his shoes before going to the grocery store because he does not want to go there, you may have to try different tactics, such as rewarding any good behavior or offering him something he would like when he gets his shoes on. Alternately, he may need some familiar item to take with him; my child, for example, often behaves better in stressful places if he is carrying something of his own.

Reward Positive Behavior. Too often we take good behavior for granted, and just focus on the negative. If you do not reward good behavior, your child will see no gain for continuing or repeating the behavior. For example, at mealtime, praise can go a lot farther than criticism when he eats neatly and with proper manners. Reward does not need to be material; it can just be praise.

Time Outs. When all else fails, use time out. Sometimes we all need it! It may mean that you need to send your child to his room while you both calm down. Time outs can be a necessary cooling off period for both parent and child. Both you and your child are capable of digging your heels in further and further until a total "stand-off" is reached. Because it is unlikely that your child will see time out as necessary, you as the adult must choose this option for both of you, especially when your temper is escalating. Time outs are far superior to losing your temper. Therefore you need to be able to sense when a situation is getting out of control and take the opportunity of time out to prevent things worsening. For example, you may need to put on some soothing music for your child and then go and sit down yourself or take a walk to calm down.

Consistency and Flexibility. Be consistent, yet remain flexible. Although being consistent must be the mainstay of your behavior management, sometimes it pays to be flexible. You may find that your child can be just as stubborn as you, if not more so. Stand back and try to find a different approach to avoid the feeling that you have both lost. Remember that you are the adult and you should be capable of thinking in a mature manner. Sometimes we have to remind ourselves not to descend to child-like behavior over principles. For example, it is easy to end up shouting at your child when you want something done "Because I say so" or "Because I am the parent." Often the reason is that you have experienced what will go wrong if it is done any other way. How-

ever, sometimes you should carefully let your child find out the pitfalls for himself—he may remember better the next time and do it your way.

Model Appropriate Behavior. Try to take advantage of your child's special skills. We know that children with fragile X syndrome tend to copy behaviors. If you are hoping for good behavior from him, you will have to ensure the same from others around him. It is no help to allow poor behavior from brothers and sisters. If you can get siblings to model good behavior, you increase the chance that your child with fragile X syndrome will too.

Medication. There are times when medication may help with behavior. This may be particularly so if your child has ADHD. If your doctor is proposing stimulant medication, often prescribed for ADHD, be sure you understand its advantages and disadvantages. These medications may help him because they stimulate the parts of the brain that control concentration. These medications may calm him down and allow for better attention span. See Chapter 4 for more information on medications.

▪▪ Give Your Child Responsibility

Where to Start

All children (and all adults for that matter) have a need to feel needed. This is especially true in family settings with a child who has special needs. It is important to try to make all your children feel needed and valued. Everyone should contribute to the family, and feel good about it.

Involve your child with fragile X syndrome in family life. He can find his cup and his place mat. He can set the knives and forks on the table. They may not be in the right place, but never mind—by praise and reinforcement he will learn where the correct places are. And at the end of a meal, he can learn to help collect dishes and take them to the kitchen for washing. Also, when returning to your home with groceries, he can help unpack and put things away; this is a good opportunity for praise and reward. Many children with fragile X syndrome like to vacuum (they like the noise and the vibration) and it seems to calm them down.

Take advantage of the fact that your child likes repetitive behavior. This can sometimes be an advantage when doing something seemingly tedious, like cutting the grass. My son loves to help collect the clippings and put them in the wheelbarrow. He has his own little wheelbarrow and when both are full, we wheel them away together. This is a real contribution to our family's chores, and he feels like a part of the team.

Seek to build your child's self-esteem. By encouraging your child to participate in your family life, you will encourage his confidence and self-esteem. Tasks can be something straightforward like watering plants or helping to feed a family pet. Have expectations that are reasonable so that, for example, the first time you let him help clear the dishes, don't use the best china. This unnecessarily raises the stakes and adds stress. However, do not give him only tasks you know he can do easily; challenge him to learn and grow.

Praising Your Child

Praising needs to become a habit. Really it should be a regular part of the upbringing of all children, but too soon we tend to forget it and move into a negative mode. "How many times do I have to tell you to clear your plate away after you've finished eating?" After a while we expect our children to have learned to do things regularly without being asked. However, most children dislike the household chores as much as we do, and don't see it as their role to do these things. If praising can become a regular part of the way a family works, things flow along better. With a child who has a learning disability the praising may need to be exaggerated to ingrain the behaviors that you want to achieve. Try it and you may be surprised. I do not believe that it is possible to overdo praise for a child with fragile X syndrome, but it may become boring for you and others. Strike a balance.

Setting Goals Your Child Can Achieve

Try to give your child tasks that are achievable. When you give your child a job to do, it is important to talk with him about it so he knows what to expect. Many children with fragile X syndrome cannot handle complex sequencing well. They may not be able to process "Put the knives, forks, and spoons in each place on the table, then get the glasses, then sit down." It may be necessary to break down the main task into smaller tasks that are within your child's ability. The above task could be broken down into:

1. Find four knives from the drawer
2. Put them on the table
3. Find four forks from the drawer
4. Put them on the table
5. Find four spoons from the drawer
6. Put them on the table
7. Help me put one knife in each place
8. Help me put one fork in each place
9. Help me put one spoon in each place
10. Get four glasses from the cupboard
11. Put them on the table
12. Put one glass at each place
13. Sit down in your chair

This may seem elaborate, but it gives you plenty of opportunity to praise success for each step along the way. One hint: Remember that your child may try to do everything too fast.

Parents will need to look at the tasks they want their child to learn. Even a task such as "get undressed" can be broken down into: 1) sit on the floor, 2) undo your shoe, 3) take your shoe off, 4) take your sock off, and so on. Gradually you will find that correct sequencing will occur, but you may find that if one stage is missed, your child will not be able to make progress. For example, it may be hard for him to undo his shoe until he sits down.

Evaluate Your Expectations

If your child does not achieve a task, you may be setting your goals too high. Evaluate the situation. If you are, there will be little reward for either of you. Sometimes you may need to see where learning a task has gone wrong. You may need to break it down further or simply guide or demonstrate to your child how the task is performed. It is reasonable to expect your child to gradually extend his range of abilities, but he will need to see that he is succeeding.

Teach Your Child to Finish

A child with fragile X syndrome may have difficulty concentrating. He may be keen to get to the end of a task without going through all the necessary steps or may get distracted before he is halfway through the task. You may need to remind him how to do a task until the pattern gets imprinted in his memory and stay with him until the task is finished. For example, learning to dress may require lots of repetition until learned by rote. Once learned satisfactorily, it will stay. Children with fragile X syndrome can often do surprisingly complicated tasks once they understand the sequencing. For example, my son can manage computers quite well even though he has significant learning difficulties. From experience he has learned to plug it in, switch it on, put in the correct CD/ROM or disk, find the correct icon with the mouse, and start his program. In fact, I have had to put a password on the computer to prevent him from spending all day on it.

Generalizing Skills

Once your child has achieved a goal and can repeat it without prompting, you may be able to consider extending the same activity elsewhere. However, beware that there are all sorts of pits and traps into which you and your child may fall. Just because he can manage to

sit and eat quietly at home does not mean that he will do the same when you take him out to eat at the mall. You have to remember that at home he is on familiar ground and just the change of location may be enough to tip the balance. So if you are going to try to extend the process, make sure that your child knows what is going to happen in advance, and start slowly and gradually.

Experiment with your child when there are not too many other people around. For example try eating at a friend's house first before you go out to a restaurant. Most of us can recount experiences that we would prefer to forget when we've tried to push our child too far. My own have been in crowded places where I least wanted a scene and least wanted to be seen manhandling a kicking, bawling child. We get the usual response, and it's not our child who gets embarrassed, it's us!

In summary:
1. Give your child verbal and visual directions and reminders;
2. Motivate your child by positive praise;
3. Reward your child when he achieves the goal. Often praise, a hug, or a cuddle may be enough, but sometimes you may want to reward him with a treat.

▪▪ Taking a Break

Separating—You May Need It

Surprisingly few people recognize that having a child alters your life more than any other episode in your life. Before your child came along, you were at least relatively free to make choices about what you did and when. Once a child comes into the family, the whole emphasis shifts, and you can no longer do precisely what you want without taking your child into consideration.

With a child who has special needs the parent-child bond exists to a seemingly greater degree. It is often extremely difficult, logistically and emotionally, for parents to take time away from their child with fragile X syndrome. This bond can be perceived as insoluble, a millstone, with an incredible amount of guilt attached to it. There are few parents who haven't thought to themselves, "Why has this happened to us" or "If only this child had not come along." It becomes easy to slip into this frame of mind and it becomes very hard to be positive about your child.

Help is needed before you reach despair, but we don't often seek it until we get this low. It is a hard road we tread with a child who has special needs. There is hard work, patience, adjustment of life goals, and guilt along the way, especially for mothers as they have the knowledge that all these issues were inherited. It is important, therefore, to stand back from time to time to evaluate the effect that your child has on you, your other children, and your family life.

Mothers of Children with Fragile X Syndrome. It needs to be remembered that mothers of children with fragile X syndrome have a higher incidence of depression than mothers of other children who have a learning disability. In one study, between three and four out of ten suffered from major depression or recurrent depressive disorders. Precise reasons for this are not yet known, though it may be related to the biochemical make-up of females with fragile X syndrome. If a mother of a child with fragile X syndrome is depressed, she may be unable to cope with the demands put upon her. Depression is nothing to be ashamed of. It needs to be recognized and given the appropriate consideration and, if necessary, medication or therapy.

Depression may affect mood, energy, appetite, libido, sleep, and general well-being. One of the most frequent and persistent symptoms is insomnia, especially early morning wakening followed by an inability to return to sleep. This situation needs to be noticed and appreciated for what it is by spouses and professionals; otherwise it can all too easily be pigeonholed as "a mother of a child with a disability who just can't cope." Mothers of children with fragile X syndrome should recognize that this is a potential problem. It may, however, require the family physician to confirm it because sometimes a depressed person and his or her family cannot see it clearly.

Parents in General. All parents need some "me time." We all need to be able to do things just for ourselves. There should be no guilt attached to this need. It is a healthy and necessary part of everyone's life and existence. There is a great temptation to doggedly and tirelessly give your all for your family, to become immersed in meeting its needs. Sometimes you can give your all, but yet life still seems like an uphill struggle. We all need chances to look after ourselves, our mental and physical health. We also need to be able to see when our spouses need relief, rest, and recuperation.

Much is written about maintaining physical fitness, and there is much hype and far too many fitness fads. However, getting regular exercise and keeping your body fit has been shown to have positive benefits on mental health. So, even though it may be hard to find the time, try to make the effort several times each week. There is an endless variety of things you can do. Just find an activity you enjoy—one that will focus your mind *away* from your other responsibilities in life. On top of this, seek out some other forms of mental stimulation. Try to find an activity or interest outside of your family or your work. Try not to let your family or your child's condition consume all your thoughts. If you can concentrate on something of interest to you, it refreshes your mind.

You may dismiss this as just the pat advice of a detached professional, but I try to follow this advice myself, and it helps me tremendously. Perhaps you and your spouse can take turns getting time off. Perhaps a babysitter can be found or families can pool respite care. There are many ways you can find time to get away to refresh. It will do a lot to help you face your responsibilities with energy and inspiration.

Siblings. In some families there may be more than one child with fragile X syndrome, and so double or triple the challenges. There may be sisters who are carriers. There may be siblings who are unaffected. In most family groups the child who is most affected by fragile X syndrome may demand and need the most attention, sometimes to the detriment of his siblings. Again, you need to stand back and look at your entire family to see what effect the presence of this child has on your other children. Often it means that you cannot do things as other families do "because we have to take Thomas along and he might have a tantrum." In the same manner, your other children may have to take supportive roles to help keep the family going. "Can you look after Thomas for a while, so I can go food shopping?" It is also important to allow your other children some time alone with you, with the knowledge that it will not be interrupted by your child with fragile X syndrome.

Good for Parent and Child. There will be times when it would be nice to have time away from the issues fragile X syndrome brings, such as ordinary time alone with your spouse. In addition, there will be times when you will simply not be able to do something if your child with fragile X syndrome is along. For example, going to a movie or to a concert may be too much for your child to handle; you are left with the choice of leaving him home or foregoing the activity.

Remember that separation can be beneficial for both you and your child. Time away allows for some "me time," it gives you a chance to be with your spouse in peace, and it allows for time to be with other members of the family. Simply put, it allows a brief recess from the stress that comes with raising a child with a special need. It may also allow you the chance to learn that someone else can look after your child competently and safely for a while. It can be good for your child because it gets him familiar with other situations and other people outside his own family. This lays the groundwork for future times you take a break.

Don't be stopped by guilt. Initially there may be vast amounts of guilt attached to the process. So at first, try it for just a couple of hours. You will find that the guilt rapidly disappears and is replaced by relief that you have some breathing space. And with some breathing space, you are refueling yourself for the next day's challenges.

Finding Care

Babysitters. Good babysitters are always in big demand. However, select your child's babysitter carefully. Consider looking for an older person to sit for your child. You may find an adult might be more tolerant and understanding than a teenager. There are many sources of potential babysitters: other parents, teachers, colleges (particularly special education students), and friends. Some areas may also have programs sponsored by schools, social service agencies, and non-profit organizations (such as your local branch of The Arc or ACL) that can provide babysitters as part of a respite care program.

Once you have found a babysitter, you need to invest some time with him or her. First you need to meet and get to know your child's babysitter. Then your child should meet the person you have chosen. Pick a time when the babysitter can come to your house when you are all at home, so your child can get used to her or him being around. You will need to explain about your child's routines and how following the usual pattern will make life easier for both of them. When the occasion comes, go out with a clear conscience, leaving a phone number of where you may be contacted if necessary. Do not be deterred by the displeasure your child may display.

Respite Care. Respite care offers the chance for more extended periods of time away (like an entire evening or weekend). It can be either center-based (where your child goes to a center) or home-based (where care is provided in your home). It may take some time to find these services, but they are gradually becoming more common.

Sources of respite care will vary from area to area. You should be able to get advice from your child-care social worker or from local agencies such as The Arc or ACL. Once you have obtained addresses and phone numbers, visit the establishment and see how you find the atmosphere. With many centers it may be difficult to visit initially, as it may be a painful reminder of your situation. However, grit your teeth and you may be pleasantly surprised. Ask what the approach of the center is, and what conditions and terms they expect. Once you have found somewhere that you think may be suitable, take your child for a short while. Initially your child may cling to you and there may be tears when you leave, but usually on your return you will find the tears dried and your child engaged in play. Fortunately children with fragile X syndrome are basically happy and are not difficult to keep occupied.

In some areas respite families exist. My son goes to a respite family every third weekend and always seems to have a good time. In fact, once we used our respite family, plus our local respite care service, for two weeks to look after our son while we took a trip. It was infinitely better than subjecting him to the ordeal of going on an airplane, which proved too much for him on a previous family holiday.

▪▪ Conclusion

Everyone is somebody and everyone has something to give in this life. It may seem at the beginning, soon after diagnosis, that life looks bleak and hopeless. You may not have ended up with the child you had hoped for, but is anyone's child the "perfect child"? You may have to set your sights differently for yourself and for your child, but once you have done that and accepted it, life becomes easier. Establish a routine, enforce your family rules, expect your children to help with family chores. In short, be a typical family that just happens to have a child with special needs.

Having a child with a disability will change your perspective over time. You will find that you get joy from different achievements. There are accomplishments for both of you. It may be only a cheeky grin or a funny expression, but things will give you joy. Relish them.

How lucky I am? All of us will feel at times that we have been very unlucky to find ourselves in this situation, but self-pity will not change your position; if anything it will only worsen it. Sometimes you may have to consciously count your blessings, and try to keep your sense of humor. Don't plan too far ahead: most families who have children with a learning disability don't either. Just try to keep going from day to day.

One last important piece of advice: Find support. Support comes in all sorts of shapes. All of us will need support at times, especially in the early years. There is no shame in asking for help with your child. Talk and share with friends and relations, and you will find that they will rally around you. You can also receive professional support from many agencies. There is a excellent network of families with fragile X syndrome throughout the world, too. Over time, you will feel part of a larger community of parents and families, all of whom root for each other.

■■ References

Gibbs, C. "Educational Issues for Primary and Secondary Children." A report of a conference, "Fragile X and Education." Fragile X Society (UK), July 1994.

Reiss, A.L., Hagerman, R.J., et al. "Psychiatric Disability in Female Carriers of the Fragile X Syndrome." *Archives of General Psychiatry* 45 (1988): 25-30.

Turk, J. "The Fragile X Syndrome: On the Way to a Behavioural Phenotype." *British Journal of Psychiatry* 160 (1992): 24-35.

■■ Parent Statements

Brushing calms our son.

Tony loves the trampoline. If I let him, he would probably stay on all day.

Patrick loves water. He stays in the bathtub or the pool for hours.

Our son was not toilet trained during the day until he was six. Who knows when the nighttime training will come?

Patrick has basically good behavior if I play with him—whining occurs if he is left for a time by himself.

What can really set my son off is unstructured or unfamiliar surroundings, too many people around him (especially if it's noisy), large disruptions to our sequence of routine, and people expecting too much of him.

We live with perseveration and routine.

We cut out pictures from the boxes of his favorite snacks, pasted them on index cards, covered them with contact paper, and used them with Lucas so he could show us what he wanted

Both of our children do best in transitions when they fully understand what is likely to happen and what their role will be. It is important to give them enough advance warning so that they can fully understand and even rehearse the transition, but not so much that they get nervous about it. It also helps to include them in any decision-making.

Our son has such a difficult time with transitions. If we get up in the morning on a weekend and decide we want to go to a park, the first thing our son says is "no." After letting him process the information—sometimes for up to an hour—he can't wait to go.

As a carrier of the fragile X gene, I find that I have a difficult time with transitions too. It's just that I have developed strategies to deal with it and I can implement them myself.

I tell Tony what we are going to do before we start. This isn't a major problem for him.

If whining or crying persists, without cause, I use time out.

One special form of time out has been helpful. When one of the boys did something unacceptable, he was sent to his time out place with instructions that he could return when he was ready to perform the desired action, such as pick up the blocks or apologize nicely to his brother. In effect, we were teaching the boys that they could leave a situation when it was overwhelming, and return when they felt better organized. They still do that, although we have not enforced a time out in years.

Talking firmly about the misbehavior and perhaps losing a correlating privilege is all that's necessary. He's very tender hearted and anything harsher simply scares him and hurts his feelings.

Tony's jobs: feeding the dog, picking up his toys, unloading the dishwasher, and windexing glass.

Jobs give all children purpose and build self-esteem.

When he is given a job that is important or desirable to him, he is so focused, self-assured, and competent. It gives him such a thrill to be needed and productive. The task has to be authentic not just busy work or pretend.

Within the last two months we have gotten a new babysitter. This is the first success I have had with leaving him. I still can't leave him at night.

I have tried everything to find a babysitter. I finally placed an ad with very specific details that would help my son feel more comfortable and then I interviewed them. I selected a most loving, responsible patient woman.

Neighborhood children did not work out at all. We had to get college age and older and pay them $10 an hour.

Babysitters are no problem for us. We live in a great neighborhood and the teenagers are very responsible. Until about age five, separations were difficult and tearful. After that, he seemed emotionally and cognitively able to understand (most of the time) that I would be back. Even now at seven years old, he needs reassurance such as "She loves you even when she's away" or "It's only for one night and then they will be back".

One behavior Tony has which is consistently predictable is his turn-away arch-and-yell response to any stranger who comes too close and speaks to him with direct eye contact. Since many women in particular tend to do this in public places (stores, doctor's offices, therapy clinics), outings can become rather embarrassing or just plain difficult. Shopping during quiet hours at the grocery store or mall, and avoiding line-ups (for anything) as much as possible helps to avoid this situation. Sometimes I simply have to say, "He's shy and doesn't understand you," for someone to give him a little more space.

As the boys have grown, their behavior has been a minimal concern. We do not press them to do fun things, if they choose not to. Each son has found a level of activity with which he is comfortable. While we wish one of our sons had a more active social life, we are learning that we have to honor his preferences, not ours.

William has been a hitter and a thrower since the day he was born. We have to be very proactive in our behavior management.

In general, outbursts mean that my child is over-burdened, frustrated, cannot meet expectations, or is uncertain about his environment. That is why having calm time alone is the best way of dealing with such behavior when it happens.

Ours lives are great on a day-to-day basis because he does not cry anymore and he sleeps at night now.

It almost seems like each day has a heightened awareness to it. We are always very aware of where Tony is emotionally all of the time. We have just gotten used to it and don't really think about it.

The days go well when Patrick is doing well; they can be a challenge when he's not.

6
FAMILY LIFE

Jayne Dixon Weber

▪▪ Introduction

Family. Webster says it is "a fundamental social group in society consisting especially of a man and woman and their offspring." He also defines it to be "a group of people sharing common ancestry." And finally, Webster defines family as "distinguished lineage."[1] I like that one the best. I like to think that what I passed on to my son is considered "distinguished." It certainly is distinguishable!

What's life going to be like in a family that has a child with fragile X syndrome? Let's assume you did not grow up in a family with a sibling or a parent who had a disability. How you envision your own family is often based largely on what your family life was like when you were growing up. Maybe you grew up in a big family and you wanted the same thing—to have lots of children. Or maybe you grew up in a big family and you wanted the opposite. Maybe you remember the good feelings you had when you did things together as a family—from playing in the backyard, to going to the zoo, to going on vacations—memories you want to create for your own children. While your family life will be different, that's all it will be—different. It will be *your* family. It won't be like when you were growing up, it never could, even if you did not have a child with fragile X syndrome. But it will be the family life your children will remember.

Were there some traditions that were a part of your family when you were growing up? Activities that have been passed from generation

---

[1] Webster's II New Riverside University Dictionary. Boston: Houghton Mifflin Co. (1984)

to generation? Things you did year after year? This is what will make your family different from everyone else's. Maybe there are some traditions you hope to continue with your own family. Maybe there are some traditions you will develop that will be unique to your family. Traditions are an important base for every family. When it is something the whole family does together traditions instill a sense of belonging for each member.

In your imagining you probably also remembered some of the hard times your family had when you were growing up. We want to forget them and remember the good times. But they are both a part of life. What do I mean by hard times? It could be a death in the family, job loss or relocation, divorce, problems with school, or dealing with the challenging behavior that comes with adolescence. There will be hard times in your own family too. Try to keep a long-term view of your family during those times. They will cycle in and out of your lives, but they will pass.

In your imagining, did having a child with a disability, much less fragile X syndrome, ever occur to you? It is probably something you never thought would happen to you. And if it ever did cross your mind, you probably didn't even give it a second thought: "It won't happen to me." Couple that with the fact that many people have not even heard of fragile X syndrome.

I imagined I would have a family that would be pretty much like the family I grew up in. The only difference I envisioned was that I would probably have fewer children. I have three siblings; I thought two children would be plenty. When I was growing up we played with the other children in the neighborhood, we went to school, and we made our own friends. We had our own family traditions. One of the traditions in our family was that we went on a vacation the first week of August every year. We always went at that time. The place was often the same too, but that didn't matter because we were on vacation together. We looked forward to it every year. We also sat down together for dinner most every night (I remember things like putting the vegetables back in the bowl when my mom wasn't looking. "Oh, you've cleared your plate, you can be excused now."). I wanted both of these practices to continue in my own family. We also had the usual challenges at school—no big deal—and there was sibling rivalry, but I thought we were a pretty typical middle class family. We lived not knowing that half of us were carrying the premutation of the fragile X gene.

But then the unimaginable happened in my own family. We heard the words, "Your son has fragile X syndrome." I fell back into a chair in disbelief. Family issues came up almost immediately. "What will this do to my dream of a family? Will we be able to do things as a family? Will we have a family?" I remember thinking, "I don't know how to have a family that includes a child with a disability." It was scary for me to think that I was going to have to create a family that was going to be so different from the one I grew up with.

Believe it or not your family life will be more like other families than it will be different, not that there won't be some differences. There *will* be differences and some of them will be big (they are discussed below). So, what does that do to your image of what you thought your family would be like? You may still be able to have the size family you wanted, but you might also adjust the size because of the genetic nature of fragile X syndrome. In many ways, your family can *and* will be just like the one you imagined. You can still do things together as a family. You can play in the backyard. You can go to the zoo, and you can go on vacations.

You can and should have your own family traditions. You can use some from when you were growing up *and* you can create your own. Your traditions can be as simple or as complex as you want them. It is fun to say, "We do it every year, and we have been doing it since you were a tiny baby." Maybe you will be able to tell your children that you did this when you were growing up too.

Chapter 2 dealt with the emotions of receiving a diagnosis of fragile X syndrome. Acknowledging and working through what is often a very emotional time is important for you and your family's well-being. You may never forget the day you heard the news about your child, but your life will go on, and that's the focus of this chapter. It addresses the long-term impact of having a child with fragile X syndrome in your family. It starts by discussing the importance of parents taking care of themselves, so they can take care of their children and their extended family members. There are ideas for helping your children deal with their brother who has fragile X syndrome, and for helping them deal with people outside of the family, including friends and strangers.

Some of the differences in your family life may make your life more challenging than that of your friends. But you will soon see there are good times ahead, lots of them. You will adapt. You will find what works for you and your family. It is important to remember that every member of your family has his or her own individual needs: your child with fragile X syndrome and your other children, your spouse, and you. It is a challenge to meet all of those needs, as well as your own, but that's true for any family. It's just that in our cases, yours and mine, our family's needs are greater. The needs are greater than other families not only when your child is young but also when he gets older.

When it comes to developing a life as a family that includes your child and his siblings and all of their emotions, and your extended family and friends (and strangers too), it can seem very complicated. Developing strategies to integrate them all into a family life will take time. I can offer suggestions on ways to do this. But the truth is, experience will be your best teacher.

■■ For Parents

When thinking of your own family, it is important to feel good about yourself as a parent. You do not have to be a super parent just because you have a child with fragile X syndrome. It is okay to be ordinary. Every parent has struggles in raising children and every parent makes mistakes. You will too. Do what you think needs to be done in all of the different circumstances. You have to create your own family, which means doing it in your own way, on your own schedule. Develop routines that will work for you and your family.

When a crisis situation arises, and you know they will, handle it the best way you know how. You can draw on your own life experiences, ask your friends for advice, read books, or talk to professionals who know your child to find what works for you. You will soon develop your own repertoire of responses for different situations. What works for you may or may not work for your spouse. What works in one situation may or may not work in another situation. And what works today may or may not work tomorrow. There is no one right answer in any given situation. But if it works for you, then it is the right answer, at least for today.

Taking Care of Yourself...First

In order to feel good about yourself you need to take care of yourself—both physically and mentally. Taking care of your physical needs means eating right and getting plenty of sleep. Both require a conscious effort on your part. How many times have you grabbed a cookie on your way out the door? Grab some fruit or a bagel next time. I'll be the first to admit that I don't get as much sleep as I should. The times I lose my patience the fastest is when I am either hungry or tired. Sounds like some children I know....

There are a couple of things you can do to take care of your mental well-being. Learn everything you can about fragile X syndrome, including people to contact when you have questions. Knowledge can be very empowering for both you and your family. After learning about fragile X syndrome specifically, I found I also needed some general parenting information. I realized when my son was young that he was going to have some challenging behaviors. I soon found I was not happy with the way I was parenting; I felt like I was in over my head. So I sought out information on different parenting strategies. I took a parenting class at my son's preschool.

I had no great expectations when I went in the first day, but over the course of four sessions, it opened my eyes to new parenting methods. It was different from how I was raised, but I liked the new ideas. I needed new ideas. The class gave me alternatives on disciplining, like redirection and natural consequences. It made me more aware of what I was doing and why I was reacting the way I was. I did not have any grandiose ideas about becoming a super parent; I just wanted to be a better parent. While I opted for outside help, you might not. It is nice to know you have that option.

Another thing you can do to take care of your mental well-being is to find the time to get away. This can be difficult. Schedule it. Plan it. Just do it. You need to have time by yourself doing activities that you like to do, without the responsibility of looking out for someone else. Every parent needs this time, but when you have a child with extra needs, it is even more important that you get away. You can wear yourself out trying to meet extra needs day after day after day. Your child is going to be with you for a long time. Don't burn yourself out when he is young. Getting away not only refreshes you physically (you can sit down for longer than two minutes), but also mentally. Your opportunities and types of breaks will vary over time. When children are young, you may only get short sporadic times for yourself. But as your children grow, you will be more comfortable leaving them for longer periods of time, which will increase the time you have for yourself. It may take longer for both of you to reach the comfort stage of longer separations than for most children, but it will come. When children are young, they may not understand that you will be back in 15 minutes—that's half of a day to them. Crying may be their way of telling you.

One way to get some time for yourself is to get involved in a neighborhood childcare co-op where you can trade child-care with friends. A group can range from 5 to 15 families. You can do an honor system or you can make your own coupons. Every time you watch someone else's child or children, they give you coupons; every time they watch yours, you give them coupons. This is a good way to meet new families in your area. Not only can you get some "me" time, but the co-op can also be used for time away with your spouse inexpensively.

▪▪ Creating a Family

You have the *opportunity* to create your own family life. You can make your family life into whatever you want it to be. It is actually quite a large responsibility, a responsibility that is challenging in its very nature, and a little more complicated for you too. You may have to give more thought to what you do and how you create your family.

What about the times when you want to do something as a family, but don't because your child with fragile X syndrome won't be able to handle it? It will be frustrating sometimes, no doubt about it. What do you do? How can you be a family when you can't do the stuff you want to do that other families can do? Going to parks and playing in sandboxes are going to get old after a while.

You may soon realize that even ordinary aspects of your family life can be difficult for your child. A family outing to the circus can be overstimulating. Varying a routine by going on vacation can be disastrous. Leaving your child with a baby sitter so you and your spouse can have some time alone together may turn into a battle. Take a step back and evaluate the situation. Then determine what you are willing to live with. Make adjustments. Maybe you will decide to do an activity anyway or you will go early and get used to the environment or plan on leaving early. Maybe you won't go at all. Something like the circus will always come back next year. Are you willing to instill some routine into a vacation or develop a daily schedule? And remember, a decision that is made today can always change—or at least be re-evaluated.

Families, like marriages, take work to keep them alive and growing. Raising children takes work. Parenting a child or children with fragile X syndrome is challenging and takes even more work. Work doesn't mean doing everything for your child with no expectations on his part. That is not good for anyone. All members of a family need to learn to take care of each other at different times. When your children are young, you spend the majority of time taking care of them. It is important that you share the responsibility with your spouse and that your children see that. As your children grow, they can spend some time taking care of you too. Doing chores around the house not only helps you out, but it makes children feel like they are part of the family. Responsibility helps independence to develop; responsibility helps families to grow. Taking mom a cup of tea when she's not feeling well allows the caring part of your child to come out; that's a good characteristic to develop!

It is important that every member of a family take time for themselves—including your child with fragile X syndrome. As parents, you not only need to allow this, you need to encourage it. This is another way you can be an ordinary parent. Most parents encourage this in all of their children. Your children will get breaks when you take yours, but promote these breaks from you too.

You will probably make mistakes. Learn from them and move on. Children are so forgiving. Keep your visionary goal of family in mind and continue to strive toward it. And when you want to do something that you consider simple, think of a way to make it even simpler. This is your challenge.

The Parent's Attitude

The way you nurture a family that includes a child with fragile X syndrome will be determined by your attitude toward that child. How do you feel about your child? Have you worked through the initial feelings of, "I didn't think this would ever happen to me?" "Why did this happen to me?"

If you had planned on your child becoming the president of the United States, it is going to be a real challenge for you to realize that this may not happen. It may even be difficult for you to hear that you have "lost" your expected child. You haven't lost anything. You've gained a person who is probably a little different from what you expected, but is still a very real person. In most cases, your attitude toward your child with fragile X syndrome will be just like the attitude you have toward your other children—unconditional love. Simple? Should be. It may be easier to love your child than you ever imagined. Is it sympathy? Maybe partially. Maybe our children strike a chord so deep within us that it brings out a kind of love that only children bring out, no matter their ability or disability.

Here's an attitude check. Do you see your child before you see his disability? You have a child with fragile X syndrome, not a fragile X child. You have a child in special education, not a special education child. You have a child with a disability, not a disabled child. You may have a child with challenging behavior, not a problem child. All children are special, all children are people first.

Seeing the child as a person first means there must be a degree of mutual respect from the both of you. When I was growing up, I was always told to respect my elders. Now as a parent, I realize that my children too command a certain amount of respect as unique individuals who may or may not end up liking the same things that I like. I now understand that while I have the job (which sometimes seems overwhelming) of teaching my children to become the best they can be, I can also learn a lot about life from them. They are teaching me to slow down and enjoy the simple things. I see a beauty through their eyes that I have neglected as I matured —rainbows, ladybugs, ripples in a lake. And looking through the eyes of a child with fragile X syndrome is like looking through no other—a fascination with what kind of horns vehicles have and where they are located, an interest in why some vehicles have running boards and some don't, the intrigue of where the gas goes in different vehicles. Learn to appreciate your children and what they see. You will be amazed.

One of the hardest things in maintaining a positive attitude is not letting the challenging times you have with your child or the difficult experiences you may have get you down. Every family goes through challenging periods, even with children who are developing typically. Struggles, and working through them together as a family, are part of being a family and will bring you closer together. These are the times that you will become more appreciative of each other.

Earlier I said you could be an ordinary parent. How, you may ask, can I be ordinary when nothing in my day seems to be ordinary? As you would with any child, you will develop your own style, and it will become second nature. For example, we discovered that whenever we go to any event outside the home like a movie, a basketball game, or the circus, we get there early and give our son a chance to settle in—I'm talking *an hour* early. It is almost as if he can handle the stimulus of a crowd of people if he sees them gradually arriving. We watch the crowd come in, instead of walking into a crowd. It has been interesting to see that there are usually a few other people who do the same thing—they get there early and check out what is going on. But think about how our children learn: Arriving early to an event allows them to see the "big picture" of an activity. For example, the actual basketball game is only one part of what goes on. There are pre-game activities of players warming up and music; and there are post-game activities too, even if it is mostly just cleaning up. Look at adjustments like this as being ordinary in an extra-ordinary kind of way.

Encourage your child to be a part of the family. This means not only giving him jobs to do around the house. It also means including your child in meaningful conversations with the rest of the family. Keep his developmental ability in mind and set realistic expectations when doing both of these activities so he is successful in his eyes, his sibling's eyes, and yours. Watch his self-esteem grow as his successes grow.

Now stand back and take a long look at what you are doing. You are dealing with your child who has fragile X syndrome in many of the same ways you deal with your children who do not have the syndrome. Job well done.

The Great Balancing Act

Keeping *balance* in a family often takes careful thought. When children are young, the parents have sole responsibility for maintaining some semblance of balance. As your children grow they'll help you in various ways. Yes, it may start out as a whine about going to Dustin's therapy again, but it will soon progress to helping out around the house and maybe even cooking a meal or two.

You planned and prepared the day for you and your family or you are at that stage where the whole family is in on the planning and preparing. You've talked to everybody about what is going to happen today. Tom is going to Mike's house after school. Ann has piano. Everybody is expected home for supper. The children are dropped at school. Your child with fragile X syndrome has therapy and preschool today. You stop at the store and the dry cleaners. The children are picked up from school, chauffeured to their respective places, and picked up in time for supper, which you somehow manage to cook. You clean up, help out on the homework, and get the children showered and to bed. These are just the physical aspects of each day. How do you fit in some quality individual time alone with each child and your spouse each day? What about taking care of you? How do you feel at the end of the day? You probably feel overextended in every way possible. Emotionally. Financially. Physically. How can we keep our lives balanced in all of the various aspects?

How can you deal with those overextended feelings? Sometimes when it feels like you have a lot to do, it helps to write everything down on a list. It may look like there are many things that have to be done, so prioritize the list. Then you know what has to be done and what can wait, and what really does not have to be done. Be sure to cross the item off your list when it is done. It is quite astonishing what a psychological boost it can be to just draw that line through the item you completed. It is such a good feeling to know there is one less thing to do. (Don't look at the two other things you've added to the list.) This is also where priorities come in. A sick child cannot wait. Most jobs cannot wait. Paying bills cannot wait. Housecleaning can wait. Making fancy meals can wait.

Another way to help with feeling overextended is to learn to say, "No" and mean it. "No, I can't help out at school today." "No, I'm not going to the store to buy you some new socks today." "No, I'm not going to go the supermarket to get you something special for supper tonight." "No, I can't watch your children for an hour this afternoon." "No, I'm not going to make some cookies today." Just emphasize that just because it is not going to get done today, it doesn't mean it is not ever going to get done.

So often what it all comes down to is finding the elusive "time." "We don't have the time." "We're going to be late." "There's not enough time to do that." *How* can you find more time? *Where* can you find more time? First look at your days and see how you spend your time. Are you spending a lot of time doing housework? (I hope everyone laughs at that one.) But housework encompasses cooking, dishes, laundry, dusting, and vacuuming among other things, and a certain amount of it has to be done almost everyday. Look at the amount of time you spend in the car. This is usually a big one, between running errands and running your children around. Work may take a big chunk of your time. Changes in how you and your family spend time are very personal. It's like parenting. There is no one right answer. If it works for you, it's right, and you will hear others say, "How do you ever find the time?" Find ways to make your day simpler. Start scheduling. Pick up the house, but don't worry as often about the dust; save it for the cleaning you do when company comes over. Get the children involved in washing the windows. Have them help you make the beds and sort laundry. Lower your standards. The old adage is true: "Your children will never remember how clean the kitchen floor was, but they will always remember the time you spent with them." Have your children help each other out on their homework. Find simple meals that you know your children will eat. Just sit and relax with your children. They do not have to be doing something every waking minute of their day.

Successfully balancing your act (or should I say getting your act together) allows you to stop hurrying everywhere you go and in everything you do. The object is to enjoy your day, even if there are tasks that you do not want to do. Not always being in a hurry may allow you to look at the firetruck that's down at the grocery store. See if you can eliminate the following two words from your vocabulary: "hurry" and "late."

Successfully balancing your act also allows for some of the "me" time discussed earlier. Include yourself on the list of who gets your attention and time. Remember to take care of yourself. It is hard to take care of someone else when you are not taking care of yourself.

Keeping family life balanced is truly like walking on a tightrope. All of your activities are on the pole you are carrying. If one side gets weighted too much, you are going to fall off. Re-adjust your weight and get back on. It is all in the *time*-ing!

Support

Throughout your life, the type and amount of support that you and your family require will vary. Support can be either physical or emotional, or both. By physical support I mean someone who watches your children or who helps you run errands, someone whose presence makes a difference in your life. Emotional support can come from someone who listens, and provides information and advice (only when asked, of course).

Support has a couple of sources. The first is the support found only in families. It is support through love and understanding of one another. It is acceptance of one another. It can be spoken or unspoken. And it's always there.

The second kind of support comes from outside your immediate family—extended family, friends, respite providers, doctors, and therapists. Every family needs outside supports of one kind or another, at one time or another. People outside the family can give a perspective that can get lost inside the family. However, the kinds of outside support you use

may be different from what other families use. Over your child's life, doctors and therapists may be a strong building block in your support system. They can give you ideas to try in working with your child. They usually have a sympathetic ear to lend when you need it, too. The good part is that you usually get an objective opinion. The bad part is that outside support can be very unpredictable; you might receive unwanted or unasked for advice or it may not be available when you need it. The advice should be listened to and filtered by you and your spouse. If you hear the same advice from more than one person, you may want to give some thought to what is being said even if you initially disagree. One other type of outside support is advocacy, which is covered in Chapter 10.

Your extended family, grandparents, aunts, and uncles will hopefully be a strong source of support for you. But you must know, in some cases they are and in some they are *not*. Or there may be one or two who stand out as a support for you. Either way, continue to provide information on fragile X syndrome, and also let them see you develop your own family.

Friends too are important in your support network. Your friends can give you perspective, whether or not they have a child with fragile X syndrome or any disability. Over your life you will have different kinds of friends, which is true whether or not there is a disability in your life. What I've found is that more and different kinds of people have entered my life than would have if I did not have a child with fragile X syndrome; in many respects, it has been quite fascinating to experience that. There are a lot of *good* people in this world.

One other source of support is private therapy. You can do it individually or as a couple. Therapists can give yet another perspective. Your local office of The Arc or ACL may be able to provide you with some names of therapists who are familiar in dealing with families who have a child with a disability.

Building Independence

One of our jobs and goals as parents is to build independence in all of our children, including our child with fragile X syndrome. However, this does not happen overnight. It is a continuous job that starts the day they are born, with the long-term goal that our children someday learn to be self-reliant. Your child with fragile X syndrome wants independence too just like all of the other children in the family, like all of the other children in the world. Our children can and will develop many of the same independence skills as other children. Some modifications will have to be made: modifications in what you expect and when you expect it.

When your child is young, you will work on getting your child to sit, walk, talk, and ride a trike. Depending on the age of your child, you may also have a therapist helping your child achieve some of these goals.

As your child grows, giving him responsibility will help him gain independence. Start at an early age by expecting your child to pick up toys after playing with them. You may need to model this at first, maybe even make a game out of it. If this expectation begins when your child is young, it often becomes automatic as he grows and may generalize to other activities, for example, cleaning up after himself. As your child grows, involve him in choosing the area in which he would like to become more independent. My son's kindergarten teacher told me the best thing I could do to get him ready for kindergarten was to give him a job that he was expected to do everyday. We discussed this as a family, not only how important it is to learn to do things on your own, but also how doing chores around the house is part of a family. Offer a choice and see what response you get. "Would you like to make your bed or set the table?" If he makes a choice, go for it. If your child isn't able to make the choice, then you make the choice. "Let's start by making your bed." But continue to offer choices over time. Learning to choose is the first step to thinking independently later.

As your child reaches the upper elementary years set your goal to be that he sees what needs to be done around the house for himself.

"Can you see anything that needs to be done that you would like to do?" See if your child can come up with anything on his own. And if he does, try to honor it as best you can or maybe modify it slightly to meet both of your needs. Your child says, "Guess I could clean my room." You could say, "That's a great idea." Over time (which could be as long as a year) it is okay to ask your child to spend a little more time on the activity so a better job is done. Shoving stuff to one side might be okay for a while, but there comes a time when things need to actually be put away. It is okay to modify your expectations, as long as you communicate this to your child.

Another type of independence skill is developing self-control. Here's a personal example. I took both of my children to the Denver Museum of Natural History. Neither of the children had ever been to this museum. My son was seven years old at the time. We walked into the dinosaur exhibit, I turned my back for less than a minute, and he vanished. Fortunately the exhibit was set up so the traffic flowed in only one direction. He was almost half way through the exhibit before I found him; he was cruising along. In hindsight I should have had this talk before we even set foot in the building. I told my son that I wanted him to take the responsibility of staying with his sister and me. If he wanted to move faster, he needed to tell us. If he took off again, we would sit down and not move for five minutes. I explained the safety issues involved too. Well, a minute later we ended up sitting down for five minutes. I repeated what I had stated earlier. We did not have a problem for the next two hours.

Helping your child gain independence can be challenging because the skill level of children who have fragile X syndrome can be so scattered in all of the different developmental areas. Keep your child's developmental age in mind when looking at different independence skills. My daughter demonstrated that she had the skills to cross the street independently at six years of age. That was coupled with the self-awareness and control for her to come tell me where she was going. "I'm going over to Stephanie's house." I always made a point to thank her for coming to tell me. Because I knew that when she went to Stephanie's house, it meant she had to cross a street to get there. My son was eight years at the time, but more like four to five years developmentally. I found I still had to give some cues. He would say, "I *want* to go over to Stephanie's house." I'd say, "What do you need to do?" He knew the jingle. "Stop, look, and listen." At first I stood on the curb next to him.

I wanted to make sure he went through all of the appropriate motions. Over time I could watch from the door of our house. He crosses the street on his own now.

Your child's Individualized Education Program (IEP) should also support the independence goals you have for your child. As your child moves into middle and high school, his IEP should also include goals and objectives that will help him develop independence. This is a great opportunity to work with the school and support each other.

The difficult part of developing independence is to avoid being overprotective. Every parent I know who has a child with a disability has been accused of being overprotective at one time or another. Nothing makes me angrier when another parent (of a typical child, of course) tells me not to be so overprotective of my son. "Just let him go, you don't have to watch him all of the time." You know your child better than anyone else. As long as you are aware of being overprotective, you will do things because you think it is right for your child. I'll bet you haven't been wrong very many times.

It is not unusual for parents to be more protective of their children who have a disability. Our children learn at a slower rate than their peers, so we need to be protective a little longer. We step back like all parents do, we just do it a little slower. I know it is a fine line between nurturing and overprotecting. I know that sometimes it can be more my fear than my child's (and sometimes it needs to be). It is important that your child prove to himself and you that he has the skills to do certain things. Go back to the example of learning to cross the street. You may have to observe him when he tells you, "Yes, mom, I know how to cross the street. I know to look for cars. I know to be careful." But what he says and what he does are sometimes two different things. I have seen him start to walk out in front of a car before. Spend whatever time it takes to learn safety skills.

You do have to allow your child to take some chances sometimes, but do not let yourself be pushed to a point where you are not comfortable. And you only want him to take chances where the chances of him being hurt are low. It is going to be much easier to let him go when you've laid a strong foundation. With crossing the street, lay the foundation like this: Talk about crossing the street as a family, maybe at the dinner table. Perhaps you can find a video that demonstrates the crossing skills you want to teach. Physically walk your child through the process of crossing the street while you talk about what you are doing.

Eventually encourage your child to do the talking when you *both* cross the street. Then you can gradually step back.

For example, when your child is young, you probably know where he is all of his waking moments. As he starts to walk, you may have to look a couple of extra places. But you pretty well know where he is and what he is doing. Time to step back. Start out initially by not checking on your child as often when you are at home and he is in another room. Let him know that you are comfortable with that (and you are because you have child-proofed every cabinet door and toilet and put breakable items in places that you can't even remember). Expand this concept when you go to someone else's house to visit. Let your child play by himself or with the other children without continual watching.

Two skills are actually being developed here. Your child is learning to be comfortable being away from you and he is learning how to play by himself or with other children. Both skills are important.

Your child, in his own way, will probably help limit how overprotective you can be. He will, hopefully, push you to let him have more freedom. Listen to your child and watch him; he will tell you when he is ready to take the next step. One morning when my son was in kindergarten, I drove him to school. As I was about to shut off the car engine and walk him up to his classroom, he leaned over to me, tapped me on the shoulder, and said, "Leave, Mom." I looked at him and said, "Do you want me to leave or stay?" "Leave, Mom," was all he answered. "I love you," was all I could say before he shut the door.

Notes from teachers and therapists may allow you to step back. You may have to request this. Let the observation and progress be monitored by someone else for a change. No one will see your child like you do, but a second set of eyes gives you different kinds of information. Sometimes it can be hard just to see the information about your child only on a piece of paper, but it will enable you to watch your child grow up in a new way.

One way of checking whether you are being too overprotective is to compare what you do with your child with fragile X syndrome to what you do with your other children. Look at their developmental ages and behaviors. How do you respond when your six-year-old child who has fragile X syndrome does something compared to when your other children do the same thing? My daughter is two and a half years younger than my son who has fragile X syndrome, but they are very close to the same age developmentally (six and four years, respectively). We try to treat them the same as they build their independence, but we can't do that all of the time. When we go over to a friend's house for dinner, we check on our son more often than we check on our daughter. Sometimes we have to help facilitate communication. While we now check on our son more often at a friend's house, in the past one of us used to stay with him the entire time. We call that progress.

Be aware of your level of protectiveness and you will both grow. Realizing why you do what you do will help you learn to step back when it is time. Once you get the idea of backing away and see your child have successes of his own, it will be easier to do this in the future. Celebrate both of your newfound freedoms.

∷ Your Marriage

Your marriage is a union of two people from different backgrounds and different lives. Most likely, fate brought you two together. Two people who now have a family to raise. Two people who now must shoulder the responsibility of raising a child with fragile X syndrome.

Potential Marital Stress

If you are reading this book, your child has probably already been diagnosed with fragile X syndrome. In many instances, just getting to the answer—fragile X syndrome—will have put an unbelievable amount of stress on your marriage. You may have wondered whether your child was doing age appropriate activities. Your husband may have agreed, but maybe he didn't. Your pediatrician may have agreed, but maybe he didn't. The same is true for your friends and neighbors, your own parents, and your other relatives. It is just the beginning.

There are decisions that will have to be made continually. Lots and lots of decisions have to be made, sometimes faster than you are ready to make them. What's the best way (for your family) to treat fragile X syndrome? Therapy? What kinds? How often? Who is going be responsible for taking our child to therapy? What school do we send our child to? What kind of support does our child need and how do we get it? Should we move to a different school district, to a different state?

Develop a way to make decisions, especially the big decisions. This process will be invaluable in the long run. The types of decisions will range from simple to complex, from establishing a bedtime routine to choosing a family doctor to picking a school. You may have fifteen decisions to make in one week, and you may have none the next. One way is to list, analyze, and rank the pros and cons of various alternatives. Find a way that will meet both of your needs. Maybe you need to analyze the pros and cons of various alternatives (and then pull the answer out of a hat). Go with your gut feeling. Maybe that sounds too much like hocus-pocus. But I have always been a believer in the saying, "Things always work out for the best." Don't forget that you can always (well, usually) change your mind.

There's another big decision—how do we discipline? Discipline is difficult with all children, and part of it is because the parents (you) came from different parenting styles. Melding the two styles can be hard, particularly if your child has challenging behavior. How can you agree to a course of action when different situations arise? How can you be consistent? You won't really know until you have to start disciplining. Share your stories and your responses with each other. Discuss strategies. Most important, back your spouse (even if you don't agree) in front of your children. Discuss later when the children are not around. And yes, there are exceptions to every rule....

We found discipline didn't become much of an issue until our son was about 12 to 15 months old. Here was our first issue: I was home with Ian and pretty strict about discipline. My husband would come home and not want to discipline because he hadn't been home all day. After numerous discussions, we realized that it wasn't good for Ian to have two different sets of standards—strict mom, easy dad.

There are added responsibilities of having a child with fragile X syndrome. As much as possible, divide up the responsibilities with your spouse. If one spouse works outside the home, the other will handle much of the day-to-day activities. But it is important that the spouse who works outside the home help pick up some of the work in the evenings. It is important that both of the parents get to know their child.

If both parents work, much of the time spent with their child will be in meeting his physical needs. Finding time for calm interactive play will be a challenge. Maybe you will let the dinner dishes wait until your child is in bed. Maybe you alter your work schedule so you go in early and come home early, while your spouse goes in late and comes home late. Be sure you consider how all of these ideas affect the time you spend with your spouse, and time you have to yourself.

There may be a work decision to consider. If both of you are working, should one of you quit? Do you want to? Can you? There are financial and emotional consequences if you do. This is a very personal family decision.

Develop a budget so you can watch your finances. And stick to it. Nothing can be a greater source of contention in a marriage than money—how it is spent, the lack of it. There are organizations that are state and federally funded that have funds available for families who have children with disabilities. Your local office of The Arc or ACL can give you more information. See the Resource Guide at the end of the book for more information.

What Helps

Open Communication. If that meant the same to everybody, I could end this section right here. Most likely it means something different to each of us. Communication is more than just talking about the weather or sporting events. Communication is an exchange of ideas, or learning to express yourself *and* learning to listen to others. Let your spouse know what you are thinking and feeling. Exchange ideas and information.

It is important that information be shared in a nonconfrontational way. Starting out with, "You're not going to like this, but ..." may close off some communication. You are in this together. There's no need for one parent to "look better" than the other. This is not a contest to see who can come up with the best or most ideas...or the worst.

The other side of communication is being able to listen to what your spouse is saying. Listening means not interrupting. Let your spouse finish his train of thought even if half way through you find yourself disagreeing with what is being said. Listening, really listening, takes as much work, if not more, than learning to express yourself. Listening is more than just hearing words. Listening means trying to understand the other person's point of view. Good communication takes practice and it is something that all couples have to work on their whole lives. Talking through your thoughts can allow you both to keep moving with your child with fragile X syndrome.

There are ways to facilitate better communication. Some ideas are listed below.

Find Time Alone Together. Talk without the distraction of your children, without the distraction of other people. Talk about now. Talk about the future. In order to have time alone together, it is important that you find a babysitter with whom you can trust your children. Seek out the local agencies that will help you find quality respite care. Many agencies

can refer you to people who are interested in working with your child. These people are paid like regular babysitters. You might also be able to trade nights out with a neighbor or a friend. If you can't get a babysitter, schedule a time after the children have gone to bed. Set an agenda if you have to, and there may be times you have to if you have a lot to talk about or an important decision to make.

Try Agreeing with Your Spouse. There's a novel idea! Many of your daily decisions will not have a negative long-term impact. Things like what you eat, where you go, who you do activities with, probably won't change their lives. There's a wonderful book, *Don't Sweat the Small Stuff with Your Family: Simple Ways to Keep Daily Responsibilities and Household Chores from Taking over your Life* by Richard Carlson (Hyperion 1998), that has good advice.

Single Parent Families

A single parent raising a child with fragile X syndrome experiences the same range of emotions and needs that couples do. Creating a family, however, may be considerably harder because the single parent must make important decisions alone. You may be able to lessen the burden some by asking someone you trust to serve as your sounding board. You could turn to a close friend, your brother or sister, a member of the clergy, a therapist, or a social worker.

What matters is that you have someone to talk to who will be available on a consistent basis—someone who will offer you support, but who will not be afraid to question your decisions either. Often just knowing that there is someone with whom you can discuss your concerns can help reduce some of the overwhelming feelings of being on your own with your child every day.

Single parents in this position must realize they are doing the best they can—not only for their children, but also for themselves. Everything mentioned above applies here too. You meet everyone's needs the best way you know how. Maybe that means bringing in someone to clean the house. Order out for meals. Maybe you can find friends or neighbors with whom you can trade housekeeping or childcare. There are organizations that can help out with finances. This is not the time to become "super" parent. Save your strength for hard times.

■ Your Children's Feelings

Your Child's Feelings

How your child with fragile X syndrome learns to deal with his feelings can have an effect on the entire family. Your child with fragile X syndrome has feelings like every other child. Deal with them like you would for your other children. Just plan on spending a little extra time to help your child work through whatever he is feeling.

When your child is young, you may notice that it is *your* feelings that get hurt and not your child's. You see the stares. You hear the comments. You know that your child would feel hurt too if he had the same awareness. Your child will gain awareness of his feelings at his own pace. At the preschool stage you will have to figure out what your child is feeling because he probably won't be able to tell you with words. And you will have to observe what activities or events lead to certain feelings in your child. You will be able to figure out some fairly quickly. Acknowledge your child's feelings and then help him to vocalize them. "I see you like playing with your trucks. I'm happy when I get to play with trucks." Anger, when he does not get his way may be the second. "I see that you are angry that we have to leave the park. We'll come back another time. You will be able to sense his feeling of being overwhelmed when you enter a place with a lot of stimuli. "Wow, there's a lot going on in here. There's so much to see."

You may notice one day that when your child sees other children doing activities that you know he cannot do, he may act out. And you may start to wonder if it is a coincidence or if he is acting like that because he knows he can't do that. Continue to help him vocalize his feelings. "I want to build a house with these blocks but sometimes they fall over. Maybe we can start with a house that's not too tall."

As your child grows he will discover soon enough that he is "different" from other children. He will grow frustrated with his skills. He may get irritated from constant reminders and limited choices and feel sadness or anger. Continue to help him learn to describe his feelings to you. It is important to discuss these feelings with your child and work through them.

One morning my son had something he just had to tell me. I could pick out most of the words, but there was one key word to the whole story that I just could not get (it was actually two words: "recycle truck"). He tried over and over. Finally he said (clear as day), "I can't say it, I just can't say it." My heart went out to him. I looked at him and said, "You know, sometimes I have a hard time saying some words too. But you know what else, sometimes my ears don't work very well. So let's try this again. Tell me about this word. Is there something about it you can show me?" And there was something he could show me—a toy recycle truck.

Getting your child to verbally express his emotions will take some time. The concept of emotions is pretty abstract and may be difficult for your child to understand. You can lead the way for him. Model your emotions for your child when something happens to you. Let him see that we all experience emotions. When something good happens that your child knows is good say, "I'm happy!" with a big smile on your face. Not too long ago, I got out some papers and markers for the children to do some art projects. My daughter just jumped right in and started drawing the house, the yard, and the family. My son just sat and watched her draw. After a while, he said, "I can't do that." I told him I would help him. "But *I* want to do that." We talked about how it is frustrating when you want to do something but you aren't able to by yourself. I talked about how everybody has that feeling at one time or another in his or her life. People learn different things at different rates. Everything we do—from drawing to reading to playing a musical instrument—takes practice, and often it takes a lot of practice. Gear your responses to your child's developmental level.

Your child with fragile X syndrome has unique feelings, but it does not mean he needs to be spoiled. Your family will grow when all of your children are treated as unique and valuable. Certain allowances may need to be made for your child with fragile X syndrome, such as a calming activity at the end of the day. But it doesn't mean that he gets to pick the activities all day long or all of the time. Family relationships require give and take. Everyone's needs and desires should be taken into account when looking at the day or planning an activity. For example, let's say your family decides to go to the zoo. Some children want to go in the afternoon, but you know the best time for Dustin is in the morning. Can you go in the morning and still have it be successful for everyone? Do you compromise—say early afternoon? Do you go in the after-noon and not take Dustin? Do you *make* everyone go in the morning? Maybe you go in the morning this time and do something in the after-noon next time. It's all about listening, considering everyone's needs, and taking turns.

■■ Brothers and Sisters

When you think about siblings, what comes to mind? How they drove you crazy? How fond you are of them? The fighting? The hugs? Meeting the needs of my own two children is overwhelming sometimes. My parents had four children. My husband comes from a family of six children. They've all lived to tell about it!

In meeting the physical and emotional needs of your child with fragile X syndrome, it is important that the needs of your other children be met as well, particularly the emotional needs. Don't assume that just because they are not affected they don't need you as much. They have their own needs; they are just a little different from their brother's.

Brothers and Sisters Have Emotions Too

Having a child with fragile X will bring out the best and the worst in your other children, just like it does in you. Yes, brothers and sisters will experience emotions and feelings that are very similar to the feel-ings you as parents experience; the age and developmental level will be the only difference. For example, you and your children may both feel resentment toward your child with fragile X syndrome because of the extra time he takes. You resent the time it takes to drive around to doctors and therapists, and your children resent the time that their sib-ling takes you away from them. You will both probably be embarrassed by your child (their brother) at one time or another in your lives, again for similar but different reasons. Where you may be saddened by not being able to do certain things as a family, your children will probably get mad. As they mature, they will understand why you were sad, and why you still get sad sometimes. Just as the negative emotions will come out, so will the positive. The love you have for each of your chil-dren is special. The love your children have for each other is also spe-cial. Different feelings will surface at different times, depending on the ages of your children, and they will resurface periodically, which is the same thing that will be happening to you.

It is important for you to talk to your children about how they are feeling about their brother from the time they are very young. At all ages it is good to affirm to your children that what they are feeling is very normal. You can make the most impact by talking at their level of understanding and by being available to talk about it, whenever possible, at their convenience. Their need for information may be immediate and the sooner their questions can be answered, the sooner you can put their fears to rest. The love between siblings can be nurtured by you at a very young age and can last a lifetime.

Preschool. When they are very young, children will accept their brother with fragile X syndrome without question. But the questions will start early enough. "How come other people can't understand my brother when he talks?" (Your children will probably understand their brother's speech very well.) Children are very perceptive about what is going on around them. They may not know or understand the details of a situation, but they pick up pretty quickly that *something* is going on. The emotions brought out by having a child with fragile X syndrome will be seen from a very young age. They can range from sadness when their brother won't play with them to anger and frustration when their brother won't play the "right" way. Those will be your first opportunities to talk about your child with fragile X syndrome.

Although you will see the differences in your children at this age, don't forget that preschoolers don't always have the words to tell you what is going on with them. Just as your child with fragile X syndrome sometimes speaks with his behavior, your other children may try to tell you something with their behavior too. It is up to you to figure out what the behavior is saying.

The Elementary School Years. During these years, your children will develop a good sense of fairness, everything from how much time you spend with each of your children to how their brother is being treated by others. Your children will let you know, hopefully verbally, if you are successfully balancing your time and attention. It will always take a conscious effort on your part to spend time with each of your children every day.

Some children at this age may stand up for their sibling with fragile X syndrome if he is not being treated fairly or appropriately, by either dealing with the problem themselves or seeking out an adult's help. "Some kids were making fun of Davey today, so I told a teacher." There may be a risk for your children to do this—risk of how their own friends will respond. In most cases, your children won't even give this a second thought.

Some negative emotions may come out in these years. Your children may get embarrassed by their brother's speech or handflapping, especially in front of their friends. When your children have friends over, and their older brother plays much more immaturely than they, it may be hard for your children to explain the reasons to their friends. They may get angry because they have a brother who has fragile X syndrome and they feel guilty at having that anger.

This is when your children figure out that Davey really is "different." Your children may begin to wonder if they have what their brother has or if they are going to get it. "How did he get it?" "Do I have this fragile X thing?" "Is there anybody else in the family who has it?" "There aren't other children at school like him." Your children will begin to understand what it means when someone has a disability. They will learn that not only are there different kinds of disabilities, but that *everyone* has different abilities. Every person is good at something, and every person has something that is hard for him or her. They will learn that the same is true for children with fragile X syndrome.

Adolescence. The teenage years are a challenging time for all children, not to mention their parents. As if a teenager's emotions don't fluctuate enough, having a brother or a sister with fragile X syndrome just complicates the matter. Your teenager will continue to experience a wide range of emotions like you do, but the emotions can become greatly exaggerated. Not only do teenagers not want to be seen with their parents, they *really* don't want to be seen with Davey. Embarrassment can be huge—and their brother doesn't even have to do anything to embarrass them, it's just being seen with him, sometimes it will be just people knowing that they have a brother "like that."

It's not that they don't love their brother with fragile X syndrome. Teenagers are pushing independence from the whole family, trying to figure out who they are and where they fit in. A teenager's desire not to be seen with the rest of his or her family happens to a certain extent in most every family, whether there are siblings who have a disability or not. Remember, your teenagers do love you and their family—they still need both.

If possible, talk with your child who has fragile X syndrome about his changing sister. Reassure your child that his sister still loves him. Explain in whatever detail you and your child are comfortable with what happens as people grow up. "As your sister gets older, her friends become very important to her. It doesn't mean she loves you any less, but she tends to spend more time with them than you and me. It feels lonely sometime too. We will still do activities together as a family, we just may not do as many with her."

Teenagers will become more responsible for their own schedule. They will probably not spend as much time at home as your child with fragile X syndrome. However, you should still expect them to do some things with the family. Where earlier the discussion centered on what time to go to the zoo, the discussion now will include someone who may not want to go at all. Taking turns in the family now takes on a different perspective. "You don't have to go shopping with us this afternoon, but we would like you to go out for dinner with us tonight." Allowing your teenager to do things without you becomes as important as expecting her to do things with you.

The teenage years will be an evolving time for your family. It will be a time to acknowledge and discuss the feelings your children have. Let them know you understand (or least you think you do or that you are trying to). It will be a time to pick your battles. It is also a time to hold onto the ideals of your family. Hold on to that dinner together every night as best as you can, for as long as you can.

Helping Your Children Adjust

A family who has a child with fragile X syndrome has to address the extra needs of the child, but it also has to address the needs of the other children. Look at yourself—the extra emotions and how you deal with them. Your children need skills too. Help find what works best for them.

There are many factors that can influence how your children adjust to having a sibling with fragile X syndrome. Three of the big factors are your lifestyle, financial resources, and parenting style. Your lifestyle, which includes your attitude, changes after you have a child, and that becomes a little more magnified when you have a child with fragile X syndrome. It can be even more magnified when there are others in the family who are carriers or are affected. Having financial resources will be helpful. Children with fragile X syndrome cost more than other children: doctors, therapies, glasses, and surgeries. And finally your parenting style—in some ways the most daunting factor—will stay with all of your children for their entire lives.

Communicate. Communicating with your children when they are very young not only allows you to acknowledge their feelings, but it provides a way to help them adjust to having a brother with fragile X syndrome. Remember to talk to your children at their level. "That's one way your brother is differ-  ent" to "Yeah, the doctors think it is somehow related to the lack of a certain pro- tein level in children who carry the full mutation of the fragile X gene." And when your children are ready, expand on the issue of families. Although most families do not include a child with fragile X syn- drome, most every family has some issue that affects them. These issues can range from other types of disabilities to cancer to death to other health issues to multiple births to divorce. Some come and go, and some are long-term issues. But the point to emphasize to your children is that every family has an issue they have to deal with.

You may have better discussions if you ask specific questions rather than open ended ones. Rather than saying, "How are you doing?" which may be okay in certain situations, you might ask about a specific event. "What did you think when your brother started jumping up and down and flapping his arms in front of all of your friends?" Continual dia- logue with your children will take time and work. Listen to your chil- dren, hear what they say, have respect for what they say—without judg- ing them. You can shut dialogue down real fast with, "Oh, you don't need to feel that way. He can't help it." Acknowledge what they say, let them know you understand. Humor helps too.

Reactions of Others. When your children are young, they may not notice the reactions of others or think too much about them if they do notice. Reflect back their thoughts or feelings. "I wonder why he does that. What do you think it feels like to him?"

As your children get older, they will notice how other people react to their sibling. Watch for that and stay with the matter-of-fact ap- proach. "Did you see the look on their face? They didn't know what to think." What about that look on your teenager's face that says, "Ohhh, there he goes again. I hate this." You might go up to her and whisper, "Isn't he cute?"

Information. When you talk to your children, provide accurate information. Knowledge will counteract unspoken fears. "Do I have any fragile X syndrome?" There may be issues that are nagging at your children, but they haven't been able to put their fingers on it or they don't know quite how to put it into words. Answer questions with information that they can understand. There is no need to overload your children, but don't hide information from them either. When your children are furnished with information that they understand, they are better prepared to deal with their brother themselves and to talk to others about him. They become confident about what they say. When your children can talk about their brother like he's no big deal, other people will often mirror that attitude.

Your children will also realize that there are long-term implications to having a child with a disability in the family. "What's going to happen to Davey when he gets older? Will he ever be able to drive? Will he get married? Where's he going to live? Who's going to help him take care of himself after mom and dad die?" Your children may wonder what kind of role their sibling is going to play in their lives as they get older. They will struggle with what kind of role they want to play. Be ready with some answers.

Comparisons. Your other children will eventually notice that they can do things better than their brother with fragile X syndrome. My own daughter went through a short phase of "I can do this better than Ian, can't I Mom?" The first time I heard it, I stopped the conversation and talked about it. "You're both working hard, some things are easier for you." A couple of those discussions and a couple of glares got her through that phase pretty quickly. And then it went to "Mom, look how good Ian is doing on the scooter" and "Good job, Ian!"

Balance. As discussed above, balance is much easier to describe than it is to put into practice. When you take your child with fragile X to therapy or the doctor, arrange for your other children to have something fun to do. Bring them with you and bring a game or a treat, or see if they can go to a friend's house.

You may need to schedule time with each of your children. Even if it is only 15 minutes a day, let that child know that he is the most important one in the world during that time. Other times, seize the moment. If one of them wakes up early in the morning, let him or her climb into bed with you and talk about what is going to happen that day or just listen to what they have to say. As your children get older, these 15 minutes a day will be harder to find as schedules get more complicated. It becomes difficult to schedule anything. You really have to be ready to seize the moment; it could be at breakfast, in the car, or around bedtime, and it probably won't be at the same time each day. Look for opportunities, and if one doesn't present itself, create one. Ice cream gets 'em every time!

And then everyone lives happily ever after, right? Helping siblings adjust will be an ongoing process throughout all of your life and theirs. Provide the perspective that all families deal with some kind of issue. Look at life as a series of opportunities rather than a bunch of problems, and help your children realize that this is what life is all about.

Counseling. If you have a child who is having a particularly difficult time adjusting, it may be prudent to seek outside help. Your child may need to vent to someone who is more objective than he or she thinks you are. Some signs that your child is having a hard time adjusting could be that she has shut down all communication with you, or whenever she does talk, there is a negative attitude present. This is not a one time negative attitude, but one that has persisted over a period of weeks. The type of counseling can be informal—another parent or a teacher, or you may choose to use a professional therapist. Counseling is usually most successful when your child has a say in whom he or she talks to. Reassure him or her that you'll always be there and you're always available to talk.

Helping Friends of Your Children Adjust. Helping your children adjust to having a child with fragile X syndrome in the family means also helping their friends to get to know their brother. Either by going through your children or by dealing with their friends, there are many opportunities to convey understanding and even friendship. Unless you know the child and his parents well, you may not know where the child "is coming from." When children are young, you will be able to find out pretty quickly whether or not they are going to be receptive to your child with fragile X syndrome. The best you can do is to be open with them about your child. Listen to and address their questions with information. Basically it means talking to them like you do your own children. Most likely you will start at a more basic level than your children, but that's because you've talked to your children since the day they were born (or their brother was born). Your goal is that in time the friends of your children will see that the whole issue of fragile X syndrome is no big deal.

It is good for the friends to see that your family is pretty typical in most regards. Your family does things like every other family. You go to the movies, you go out to eat, and you go on vacations. Your children like to do what other children like to do. Your child with fragile X syndrome likes to do what other children like to do. Depending on the age of your child with fragile X syndrome, you can compare it to having a younger child around. When you go places you may not stay as long, or sometimes you may go places that may seem a little "young." But it is important that you show that your family likes to have fun whenever and wherever you go out.

Here's an example of a family outing that we shared with our daughter's friends:

We all went to the circus last weekend. Our kids had never been to the circus, so we splurged and bought tickets that were right up front. We went an hour early so all of the children could look around and get used to the place before the crowds arrived and the lights went out. And because we were there so early, we got to see and talk to many of the clowns. We got to watch some of the performers practice their stunts. We got to see what is involved in setting up for a circus. When the circus started, we all found the performers were fun to watch. But about halfway through the performance, they turned out all of the lights for one of the shows. Ian chose to leave because it scared him (he thought they lost power), but he was able to come back in after they turned the lights back on. We enjoyed all of the rest of the performances. But another thing we did to help Ian get ready to go home was to stick around to see what happened after the circus was over. We watched how the arena was cleaned up and preparations were made for the next show. Getting to the circus early and staying late not only made the transitions easier, but it was interesting for all of us to see what goes on both before and after. It takes little adaptations like that to make outings successful for everyone in our family.

The friends then see that your family does activities like all families do. And you can point out the adaptations that you have made to make the trip successful, or you can minimize them, as if it is something you all like to do (which is often what they become).

▪▪ Your Extended Family's Emotions

Some of the initial reactions of extended family members were discussed in Chapter 2, but what happens a few years down the road? It's about as unpredictable as the response you got when you first told everyone about your child. In many cases, your extended family will follow your lead in how they see your child. Your attitude— that this is just the way it was meant to be—will rub off. Share with your family the things your child likes to do. Share the unique joy he brings to your family. Let them see you, your child, and your family interact. When your extended family sees that your child likes to do things that every child likes to do, when they begin to see how similar your child is to other children, they will enjoy your child like they do their other grandchildren.

When you first told everyone your child has fragile X syndrome and the genetic nature become known, the effect was felt through the extended family—grandparents, aunts, uncles, and cousins. With fragile X syndrome, we know that there can be repercussions in future generations. What do you do about testing for carriers? What do we do about having more children? What do we do about starting a family? These questions do not always have easy or simple answers.

The unknown future of your child can be difficult on your extended family. Your extended family will often have the same questions and concerns that your own children have. "What's going to happen to Ian when he gets older?" Often it is that unknown that is most difficult for many families to deal with. Help your family to answer the questions that can be answered and live with the ones that can't be answered.

Custodianship

What plans do you have for your children if something happens to you and your spouse that leaves you unable to take care of your young children living at home? Many families have made arrangements for members of their extended family to take care of the children if something happens to them. While the chances for something devastating like this to happen are low, the possibility exists, and careful thought should be given to this "what if?" Leaving something like this to fate isn't fair to your children or anyone else in your extended family.

■■ Family Friends

You will play a key role in helping your friends get to know your child. Start by giving them some information about fragile X syndrome. When you can, try to relate the information to your child. Help them to see your child as a person first, not just a list of characteristics. For example, your friend might read, "Children with fragile X syndrome have loose connective tissue." You can tell your friend what it means for *your* child. "That's why he has so many ear infections. That probably contributed to his hernia. That's why his joints are so loose and why we are careful about swinging him around. But, that's also why he will probably never pull a hamstring, and why he can touch the ground flat-handed without giving it a second thought."

Your friends will see you interact with your child, but encourage them to interact while you facilitate. Allow your friends to get to know your child in their own way at their own pace. It may take some time for them to be comfortable with your child. Like your family, they probably did not grow up around anyone with a disability. The more time they spend with your child, the more comfortable they will be. As your friends get to know your child, they will probably want to know more than the average person does about fragile X syndrome. When they ask, "Why does he do that?" it will be because they really want to understand your child.

My friends have taken different paths to getting to know my son, Ian. One of my friends asked for information on fragile X syndrome right after my son was diagnosed. As she spent time with him, she had lots of questions which were much more probing and detailed than the information I had given her. But I don't think she would have thought to ask these questions if she hadn't spent time with Ian. Playing with him made the information "real" to her and made her curious to learn more. I also had a friend who didn't want information about fragile X syndrome initially. She just wanted to get to know Ian first. She eventually asked for information, but her focus was on the person and not the "reason" behind him.

I have a need for my friends not only to accept my son, but to enjoy him too. I strive to meet their needs in order for that to happen, whether it is with information or providing opportunities for getting to know my son. After he was diagnosed, I remember wondering what effect it would have on friendships. I wondered if I would only have friends who had a child with a disability. As it has turned out, we have all kinds of friends, some who have a child with a disability, some who don't. I have my own friends, and we have a large circle of family friends. I am involved in many activities that revolve around people who have disabilities, and I am involved in many that do not. The balance has been important for our family.

When socializing and entertaining with your friends don't forget to consider your child when deciding where you will go, what time you'll go and what time you'll come home, what there will be to eat, and how bedtime will be affected. Also, the number of people who will be involved can be very important. In general, the higher the number of people, the higher the activity level. Our children thrive on routine, and whether you go to a friend's house or you have them over to your house, it is a variation to your child's routine. Talking to your child about what to expect will do wonders.

We schedule earlier dinners with our friends than we used to. Depending on where we are going, we may feed our children a small meal before we go. If there is going to be a lot of people at a particular activity, we tend to arrive early and leave early. Our son has a difficult time recovering from staying up late. He tends to get up at six in the morning no matter what time he goes to bed. But we still occasionally let him stay up late, knowing he'll be tired for a day or so. We talk to both of our children before we go anywhere or have anyone over so they know what to expect. And we often remind them throughout the evening of what's going to happen and when.

■■ Community Life

When you go out into the community you may see a variety of reactions to your child with fragile X syndrome. Just as there are different types of people in the world, so are the responses you get in public. The reactions will vary from positive to none to negative. An example of a negative reaction might be that disapproving look you get for the way you handle your child's tantrum. Or there may be a look of disgust at some of your child's mannerisms. Either way, most of the negative reactions you get will be the result of fear that others have of people who have disabilities. People have this fear because they don't know what to say or do around people who don't fit their norm. Many people fear the unknown, and do not know much, if anything, about fragile X syndrome. Most have never spent any time around people who look or act or think differently.

Other people you see in public will not give you the time of day. It is nothing personal, that's just how they are. They are people who are in a hurry, or wrapped up in some private thought. Either way, you are not a part of it (unless you get in their way!). Most people fit into this category.

And finally, there are people who give you an extra smile, hold the door, and take the time to talk to your child. These are people who see the child first. It doesn't mean they are not curious. But the disability is not what is important when they see your child, and some people can just look past it more quickly than others.

What makes some people respond positively and others respond negatively? Why do people respond so differently? Once you have acknowledged there are all different types of people in the world, look at three other factors: their information base, their life experiences, and their personality.

Knowledge can dramatically affect how people respond to people with disabilities. I'm referring to people who have studied or read about any aspect of special education or developmental disabilities. How many people have already asked you for more information on fragile X syndrome? Your friends, teachers, and therapists? These people will want to know more about fragile X syndrome, so they can really reach out to your child. It's a compliment to be asked for information, so don't let them down. Actually, you may have to be careful you don't overwhelm them with information!

Experience has a powerful influence on people's lives. Think how the events in your life have shaped you. Not just the big vacations you took, but look at all of the activities you did on an everyday basis. Look at the communication that took place in your family. How did your family talk about people who had disabilities? Did the topic even come up? What was your family's general reaction to people who were "different" from them? Did you spend time around people who had disabilities? When I grew up, not only did I have limited experiences with people with disabilities, I rarely even saw anyone who had a disability. When I look at the experiences my daughter is having as she grows up, it will be interesting to see what kind of person she turns out to be and how she relates to people with differences.

Though influential, personality is very complicated. I don't think you can use it alone in determining how someone is going to respond to your child with fragile X syndrome. Although it may seem that someone who is more laid back would respond best to our children, it doesn't mean that someone who is the opposite wouldn't do well too. Experience with people who have disabilities along with learning about or seeking information about the world of disabilities tends to enhance anyone's personality.

I have met some of the nicest people since my son was diagnosed. I have probably met some of the biggest jerks in my life too, but somehow I have been able to erase them from my mind. Well, all but a couple.... And you never know who's going to smile and who's going to frown on any given day.

Dealing with the Reaction of Others

Dealing with reactions to your child can vary from uplifting to depressing. Each day in public will be a new adventure for you and your child. Most days will be uneventful. Other days you'll get a reaction. Some days it will bother you, some days it will elate you, depending on the reaction.

One option you have in dealing with the reaction of others is to educate them. Educating others can have a big effect, but requires effort. It means talking to them about your child and his disability. You can provide details about fragile X syndrome or you can make it general information. People you talk to will see you as a parent who is truly interested in your child. You should not feel you have to educate everyone you meet on the street. Some days you are not going to feel like talking to anyone. That's okay. That's how most people are; you have a right to be like that too.

Educating a stranger takes courage. You are taking a chance by putting yourself "out there." You know nothing about the person you're talking to, so you really don't know how he or she is going to respond to what you say. Making fragile X syndrome understandable to someone with an unknown background is a challenge. Watch to see if they are getting it. You may notice that explaining fragile X syndrome will help you understand it better too. In general, educating others gets easier with time. Your confidence grows and you will learn to spot receptive people.

Helping Siblings Deal with Strangers

Your children will have experiences with strangers that will be very similar to yours; there will be both good and bad. Talk to your children about your experiences. Give them examples of what they can expect

when they walk into a grocery store with a brother who has fragile X syndrome. Give them examples of how you have dealt with different situations. Impress upon them not to take the negative experiences personally. It is hard advice to follow, but it can be very effective for them in dealing with strangers. Encourage your children to talk to you about their experiences, the good ones and the bad ones. Talking about it allows all of you to say, "Yeah, well the next time I'm going to say...." And that is often what is said the next time.

The Tantrum

Everyone who wants to have children and take on the job of raising a family should sign a contract that contains the following pledge: *"I am eager to deal with my child's public tantrums."* The reason is simple: Every parent gets his or her chance. It's a rite of passage.

What do you do? Hold fast to your discipline. If you have to walk out of a grocery store and leave a cart full of food, I guarantee it won't be the first time that it's happened at the store. It is easier to leave then than it is when you are already in the process of being checked out. If you have to walk out of a movie, no one will care.

One morning my husband took our son to the grocery store so I could get some work done. About 15 minutes after they'd gone, I heard the front door open and my son walk in. Then the door closed and I heard the car take off. My husband came back about 45 minutes later, groceries in hand. The good news: I was at home. The bad news: My husband didn't really get to experience a full-blown public tantrum...that time. It was prudent to get our son out of the store whether I was at home or not; the shopping could always have gotten done another time.

All children have their phases of testing mom and dad. When you see one coming, just lay out the boundaries. Reward the good behavior, and have consequences for the not-so-good, and maybe start doing your grocery shopping on a monthly basis...find the stores that are open 24 hours a day and go in the middle of the night!

Community Activities

As your child grows, he will also want to participate in activities that all children enjoy. He will want to take swim lessons, go bowling, go to amusement parks, and go to movies, to name a few. Put some thought into the activities so your child will have a good experience. In our community I can sign my son up for group swim lessons at the recreation center. There's even an organization that will provide a volunteer to help my son in these lessons. I can sign him up for private lessons. Or I can enroll him in a class where all of the children have some kind of disability. All of these options are available in all of the activities offered through our local recreation centers.

We have also participated in Special Olympic events. We started with track and field activities when our son was five years old. He has competed many times in various sports and thinks it is the greatest. Contact your local office of The Arc, ACL, or the Special Olympics organization. See the Resource Guide at the end of the book.

◗◗ School

Today children with disabilities are going to school with children who are typically developing; often they are in the same classes. Other children are learning that children with disabilities are children first. They are able to look past the disability quickly. Educating people at a young age makes such a big difference in their attitude. Parents of the children at school may have many of the same questions children have, but they will also have different ones. They may want to know the name and details of fragile X syndrome.

Whether you are talking to other children or their parents, it is important to point out that your child is a child like any other. His body just works a little differently. But he has feelings like every other child, which can be hurt, just like everyone else. Don't worry if what you say seems awkward at first. Over time you will gain confidence. That's because you will get a lot of practice. The people you run into will soon pick up on your attitude of "He's a great kid!"

■■ Conclusion

When I think of "family," I smile. I have fond memories as a child of our family going places and doing things together. I have tried to instill the same kind of memories in my own children. We do something every weekend as a family, even if it is just for one hour. We try to get away from the house overnight, several times a year. We take a vacation every year.

But there's more to being a family than sharing "big" events together. Families teach us how to enjoy each other and have fun together every day doing simple things. We all love to putter in the yard. We each do our own thing for a while, and then we all play together. This interaction sometimes lasts an entire afternoon. It is so nice to watch the children play and see the happiness on their faces when they play with each other. We watch television together. We laugh together.

Our son has "demanded" many of the much-loved traditions we now follow as a family. He expects certain things to happen around various annual activities. He anticipates the big holidays and delights in the "same old thing" happening every year. The inside of the house gets decorated for everyone's birthday, even mom's and dad's, and everyone chips in to help. Valentine and Easter mean candy and a little gift, and often it is the same favorite candy year after year. We have a neighborhood party every year on the Fourth of July that the whole family gets involved in preparing. As Christmas nears, our son is the first to ask about the tree. We tromp around and cut down a Christmas tree every year. I give my children chocolate marshmallow Santas every year at Christmas, just like my mom use to give me. The children expect them.

Our son loves ritual. We all eat supper together almost every night, often by candlelight. If dad has to work late, we wait for him (or maybe I should say the children refuse to eat until dad gets home!). We have family time after supper. We read books together. Making traditions and rituals a part of our life has done wonderful things for our family. We enjoy each other and we're creating memories to carry with us.

Throughout your family life there will invariably come some challenging times. There will be changing emotions in everyone. Each family member will have to learn to deal with life in the community. And it is not only for them that they will have to learn this. The family must band together to help your child with fragile X syndrome learn to not just live in the community, but to thrive in the community. That's a family!

∷ Parent Statements

In some ways we are like most other families, but in other ways we are very different. We have to do lots of planning and preparation—well, we do if we want things to go well.

Sometimes it seems like everything revolves around Patrick's world and no matter how hard we try for it not to, often that's just what it comes down to.

We are pretty much like every other family we know.

If you raise your kids with the premise of giving them what they each individually need, then it's harder to get stuck in the "equal" trap. Treat them fairly and uniquely, not evenly.

Our family is pretty different from others—we plan our whole day around being home when the mail carrier comes around because Tony likes to run alongside him.

When we visit my parents they almost always ask what accommodations they can make for William—like when and what we eat. They are aware of some of the sensory issues.

All of our friends reacted positively and encouragingly.

Our old friends got closer, and we have made some wonderful new friends, some who have a child with a disability and some who don't.

Our neighbors love our son. He takes a genuine interest in whatever they are doing, from weeding their garden, to changing a tire, to mowing the lawn, to cleaning their house.

On an emotional level, one of the hardest things for me as the mother (doesn't seem to bother my husband as much) has been dealing with the outside people in this world. The neighbors that come over to play once and never talk to you again; seeing birthday parties going on in the block and not being invited.

At a park when a mother finds out Alex has fragile X, she takes her kid to the opposite side of the playground.

There are people who, when you tell them that your son has special needs or fragile X syndrome, quickly find a way to exit the conversation. The fear element is really great with a lot of people.

I might explain in generalities like, "Sports are really difficult for him" or "He's really trying but it is really tough for him." I explain fragile X to the degree necessary.

Some people are overly solicitous toward him. Others seem confused or unable to understand his behavior. The best reaction is when people learn that fragile X syndrome is only one fraction of who he is.

When it comes to strangers, if they respond to Tony in a loving, understanding way, I react to them in the same manner. If they look down on my child—I simply don't fool with them.

Sometimes when another child is staring at my child, I revert to their behavior and stare back at them, often with emphasis.

We went to an amusement park in our city one time and all Patrick wanted to do was ride the bumper cars. We didn't go back for two years and when we did, the same lady was running the bumper cars and she remembered Patrick from the first time we were there. She let him stay on the cars almost continuously and was introducing him to other children when they got into their cars.

My husband and I went out on one date last year.

We have started meeting for lunch during the week because it is so hard to find a good babysitter.

With our children being so young, it's often hard to digest or even take in most of the information we have collected about fragile X, which focuses on older children, adolescents, and adults. It's too difficult to look that far down the road for us, when the here and now is so demanding.

We know there are no guarantees and few accurate predictions about what will be involved in raising our two boys. They are individuals with

their own unique personalities and ways of responding to the people and things around them.

This reality—that Patrick and Sam are individuals and not fragile X specimens—has been difficult to communicate to some people who learned of the boys' diagnoses. Although fragile X syndrome affects our sons in many ways, fragile X syndrome is not all they are—it is only part of who they are.

We live a happy, typical life. Fragile X syndrome has changed some things but everyone in the world has to make accommodations for someone or something in their daily life. For some it's adjusting to not making enough money, for others it's living with poor health, for us it's fragile X syndrome.

William touches the hearts of so many people that sometimes it brings a tear to my eye.

Our son wanted to invite a very popular girl in his class to his birthday party. The other four kids were boys (who seem to overlook more behavioral miscues than girls). The girl was happy to be invited and when I saw her arrive, I had to turn away and choke back tears. It meant so much that a typical child wanted to be his friend.

With two boys with fragile X, the future worries me. As the boys grow bigger physically it even scares me a bit. They do fight now and again, but we are sure to include time by themselves away from each other during the day.

My brother can be really nice sometimes, like when he lets me play with his toys. But there can be bad times too, because sometimes he hits me.

Sometimes he embarrasses me when he flaps his arms or bites his hands or makes funny noises when we're in public.

One day a lot of mail carriers in our area came to our house and gave my brother an award for helping the mail carrier in our neighborhood. It was really cool.

We get into national parks for free because my brother has a disability.

Sometimes my brother tells me to "Stop it" and I'm just sitting there. That drives me crazy. I just say, "Yeah, whatever."

Sometimes my brother is really funny. We'll be driving in the car and when we pass people he'll say "Hi Bob" or "Hi Betty" and we don't know who the people are and they'll either stare or wave back.

He knows people everywhere we go—the grocery store, the fire department, the bakery, the shoe store, the post office, and the place we get our oil changed. They know him by name! It's kind of neat.

There's no one at my school who has a brother like mine. My friends don't really know what it's like to have a brother with a disability.

7

THE DEVELOPMENT OF CHILDREN WITH FRAGILE X SYNDROME

*Ave M. Lachiewicz, M.D. and
Penny L. Mirrett, Ph.D.*

Most parents don't *really* expect their children to grow up to be rocket scientists or bestselling authors. For most it is rewarding enough to see their children progress from being helpless infants to real people with distinctive personalities and the skills to look after their own wants and needs. Few parents would trade the joy of watching their children learn to roll over, sit up, and walk; coo, laugh, and babble; wave bye-bye, recognize Mom and Dad, and play peek-a-boo for anything.

Virtually all children grow and acquire skills that enable them to become more independent. This wondrous and complex process is called development. The rate and quality of development, however, can vary widely from child to child. As the parent of a child with fragile X syndrome, you probably know this from personal experience. In fact the differences in the way your child was developing physically and mentally may have been your first clue that something was not "right."

Perhaps your child took longer to learn to sit or walk. Perhaps he did not begin to babble when you expected. It is usual for the development of a child with fragile X syndrome to be delayed in at least some ways, because fragile X syndrome is a developmental disability. That is, it is a condition that appears before the age of 21 and interferes with or hinders how a child develops.

This chapter provides a basic understanding of human development, and explains how fragile X syndrome can alter the usual course of development. By learning more about how children with fragile X syndrome develop, you will gain insight into your own child's strengths and weaknesses. This will enable you to address your child's needs, set goals for your child, and prepare for the future.

■■ What Is Development?

The term development can mean different things to different people. To parents of young children, it may mean the process by which their child learns to look and listen; laugh and coo; sit, walk, and climb steps. To parents of older children, it may mean how well their child is able to read, write, or do math; take part in athletic activities; or conform to typical behavioral expectations. To professionals in child development, development can mean all these things and more. For everyone, however, development may be defined as the process that occurs as people mature from infancy through childhood, adolescence, and, finally, into adulthood, acquiring increasingly complex skills.

The Areas of Development

Over the course of a lifetime, people develop in many different ways. Their bodies develop physically, as do their nervous systems and muscular systems. Their intellectual abilities increase, and their temperaments and personalities mature. Along the way, children improve their abilities to communicate, to move about, to socialize, and to get along in their environment. Some specific areas of development that child development specialists often monitor and measure are described below.

Cognitive Skills. Cognitive skills or cognition is the ability to understand concepts, pay attention, remember, reason, and solve problems. These skills enable us to understand our world and adapt to it. When your infant learns that an object does not cease to exist just because it is out of sight, his cognitive abilities are developing. When your child learns to read, figures out how to build a model car, or learns the mailman's delivery schedule to your house, he is using and honing his cognitive skills.

Language Skills. Language skills focus on the ability to communicate, to express, and to understand language, which can be both verbal and nonverbal. Expressive language involves the ability to communicate thoughts, ideas, and feelings with words, pronunciation, and expression. Receptive language is the ability to make sense out of spoken language. It develops before expressive language. Children below the age of two will follow a command such as getting a ball or giving a kiss before they can speak words like "ball" or "kiss." This means that your child can make sense out of the language in his world and respond even if he has not mastered speech.

The acquisition of language skills tends to proceed in a "stairstep" fashion for all children. New skills appear with an obvious change to a higher level. Children then spend some time on that level integrating and practicing the new skills. For example, when children move from single words to word combinations, they spend quite a while trying out different versions of the same forms—such as "my book," "my lunch," and "my daddy"—and then trying more novel combinations—such as "go outside," "want juice," and "more chips." Typically, children will use their favorite words and two-word combinations for several months before moving on to longer phrases.

Sensorimotor Development. This area of development includes the ability to perceive and process sensory and motor stimuli from the environment and to respond appropriately. Our sensory ability is remarkably sophisticated. It allows us to feel a light touch on the back and recognize it as a friendly touch. It allows us to filter out loud noises at the mall while holding a conversation. It allows us to maintain our balance and equilibrium while riding an escalator or a boat. We can even play with our senses; children who spin themselves in circles and then quickly stop to watch the world spin are really just enjoying their sensory system adjust.

Sensorimotor development involves several "systems" that together keep us connected to our world and its many sensations. They include what we commonly think of as our senses of sight, smell, hearing, taste, and touch. But there are other more complex yet equally important sensing "systems" our bodies depend upon. These are the tactile, proprioceptive, and vestibular systems.

Humans are able to "feel" or sense things in the world such as hot soup, cold water, and rough fabric. These all involve the tactile system. It enables us to feel pain and pleasure, to receive complex information from the environment, and to tell the difference between objects. Our sense of touch is part of the tactile system.

The proprioceptive system tells our bodies about its movement and position. For example, proprioception tells us about our distance from

other people or objects. Our nervous systems have receptors in our muscles, tendons, and joints, called proprioceptors, that transmit information so that our brains are aware of where our body and limbs are. This helps us perform some movements quickly and automatically. For example, when someone throws a ball to you, your proprioceptive system allows you to automatically shift your body and hands to be ready to catch it.

Another part of the sensory system, the vestibular system, regulates balance and maintains equilibrium. Receptors around our body send messages to the inner ear about the orientation of our body in space and the position of the head in relation to the rest of our body. This is the part of our sensory system that responds to the position of the head in relation to gravity and allows us to sense accelerated or decelerated movement. For whatever reason, if you start to lose your balance and fall, the "righting mechanism" in your middle ear responds to help you regain equilibrium. The response is reflexive or automatic, but is based on sensory information from the rest of the body. For example, when you unexpectedly step into a hole, the vestibular system helps you balance yourself so you do not fall. Other visual receptors help us understand movement and allow us to distinguish our movement from movement around us.

Gross Motor Skills. Gross motor skills refer to the use of the large muscles of the body, such as the arms and legs. Walking, running, and throwing a ball are all examples of gross motor skills.

Fine Motor Skills. Fine motor skills, also referred to as hand skills, involve the small muscles, such as the hands and fingers. Grasping, buttoning, drawing, writing, and opening a lid are examples of fine motor skills.

Self-Help Skills. Sometimes referred to as adaptive skills, self-help skills enable us to function in our environment—at home, school, and work. These are the skills that enable us to take care of ourselves. They include the ability to feed, dress, clean, and toilet ourselves .

Social Skills. Social development is the process of learning how to function in groups. As we grow, we learn how to relate to others and how to function in society by its rules. Some important areas of social development include learning to bond or form relationships with our parents and later on to make friends. Another important social skill is the ability to gauge and understand how someone else is feeling, and to learn how to please someone. On a broader level, social skills enable people to understand and obey society's moral rules.

All of this social and cultural knowledge which most of us take for granted involves a very complex array of concepts and "awareness" which we utilize whenever we interact with other human beings. One critical aspect of this social awareness is referred to as "pre-supposition." Whenever we make social contact with someone, we pre-suppose a degree of understanding about the topic to be discussed. The knowledge we call upon to make these split-second decisions is based strongly on our knowledge of local culture, past encounters of a similar nature, and our general command of the language. Our social skills, learned over a lifetime, enable us to pre-suppose well enough to get along with other people.

All areas of development are important and also interdependent. That is, development in one area depends on development in others. For example, self-help skills can be delayed when there are delays in motor development; a child with delayed fine motor skills will have a harder time learning to use a toothbrush. Delays in the cognitive, sensory, and motor areas can make sitting at a desk in school very difficult. A poor vestibular system will cause delays in learning motor skills because it will make physical activity more difficult.

Developmental Milestones: The Sequence and Timing of Development

Development usually occurs in an orderly sequence. Children typically acquire the most basic skills first, followed by more sophisticated skills. Each of these early skills lays the groundwork for the acquisition of future, more complex skills. For example, children must develop a pincer grasp before they can scribble with a crayon; they must learn to walk before they can climb stairs; they must understand cause-and-effect before they can solve problems. These types of basic skills which underlie future development are known as milestones. Milestones are a way to measure typical development. Most typical children reach developmental milestones in about the same sequence as other children, and at about the same age.

■■ TABLE 1. DEVELOPMENTAL MILESTONES FOR CHILDREN ....

Age	Gross Motor
6 months	Sits
12 months	Cruises (walks while holding on to support)
2 years	Climbs
3 years	Walks up and down stairs
4 years	Uses outdoor toys such as a tricycle
5 years	Plays some sports such as swimming; may dribble a basketball or play baseball

Age	Fine Motor
6 months	Grasps with whole hand
12 months	Uses good pincer grasp
2 years	Scribbles
3 years	Draws a circle
4 years	Draws a square; draws a simple person
5 years	Writes name; tries to tie shoelaces; buttons shirt and zips pants

Age	Language
6 months	Babbles (e.g., "dah-dah-dah" or "ah-eee-nah-nah")
12 months	Says first words (e.g., "uh-oh"…or "ma-ma" with specific meaning)
18 months	Says first generic word combinations (e.g., "love you" or "want some")
2 years	Speaks 50 words and short phrases
3 years	Speaks 1000 words; full sentences
4 years	Asks many questions
5 years	Looks at a picture and describe actions

Table 1 shows some typical skills that children usually acquire between the ages of birth and five. However, a child can reach any given milestone somewhat earlier or somewhat later than other children do and still be considered to be developing "normally." Children may also develop more quickly in one area than another. For example, even though a child is not talking at age two, he might still be considered to be developing "normally" if his motor skills are typical for his age and he seems bright and alert. Sometimes young children start out

··········· BIRTH TO AGE FIVE YEARS

Age	Self-Help
6 months	Holds bottle
12 months	Feeds self finger foods
2 years	Feeds self with spoon and cup
3 years	Uses toilet independently
4 years	Dresses self in pullovers and stretch pants
5 years	Dresses self in more complicated clothes with zippers and buttons; gets a snack such as a cookie or yogurt

Age	Social
6 months	Smiles, laughs
12 months	Shows stranger anxiety; prefers certain people
2 years	Imitates chores or activities—tries to sweep the floor or talk on the phone
3 years	Understands taking turns
4 years	Plays interactive games with other children
5 years	Plays pretend—with costumes, jewelry, or other people's clothes

Age	Cognitive
6 months	Looks for a fallen object
12 months	Puts several blocks into a cup; has many hand gestures like "bye bye," "so big," "patty cake"
2 years	Inserts forms into a formboard
3 years	Knows concepts like up/down and loud/soft
4 years	Knows colors
5 years	Recognizes penny, nickel, dime

with delays in one area but then catch up. Professionals therefore look at the big picture in evaluating development.

Developmental Delays

Usually all areas of development flow together so well that most people do not give it a second thought. You may know someone who is extremely capable and accomplished and not realize that it is because all the different aspects of his or her development came together at the right time and in the right order. It is when development does not go as expected that we stop to wonder why.

There are many causes of developmental delays. Some causes are termed congenital or genetic; these are developmental delays caused by a difference in the physical or neurological makeup of an individual. For example, cerebral palsy, Down syndrome, and fragile X syndrome, which cause developmental delays, are congenital; people are born with these conditions. Fragile X syndrome and Down syndrome are also genetic: they result from a difference in a person's genes. Delays in development can also result from medical or environmental causes. For example, chronic ear infections can hamper speech and language development, and prolonged lack of stimulation by caregivers can lead to delayed cognitive development. Usually, however, if these problems are treated or conditions improve, the delays are temporary and the child's development catches up.

Other more permanent developmental delays can be caused by acquired physical or neurological problems such as cerebral palsy, which occurs at birth, or head injury, which can occur at any time due to an accident, or disease such as a tumor or meningitis.

In children with developmental delays, the rate, sequence, or overall quality of development is different. For example, children with fragile X syndrome may achieve some or all of the milestones in Table 1, but they may acquire them a few months or even years later than other children do. Or they may acquire the skills in the list, but the quality of those skills may be different. For example, their walking skills may look different from those of other children. There can also be a wide range of how their condition affects their development; some will experience only mild delays while others will experience bigger delays.

Other factors can also affect a child's development that are not related to fragile X syndrome. Children inherit a full array of genes from their parents in addition to their fragile X genes. These genes also have a tremendous impact on development in both subtle and obvious ways. For example, each child's temperament can directly influence daily experiences. Some children are basically "easy going" and cope well with challenges. Other children are more volatile by nature and may have behavioral challenges that become roadblocks to development. Even more subtle aspects of temperament or personality can influence development. For example, a child who is eager to please and is motivated by praise is likely to have more numerous and longer interactions with teachers and other caregivers.

Scientists have learned what parents have long understood: A child's environment can affect his development tremendously. A healthy, loving, and engaging environment will foster any child's development, as will good educational services. Thus, in viewing your child's development, be careful not to attribute every single developmental delay or problem solely to fragile X syndrome.

For children with fragile X syndrome, it is usually impossible to predict prior to puberty what the eventual endpoint of their development might be. This is because fragile X syndrome can affect each child in many different ways. For example, one child may be born with a severe mental impairment, while another may have mild learning disabilities. Children can also have different mixes of developmental strengths and weaknesses. One child may have mental retardation, but have good motor skills, a special talent in art or music, and a great personality. That child may develop into a more independent adult than one who has milder mental retardation, but who also has difficulty with motor and social skills. And as mentioned above, a child's environment can either help or hinder his development. A supportive family life (discussed in Chapter 6) and appropriate educational services (discussed in Chapter 8) can have a positive effect, while abuse or neglect can have a negative effect on the development of children with fragile X syndrome. These factors make it impossible to predict the path or boundary of your child's development.

:: The Development of Children with Fragile X Syndrome

There is no single perfect example of a child with fragile X syndrome; every child is unique, with his own array of developmental strengths and weaknesses. Not only is there often tremendous variation between boys and girls, but also within each of the sexes a wide variation can be seen. Consequently, describing the development of a typical child with fragile X syndrome can be misleading. There are, however, certain developmental characteristics that are common to children with fragile X syndrome.

Many boys will experience delays in several developmental areas, including cognition, language, fine motor, self-help, and sensorimotor skills. Some boys have obvious delays at a very young age, while others appear to develop fairly typically for the first three or four years. Girls who have fragile X syndrome are typically less affected, but also experience a range of delays in their development. And both girls and boys can have hyperactivity and challenging and inappropriate behavior.

Because your child's health can directly affect development, it is essential that you and your doctor closely monitor your child. Problems like seizures, vision problems, and frequent ear infections can hinder development. Health issues are discussed in detail in Chapter 4.

Although this chapter focuses on the developmental delays of children with fragile X syndrome, this is far from the whole picture. Children with fragile X syndrome often have significant developmental strengths—skills that stand out. These include:

- *An extensive vocabulary* for the objects and people in their world. Their receptive language often far exceeds their ability to express themselves.
- *Good gross motor skills.* Many children with fragile X syndrome love to ride bikes, swim, and play soccer.
- *Good visual memory.* Children with fragile X syndrome are able to remember much detail about their environment. For example, some can memorize the route of a long bus ride home or match up all the lunch boxes with the children in their class.
- *Good imitation skills.* Many children imitate much of what they see around them. For example, some children are able to learn sign language quite early because they can imitate what they see so well.
- *An excellent sense of humor.*

Your child, of course, may have other remarkable developmental strengths or talents. Like all children, your child is unique and has a wide range of abilities and interests. As you read through the following sections, remember these are only generalizations about children with fragile X syndrome. Your child may have only a few of the developmental delays described, or he may have many of them. He may have them to a minor degree, or to a greater degree. Remember, too, that some delays are more common in boys than girls, or vice versa. Either way, identifying your child's developmental concerns is the first step in doing something about them.

Cognitive Development

Generalizing about the cognitive development of children with fragile X syndrome can be very difficult. Your child is born with a wide range of cognitive potentials. Although some children have "normal" intelligence, many have some degree of what is called mental retardation; still others have learning disabilities. The majority of children with fragile X syndrome have both mental retardation and specific learning disabilities. Conditions such as attention deficit hyperactivity disorder (ADHD) and seizures can also affect your child's ability to learn.

Still, parents and others often notice certain common cognitive strengths among their children with fragile X syndrome. Parents often describe their child as "smart." They may report that their child understands everything that is going on around him. They may observe that their child knows the neighborhood inside and out, can direct a taxi driver to their home, or has an uncanny ability to remember everyone's schedule. They almost always describe their child as having an excellent memory for people, places, and events. Parents also describe a strong empathy with other children and awareness of others in distress.

The cognitive weaknesses in children with fragile X syndrome include difficulties with:

- *Memory*—Sequential learning refers to tasks that require step-by-step processing or putting things into a sequence. For example, processing verbal directions that have several parts is often difficult because these tasks require keeping both the instructions and their sequence in mind.
- *Organizational skills and impulsiveness*—Children with fragile X syndrome have a distinct processing style. It is difficult for them to hold information in their short term working memory as they attempt to complete a task such as arranging pictures in the correct order. They may rush and complete the tasks poorly. The ability to orga-

nize activities is called "executive function" and this is difficult for children with fragile X syndrome.

■ *Counting and math skills*—As a result of the difficulties with sequential processing, your child will likely struggle with some of the processes in math. The sequence of steps for counting, adding, subtracting, and performing other math functions must be followed exactly.

■ *Abstract reasoning*—Children with fragile X syndrome tend to think in concrete terms and have trouble with concepts that they cannot see, hear, or touch. This makes problem solving more difficult, and creates other challenges. For example, many children with cognitive delays have troubling understanding concepts like "danger." As a result, it may be harder to calm their fears of dogs or thunderstorms.

■ *Auditory memory*—Although memory for places and events is often excellent (such as when memories are tied to a visual image), memory for new information, particularly verbal information, memory for facts, or for steps in a sequence is often limited.

Cognitive delays, whatever their cause, can delay development in other areas as well. Motor, social, and language skills can all be affected. For example, if a child does not have the cognitive ability to understand grammatical rules, his language skills will lag. If he has trouble understanding gestures or facial expressions, his social abilities will be affected. Understanding your child's cognitive development can therefore help you understand his development in other areas. The sections below discuss different levels of cognitive delays.

Mental Retardation. No parent likes the term mental retardation. However, it is the term used by doctors and teachers to describe how some children with fragile X syndrome perform on IQ (Intelligence Quotient) tests. These tests were given to thousands of children; the results were analyzed to determine what "average" intelligence is. Children who score in the lowest three percentiles on these tests are said to have mental retardation. Whatever term you use—mental retardation, cognitive delay, intellectual impairment, or some other term—it is important to understand what it means for your child's development.

Scientists have tried for years to compare how mental retardation affects different people. There are now two common systems for comparing people who have mental retardation. Under the older and more common system, there are four degrees or levels of mental retardation, and they are determined by IQ test scores. People with IQs between 50 and 69 are said to have mild mental retardation. People with IQs of 35 to 50 are said to have moderate mental retardation. People with IQs of 20 to 35 are said to have severe mental retardation. And people with IQs of 20 and below are said to have profound mental retardation. According to this system, 85 to 89 percent of all people with mental retardation fall into the mild category; 6 to 10 percent fall into the moderate category; 3 to 4 percent fall into the severe category; and 1 to 2 percent fall into the profound category. In the past these labels were used to determine what kind of education children would receive and what kinds of skills they would be taught.

According to how people with mental retardation are categorized, there is tremendous variety in the cognitive skills of children with fragile X syndrome. But here is what is known: 80 to 90 percent of boys with fragile X syndrome are classified as having mental retardation. The majority of the children test in the range of moderate mental retardation, but some test in the severe range. The remaining 10 to 15 percent of children test above the mild mental retardation range. Among girls, 30 to 35 percent test in the range of mental retardation, with roughly 25 to 30 percent of those testing in the mild range. Twenty to 30 percent of girls with fragile X syndrome test in the borderline "normal" range, while 40 to 50 percent test in the "normal" range. At least half of those girls with "normal" IQs have learning disabilities. These numbers may change, though, now that DNA studies are available and more females are being diagnosed.

Although almost all males with fragile X syndrome who have the full mutation have mental retardation, the degree of impairment ranges from mild to severe. Researchers have found that the degree of mental retardation is mild to moderate in most males through the early childhood years. It is likely that declines of test-measured IQ results during adolescence is caused by the fact that the skills tested at older age levels emphasize language-based knowledge and abstract reasoning.

A newer system of categorizing mental retardation was devised a few years ago by the American Association on Mental Retardation. It is designed to provide more useful information about how people with mental retardation function. It is intended to rely less on IQ test scores which provide little practical information. In the newer system, there are also four categories, but the categories are based, not on IQ score, but on an assessment of the support a person needs to get along in his environment. The four levels are:

1. *Intermittent:* does not require constant support, but may need short-term support for special times and occurrences such as a death in the family or finding a new job.
2. *Limited:* requires some supports consistently, such as handling finances, maintaining job skills, and training.
3. *Extensive:* needs daily support in some aspects of living, such as job support, and nutrition.
4. *Pervasive:* requires constant, intense support for all aspects of life.

This system allows how each person functions in his world to determine the category that applies to him. Although useful, this newer system has not been widely adopted; you will likely continue to hear mild, moderate, severe, and profound used as categories.

As explained above, all areas of development depend on each other. In fact what makes mental retardation different from delays in specific developmental areas is its effect on development in all areas. Thus, a person with mental retardation will show across-the-board delays in several developmental areas. It is this characteristic that distinguishes "mental retardation" from "learning disabilities," which have a far more limited impact on development.

A child who is classified as having mild mental retardation is usually expected to learn to read and write to about a fifth or sixth grade level. As an adult, he may get married, master job skills, pay taxes, and function well in society with some support, such as job training. Most children labeled with moderate mental retardation are expected to learn to read functional words like "men's room," "exit," and "stop." They will take care of their own personal needs like bathing, dressing, and eating. An adult with moderate mental retardation will be expected to live semi-independently and work with support, such as ongoing job coaching, but will not be expected to raise children or take care of someone else. They often have trouble learning abstract concepts and have more limited memory. This especially affects their ability to learn more academic skills like math. Children labeled as having severe or profound mental retardation usually have suffered a major medical disorder, traumatic brain injury, uncontrolled seizures, or untreated metabolic disorder. Most people with severe or profound mental retardation rely on family and society for help with most of their needs. If there are no physical handicaps associated, there is the opportunity for supported employment, group residential living, and recreation.

Learning Disabilities. The definition of learning disabilities is quite specific. It means that a child has difficulty in learning one or more language-based or academic skills, and his IQ is 70 or above. Consequently, the term is most often applied to children who have no significant developmental issues other than specific learning disabilities. Although some children with completely typical development and high scores on IQ tests have learning disabilities, almost all children with fragile X syndrome have some form of learning difficulty in addition to mental retardation. These roadblocks to learning and academic progress likely have their roots in some of the language and cognitive delays already discussed; however, they need to be addressed using techniques that focus on the curriculum they need to master to move on; that is, the curriculum used for children with learning disabilities. For example, children with fragile X syndrome often have persistent difficulties learning to read with a phonetics-only approach. Their difficulties with phonics result from their problem with sequential learning. As a result, reading instruction needs to *incorporate* whole word and whole language approaches, like you might use for a child whose only struggle is in learning to read.

There are many types of learning disabilities, and every learning disability is unique in its impact on learning. There are math, reading, and writing disabilities to name just a few. Professionals also label learning disabilities according to the cognitive or sensory process involved or affected by the disability. These include:

- visual perception and visual processing
- auditory perception and auditory processing

- fine motor and visual-motor processing
- motor planning
- memory
- sequencing
- language
- organization
- metacognition (knowing how to figure out how to approach a task)

If your child has or is found to have a learning disability in one or more of these areas, try to learn *how* the learning disability affects him. There are several organizations listed in the Resource Guide of this book that can provide you with information about learning disabilities.

Like mental retardation, learning disabilities can be mild, moderate, or severe in their impact. The severity of a learning disability is not directly related to overall level of intelligence. Cognitive ability will affect the specific intervention strategies used to treat learning disabilities. Children with mild learning disabilities may learn to easily overcome their particular problem, while children with more severe learning disabilities may require extensive intervention to function well. Some children overcome their learning disabilities, while others learn how to compensate for their problems. They learn what are called bypass strategies to enable them to avoid or "get around" their weaknesses. For example, people with poor writing due to weak fine motor skills can learn to write using a computer instead of learning handwriting. A child with poor memory can learn to use lists. These bypass strategies do not eliminate the underlying disability, but can enable your child to function almost as if he did not have a problem. Although the weaknesses that cause learning disabilities in childhood may not entirely disappear, many adults master good bypass strategies.

Conditions that Can Affect Cognitive Function. Conditions like attention deficit disorder, anxiety, and hyperactivity can have an impact on how your child uses his cognitive abilities and on how those abilities are tested. As with typically developing children, attention deficits make learning harder by limiting the time children are "available" for learning. They also make cognitive testing more difficult because most intelligence tests require extended periods of concentration.

Anxiety can also affect cognitive performance. Almost all boys with fragile X syndrome experience significant anxiety, often beginning at a very young age. This anxiety usually appears first as separation anxiety—your child might become hysterical when you are out of sight. Later it appears as difficulty with unfamiliar places, new routines, and transitions. Extreme anxiety may lead to temper tantrums or aggressive behaviors. Girls with fragile X syndrome most often display anxiety in social situations.

Anxiety is not voluntary. Its usual cause is low levels of the neurotransmitter serotonin. Low serotonin levels cause fear and anxiety, while normal levels of serotonin keep us calm. Although behavioral strategies to counteract anxiety are important, medication can also help. Some medications that elevate serotonin levels are known as "SSRI's" or Selective Serotonin Re-uptake Inhibitors. They include Paxil™, Luvox™, Prozac™, and Zoloft™. Stimulants like caffeine can make anxiety worse.

These difficulties can have a cumulative impact on learning and development. New or over-stimulating environments can cause your child to be overwhelmed by his own powerful responses. This may render him unable to attend to new information and lead him to avoidance or escape behavior. All his energy is diverted to random attention to new stimuli, excessive or repetitive movements, or emotionally draining fear and flight responses. This is an area where behavior management plans, implemented by parents, caregivers, and teachers (discussed in Chapters 5 and 8), can help.

Cognitive Assessment. Evaluating your child's cognitive level is a difficult task. Cognitive assessment is not an exact science; it requires several tests, interpretation, and lots of information about your child. In the end, testing, assessment, and an IQ score give only a partial picture of your child's true abilities. Your challenge as a parent is to help everyone—family, school, and community—to see beyond an IQ score.

There are dozens of developmental tests, many of which test cognitive ability. IQ tests are designed for children within specified age ranges and evaluate different skill areas. In addition, tests in one developmental area may be used to draw conclusions in others. For example, the Bayley Scales of Infant Development that is used to test children 30 months and under also assesses fine motor skills of young children. Children who do well on the Bayley Scales are considered to have "normal" intelligence. Other tests that may be used include the Kaufman Assessment Battery for Children, the Batelle Developmental Inventory, the Wechsler Scales, and the Mullen Scales of Early Learning.

Although developmental tests may be useful in general, they do not always reflect the true potential of any child. For example, a young child with cerebral palsy may do very poorly on early Bayley tests because of poor fine motor skills and yet may have strong cognitive skills. Tests for school-age children place heavy emphasis on language development, math skills, and abstract reasoning. Some tests are timed. The wording of the questions can be rigid, and the instructions may not be repeated. Other factors like limited exposure to language-based experiences, ADHD, or a health problem can also affect test performance. The consequence is a test result, and an IQ score, that may not accurately reflect true ability.

Other factors can skew the assessment picture. An IQ score is an average of several tests. Viewed alone it tells very little; it does not show the child's particular strengths and weaknesses in *any* detail. Your child's cognitive ability is more complicated. For example, although many children are labeled with mental retardation because testing shows delays in several areas of development, that is not always the case. Some cognitive skills may actually be in the "average" range. Identification of vocabulary words from pictures (selecting from four pictured choices) may be a particular strength as may be sentence repetition. As a result of all these factors, it is important not to just look at the overall score, but to ask your child's teachers and school psychologist for detailed information about specific strengths and weaknesses in each developmental area.

Self-Esteem and Learning Disabilities. One major concern for children with learning disabilities or mental retardation is self-esteem. Children who have to try so hard to learn can become frustrated; sadly, some just give up. Because of this, children require praise for good work and good effort. Do not set your standards too high, do not make too many demands at the same time, and gauge your expectations to your child as he is. Pace your child's learning and plan ahead. For example, although during summer vacation almost all children will forget some of what they learned in school, your child may lose more and have a harder time picking the information back up in September. Summer tutors may be a good idea for your child so that he starts the school year where he left off the previous spring.

Another useful strategy is to work on developing your child's areas of strength. This can help him build his self-esteem because it shows him what he does well. For example, if your child has trouble reading but loves sports cars, help him build a model sports car collection, subscribe him to sports car magazines, and buy some books on the subject. Help him become the "local expert" in his area of greatest interest. Along the same line, if your child has good athletic ability, help him pursue his interests in that area. This gives him the chance to experience an area of learning without frustration. These strategies can also help your child build friendships with children who share his interests.

Speech and Language Development

All children with fragile X syndrome have delays in learning to understand what is said to them and in using first words. Typically boys begin to use first words, such as "bottle," "out," and "mine," in their third year and begin putting some words together, such as "go outside," "want cookie," around age four. Girls usually begin talking much sooner, before age two, and often begin conversing in full sentences by age four. Of course, individual children may demonstrate a very different pattern. The good news is that almost all children with fragile X syndrome eventually develop functional speech. They are able to greet people, ask for basic wants, and respond to simple questions. A few males (roughly 10 to 15%) do not develop useful speech; this appears to be related to oral-motor planning problems (dyspraxia), but these children can learn to use alternate means of communication, such as hand-held devices that talk when a key is pressed.

Often the first major concern that parents have about their child is that his speech and language development seems delayed. They may attribute the delays to other reasons, not suspecting fragile X syndrome. For example, if your child has frequent ear infections, you may be lulled into attributing his language delays to the infections. If your child is experiencing difficulty in this area, he should be evaluated by a speech and language therapist.

Many factors can affect speech and language development. A child's cognitive abilities can make learning all skills, including speech and language, more difficult. Poor muscle tone can make it harder to form sounds correctly. Difficulties with sensory integration (explained below) can make it harder for your child to plan the oral muscle movements necessary to make word sounds. Because of the variety of potential causes of speech and language delays, the therapy your child receives will have to be carefully designed, focusing on his individual strengths and weaknesses.

Before Your Child Speaks. Your child's early talking may be delayed and may also advance in fits and starts. It usually takes longer for language skills to emerge and they do not always evolve in the expected sequence. As mentioned, low muscle tone in the face and mouth may contribute to the delayed start of speech. This may also cause your child to drool more than other children and cause his mouth to stay open. As boys learn to speak, they may use words with few syllables and shorter sentences of one to two words. This is their attempt to make speech easier for themselves.

During this time it is very important for children with fragile X syndrome to have a speech and language therapist to help them learn oral motor planning (learning the correct sequence of mouth movements to produce the desired word) as well as language (learning to listen and understand what is said). While awaiting the emergence of speech, it may help to teach sign language to help them communicate their needs and wants. Sign language is quite simple and helps children learn the basic cause-and-effect of communication; they learn that words (such as the sign for "cookie") can cause positive results (the cookie). Words like "more," "all done," "help," and "eat" are some of the essential signs that can help your child learn to communicate before he learns to speak. Using sign language will not delay the emergence of speech.

Pictures can also be used in many ways to help teach your child to communicate. As with sign language, pictures can be used to teach the basic concept of communication. If you have a collection of pictures of food items, your child can pick a picture of the specific food item he wants. He can also have a book (or computer) with pictures and symbols that he can use to convey his wants, needs, feelings, and responses. Pictures can also be used to show your child what to expect during his day. For example, your child can be prepared for an upcoming trip to the doctor with pictures that allow him to see what to expect beforehand. Some parents put together books that show daily schedules, daily routines (morning, bedtime), and school routines using pictures.

Pictures can also be used to help build vocabulary. It is often helpful to label everything around the house with simple pictures of the object and the word printed below, and to place these labels at the child's eye level. The picture labels serve as cues for your child to say the name. For example, pointing to the picture, you may say, "We're going out the _____," and then wait for your child to say "door." You can also place two or three pictures and word labels for things your child may want to ask for. For example, it may work to place words and a picture of "juice," "milk," and "cheese" on the refrigerator door at your child's eye level. When he goes to the refrigerator, "play dumb" and direct his attention to the pictures. Say, "Do you want juice or milk or cheese?" This may not result in immediate success, but when the ritual is repeated frequently, your child will eventually try to state his choice.

When Your Child Is Speaking. Once your child is speaking, some unusual speech and language patterns may emerge. The good news is that children with fragile X syndrome are very motivated to communicate verbally because of their social nature. In addition, most are very eager to please and will almost always respond, at least briefly, to cues or cajoling by adults or peers asking them to "use your words." As you read the following list, remember that not every child with fragile X syndrome has all or even any of these speech and language patterns. In addition, for most children, the situations they encounter will affect how well or poorly they speak. For example, in unfamiliar situations, when meeting new people, or when transitioning to a new activity, more typical speech patterns will tend to fall apart. This is usually caused by anxiety. Try to be supportive at these times, but do not preempt or help your child avoid these situations. Supported practice will help him learn to speak appropriately in a variety of situations.

The following list explains the speech and language patterns children with fragile X syndrome most often have:

- ▪ *Poor Topic Maintenance.* Some children seem to jump from one topic to another in their conversation. This is known as tangential speech. In a discussion they may have to be brought back to the main topic several times. For example, when asked, "Did you go swimming this summer?" a child might respond, "Yeah, my friend has a pool. His dog ran away." They may be better at discussing a topic when they bring up the subject, but have trouble when the conversation is directed by someone else.

- **Perseverative Speech.** Some children may repeat a sentence, phrase, or word over and over. This is often referred to as perseverative speech or just perseveration. For example, a child may speak to his mother, saying "go home, mommy, mommy, home mommy, home." It is not known exactly why repetitive speech occurs, but it may be related to poor skills at finding the right word to express a thought (called word retrieval, explained below). Perseverative speech also occurs more frequently when children are anxious or frustrated. For example, when faced with a task that is difficult, children with fragile X syndrome may repeat "Put it in the bag...put it in the bag...put it in the bag..." over and over in an attempt to end the activity.

- **Echolalia.** In this condition, seen often in children with fragile X syndrome, children repeat back questions or statements rather than responding to them. For example, if a child with echolalia is asked, "What time is it?" he may reply by saying, "What time is it?" Although some typically developing children may have some echolalia, in children with fragile X syndrome, the condition can persist much longer.

- **Poor Word Retrieval.** Some children have trouble finding the right word or words with which to answer a question. For some children, this results from limited flexibility in word use. That is, children with fragile X syndrome seem to rely on a familiar "script" for their responses. Thus, children may use specific words without hesitation in a familiar context, but be unable to use the same words in a different situation. For example, your child may tell you each morning, "Pack my lunch." However, when the teacher asks him, "What are we going to eat now?" he may be unable to come up with the word "lunch." At other times word retrieval may fail because your child does not understand exactly what is being asked.

- **Direct Language.** Children often have trouble with abstract concepts and their interests may be limited to everyday life experiences, such as school, TV, family, and friends. In conversation they may be quite literal in expressing things and in reacting to what someone has said. Sometimes this directness can be embarrassing. For example, some children might tell people who are overweight, "You have a big tummy."

- **Difficulty with Oral-Motor Coordination.** Some children have trouble coordinating the sound-making movements of their mouth and tongue. This condition can persist beyond childhood and affect speech permanently. Children may speak less or may use smaller, simpler words. They may also drool more. And they may pronounce the same word differently each time they try to say it. A child may say "duhdehdeee" or "sketteee" when he means "spaghetti." Sound errors like the above are not unusual or any different from the errors typically developing children make when they are learning a new word. What is different in children with fragile X syndrome is their tendency to talk much less clearly in conversation than they do when using one word at a time. In addition to these oral motor problems, 10 to 15 percent of children with fragile X syndrome (almost always males) have a specific speech difficulty called verbal dyspraxia. In this condition, the brain has an inability to transmit sound sequencing information to the speech muscles. Another way to look at it is an extreme difficulty imitating sounds and sound sequences. This particular speech difficulty is often misdiagnosed as "lack of cooperation" or extreme attention problems. It is also difficult to diagnose in children with fragile X syndrome because the vast majority of them have good verbal imitation skills.

- **Dysfluency.** Children with fragile X syndrome often have more trouble speaking smoothly than do other children. Although the terms stuttering and stammering have been used in the past to describe these problems, they are loaded with negative images that are not necessarily accurate. Dysfluency may take many forms, including hesitations, pauses, repetitions of words or syllables, and prolonged sounds. For example, a child who is trying to pronounce

the word "apple" may get stuck on the initial "a" sound, and the word may sound more like "a-a-a-a-a-ple."
- **Cluttering.** Sometimes children, especially boys, speak very fast and at an erratic rhythm. The result is that words get crammed together, making the speech harder to understand.
- **High Pitch Voice.** Some children speak in short sentences and in a high-pitched voice.

Speech and language therapy, carefully planned and diligently implemented, can help to minimize the patterns listed above. Although it may not be possible to eliminate all of them, they can be controlled, and your child can learn how to deal with them. Work closely with your child's speech therapist, and try to follow through at home with exercises and techniques the speech therapist works on with your child. In addition, here are some other suggestions:

- Minimize extended or particularly stressful situations. Provide lots of practice with novel or somewhat stressful situations, such as meeting new people or calling family members to dinner. This helps reduce perseveration, repetitive speech, and dysfluency.
- Allow your child more time to answer questions or respond to you.
- Monitor your child closely for ear infections to make sure no medical problem is interfering with language development.
- Offer your child verbal choices. Do not always supply the whole response or give him what he wants without expecting a verbal request. For example, when your child points to toys he wants, play innocent and ask a few questions like, "Do you want the big robot or the little robot?" or "Do you want your cars or your animals?"
- Provide lots of verbal cues about what's coming next so your child can get ready. For example, before giving a direction say, "Listen to my words." When your child points to what he wants without saying anything, say "Use your words" or "I don't know what you want. Do you want the _____ or the _____?"

Most girls with fragile X syndrome have strong verbal skills, but like boys may have a distinct conversation pattern even when they are not feeling socially anxious. When comfortable (on the telephone), they tend to speak in a "run-on" fashion without pausing between sentences and without providing expected transitions between topics. Their speech can also be referred to as "tangential." That is, one topic reminds them of something else and that triggers yet another topic and so on. They can be very difficult to interrupt; they benefit from "verbal cues," such as "Stop, my turn to talk," to get them back on track. Boys who are highly verbal may also have this style of "run-on" speech with poor topic maintenance; but the majority of boys are not as verbally fluent as girls and are more likely to perseverate or repeat the same thing over and over. That is, they often get stuck on one topic and have trouble moving to a new topic.

Although there is tremendous variation in the listening and talking skills children with fragile X syndrome develop, the vast majority do develop functional, intelligible speech. For the 10 to 15 percent of children who may not develop useful verbal skills or do not develop words until they are eight or nine years of age, it is critical to provide alternate means of both input and output. The devices available through assistive technology programs provide some excellent options. The technology, which continually improves, can be used in the classroom or at home. For example, small electronic "talking" devices can be suspended around your child's neck or attached to a vest with Velcro. Your child can start with very simple responses, such as "yes" or "no," and advance to more sophisticated requests and responses like "I want to _____." In addition, most assistive technology programs provide free consultation from experts in the field and will allow the parents or the classroom teacher to borrow devices for several weeks of trial use before purchasing anything.

Sensory Processing and Sensorimotor Integration

Sensory processing is a common area of early concern for parents of children with fragile X syndrome. As discussed earlier, sensory issues encompass a very wide range of complex processes that most of us take for granted. Sensorimotor integration begins when the brain takes in information from the senses of sight, hearing, touch, and taste, as well as information about body movement, position, and the pull of gravity. The brain then processes and interprets the information and generates appropriate responses.

Our sensory systems perform hundreds of critical tasks that most of the time go completely unnoticed. One such task is tuning out or ignoring information that is not important so that we can focus on what is important. For example, if we are in a mall or at a basketball game, our auditory system automatically tunes out the many loud, yet irrelevant, noises such as crowd noise and background music. In quieter environments, like an office or classroom, we can tune out noises like the heating system, air conditioning system, shuffling feet, pencil sharpeners, whispering, or telephones.

Our sensory systems are remarkably sophisticated. Visual processing involves observing objects in space and processing how they relate to each other. For example, the only difference between a lower case *b* and *d* is how the letters are oriented in space. Children with good visual processing skills can distinguish minor differences in printed lower case letters relatively easily, respond well to visually based whole language teaching techniques, enjoy puzzles or maps, do well shopping because they can find their way easily, have a good sense of direction, be good at fixing things, and recognize people readily.

Sensory processing requires meshing sensory input from several sources. In visual-spatial processing, information is gathered by the eye and processed in the visual system and then combined with input from the muscles, joints, and vestibular system. Visual-spatial processing allows us to orient where we are in space in relation to solid objects and structures like the floor or walls and in relation to gravity. The brain learns to actually "feel" distances in physical space. If this system does not become well integrated during early development, it leads to poor judgment of distances and spatial relationships and, also, to insecurity in space and movement. For example, with most people, if we are standing on one foot and begin to sense we are tipping, our other foot will quickly right us. If we have trouble with visual-spatial processing, we may lose our balance more easily and our sensory system may cause us to undercompensate or overcompensate; the result is we may fall over.

Sensorimotor integration is a broader concept that refers to our ability to pull together information from various senses, tie the information together, and respond appropriately. Children with fragile X syndrome may have trouble smoothly processing one or more different types of sensorimotor input. This may lead to unique reactions or behavior. For example, many boys dislike being touched, and may cry if they are gently patted by a teacher or parent. As babies they may resist being cuddled, and may not want to be picked up or held. They may avoid wearing clothes with textures they do not like, and may insist on only the fabrics that feel good to them. Doctor examinations, haircuts, or toothbrushing may overwhelm their sensory systems. This aversion to touch is technically known as tactile defensiveness. Tactile defensiveness can cause many difficulties, ranging from behavioral outbursts to a fear of strangers. It may contribute to fine motor problems because of the possible aversions to touching toys and art materials.

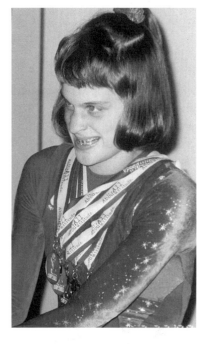

In addition to tactile defensiveness, boys with fragile X syndrome are also extra sensitive to sounds in their environment. At a crowded mall, a fairground, or a big family reunion, for example, they may be overwhelmed and begin to panic or cry. Often parents say that athletic events or Special Olympics are nightmares for their children because they are terrified by the sound of the gun that heralds the start of events. Sounds, even faint sounds, may also prevent a child from paying attention to anything else; they may not be as capable of tuning out certain sounds. For example, one child was unable to continue his work or play whenever he heard a trash truck; and he would stay distracted until the sound was completely gone.

Many boys with fragile X syndrome can also become visually overwhelmed. They may have extreme gaze aversion, or a dislike of making eye contact. Often they appear overwhelmed by faces and will look at people for only a few seconds at most. They may even have difficulty looking at a page for more than a few seconds. This can result in difficulties establishing relationships as well as working on school tasks.

Like other sensitivities, boys may also be sensitive to smells. For example, they may sense smells (like popping corn) long before other people sense them. They may also become overwhelmed by an odor before it would bother other people. Hypersensitivity in this area can affect many different areas of development, including social and self-care. This has not been studied much.

Although females with fragile X syndrome may not show extreme reactions to sensory input, they may have more subtle difficulty screening out various stimuli. This may appear as ADHD. Difficulties tolerating excessive visual and auditory stimuli may also contribute to social withdrawal or anxiety in some girls.

Most boys and girls with fragile X syndrome seem to have what are called gravitational insecurities. That is, they may have trouble with activities that require them to lift their feet off the ground. This has to do with poorly developed responses to the changing gravitational forces during movement, particularly with sudden or complex movement patterns, such as suddenly being lifted or tipped off balance. For example, your child may cry when placed on a counter to have his shoes tied. He may be frightened when he has to walk down a steep flight of stairs or ride an escalator. His balance may be very weak, making him fear everyday physical activities that would foster his motor development.

The area of sensorimotor skills is quite complicated; with so many connected and interrelated systems, it is strongly recommended that you consult a professional who has been trained and has experience in this area. Usually this person is an occupational therapist (OT). In general, therapists who are NDT Certified have had extensive training in a specific approach to integrating the various motor and sensory systems. The training they receive is called Neuro Developmental Therapy (NDT). A majority of NDT trained therapists have a background in occupational therapy, but there are also excellent NDT therapists whose degrees are in physical therapy or speech-language pathology. The therapist will try to determine through assessments which areas most need treatment and which are less important. In doing so he or she will focus on the problems that cause the most developmental disruption.

As with all therapy, it is important for parents to mirror the therapist's work so that there is consistency. Although sensory integration problems will not disappear completely even with therapy, it can help reduce the negative impact of stressful situations and enable your child to focus on learning or enjoying an activity.

Motor Development

Fine Motor Development. Children with fragile X syndrome, especially boys, can have fine motor delays. As infants and toddlers, this delay may appear first as difficulty with self-feeding or as a lack of interest in playing with crayons or pencils. As he grows, he may grasp objects like pencils using a different grip than other children use. He may also pick up objects using a raking movement rather than a pincer grasp (using the thumb and forefinger) for a longer time than other children do. Once he has picked up something, he may have trouble letting go of it, making activities like building a block tower more difficult. Some children with fine motor delays seem to know what skills are involved in a task, but just cannot seem to make them work. For example, your child may know where a peg should go in a pegboard, but be unable to physically maneuver it there. Over time, delayed fine motor development can lead to difficulties with basic skills like writing and dressing.

The exact cause of motor development delays is not known, but there are many suspected factors. Hyperextensible finger joints, caused by loose ligaments and tendons, can delay fine motor development. In addition, tactile defensiveness, discussed above, can deprive your child of many opportunities to use his hands to learn and practice fine motor skills. Weaker muscles, ADHD, and low muscle tone may also play a role in impeding fine motor development.

Early intervention is usually recommended for children who are at risk for delayed fine motor skills. As soon as your child is diagnosed, he should be referred for consultation or assessment with an occupational therapist. OTs are trained to work with your child to foster good fine motor development and to learn ways to overcome fine motor difficulties. The therapist may begin by providing activities for you to do with your child at home or he or she may recommend a combination of therapy and home intervention. The therapist may suggest a number of different tasks for your child to develop fine motor skills. Many of the activities suggested are designed to provide resistance and to develop strength in your child's fingers, hands, arms, and shoulders. Playing with clay, kneading bread dough, or pulling against resistance on a string or rope are examples.

At home it is important for you to encourage your child to use his fine motor skills. However, doing this requires patience and tolerance. Early finger feeding is an extremely important early skill; let your child begin to feed himself despite the mess. As T. Berry Brazelton, the well-known child development expert, advises, you may have to wear a raincoat to dinner while you are teaching your young toddler to self-feed, but it is worth it for his development. Another important skill, self-dressing, should also be encouraged as much as possible. Tolerate the time it takes for your child to do it himself. Other fine motor activities include: cooking, including making meatballs or cookies; drawing or working with a computer; and working with a parent, such as helping dad in the tool shed. Let him be messy outside; sidewalk chalk is a great favorite. The goal is not to turn you into a therapist, but to provide your child with fine motor activities in his everyday life. The opportunities are everywhere.

Gross Motor Development. In general children with fragile X syndrome are more likely to have delays in fine motor than gross motor skills, although early milestones usually are delayed for both. Many children love to take off on their tricycles and Big Wheels, play ball, or run, and their gross motor abilities are often regarded as areas of strength. Many boys and most girls with fragile X syndrome develop gross motor skills that are well within the normal range. It is also typical, however, for initial gross motor milestones, such as pulling to stand or taking steps independently, to be delayed in males. This section explains the gross motor delays that boys are most likely to have. Consult a physical therapist if you have concerns in any of the areas.

Many boys will have gross motor delays that parents notice during the first year of life. Some children have difficulty learning to sit or stand. Some walk later than usual. Although these delays cause worry, almost all boys learn to walk before they are two years old. As children grow, gross motor skills usually increase as well. Older children may acquire skills later than their typical peers, but they will acquire them. Bike riding, climbing, and team sports with peers are not unreasonable activities for children with fragile X syndrome to participate in with supervision. Many coaches volunteer to mentor children who wish to be involved in team sports but need some help with directions, judgment, or safety issues.

Many factors can contribute to gross motor delays. For some children, cognitive delays can delay attainment of all developmental milestones, including motor skills, even if nothing physical causes the delay. In addition, many children with fragile X syndrome have low muscle tone, and this may contribute to delays. Because of the sensory integration difficulties discussed above, some children have poor motor planning ability and poor balance; this may lead to delays in learning skills like running, climbing stairs, or other more complex motor skills. Hyperextensible joints and flat feet can also impair motor skills.

Some children with fragile X syndrome walk on their toes, possibly as a way of helping them compensate for difficulties with sensory integration such as poor balance; it may provide their brain with additional proprioceptive input. The result, however, is that toe walking may impede gross motor skills and lessen endurance. This in turn hinders motor skill development further. Another potential contributor to poor motor skills is lack of opportunity. Some children lack friends to play with at home or in school; this limits their chance for motor-oriented play. Some spend too much time watching television when they could be outside playing.

Although gross motor skills can be significantly delayed for children who are severely affected by fragile X syndrome, most children are able to enjoy many different activities. With appropriate physical therapy, support at school and home, and good health, there is little to stop good motor skills development. Each child's physical therapy program should be designed for his individual profile of strengths and weaknesses, preferences, and attention tolerance. However, activities that are almost always beneficial when supervised are swimming, trampoline jumping, bicycle riding, and small group activities like relays or short races that are high interest and of short duration.

Self-Help Development

Although the self-help skills of children with fragile X syndrome may be slower to appear, this is an area of development that in time becomes an area of relative strength. At about a year of age, you might notice your child having difficulty with finger feeding. Later your child may have trouble handling a drinking cup or becoming toilet trained. This section explains the possible causes of the delays children can encounter in learning self-help skills, and offers some advice on how you can foster good development in this area.

Self-help development depends on abilities acquired in other areas of development. Development in this area builds on the skills learned in developmental areas like fine motor, cognitive, and sensory integration. For example, a child with hypersensitivity in his mouth will resist learning to brush his teeth. Children who have not acquired sufficient fine motor skills may not be able to tie their shoes or button their shirts. And children with cognitive delays may have trouble learning toilet training. As a result, the best way to ensure your child learns good self-help skills is to work for good development in the "foundation" skills. Eventually the

vast majority of children with fragile X syndrome master the most important self-help skills even if it takes more time and effort.

Here are some suggestions for fostering your child's self-help skills:

- **Clothes.** Because of their fine motor delays and hyperactivity, it is a good idea to make dressing as quick and easy
as possible. Choose clothes that are easy for your child to
pull on and off. Try Velcro fasteners instead of buttons.
Sweatpants and sweatshirts may be better choices for your
child if he is just learning to dress himself; jeans and
buttoned shirts may cause frustration for you both. Shoes
with Velcro fasteners make sense for smaller children.
Encourage your child to make some choices about his
clothes; allow him free choice within a range that you set.
For example, allow him to choose among three shirts you
choose, making sure his favorite red cowboy shirt is
among the choices.

- **Food.** As with clothes, adapt food choices that enable
your child to feed himself as much as possible. For
example, if he has not learned to use utensils, offer finger
foods. This teaches and reinforces the concept that he is
responsible for getting food into his mouth. Also remember that, within limits, it is more important for your child
to learn these skills than it is to have a spotless kitchen.
Unbreakable dishes and cups will be easier on you. To
avoid large messes, try giving limited amounts at a time;
fill his cup with a little milk each time, rather than risk
cleaning up a big spill. This takes some of the stress out
of encouraging his independence.

    Food choice can also be affected by your child's level
of tactile defensiveness. Your child may eat only foods
that feel right in his mouth, and may develop a restricted
diet as a result. Some children prefer food textures that
are more substantial like roast beef, pizza crusts, or dill
pickles than cupcakes and ice cream just because of how
they feel.

    It is important to continue to offer food textures that
your child rejects. Forcing him to eat certain foods is not
a good idea, but if you keep a log of what foods were "off
limits" and when, try them again a month or two later

and you may find the aversion has lessened or disappeared. Some children will never tolerate certain foods or textures, but there are also a number of ways to alter texture or temperature or combine foods to provide balanced nutrition your child will eat. It is important that your child has a balanced diet even if the food choices are limited. It might prove very helpful to consult with a registered dietician at least once a year or as long as your child exhibits food preference problems.

- **Toothbrushing.** For some children with fragile X syndrome, this can be a very difficult task to learn. Some children have an overactive gag reflex and choke on the toothpaste or toothbrush. Some children may be too hyperactive to spend an adequate amount of time on this task. And some may be tactilely defensive to anything around or in their mouths. For these children, try a gradual approach; start with a washcloth or your finger. Add a bit of toothpaste. Some children may do better with just water. For some children, an electric toothbrush may eventually be a good option. The vast majority of children do learn to brush their teeth independently, although they may continue to require reminders.

- **Toileting.** Like other self-help skills, toilet training requires development in other areas. Children need the cognitive skills to use the toilet independently. For some children with fragile X syndrome who have more severe cognitive impairments, this can be difficult. Children also need the fine motor skills to remove clothing. Their sensory skills have to alert them when their bladder and bowel are full, and it has to alert them to the discomfort of walking around with wet or soiled clothes. And they need the language skills to communicate their needs. In typical children, these different skills and abilities come together to allow toilet training around age three. In children with fragile X syndrome, delays in one or more of these areas can delay toilet training.

There is a wide variety of advice about toilet training from a wide variety of experts, including parents (the true "experts"). Our advice is not to attempt toilet training until you are sure your child has all the skills he needs to succeed. Once you feel your child is ready, try frequent trips to the bathroom and frequent reminders to use the bathroom, and keep clothes simple. Most children with fragile X syndrome will achieve daytime toileting skills by the age of 6 to 7. Bowel movements are generally mastered next, and nighttime training is typically 1 to 2 years later.

Social and Behavioral Issues

Developing good social skills is an essential step toward independence. No matter how strong a child's cognitive, speech, and other skills might be, he won't function well in society unless he can behave in ways that others consider appropriate. This makes it important for you to understand how your child's behavior may differ from others.

Children with fragile X syndrome are quite sociable. They like to be around other people and are eager to be accepted, but sometimes cannot handle new faces and situations. You might notice your child run to see who is at the door, run away, then run back again to see who it is, or say "hi" and then run away again. Another greeting behavior you may see is for your child to extend his hand while leaning and/or looking away from the person being greeted. In general, almost all children with fragile X syndrome want to interact, but at the same time are overwhelmed by the sensory input involved in social interactions.

Despite their sensory difficulties, children with fragile X syndrome do seek attention and contact. For example, many boys thoroughly enjoy bear hugs. This preference is likely related to their sensory integration problems, but they soon learn to give and request hugs because of the social contact they bring.

On the other hand, as Chapter 1 discusses, there are other behaviors that children with fragile X syndrome may have. These include hyperactivity, impulsivity, hand-flapping, aggressiveness, perseveration, and autistic-like behaviors. Depending on which behaviors your child has and to what degree he has them, they may interfere with social development.

Attention deficit hyperactivity disorder (ADHD) is probably the most common condition that will affect your child's social development. Because of the impact of this condition—impulsivity, short attention span, and distractibility—children have a harder time making and keeping friends and engaging their peers. For example, a child who cannot sit still long enough to play in a small group will miss the opportunities to learn about social groups and social behavior. Children who act impulsively make it harder for other children to befriend them. The treatments for ADHD can help your child control this behavior.

Autistic characteristics cause the most serious behavioral concerns associated with fragile X syndrome. Their impact on social development can be significant. Although most children with fragile X syndrome are not diagnosed with autism, some will have autistic-like behaviors. These include verbal perseveration, poor eye contact, and more limited social awareness. All of these behaviors can impede your child's social development by making it more difficult for him to engage other children.

Behavioral outbursts, aggressive behaviors, and temper tantrums can be a major problem for some children with fragile X syndrome. These behaviors can greatly impede social development. Children will not want to play with a child they fear or whose behavior is volatile.

The cause of aggression and behavioral outbursts in children is not clearly understood. In fact, there may be many different contributors. These behaviors may result from frustration with tasks or from language and communication difficulties; they may be a child's way of expressing frustration, anger, or fear. For example, your child may act out the frustration he feels in not being able to effectively express what he wants, needs, or feels. Outbursts may result from sensory overload your child does not know how to handle. Severely restricted choices and lack of control over basic aspects of their lives may also be a cause of outbursts and aggression. So too can boredom. It is important for you to work with your child's teacher, therapist, and psychologist to sort out the cause or causes. Quite often, meeting your child's needs reduces the behaviors.

Although it is unlikely that aggressive behaviors or self-injurious behaviors (such as hand biting) stem directly from a desire to communicate, they often come to serve "escape" or communicative functions over time. For example, if your child is struggling in a math class, he may strike out knowing that he will be able to "escape" or be removed from the class. This is important to keep in mind when medications or behavior modification programs are used to eliminate these behaviors. Usually it is well worth it to spend a few days or even a week observing what conditions or events seem to bring on aggression or behavioral outbursts. Then it will be much easier to anticipate outbursts and plan how your child can learn to control them himself. When a child's behavior problems persist, parents will often conclude that a drug is not working or that a behavioral program is not working, but the real reason may be that the root causes of the behaviors have not been adequately understood.

Girls with fragile X syndrome can also have difficulties with their social development. Girls can experience shyness, ADHD, social withdrawal, anxiety, depression, and low self-esteem. They will often avoid talking or refuse to answer direct questions because of shyness. When this occurs it is often misinterpreted as "dullness" or rudeness; the listener may avoid the girl or react negatively because of their misinterpretation. If this cycle continues, social development could be impeded or be channeled toward inappropriate behaviors. It is important to work with teachers, counselors, and therapists to help your daughter work through these problems; this will enable her to make friends, work with her peers, and grow into a well-rounded person.

Social skills development is probably one of the most poorly understood aspects of fragile X syndrome. What we do know is that different developmental skills need to come together, including language skills, sensory integration, impulse control, cognitive skills, and listener intuition and understanding. It is probably safe to make two somewhat contradictory statements: 1) All children with fragile X syndrome (both male and female) have some social skill difficulties and 2) All children with fragile X syndrome are sociable by nature with the exception of the 10 to 15 percent who have severe autistic symptoms. Even many of the boys who seem quite "autistic-like" at some stage in their development often improve and become much more social over time. The truth is that this area is just beginning to be studied in depth and from a variety of perspectives; so much will be learned in the future.

▪▪ Developmental Evaluations

In addition to the tests discussed above to assess cognitive development, there are numerous developmental evaluations that are used to assess children with fragile X syndrome and other disabilities. They are very useful in: 1) determining your child's developmental level and 2) designing his treatment, therapy, and educational placement. During evaluations professionals try to measure your child's development compared to other children his age. IQ tests are given by child psychologists; educational assessments are performed by educators or psychologists to evaluate reading, writing, and math skills; fine motor testing and sensory integration testing are done by an occupational therapist; and speech and language testing are given by a speech and language therapist. Adaptive skills and behavioral problems may be assessed by a social worker or psychologist. And a physician may assess your child's overall health, checking for seizures and ADHD.

With preschool children it is important to look at nonverbal as well as verbal skills, to ask "How does your child get what he wants?" It is also important to look at your child's ability to follow directions (with and without gestures or other cues) and what sounds, word approximations, or word combinations he imitates or is starting to use appropriately. With motor development, it is important to look at the quality of his walking, jumping, and running, the quality of his eating skills, and any related behaviors, such as drooling. In addition, his ability to hold a pencil or crayon and his interest in scribbling or imitating shapes or simple figures like a happy face should be examined. It is important to assess beginning problem solving (how your child finds something hidden or reactivates a toy) and early memory skills (retrieving a favorite object on request without cues.) In addition, it is important to ask both mom and dad what they see as both strengths and weaknesses. Your input as a parent is critical to an accurate assessment.

There are many different tests that can be used to assess your child's development level. In fact, there may be several tests that can be used to test the same developmental area. In addition to using a variety of tests to assess your child in a developmental area, professionals may repeat tests or a series of tests to get a better or a different measure of progress. In most states, schools are required to fully evaluate children with disabilities every three years.

As discussed above, children with fragile X syndrome may not perform as well on developmental tests as expected. ADHD, anxiety, weak fine motor skills, and poor language may all contribute to poor results. The result: Children with fragile X syndrome may perform below their actual developmental level.

Because children with fragile X syndrome tend to test poorly, it is important to maximize the testing environment for them. Make sure your child has a good night's sleep and eats a good breakfast. If possible before the test, introduce your child to the examiner so that he or she is not a stranger. If your child takes medication for ADHD, make sure he takes his dose. Finally do not overrate the tests; although you do have to accept the reality of your child's disability, you do *not* need to blindly accept the picture of your child that a test may paint. Remember your child's real strengths, talents, and subtle abilities that testing may miss.

■■ Enhancing Your Child's Development

Since fragile X syndrome was first identified in the 1970s, much has been learned about effective ways to help children overcome their developmental delays. Much more needs to be learned, however. There are several methods of helping children that have been identified. These methods are: 1) treating medical conditions that impede development; 2) providing appropriate special education and therapy; 3) providing a supportive environment at home that encourages learning and growing; and 4) working with trained and caring professionals—doctors, teachers, and therapists.

Health

Although there is no medical cure for fragile X syndrome, there are effective medical treatments for many of the conditions that can accompany it. Many children are helped by medications to control ADHD, aggression, anxiety, or depression—conditions that can affect social development and education. In addition, medications can usually control seizures, making it easier to learn. Frequent ear infections can be treated effectively with antibiotics or ear tubes. This is especially important in optimizing speech and language development. Problems with vision or cleft palate can also be treated. Strive for wellness for your child—proper nutrition, regular health checkups, and treatment of medical conditions.

Early Intervention, Special Education, and Therapy

Your child can also receive important developmental assistance through his early intervention or special education program. Laws exist (explained in Chapter 9) that guarantee your child early intervention and special education services if he is found to need them. Special education teachers, for example, will work to understand your child's learning strengths and needs, and then tailor their teaching methods accordingly. A teacher might notice that your child, like many children, seems to learn better if he is presented with new concepts in visual ways that are meaningful to him. For instance, if your child loves baseball, he might master counting skills if he is asked to count baseball players rather than sticks. The special education teacher could also help your child learn to use computer programs designed for children with disabilities. These programs can offer a stimulating way of helping your child improve many cognitive skills. It may also be easier for your child to use a computer than a pencil if his fine motor skills are delayed.

Occupational therapists (OT) can help your child develop fine motor skills. A good OT can help your child's classroom teacher modify classroom activities to help your child succeed. For example, if your child has difficulty with sensory integration, the OT can help arrange the classroom so that it is comfortable for your child. This may include allowing your child to sit in a beanbag chair or recommending natural lighting for the classroom. Occupational therapists who are NDT Certified can help your child with tactile defensiveness and gravitational insecurities. Some occupational therapists are also experts in using various calming techniques to help children relax so that they are more receptive to learning and therapies, and less prone to behavioral outbursts.

Speech and language therapists can assist with your child's language development and language content. He or she may work one-on-one with your child or in small groups. The speech therapist can also help your child's teacher pick learning activities that will help the language development of the entire class as well as your child. This might include singing or role-playing. It is even possible to accommodate a child who is anxious in the classroom; lessons can be given outside during an enjoyable, but educational, activity.

Child psychologists can provide your family invaluable help with behavior management. Although many psychologists work in private practice or in medical centers, some early intervention and special education programs use psychologists as consultants. Psychologists can help your family establish a system of rewards and punishments to enhance your child's behavior and development. They can help establish structure at home and school to decrease temper outbursts and help your child function to the best of his ability. They can help figure out if behavior management concepts like time-out really work for your child or whether it makes more sense to redirect instead. Along with your child's teachers and therapists, the psychologist can help you decide how far to push your child or when to try something new.

There are many other professionals who can help with your child's development. In many communities music therapists, art therapists, or recreation therapists help children learn or become stronger through sports, art, play, or song. These types of therapies can be very beneficial for children with fragile X syndrome, especially if they have special interests in one of these areas.

No matter what educational and medical assistance your child receives from professionals, there will also be many ways that you, as a parent, can help enhance development. First reassure your child that he is loved and accepted in his home and community. Children with a solid family foundation of love and acceptance are better equipped to face the challenges of school and life.

Regardless of the therapy used or the professional involved, it will be important to extend the teaching or therapy into your home. Make sure that what you do at home supplements and reinforces what your child learns at school and vice versa. For example, if the speech and language therapist is focusing on colors, emphasize the same color words at home. If the color of the week is red, dress him in red clothes or use red paper plates at mealtime. Use your imagination, but don't let it become a burden.

In helping your child learn or improve skills, be sure not to stress him beyond his ability to cope. For example, your child may not be able to read stories for more than five or ten minutes at a time. Take lots of breaks and do not force him to continue with an activity beyond his attention span or patience. At the same time, do not hesitate to gradually prod him to try new experiences and activities. You can help your child with fine motor and sequencing skills in a million ways, from making cookies to decorating a Christmas tree with homemade ornaments. You can help him develop his language and social skills by including him in almost any activity involving other people—helping in the kitchen or the garage, going fishing, or going to Sunday school. Creating opportunities for your child to be with people in typical settings may be the best way to make sure your child will grow up to function in the work force and your community.

To make sure your child feels involved, don't just do things with him that *you* are interested in doing. Try to capitalize on *his* interests to create learning situations. For example, if your child loves baseball, take him to a baseball game and use the time to count the players, discuss the plays, or maybe just enjoy being out in the stadium. You may find that your child's challenging behaviors lessen if he is doing something that interests him. For instance, he might not be able to tolerate loud noises at the mall, but he may not mind loud noises at a baseball game.

If things start to become too stressful for your child, stop and think. Be flexible; follow your child's cues. This might mean going home early from a shopping trip or going to sit in the car for a little while. It might mean taking your child to a quiet room if he becomes overloaded at a family event or gathering. Some children just need to settle back with a toy or game to help recover from stress.

Give your child lavish praise whenever he makes attempts that are on the right track. Do not expect him to perform up to your adult standards the first few times he tries something. It may take many tries for him to learn to tie his shoes correctly or write his name perfectly. Praise the small steps along the way to these skills such as when he learns the first cross-over motion for shoe tying or when he learns to write his first name. Make sure your other children share in the praise; bring the whole family to the celebration of all your child's big and small victories.

∷ Conclusion

In fostering your child's development, do not forget that every child with fragile X syndrome is different. In addition, scientists, doctors, educators, and therapists simply do not know everything about fragile X syndrome; the condition is too "new." In raising your child, do not hesitate to be creative and imaginative in looking for solutions that work best for your child. Use your intimate knowledge of your child and reach out to other parents for advice and information to help your child reach his potential. And throughout your journey with your child, never give up. Your child will not let you.

❚❚ References

American Psychiatric Association. *Diagnostic and Statistical Manual of Mental Disorders* (4th Edition, Revised). Washington, DC: American Psychiatric Association. 1994.

Ayres, A.J. *Sensory Integration and the Child.* Los Angeles: Western Psychological Services. 1991.

Braden, M. *Fragile: Handle with Care, Understanding Fragile X Syndrome.* Colorado Springs, CO:1996. Contact: 100 East St. Vrain, #200, Colorado Springs, CO 80903; 719/633-3773.

Freund, L.S., Reiss, A.L., Abrams, M.T. "Psychiatric Disorders Associated with Fragile X in the Young Female." *Pediatrics* 91 (1992): 321-328.

Hagerman, R.J. and Cronister, A. *Fragile X Syndrome: Diagnosis, Treatment, Research* (2nd Edition). Baltimore: The Johns Hopkins University Press. 1996.

Hanson, D.M., Jackson, A.W., Hagerman, R.J. "Speech Disturbances (Cluttering) in Mildly Impaired Males with the Martin-Bell/Fragile X Syndrome. *American Journal of Medical Genetics* 23 (1986): 195-206.

Harris, J.R. and Liebert, R.M. *The Child: Development from Birth through Adolescence* (2nd Edition). Englewood Cliffs, NJ: Prentice-Hall, 1987.

Reiss, A.L. and Freund, L. "Behavioral Phenotype of Fragile X Syndrome: DSM-III-R Autistic Behavior in Male Children." *American Journal of Medical Genetics* 43 (1992): 35-46.

Schopmeyer, B.B. and Lowe, F. *The Fragile X Child.* San Diego: Singular Publishing Group, 1992.

Sensory Integration International. *A Parent's Guide to Understanding Sensory Integration.* Torrance, CA: Sensory Integration International, 1991.

Short-DeGraff, M.A. *Human Development for Occupational and Physical Therapists.* Baltimore: Williams and Wilkins. 1988.

Spiridigliozzi, G., Lachiewicz, A., MacMurdo, C., Vizoso, A., O'Donnell, C., McConkie-Rosell, A., Burgess, D. *Educating Boys with Fragile X Syndrome.* Durham, NC: Duke University Medical Center. 1997.

❚❚ Parent Statements

He sat up, walked, and talked a little later than many kids do, but not by a great amount. The biggest difference wasn't when he reached these developmental "landmarks," but how slow the progression was after that—being able to turn individual words into sentences and then conversation, turning walking into coordinated running or skipping.

He has great difficulty with abstract thinking and problem solving.

His language is perseverative and tangential, so conversational skills are way behind.

He's hypersensitive to people's touch, to loud voices, certain types of clothing, and changes in structure.

Bathroom skills came slowly (4 years when complete).

He still can't button, snap, or zipper things with mastery.

Athletics are becoming of interest to him but his lack of coordination is an impediment.

Socially, he's very outgoing when he gets comfortable with people, but he doesn't know what to say or do so he can't maintain a conversation more than a minute or so. He tends to get overstimulated in social settings.

We still have to find "snap" pants and shorts because he can't do the button.

Tony is four years old and functions at a two-and-a-half-year-old level.

We don't miss a stage, that's for sure. For example, you get to see every little thing it takes to learn to sit up or walk. Things don't happen overnight like they do with typical kids.

At four years of age, Patrick only says a few words.

As my son gets older, I really see how slowly things come to him.

I don't compare because I want my son to be someone or something he's not. I compare to see what the range of abilities are within an age bracket or classroom and as a gauge of how far we've come and what needs to be worked on the most.

When I compared my son to my daughter who doesn't have fragile X syndrome, I thought at first she must be gifted because things came so easily and quickly to her. I soon realized she was just a typical child.

I don't think our pediatrician was given the background in medical school to identify various developmental delays so we went to a developmental pediatrician. He did formal cognitive testing, a physical exam, we filled out parent questionnaires, and he ordered an EEG, chromosome testing, and a thyroid panel.

It was helpful to have a professional who looked at the whole child rather than just his school records or his medical history and then tie all the data together.

Motivation seems to be the key to each of the boys' learning. And both were best motivated by having lots of contact with their peers. For example, after years of speech therapy each boy developed speech most effectively when he had to communicate with others in summer camp, in an integrated classroom, or in another integrated setting.

We try to maintain his good self-esteem with lots of encouragement, love, and support. We read as much fragile X literature as we can, we talk to other parents of typical and special needs kids about our struggles and successes, and we share ideas. We also try to complement what is being learned in school with what is going on in private therapy so that they reinforce one another.

8

EDUCATION

Marcia L. Braden, Ph.D.

▪ Introduction

One of the most exciting moments for parents is sending their child to school for the first time. A flurry of hopes and dreams flash through the mind as the youngster goes off to school. If your child has fragile X syndrome, that experience may be more turbulent because fear and uncertainty may be blended in with those hopes and dreams. You may worry that your child will not be able to benefit from traditional educational experiences. You may also have to adjust your role as a parent from primarily supporting your child to advocating for an appropriate education. This chapter will help prepare you to support your child's education. It explains how to get your child started in his educational programming and examines the best learning methods and strategies for children with fragile X syndrome.

If your child's fragile X syndrome prevents him from receiving reasonable benefit from his education, he qualifies for special education under the federal law known as the Individuals with Disabilities Education Act (IDEA). This law establishes your child's right to an appropriate education, like all other children.

How do you know if your child needs special education? In young children with fragile X syndrome, educational professionals may look at language delays and speech patterns that seem inconsistent with typically developing children. In other cases, behavioral difficulties may lead to services. You may have noticed behavioral symptoms like sleeping difficulties, eating and toileting problems, behavioral outbursts, and self-abuse, which may indicate a need for special education. These are the most common ways children with fragile X syndrome qualify for special education services under IDEA. Even though your child's eligibility for special education is not automatically guaranteed by the diagnosis of fragile X syndrome, most children do qualify for services. It is important to consult your school district's special education department about eligibility.

▪▪ Identification

The overall process of obtaining services under IDEA begins with a perceived need for an evaluation. The request for an evaluation usually comes from you or the classroom teacher if your child is older. You may also be encouraged by your pediatrician or other specialist to make this request. A call to your local school district's special education department will give you the information needed to obtain the evaluation. The results of the evaluation will most likely lead to the development of an Individualized Family Service Plan (IFSP) if your child is under age three and an Individualized Education Program (IEP) if your child is three or older both of which describe the services your child will receive.

▪▪ Qualifying for Special Education Services

If your child is found eligible, he has a right to early intervention services and special education through the Individuals with Disabilities Education Act (IDEA). The intent of this comprehensive law is to enable children and their parents to access the services they need. IDEA is described in detail in Chapter 9.

Birth to Three

Part C of IDEA applies to children under age three who have an identified disability or who are experiencing developmental delays. States receive funding for Part C by submitting a program to the federal government. Most states have Part C programs in place.

Under Part C, your child must be evaluated to determine eligibility for services. If the child is found to be eligible, a plan for services, called an Individualized Family Service Plan (IFSP), is written and services begin. A service coordinator will help you coordinate the different services your child receives.

Screenings and Multidisciplinary Evaluations—Qualifying for Supports and Services. A screening is like a "quick check" to see if a child has a disability or is "at-risk" for experiencing a developmental delay. The results of a screening may or may not lead to a more in-depth evaluation of your child. Generally, children with chromosomal conditions like fragile X syndrome qualify for services under Part C. Developmental skills that are examined include: 1) communication; 2) cognitive; 3) physical and motor; 4) sensory; and 5) adaptive ability. Children with the condition often qualify for services because of delays or problems in these areas sometimes even before fragile X syndrome is diagnosed.

Most evaluations use a multidisciplinary approach, where children are observed and tested by a team of professionals. The professionals may all observe your child at the same time when he performs a task or participates in an activity, or they may assess your child individually. The professionals then meet with you to discuss their findings. The role these professionals play in the evaluation and education of your child is discussed later in this chapter.

Individualized Family Service Plan (IFSP). When your child qualifies for early intervention services, an IFSP is generated by a team of people that includes the parents, and it addresses the needs of your child and your family. This program incorporates the family into services because Part C views the family and community as the support on which the child's development rests. The family is empowered to help direct the services rather than relying solely on professional diagnosis and treatment. In addition, IDEA requires that services and support be provided in the natural environment. The natural environment is the place infants live and play at this time of their lives, places such as the home, the local community or recreation center, and parks.

IFSPs include the following:

- Your child's present level of development—List the skills your child has already demonstrated, along with his strengths, interests, and weaknesses.
- Your family's resources, priorities, and challenges—Do you need additional resources, such as money or emotional support? What is important to your family, for example, your ideals and values? What are your concerns for your family and child?
- Goals for your family—List both short and long term goals.

- Supports and services—What services do you need to reach your goals?
- The name of the primary service coordinator—A service coordinator oversees all that is going on with the family. This person may be assigned to the family, chosen by the family, or the family can choose to be their own service coordinator. This is covered in more detail in the next section.
- A written transition plan—Funding sources change when your child turns three years old. The IFSP must provide a transition plan to ensure continuity of services, and the planning for this transition should begin at least three to six months before your child turns three.

The IFSP should be reviewed every six months by the entire team.

Service Coordination. A child who qualifies for services under Part C is entitled to service coordination. A service coordinator may help your family with any or all of the following:

- Ensuring an evaluation is completed if needed
- Facilitating the development and regular review of the IFSP
- Helping to identify service providers
- Coordinating the delivery of services
- Providing information about the availability of advocacy services
- Coordinating health related services, if needed
- Facilitating the development of the transition plan at age three

Ages Three to Twenty-One

Part B of IDEA applies to children three years and older. Similar to the requirements of Part C, children of this age must also qualify for special education services. They must undergo an evaluation, which is the responsibility of the local school district. If the child is found to be eligible, a plan for services, called an Individualized Education Program (IEP), is developed (discussed below).

The evaluation team should include:

- The parents
- A regular education teacher

- A special education teacher
- A representative from the school district
- Individuals who can interpret the results of the evaluations
- The student, when appropriate
- Anyone else the parents want to include

Evaluations are conducted to:

- ***Determine whether your child has a disability***—A variety of testing methods are used to gather functional and developmental information about your child. The specific eligibility requirements vary from state to state, but basically your child must be delayed in at least one of the developmental areas listed previously under Screenings and Multidisciplinary Evaluations. The amount of delay usually must be one to two years.

- ***Determine your child's current level of development***— Evaluations generally examine four areas: 1) cognitive; 2) behavioral (social-emotional); 3) physical (vision and hearing); and 4) developmental (speech and language development, fine and gross motor development). Determining a child's current development provides a starting point for instruction and the development of goals and objectives that are a major part of the IEP. For example, a child who knows how to count will have goals and objectives that are different from a child who does not know his numbers.

- ***Determine your child's unique strengths and weaknesses***—Understanding what is hard for your child to learn and what is easy can help tremendously with designing an effective education program. Weaknesses form the basis for teaching goals and objectives. But strengths are just as important because they can be used to help your child compensate for his weaknesses. For example, if counting and math are difficult for your child, look for a strength around which to center the teaching. High interest areas, such as money, buildings and construction, or calculators, can be the focus of math instruction to make it interesting and real to your child.

- ***Determine your child's rate of learning***—Your child's rate of learning will assist in setting goals and objectives that are realistic for your child. For example, depending on his rate of learning, it may be more appropriate to expect your child to learn to recognize his printed name than it is to be reading within a year.

- *Explore ways your child may learn*—Through testing, you may discover that your child learns better when information is presented pictorially. Testing may uncover areas of high interest such as trucks, books, or cooking. You may find that regular movement is essential for your child to do quiet work. This sort of information is critical to develop an IEP.
- *Review existing evaluation data, including data from the regular education classroom*—This allows the team to look at the child's behavior in the regular classroom and how to best provide services in the classroom.
- *Determine your child's educational needs*—The results of the evaluation are used to develop programming goals and placement that are written in the IEP.
- *Determine the supports and services needed*—What is needed to meet the goals and objectives in the IEP, including the supports needed to enable your child to participate in the regular education classroom and in the general curriculum.

Types of Evaluations. The two different types of evaluations that are required in special education are an initial evaluation and a triennial evaluation. Both evaluations serve important roles in your child's special education placement and programming.

The initial evaluation is performed when your child is first placed into the special education system. You may also hear it referred to as an eligibility determination. Standardized testing and observation are both used, and your input as the parent is essential. The testing specialists will meet with you after completing the testing to discuss test results and determine the best way to meet your child's educational needs.

Triennial evaluations take place every three years after the initial evaluation. This staffing will be much like your initial staffing for which your child was extensively evaluated by a number of professionals. The purpose of the triennial review is to provide an in-depth account of your child's current level of functioning. This will help the school and you to measure progress. Your child's education program and how education services are provided to him may be adjusted based on the progress noted. It may be necessary to add, discontinue, or modify services. Remember, if you think your child needs an evaluation, you or your child's teachers can request one at any time. Also there must be an evaluation or review of progress before it is determined that a child is no longer eligible to receive special education services.

Annual Reviews. Once your child is receiving special education services, his progress will be reviewed annually to determine whether there needs to be any changes in services or goals. The annual review does not require an in-depth re-evaluation as was initially required for placement eligibility. It lets you track your child's progress in his education program. This is an opportunity to discuss areas of slow progress along with strategies to promote change and devise ways to capitalize on areas of good progress. Also know that while there is a requirement that your child's IEP be reviewed annually, you may request a meeting to review your child's progress at any time.

Don't be discouraged by annual reviews that do not show good progress across the board. Developmental and educational plateaus are fairly common with all children; they are just usually more pronounced with children who have fragile X syndrome. For example, if your child is making great gains in his motor abilities, his talking may seem to come to a standstill. And just when your concern reaches its height, he'll start talking with the same or greater ability. Or, sometimes children exhibit behavior that is out of control right before great strides are made in one area or another. As parents, it is sometimes hard to tolerate these plateaus, especially when you are right in the middle of one, but rest assured that more often than not it is a part of your child's developmental pattern, and he will continue to make progress.

Who Evaluates Your Child?

Your child must be evaluated to determine his eligibility for early intervention and special education services. Because IDEA mandates that more than one developmental area be assessed, your child will most likely meet with a variety of professionals. As each specialist has an opportunity to observe your child, they will begin to weave a cloth of needs and services that will form the basis for his educational plan. One important reminder: Although professionals will have an expert point-of-view, no one knows your child better than you do. Make sure each professional hears what you have to say about your child and takes it into consideration in forming their conclusions and recommendations.

It is important that the evaluation take into account your child's unique characteristics. Typically, standardized testing requires children to withstand intense and direct interaction with the examiner. This testing experience may provoke anxiety in your child. The anxiety can prompt a flight or fight reaction, which will clearly affect test results. Often the results are inaccurate due to the impact of behavior. Because of this, it is difficult to view the results with complete confidence, unless the examiner is an expert in testing children with fragile X syndrome. Later, this chapter discusses each of the professionals and the role they play in evaluating and working with your child.

Private Evaluations

You are always allowed to seek an independent evaluation in order to assess your child's ability level and address treatment methods. Some parents choose to do this because they disagree with the school district's evaluation or want the evaluation to be conducted by a professional with specific expertise in fragile X syndrome. Because fragile X syndrome is under-diagnosed and its prevalence low, there are few professionals who have extensive experience working with them, and even fewer with experience evaluating them. Consequently, the professionals the school district provides to perform the evaluation may not have the necessary level of expertise with fragile X syndrome.

IDEA allows you to opt for private psychological, speech and language, occupational, or educational testing. This means that the cost will be paid directly by you. You may want to contact your health insurance carrier to investigate the possibility of third party reimbursement. In some cases, it may be possible to convince, or even force, the school district to pay for the evaluation. Often due to monetary constraints, a school district will prefer to use their own staff. In that case, you can either accept their test results or attempt to prove that the person evaluating your child by the school district lacks the expertise to accurately evaluate your child. Even if you choose to bear the financial burden of a private evaluation, the school district may not always utilize the results. You may wish to pay the private evaluator (psychologist, tutor, speech-language pathologist) to attend the IEP meeting to make sure they provide input into the IEP process. If you are willing to bear the financial burden, most districts welcome additional information provided by members of the private sector.

∷ Education

What is Special Education?

Special education is not a place. It is a service provided to children who have disabilities, designed to help them learn. Serving children with disabilities, however, does not happen in a day or a month. It is a process— a process that begins with identification, and goes from assessment, to determining eligibility, to developing an Individualized Education Program (IEP), to determining placement, and ultimately implementing the IEP.

Preparing for the IEP Meeting

The IEP meeting is really a business meeting. It is not the time or the place to build relationships. It is a meeting with an agenda that is pretty much set by the requirements of IDEA. It is a meeting to learn and share information about your child and to make important choices. With that in mind, there are a few things you can do ahead of time to be prepared:

- Know the time and location of the meeting, which must be mutually agreed upon.
- Make sure you are informed of everyone who is going to be there.
- Exchange information ahead of time, if appropriate.
- Obtain a copy of the IEP forms currently in use because school districts continually change their forms to keep up with changes to IDEA.
- Prepare a list of needs for your child and questions about strategies and programming.
- Bring any records you think may be appropriate—recent doctor checkup, information on medication changes, health changes, and recent illness.
- Come prepared to take notes at the meeting.
- The staffing process can be emotional. Make sure you have support before and after the meeting.
- You are always permitted to bring a friend or support person with you.

The Individualized Education Program (IEP)

The IEP contains the information necessary to provide individualized educational instruction to your child. It is a legal document that binds the school district to the goals and objectives in it. The components of the IEP that are listed below should be found in your IEP in one form or another:

- **Demographic information** about your child
- **Type of IEP meeting**—Is this an initial or a triennial meeting?
- **IEP Review**—Is this an annual review or a requested review, and if the latter, the reason for the review?
- **Present Level of Functioning**—Under each area there is space to list the types of assessments that were used, a summary of the results, the strengths and needs of your child, or to put it another way, areas where you would like to see growth or progress. Not all areas will apply to every child.
- **Cognitive**—How your child thinks and solves problems, along with a description of his learning style.
- **Educational**—How your child performs within the general curriculum and on tasks that are age-appropriate.
- **Social, Emotional, and Adaptive Behavior**—How your child handles his own and others' feelings. How your child functions in group situations. How he handles change. This section is also where the need for a behavior plan is documented. Dealing with behavior issues and developing behavior plans are explained later in this chapter.
- **Life Skills, Career, and Transition**—This section of the IEP is mandated for children 14 and older to prepare for the transition out of public education into employment.
- **Health**—Your child's overall health, including vision, hearing, current medication, developmental history, genetic testing, and medical history.
- **Physical and Motor**—Your child's gross and fine motor abilities.
- **Communication**—Your child's receptive and expressive communication abilities.
- **Determination of Eligibility**—This section lists and prioritizes your child's educational needs. The specific type of disability or disability label is usually stated on this page. A separate sheet must document how the decision on the disability was reached. The purpose of

determining a disability is to establish qualification for
funding, not for placement into a specific program.

■ *Annual Goals and Objectives*—Based on how your child's
needs are grouped and prioritized, annual goals are created.
Annual goals are educational outcomes that a student can
reasonably attain in one year. Objectives are the steps needed
to reach the goal. The next section explains this in detail
and provides examples of goals and objectives.

■ *Characteristics of Service and Accommodations*—This
section of the IEP explains how services and accommodations will be provided in order for your child to accomplish his goals and objectives. Examples of services
include ways the curriculum might be adapted to better
meet your child's needs, classroom and school accessibility, supplies and equipment modifications, extra curricular activities, and health and medical accommodations.

■ *Special Education and Related Services*—This section
specifies what services will be provided, who will
provide the services, and for what amount of time each
week. For example, a special education teacher may be
assigned 10 to 15 hours per week of direct time with
your child. A speech therapist may be assigned one hour
per week of direct time with your child. There may also
be indirect time assigned; this can include time for
consultation with others on the team. Other services
specified may include occupational therapy, time with a
social worker, and transportation.

■ *Placement in the Least Restricted Environment*—IDEA
requires that, "to the maximum extent appropriate,
children with disabilities are educated with children who
do not have disabilities." The IEP team is responsible for
considering and documenting their rationale to provide
the specified special education services in the least
restrictive environment. They must also specify how much
time your child will spend in the regular education class
compared to the special education class. Placement
options are discussed later in this chapter.

■ *Staffing Participants*—Everyone who attends the meeting
is requested to sign the IEP form. The signature denotes

attendance only and does not signify agreement. As stated above, some people are required by law to attend.

- *Parents' and Students' Rights*—IDEA establishes many rights for parents and students (discussed in Chapter 9), and a copy of these rights should be reviewed during the creation of every IEP. You may request a copy of your rights prior to or any time during the staffing process.

Annual Goals and Objectives. The actual services your child receives are determined largely by the goals and objectives listed in his IEP. Based on the evaluation of your child, or on the experience with your child during past school years, these goals and objectives will dictate the type and frequency of his special education services. In short, services should closely follow the goals and objectives in the IEP.

Table 1 (see pages 256-57) presents goals and objectives that have been used in the past in the IEPs of children with fragile X syndrome.

In the following examples, the child's strengths and needs are presented, followed by the development of a goal and objectives. Supplementary services are then identified, along with the educational materials and techniques needed to achieve the objectives.

Example: Jack, a four-year-old student with fragile X syndrome at Lovington Elementary, has an IEP that includes the following:
Needs:
    To write his name.
    To use scissors.
    To color pictures with crayons and markers.
Strengths:
    Jack likes to work with Play Dough.
    Jack likes to draw lines and circles in shaving cream.
Goal:
    Jack will improve his fine motor skills.
Objectives:
    Jack will write his first name by January 1; last name by
        May 1.
    Jack will use scissors to cut squares and circles.
Supplementary Services:
    Jack will have small group instruction for writing his name.
    Jack will have access to computer to write his name.
    Hand-over-hand scissors will be available.

Example: Tony, a five-year-old student with fragile X syndrome at Berger Elementary, has an IEP that includes the following:
Needs:
    To learn how to read.
    To understand the importance of reading.
Strengths:
    Tony loves to have books read to him.
    Tony loves to sing the ABC song.
Goal:
    Tony will develop reading readiness skills.
Objectives:
    Tony will recognize ten logos.
    Tony will develop a sight word vocabulary of 25 words.
    Tony will listen to a story for 15 minutes per day.
Supplementary Services:
    There will be 1-to-1 instruction for 30 minutes per day.
    A visual approach will be used that matches photos to words.
    Stories will be developmentally appropriate and of high
        interest to Tony.

❚❚ TABLE 1. SUGGESTED GOALS FOR AN INDIVIDUALIZED EDUCATION PROGRAM (IEP)

Therapy Services

Physical therapy to:
- a. Improve muscle tone in the trunk
- b. Develop hand-eye coordination
- c. Increase body awareness
- d. Improve balance
- e. Improve overall gross motor ability

Occupational therapy to:
- a. Improve fine motor skills
- b. Decrease tactile defensiveness
- c. Improve motor planning skills
- d. Improve self-help skills

Sensory integration therapy to:
- a. Decrease sensitivity to sensory stimuli
- b. Develop strategies to successfully transition
- c. Increase ability to modulate incoming stimuli, that is, to gain awareness of when the environment is becoming overwhelming
- d. Increase repertoire of self-calming strategies

Speech and language therapy to:
- a. Improve oral motor planning—learning the correct sequence of mouth movements to produce the desired sound or word
- b. Increase receptive and expressive language skills
- c. Increase use of sign language or picture exchange
- d. Increase ability to maintain topic of conversation
- e. Increase ability of sequencing in telling or retelling stories
- f. Increase frequency of independently discussing feelings or concerns

Educational services

Classroom behavior to include:
- a. Increase entry level learning behaviors such as attending, waiting, imitating
- b. Increase compliance with teacher directions using indirect strategies

   c. Increase consistency of behavior among adults and environments
   d. Decrease anxiety responses to change

Math goals to:
   a. Develop one-to-one correspondence and number value
   b. Identify and write whole numbers
   c. Complete one-digit addition problems independently
   d. Use numbers in problem-solving situations
   e. Improve the functional understanding and use of math skills, for example, measurement, money, time

Reading goals to:
   a. Develop reading readiness skills
   b. Increase ability to listen to acquire information when read to—Who? What? Where?
   c. Read to acquire information—Who? What? Where?
   d. Read and understand a variety of written information such as recipes, shopping lists, schedules, newspapers

Writing goals to:
   a. Trace and then write letters
   b. Copy words and sentences
   c. Express a thought in writing
   d. Write a shopping list, note, telephone message, letter or story

Independence goals to:
   a. Increase personal independence—dressing, grooming, toileting
   b. Develop knowledge of safety—crossing the street, fire hazards, strangers
   c. Complete school work assignments independently
   d. Express needs or wants without prompts
   e. Expand repertoire of strategies for making transitions independently
   f. Learn when to use self-calming strategies
   g. Learn how to set and attain personal goals

Social goals to:
   a. Interact appropriately with a peer and maintain a friendship
   b. Develop problem solving strategies within a social setting
   c. Develop ability to give and receive compliments
   d. Meet and greet others

Example: Larry, a six-year-old student with fragile X syndrome at Frene Creek Elementary, has an IEP that includes the following:
Needs:
  To make transitions independently.
  To express his needs and wants appropriately.
Strengths:
  Larry loves to move around.
  Larry likes to do what the other children are doing.
Goal:
  Larry will make four of six daily transitions independently.
Objectives:
  Larry will develop and use a daily pictorial schedule.
  Larry will develop calming strategies.
  Larry will ask for help with prompts, then without prompts.
Supplementary Services:
  Larry's daily schedule will use a picture format.
  An aide will review Larry's schedule with him in the morning.
  An aide will help Larry use his schedule throughout the day.
  Schedule for the following day will be reviewed a day ahead.

Example: Joan, a six-year-old student with fragile X syndrome at Benedict Elementary, has an IEP that includes the following:
Needs:
  To develop a sense of numbers.
  To use numbers in problem-solving situations.
Strengths:
  Joan is interested in money.
  Joan likes to write.
Goal:
  Joan will demonstrate one-to-one correspondence from one to ten.
Objectives:
  Joan will match the correct number to a given number of items.
  Joan will count and write the correct number to a given number of items.
  Joan will count different types of money, up to ten coins.
Supplementary Services:
  Books will be at a preschool reading and interest level.
  Activities will be modeled for Joan prior to asking her to do it.
  Joan will have a book on counting read to her two to three times/week.

Annual goals should focus on the big picture—what you want your child to learn in a year. Objectives are the individual steps taken to reach that goal. In the following examples, the goals and objectives are developed after the present level of functioning has been discussed. The examples will, of course, need to be adapted or modified for your child.

John

Present Level of Functioning:
Writing is difficult for John, although he does do some printing. He often uses the Alpha Smart to put sentences together. He also likes to use the computer. John will often tell his thoughts and stories to an adult, who will transcribe them, and he will put them on the computer using the Alpha Smart. Because John likes cooking and shopping, writing lists for groceries and recipes are a good incentive.

Annual Goal:
John will select a recipe and complete a shopping list using the Alpha Smart.

John's Short-term Objective(s) and Criteria	Evaluation Procedures
1. Three cooking recipes will be read to John and he will select one recipe.	Observation with data
2. John will correctly identify the ingredients needed for the recipe and then make a grocery list for the necessary items using the Alpha Smart.	Shopping list
3. John will correctly copy the recipe onto the computer using the Alpha Smart.	The recipe

Arthur

Present Level of Functioning:
Arthur likes areas neat and clean and, as a result, he sometimes opens private desks and drawers to clean and put supplies where they belong. He is not always aware of private space and the need to respect it. Most of his peers are aware of his difficulty respecting others' personal space. This can sometimes be confusing to Arthur because some adults allow him to enter

personal space while others do not. It is important that Arthur learn the boundaries for himself.

Annual Goal:
Arthur will respect the personal items of others at an age-appropriate level of proficiency.

Short-term Objective(s) and Criteria	Evaluation Procedures
1. Arthur will be able to discriminate his items from others 100 percent of the time.	Observation with data
2. Given a script and practice, Arthur will share his personal items when appropriate four out of five times.	Observation with data
3. Given a script and practice, Arthur will ask to use items belonging to someone else in 3 different environments.	Observation with data
4. Arthur will share his personal items when appropriate and ask to use items belonging to someone else 100 percent of the time.	Observation with data

Peter

Present Level of Functioning:
Peter seems more comfortable around adults than peers. If he had peer friends, he could be involved in more activities. Usually when a peer asks him to join in an activity, Peter will decline. In order for Peter to rely less on adults, he needs to learn to develop friendships of his own, which, in turn, will help him be more independent.

Annual Goal:
Peter will demonstrate a variety of social skills to develop and maintain friendships with three peers.

Short-term Objective(s) and Criteria	Evaluation Procedures
1. Given modeling and a script, Peter will respond to others' requests to participate in an activity four out of five times.	Observation with data
2. Given modeling and practice, Peter will initiate an interaction with a peer with prompting two out of three times.	Observation with data
3. Given instruction and modeling Peter will initiate interaction with a peer on four different occasions without prompting.	Observation with data

Academic vs. Functional Skills. Parents developing IEPs for their children must often make choices about the direction of their child's education. The types of skills that children learn can generally be broken down into two categories: academic and functional. Academic skills include reading, writing, mathematics, geography, history, social studies, biology, and chemistry. Functional skills are often referred to as self-help skills or independence skills. They may include dressing, personal hygiene, shopping, purchasing personal or household items, working, budgeting, following schedules, paying bills, and recreation. All children, including children with fragile X syndrome, need to learn skills from both of these categories.

The challenge is to find the right balance between teaching academic and functional skills. Some level of academic knowledge is needed in order to teach functional skills. For example, you have to have some basic reading skills before you can read directions to prepare food or read a menu. You have to have an understanding of some math and numbers before you can make a purchase or pay your bills. In addition, certain levels of functional skills are needed for children to learn academics. For example, students need to be able to take care of their toileting needs in order to participate in a classroom.

Some parents have difficulty achieving this balance for their child with fragile X syndrome. Eventually most children with fragile X syndrome will leave the comfort of a protected home environment and move into the community. Your child's level of independence will dictate both his employment and community living opportunities later on. If your child is capable of taking care of himself, it will enable him to access a broader range of opportunities and services.

Academic Skills. Many children with fragile X syndrome experience learning difficulties. Through study and teaching experience, the strengths and weaknesses typically seen in children with fragile X syndrome are well understood. Generally, math is more difficult than reading. However, the way material is presented often determines learning success or failure in math or in any subject. The knowledge of how children with fragile X syndrome learn best should be incorporated into each child's IEP. The Resource Guide at the end of the book lists educational materials and software that you may find useful.

■ *Math.* Math may be more difficult because math concepts move from the concrete (counting, ordering, and grouping) to the abstract quickly. It is easier to count the number of blocks or tokens than it is to put them into groups of ten for adding. Children in second and third grade are expected to understand regrouping and subtraction, which require complex sequential ordering. This can be difficult for children with fragile X syndrome. Consequently, it may become difficult to keep up with the typical progression of the math curriculum. There are a number of math programs that utilize more visual methods to understanding numbers and the function of math. These kinds of programs generally help children with fragile X syndrome understand math concepts.

- **Reading.** Success in reading and spelling relies less on sequential processing and can be mastered using a number of different methods. For example, although a phonetic approach to reading uses a sequential system of blending sounds together to form words, other approaches use whole words and sight words. Children with fragile X syndrome are not penalized by this processing preference in the areas of reading and spelling because there are alternative methods to teach those subjects. How words look along with their context can provide the basis for successful reading and spelling for children with fragile X syndrome. This is referred to as a simultaneous learning approach and is discussed in the next section.

Functional or Self-Help Skills. There are many ways to teach self-help skills. The significance of these skills cannot be stressed enough and should be included in an IEP at every developmental stage. At an early age, the skills include dressing (distinguishing front and back of clothing, buttoning, lacing shoes), toileting (indicating a need to urinate, wiping, washing, and drying hands), and eating (verbalizing desires, making food choices, using utensils, wiping mouth, chewing). As children get older they need to learn how to groom themselves (bathe, brush teeth, comb hair, iron clothing, apply deodorant) and access their community resources (place telephone calls, ride mass transit, meet work schedules, develop a budget, and shop).

The need to master self-help skills and gain independence is critical to the self-esteem of any youngster. It helps build confidence and independence, two essential elements for successful living. Perhaps the most important gift a parent can give a child is that of fostering self-help. So when planning your child's IEP, be sure to consider self-help skills in addition to academics.

Characteristics of Services and Accommodations

Whether it is for your child's IFSP or for an IEP, how services are provided can make the difference between success and frustration. Like all children, your child with fragile X syndrome learns best in certain ways. As you think about how your child learns best, and how educational services can best meet his needs, make sure there is a direct connection between his learning style and the teaching methods. This section explains the factors that can affect learning and provides some examples of services and accommodations that may be needed for your child.

Learning Style. Although each child with fragile X syndrome is a unique individual, there are similarities in the way information is processed. It is critical for you and your child's teachers to understand this processing style so that the best educational strategies are used with your child. Here is what is known about how children with fragile X syndrome process information and learn:

- *Performance*—Children with fragile X syndrome perform better on achievement tests than cognitive tests. It is often assumed that cognitive ability determines achievement, but children with fragile X syndrome outperform predictions based only on cognitive test scores. It is most likely due to long-term memory and repeated exposure to material. In addition, familiar tasks that have been taught within a context are remembered better.

- *Inflexibility*—Children with fragile X syndrome tend to be inflexible in their thinking, and, like children with autism, may become over-selective about the stimuli they attend to. They may have to always use a certain type of pencil or paper. They may want to sit in a certain seat or may require that others also sit in certain seats. This learning characteristic may promote perseverative thinking about unrelated aspects of a task. In other words, it is easy for them to get stuck on something that is extraneous and unimportant.

- *Executive Functioning*—Children with fragile X syndrome show a lack of executive function, the ability to formulate a plan in total and to execute it. Executive function also requires flexibility in problem solving.

- *Closure*—Experience has demonstrated that children with fragile X syndrome need completion or closure. It is not uncommon to observe a child finishing a puzzle before moving on, or filling in a blank before leaving a task. This sense of completion can often become a compulsion that may interfere with daily functioning or transitions. Rather than focusing on the negative association, educators are now using it as a means to elicit verbal and written responses. For example, if a child is disturbed about an experience at school and is unable to verbalize the sequence of the interaction, a parent may use a closure technique to glean information. Instead of asking, "Who hit you?" or "Where did this happen?", you may say something like, "Today on the playground you got _____. When you were hit, Susie said _____." As you piece the incident together, you can gradually add more specifics to the story line and understand from your child's perspective what happened.

- *Simultaneous Processing*—Rather than learning one step at a time, children with fragile X syndrome tend to learn best by taking in a whole image. For example when learning to read, most children learn letters, then sounds, then words, then phrases, and so forth in a sequential manner. Math is also usually taught sequentially with one numerical operation building upon another. By contrast, simultaneous processing uses intuition to organize and

recall information. Children with fragile X syndrome learn facts or concepts by taking in multiple stimuli because that offers them more information—more building blocks—for forming an image or idea or for solving a problem. For example, a child with fragile X syndrome is more likely to correctly identify a missing part from a whole image than he is to identify a whole image from the individual parts. As you can imagine, this requires a different teaching approach.

- **Associative Learning**—As a result of their simultaneous learning style, it is easier for children with fragile X syndrome to recall information if it is related to or associated with a bigger whole. For example, your child may learn the whole ABC song before he is able to distinguish the different letters. Because individuals with fragile X syndrome often have attention deficit and hyperactivity, information that is presented in isolation without association is often distorted or forgotten. That is why it is important to weave high interest materials into your child's school programming. In order to develop high interest materials, you can use an interest inventory (See Table 2). This inventory, completed by parents, teachers, and caretakers, provides educators with a variety of ideas from which to create teaching materials. For example, one student interested in television weather maps used the maps to learn geographical locations, states, and capitals.

- **Direct Questioning**—It is not uncommon for children with fragile X syndrome to become stymied by a direct question like "What was your favorite part of the story?" A direct question in isolation may force a response without the benefit of contextual information. The same question asked in a more relaxed format will result in spontaneous

■ TABLE 2.   INTEREST INVENTORY

Date: _____

Name: _____

Favorite People
1. _____
2. _____
3. _____
4. _____
5. _____

Favorite TV Shows
1. _____
2. _____
3. _____
4. _____
5. _____

Favorite Videos
1. _____
2. _____
3. _____
4. _____
5. _____

Favorite Subject Areas
1. _____
2. _____
3. _____
4. _____
5. _____

Favorite Restaurants/Food
1. _____
2. _____
3. _____
4. _____
5. _____

Favorite Sports/Sports Teams
1. _____
2. _____
3. _____
4. _____
5. _____

Favorite Activities
(even those that are perservative and seem non-productive)
1. _____
2. _____
3. _____
4. _____
5. _____

recall. "When Bob came up to Cheryl and scared her, she
_____." School performance may differ considerably
from that at home due to performance anxiety.

- **Long-Term Memory**—Generally, children with fragile X
  syndrome have good long-term memory skills. Simultaneous processing contributes to good long-term memory
  through repeated exposure. In addition, long-term
  memory can be triggered by an association. For example,
  showing your child a map may conjure up questions
  about a relative living in another state, or seeing an old
  friend may prompt dialogue about an experience that
  happened several years earlier with that friend.

Classroom Environment. Understanding how children with
fragile X syndrome process information, and matching educational methods to that style, are essential to meeting the needs of the student with
fragile X syndrome. However, even with sound educational methodol-
ogy in place, environmental conditions can compete with learning if
they are not considered. Children with fragile X syndrome are affected
by their environment a great deal. This in turn affects how (and sometimes whether) they learn. For example, many children with fragile X
syndrome experience extreme anxiety whenever they confront change.
If the task is new and unfamiliar, your child may become anxious and
attempt to avoid it. If the physical environment of the classroom changes,
it too may interfere with his ability to work. A substitute or new teacher
may provoke anxiety and in turn disrupt learning.

As discussed in other chapters, arousal of the sensory system can
be caused by environmental conditions. The level of noise, lighting,
and tactile input can interfere significantly with learning. Interaction
between the teacher and the learner can also cause anxiety and heighten
arousal. Indirect teaching strategies that utilize another student as a co-
instructor may yield better results in getting children with fragile X
syndrome to respond.

The classroom is the key environment for most learners. If that
environment is controlled to avoid arousal and distraction and to encourage simultaneous processing, children with fragile X syndrome will
have the best opportunity for learning. The following adaptations are
recommended to maximize the learning and classroom performance of
children with fragile X syndrome.

- **Class Size.** Large groups of students usually generate a high noise level. This can cause distraction and lack of focus, ultimately resulting in reduced learning for your child. If your child is using his energy to control his arousal level, he will most likely miss instruction. Consequently, like so many children, small classes are preferred. Larger classes may be more suitable for physical education, music, and art. Small classes may not always (or ever) be available. In this case, it may be necessary to follow a plan to desensitize your child to large group activities by gradually increasing the number of students, noise level, and size of the room.
- **Noise.** One of the biggest issues for children with fragile X syndrome is noise (auditory stimuli). It is not uncommon for them to engage in hand flapping, rocking, and covering their ears as the noise level increases. Every attempt to eliminate extraneous noise should be made, especially when children are young and lack the experience to cope with noise. Intercoms, telephones, loud bells, fire alarms, and the general level of the classroom noise should be decreased whenever possible. Just having an awareness of this issue may provide the incentive for teachers to adjust background noise or to reduce other auditory distractions.
- **Lighting.** The use of fluorescent lighting may cause difficulty and contribute to hyperarousal. The flickering of incandescent lighting can also become distracting to the point of interfering with the ability to do any work. Natural lighting whenever possible seems to quiet the sensory system and decrease the arousal levels in children with fragile X syndrome
- **Routine and Schedule.** The predictability of your child's schedule is critical to decrease anxiety. Sudden changes without warning can be catastrophic because the anticipation of the change may itself create more anxiety. Pictorial schedules have been used effectively to create predictability and consistency for children with fragile X syndrome. As the schedule changes, so do the pictures, because they serve to cue your child to an upcoming

change. The reassurance of knowing the full layout of the day ahead of time can reduce anxiety. At home, it is a good idea to explain the day's schedule of activities and to answer scheduling questions as they arise. This creates trust in your child and reduces his anxiety.

■ *Visual Cluttering.* Like noise, too much visual stimulation in a classroom may be distracting. Many teachers choose to reduce extraneous visual cluttering on walls, worksheets, and visual aids. As your child becomes more relaxed and adapts to the classroom, additional visual stimuli may be introduced. Sometimes a special corner or "office area" can be made available where there is less visual clutter.

Following are some examples of the accommodations that help children with fragile X syndrome learn:

■ *Instructional Accommodations:*

  * Provide small group instruction whenever teaching a new skill
  * Offer one-to-one assistance as needed for academic tasks
  * Schedule regularly occurring opportunities for movement throughout the day
  * Keep noise level to a minimum
  * Use a personal picture schedule
  * Require fewer writing tasks—use alternatives such as a computer and a tape recorder
  * Offer choices whenever possible (but the child is required to choose one)
  * Provide leadership opportunities, along with opportunities to assist others
  * Wait longer for verbal responses
  * Modify reading material to appropriate grade level
  * Use sign language or visual picture cues to teach new skill
  * Offer a school job with coaching
  * Print daily schedule on the board and review at the beginning of every day
  * Modify worksheets to limit the amount of visual distractions

- *Classroom Accessibility:*
    - * Place child's seat at either the front of the class or the back of the class, but never in the middle of the class
    - * Move desks only when the child is present
- *Facility Accessibility:*
    - * Provide daily tours of the school during the first week or until the child demonstrates knowledge of location of classes
- *Supplies and Equipment Modifications:*
    - * Use calculator, computer, tape recorder, video camera, telephone, microwave
- *Extracurricular Programs:*
    - * Encourage parents to pursue options for their child, such as swimming, cycling, or basketball
    - * Include the child in after school programs, sports (as a team manager)
- *Standards Based Education:*
    - * Exempt the child or take a modified test
- *Communication:*
    - * Use a notebook to communicate on a daily basis.

Teaching Girls

As mentioned in Chapter 1, girls with fragile X are generally affected to a lesser extent than are boys. However, many girls with fragile X syndrome do have both learning disabilities and difficulties with social interactions. It is just that girls often function so "normally" that early identification is unusual. Table 3 lists characteristics that are often seen in girls with fragile X syndrome. It is important to note that learning disabilities are also seen in many girls who are carriers of the fragile X gene.

Even though much has been written about girls with fragile X syndrome, there is very little written about teaching girls. Girls are often recognized for their creative writing ability and enjoy written language and English classes. However, they also have difficulty in areas of math, auditory memory, and visual organization. Table 4 lists those areas of concern and provides strategies that have proven successful.

■ TABLE 3.   SYMPTOM CHECKLIST: GIRLS

Name: _____

DOB: _____   Age: _____

Full mutation   **Premutation**
# of CGG repeats _____   Year DNA Tested _____
Current medications _____   Dosages: _____
_____   _____

	mild	moderate	severe
1. Aggressive/behavioral outbursts			
2. Anxious			
3. Cognitive delays			
4. Closes eyes while talking			
5. Clumsiness, poor motor planning			
6. Diagnosed bi-polar disorder			
7. Hyperactivity			
8. Impulsive			
9. Interpersonal problems			
10. Lack of initiation			
11. Language delays (odd communication patterns)			
12. Math difficulties			
13. Mood instability			
14. Outgoing, gregarious			
15. Panic attacks			
16. Premature puberty			
17. Sensitivity			
18. Shy			
19. Social anxiety			
20. Visual/spatial difficulties (gets lost, directions difficult)			

Please add any additional symptoms not included above: _____

▪▪ TABLE 4. SUGGESTED STRATEGIES: GIRLS

Suggested Strategies for Math

- Use concrete manipulative materials to teach concepts and mathematical operations.
- Use visual cues whenever possible to reinforce mathematical operations.
- Allow additional time to reduce the possibility of provoking performance anxiety.
- Minimize auditory distractions during time periods when concentration is required (computation, problem solving).
- Use diagrams, illustrations, and visual patterns whenever teaching a new concept.
- Use repetition and patterning whenever rote memory tasks are required.

Suggested Strategies for Auditory Memory

- Give specific instructions in a slow, simple, and concrete manner.
- Place the student close to the instructor to ensure attention and concentration.
- Structure the environment to eliminate auditory distractions— use earphones, carrels, or seating arrangements.
- Vary presentation to include frequent breaks to avoid attention difficulties and lack of concentration.

Suggested Strategies for Visual Organization

- Limit amount to be copied from printed or written materials.
- Simplify visually presented materials to eliminate a cluttered or excessively stimulating format.
- Provide visual cues—such as color coding, numbering, and arrows—to organize written tasks.
- Give specific concrete cues when giving oral directions that require an organized format.
- Give additional time for written assignments, when needed.

When it comes to social interaction, girls can be well-behaved and cooperative at school, but unhappy and insecure at home. Parents will often find themselves frustrated by the lack of assertion their daughter demonstrates at school while exhibiting a controlling nature at home. Parents hear constant complaints about school, while teachers hear few. Girls with fragile X syndrome can often benefit from social learning groups at school and in private therapy. Social skills can be taught in much the same way as academic skills. It is important to advocate for appropriate support within the school setting. Be sure to speak with your daughter's teacher about academic and social issues. Question her social functioning and ask if she is participating in class and interacting with her peers. You may want to request assistance from a school social worker or counselor in providing emotional support. Whatever the need, be aware that support now may reduce the need for it later.

Placement for Least Restrictive Environment— Special Education Settings

IDEA endorses a free and appropriate education (FAPE) and requires that students with disabilities be educated in the least restrictive environment (LRE). Because children with fragile X syndrome have unique needs that are addressed individually in their IEPs, LRE will look different from child to child. At school, LRE can be viewed as a continuum: from full inclusion in the regular education classroom to complete segregation in a self-contained classroom or building; from continual contact with peers who do not have disabilities to none. Programs for infants and toddlers also have a range of inclusiveness that are different from school programs. Exactly how your child will be included in school or preschool should be spelled out clearly in his IFSP or IEP. This section explains options for inclusion of children with fragile X syndrome from early intervention through school age.

LRE During Early Intervention. Under new provisions of IDEA, providing supports and services in a child's natural environment is an important goal. Natural environment means those places where other children their age who don't have disabilities would be. Natural environments for children in this age range may include the home, daycare, parks, swimming lessons, a dance class, or a playgroup. While some families may opt for services in natural environments, some may not out of concern that their child's needs can best be met in an individual therapy session at a medical facility.

LRE During Preschool. Preschoolers with fragile X syndrome can be served well in inclusive public or private preschool programs. This involves including them with their peers. Often related services such as speech and occupational therapies can be provided right in the classroom. On occasion your school district may opt to fund the tuition charges for private programs instead of creating their own preschool program. There are times, however, when a child with fragile X syndrome may require instruction in a self-contained classroom with appropriate related services such as speech therapy and occupational therapy. It is important that you investigate all your options and find one that best suits your child's needs. Your child's IEP should reflect this choice.

LRE During School Age. Figure out the types of programs and services your district offers and lobby to get what your child needs. Your options may include the following:

- *Full inclusion in the regular education classroom—* Your child would attend class or classes like any other child. He would probably have at least the part-time assistance of a paraprofessional or aide if he needed help in class or if the classroom teacher needed help adapting or modifying the curriculum for your child. The paraprofessional would function under the guidance of a special education teacher. The amount of paraprofessional time your child receives should be specified in his IEP. In this type of placement, your child's teacher would ideally be the regular classroom teacher who would view your child as his or her student, like all the other children in the class.

- *Most of the school day included in the regular education classroom, with some time spent in a special education classroom—*Your child would still spend most of his time in the regular education classroom, probably with occasional support from a paraprofessional, but would also spend part of his day pulled-out in a special education classroom. In this classroom, he would have direct one-on-one or small-group instruction. The instruction would be provided by the special education teacher or by a paraprofessional. For example, your child may be pulled out for direct instruction of reading or math.

- *Time evenly split between the regular education classroom and the special education classroom—* Same as above, except less time in the regular education classroom and more in the special education classroom.
- *Most of school day spent in the special education classroom, with some time spent in the regular education classroom—*Your child might be included for art, music, library, and physical education, or some combination thereof.
- *Full time in a self-contained classroom—*This placement could either be in your neighborhood school or it could be in a completely separate building, also known as a center-based program. Your child would have little to no contact with children who do not have disabilities, particularly if your child is in a separate building. Otherwise recess may be the only contact your child has with typical children. There would probably also be paraprofessional support in this type of classroom too.

The advantages and disadvantages of inclusion have been debated for years. IDEA answers that debate with its policy that is clearly in favor of inclusion. The advantages of inclusion for children with fragile X syndrome are far reaching. Because children with fragile X syndrome tend to model other children's behavior, typically developing children provide good role models. Your child will learn skills needed to live in the "real" world. He will learn that there are children who can do things that he can't do. He will form relationships with children who live in your neighborhood and community. Other children will learn to value diversity.

There can also be disadvantages to inclusion. Learning academics may suffer because there may not be the time or ability to adequately modify the material for your child. Your child may have trouble dealing with not being able to do what other children can do. Regular education classrooms generally have larger class sizes and sensory stimulation may be more of an issue.

Choosing the Location of Services for Your Child

When it comes to placement in the least restrictive environment, options may vary from district to district, and from state to state. Always keep in mind, however, that it is the district's responsibility to provide a free and appropriate education and not your responsibility to uproot your family to find the right school. Also remember the option of a due process hearing that may force your district to develop a program within your home district.

Before you make a decision about school placement, look at your child's educational needs and determine what setting or settings will best meet your child's unique needs. Look at the different ways inclusion is accomplished as well as the related services. The location of the school may be another factor to consider. This is an area in which you will have to research and advocate. Your child may benefit from different types of settings at different stages of his development.

As you visit different schools remember that the teaching staff may not be available to talk to you during your visits. You may need to schedule time outside the regular school hours. Even though the staff may seem particularly competent, teacher turnover rates vary and the staff you interview may not remain intact for the following school years. Look at the entire school and find out as much as you can about all grade levels, the support staff, and the principal.

When you walk into a school you will sense a certain comfort level. This may depend on how you are first received by office staff, the building appearance, and your overall first impression.

When you visit a potential classroom, consider the class size and student-teacher ratio. Look at the size and layout of the classroom. Does it seem organized or cluttered? Note the teacher's style and method of interacting with the children. Often children with fragile X syndrome respond best to calm voices, predictable schedules, and organized classrooms.

Pay particular attention to the visual cues, schedules, and nonverbal information. Is there a daily routine and is it posted somewhere? Does the teacher augment her verbal instruction with pictures or other visual supports?

Notice the teaching style. Does the teacher vary instruction and are there opportunities for experiential learning? Are there other children with disabilities in the classroom? How are they treated by the teacher and children?

If you witness any correction by the teacher following a behavioral episode, how is it handled? Do you notice discomfort or frustration in the teaching staff?

Visit the entire school and note the opportunity for support from a speech and language pathologist or an occupational therapist. Are there therapy rooms available and within close proximity of the classroom?

Professionals

There will most likely be a variety of professionals who evaluate and work with your child at school. Each of the professionals, for the most part, has an area of expertise. So it takes a team of people who not only evaluate but also work with and address your child's various needs. In addition, the professionals usually work closely together to come up with ideas and strategies to help your child learn.

Special Education Teacher. The special education teacher is trained in the acquisition of academic (and pre-academic) skills and in assessing special education needs. When evaluating your child he or she will look at how well your child understands basic concepts such as colors and shapes, letters and words, numbers and counting, patterns and sorting, prepositional terms (up, down, behind, between, over, under), relational terms (longer, bigger, longest, biggest), and his overall readiness to learn.

The special education teacher will use the results of the testing to provide input into all aspects of the IEP. However, the same teacher may not be directly involved with your child in the classroom.

When teaching your child, the special education teacher is able to evaluate and understand your child's unique learning style and use his strengths to improve his learning. He or she is also trained in methods to accommodate your child's learning style. Often the special education teacher acts as a consultant to other IEP staff members and the regular education teacher by coordinating services and classroom adaptations. It is important that the special education teacher understands how your child learns so that he or she can advocate for proper curricular adaptations. In addition, it may be necessary for her to work with your child directly or in a small group for part of the day. Her role is to facilitate learning whether it is in an individualized, self-contained program or with typically developing peers in the regular education classroom.

Regular Education Teacher. A regular education teacher does not formally evaluate your child. However, he or she is a member of the IEP team and attends the meeting at which the IEP is developed. He or she usually reports on your child's abilities and behaviors that have been observed in the classroom. The IEP meeting is also when the regular education teacher may ask for additional ideas on teaching or support in working with your child. The support may take the form of a paraprofessional assisting your child or modified materials that can be used in the classroom. It is important that the regular education teacher see your child as a member of his or her class and not as a guest. Ensuring he or she has the support to work with your child is the basis to making inclusion successful. As mentioned above, the special education teacher usually takes the lead in providing the necessary supports for the regular education teacher.

Speech and Language Pathologist (SLP). The speech and language pathologist (SLP) is trained in both communication and speech development. Delayed language development is often the keystone for early diagnosis of children with fragile X syndrome. The speech and language pathologist may be one of the first professionals you consult.

SLPs are not only trained in the assessment of how your child speaks, but are also able to address how well your child's language is developing. Even though your child may not speak out loud or make other sounds, he may have developed an internal language system. He may use gestures to communicate basic needs by pointing to what he wants. He may have learned to get your attention by crying, whining, or screaming. He may laugh or smile or clap his hands to indicate pleasure. He may easily communicate choices by pushing away a food he does not enjoy or grabbing for what he wants.

A SLP can use a number of different tests to evaluate speech and language development. He or she may use standardized and non-standardized measures depending on your child's cognitive ability and behavior. Sometimes for children with fragile X syndrome, it is important to evaluate the function of language and to what extent language is used to communicate. A SLP may use a language sample to evaluate your child's spontaneous language. A language sample is simply a verbatim transcript of what your child says. The SLP writes down the words uttered by your child and then analyzes how your child uses the language. In addition, the SLP can identify language concerns, such as perseveration and the relationship it may have with anxiety, because sometimes the intelligibility and appropriateness of speech is affected by situational discomfort.

How speech and language therapy is provided to your child is determined by his needs, but make sure the services take your child's unique learning style into account. For example, engaging your child in a side dialogue in the regular class may be a better approach than direct instruction or individualized drill. Often the intensity of direct therapy or instruction can elevate anxiety and reduce the effectiveness of the intervention.

Sometimes a social language group will be recommended. In these groups, youngsters provide indirect interaction, thereby reducing the threat to children with fragile X syndrome. The SLP can use the language of other children in the group to stimulate spontaneous language. The instruction revolves around appropriate social language such as greetings, asking for help, and responding appropriately to others.

If your child does not develop expressive language, the SLP and special educator may recommend an alternative or augmentative form of communication. Because communication is essential for learning, socialization, and the development of appropriate behavior, a significant emphasis should be placed on communication skills. There are a number of visual and electronic devices available to augment speech. These can help give non-verbal children a voice and a way to communicate with their world. The SLP should be able to guide you toward the best augmentative communication system for your child.

Occupational Therapist (OT). A person who specializes in the knowledge of fine motor skills is called an occupational therapist. The name is confusing because some OTs consult with older patients about ways their work performance may be enhanced. Others work with rehabilitating adults who have been physically injured. An OT who works with children or within a school system, however, provides a much different service. Because children with fragile X syndrome often demonstrate difficulty with motor planning or coordinating fine motor responses, an OT will often be consulted.

An OT will evaluate your child in the following areas:

- *Muscle tone*—particularly how it affects movement of the hands and arms
- *Quality of hand movements and skills*—grasping, holding, stacking, writing
- *Eye-hand coordination*—throwing and catching
- *Skills needed for daily functioning*—eating, toothbrushing, dressing
- *Development of spatial abilities*—skill at putting together puzzles

- *Sensory modulation and integration*—ability to tolerate certain fabrics, textures
- *Play skills*—turn taking, imitation, parallel play

Like other professionals who evaluate your child, the OT will use a variety of tests. In addition, he or she will observe your child and should, of course, gather information about your child from you. It is critical to the fine motor assessment to share information about what you see your child doing at home.

When providing occupational therapy, the OT will work with your child on a wide variety of skills. The focus of his or her work will be on developing your child's fine motor skills. Activities that your child may participate in include self-help skills such as buttoning, zipping, tying shoes, eating, drinking, brushing teeth, and washing his face. To improve his fine motor skills, the OT may teach your child to write and draw with a variety

of materials such as shaving cream, crayons, markers, paint, chalk, pencils, and pens, and he or she may do this in a variety of positions: sitting, standing, on the floor, and laying down. The OT will also work with your child using play dough, clay, glue, and scissors. Working with these different materials helps reduce tactile defensiveness. Some OTs also use a brushing program to reduce tactile defensiveness. The OT may also help your child improve motor planning skills by helping him carry out a sequence of movements such as climbing a ladder and getting on a tricycle or bicycle. And to help your child's eye-hand coordination, the OT may have your child bounce on a large ball, and catch and throw a variety of materials such as a ball, balloon, Velcro balls, or a Frisbee. Like all education and therapy services, OT services should be provided in the way that best suits your child's learning style.

Because children with fragile X syndrome often experience sensory problems, using an OT who has training in sensory integration (SI) may be necessary. Sensory integration has been studied by OTs for many years, and can be very helpful in assessing your child's sensory abilities.

Sometimes OT and SLP therapists work together to stimulate spontaneous verbal responses. Experience has taught that when a child with fragile X syndrome is moving or being stimulated using a variety of sensory systems, the child is able to verbalize with better flow and rhythm.

Physical Therapist (PT). Physical therapists are trained in evaluating and treating posture and body movement. They have expertise in how the large muscles (such as the legs and torso) move together and how they stabilize the body for fine motor activities. When a PT evaluates your child, he or she will look at:

- Quantity and quality of movement
- Large muscle strength and tone
- Balance
- Joint flexibility
- Body stability

A PT will also use a variety of tests when evaluating your child. She will assess all of the areas listed above through the use of standardized tests, observation, and input from you.

In therapy, physical therapists work on the development of gross motor skills. Physical therapy is often needed for children with fragile X syndrome because of hypotonia (discussed in Chapter 4). Hypotonia must be addressed because tone in the torso area is needed for the development of most gross motor skills. Gross motor skills include crawling, sitting, walking, climbing stairs, and riding a bike. A PT may include some of the following activities when working with your child: upper body exercises, practice in balance activities, and practicing the skills listed above.

Social Worker. A social worker is trained to help people and families function well together. He or she may provide counseling, service coordination, or case management services, and will consult with you about your family life. The social worker seeks to understand how, as a family, you are getting along. They are particularly useful when your child receives early intervention or when your family is first adjusting to the diagnosis of fragile X syndrome. The social worker may ask about:

- *Financial resources*—What is the impact of your child with fragile X syndrome on your family finances?
- *Emotional resources*—Are there family and friends to call on when you need to talk? Is there respite available?

- **Sibling relationships**—How are things at home between your child with fragile X syndrome and his siblings?
- **School relationships**—How is the communication between you and the school, and how is your child doing with other children in the school?

Some of the questions may be very personal. While your discussions are confidential, only discuss the information you are comfortable sharing.

A social worker may work with your child in a small group setting to improve his social skills. The children may take turns asking and answering questions. They may have opportunities to talk about their feelings around different situations. In groups each person can talk about ways to deal with negative feelings. What do you do when someone says something to you that is not nice? What can you do if things don't go the way you planned them? What if you make a mistake? And on the opposite side they may talk about things they should say or do if they hurt someone else's feelings. Role-playing can be a helpful technique during group sessions. These social skill groups may be beneficial at different times in your child's life.

Psychologist. Psychologists are trained in understanding human behavior. They are most often involved in testing the cognitive ability of children during the evaluation process. In addition, a test of how your child adapts to and functions in different situations, called an adaptive behavior checklist, may be used to augment the cognitive assessment.

As explained in Chapter 7, standardized IQ tests do not always accurately measure the cognitive ability of children with fragile X syndrome. As a result, the psychologist may choose not to rely exclusively on standardized tests, and instead utilize a non-standardized assessment. This type of assessment often includes an observation of your child's behavior. The psychologist may use this information to develop learning strategies for school or define the function of the observed behavior so that your child's behavior can be modified, if needed. The psychologist will share the results of your child's cognitive testing at the IEP meeting.

Even though your child's cognitive assessment (or IQ) is important, there are other aspects the psychologist should observe during the evaluation that are equally important. For example, it is essential to understand cognitive strengths and weaknesses in order to plan for effective educational programming. So, while the psychologist is evaluating your child, he or she will be checking off correct and incorrect responses and observing how your child processes the information given.

Medical Professionals. A variety of medical professionals may also be involved in your child's assessment, during both the initial and the triennial evaluations. Their role is to identify issues that are more medical in nature and that could be affecting development.

Registered Nurse. A registered nurse is the medical professional who usually takes part in evaluations. During the initial evaluation she will ask about your child's medical history, including birth history, childhood illness and sickness, the age at which developmental milestones were met, and possibly your family pedigree. Also during the initial evaluation and during subsequent evaluations she will inquire into your child's current health status. She will be interested in:

- Developmental and social history
- Vision and glasses
- Eating, allergies, weight gain, and growth
- Ear infections and hearing
- Recent or recurrent illness
- Medical checkups
- Medications your child receives—types, quantities, and side effects
- Any other concerns you may have

Your child's health can have a tremendous impact on how well your child does in school. It is important to address medical issues as quickly and completely as you can.

Other medical professionals your child may see include a pediatrician, developmental pediatrician, psychiatrist, neurologist, geneticist, ophthalmologist, or audiologist. Generally, these professionals will only be seen if referred by one of the specialists listed above. They are not usually members of the IEP team.

Paraprofessionals. Also known as a para-educator or an aide, these valuable people are not involved in the evaluation of your child. They do, however, help in the education of your child in many ways. They may work directly with your child in the classroom or operate as an assistant to the regular or special education teacher. When they work with your child, they may utilize material that has been modified for them by the teacher or use material they modified themselves.

Some children with fragile X syndrome who have higher needs may require the services of a one-on-one paraprofessional. Most likely your child will need assistance off and on throughout the day, depending on the activity. It is important to have a systematic procedure in place to have the paraprofessionals "move in and move out" of your child's activity. A parapro is there to assist, not "do." It is important that your child, and the other teachers and therapists in school, not learn to rely too heavily on this person.

Working with Education Professionals

Education, especially special education, is a team effort. You, as your child's parent, are an important member of that team. So, it is important to develop working relationships with the other people on the team. Development of these relationships takes time and energy. While the IEP meeting is not the place to develop relationships, a positive relationship with the staff during the school year can only enhance your child's educational development.

You may want to focus your energies on your relationship with your child's special education teacher because she or he will probably have the most interaction with your child. A good way to start is by offering literature on fragile X syndrome. The experiential background of the teacher will dictate the type of information you share. A very experienced teacher who has knowledge of fragile X syndrome may be more interested in teaching strategies and behavioral intervention. A new teacher who has had less experience will want to understand the basic characteristics and learning styles.

When developing a relationship with educational staff remember that communication is important in every relationship. The exchange of a notebook on a daily basis is a good communication tool. You can write down what is happening at home and the school personnel can write what they do at school. The notebook can be used to get questions answered about certain classes or activities that occur at school. The notebook can also be used to relay a concern; however, depending on the nature of the issue, you may want to request the teacher contact you. Use the notebook to offer suggestions: "Something that works really well at home ...." Ask the teacher for ideas to try at home, like getting homework done and using reward systems.

When you talk to the teacher or other school personnel, be aware of your communication style. Using "I" statements are usually more effective than "you" statements. Try to be an active listener and be open to their thoughts and ideas. Be aware of how you speak. Information delivered unemotionally is viewed differently than information delivered with frustration or tears. Also, starting off the school year with regularly scheduled monthly meetings is a good way to keep communication open and address issues before they become problems.

As in every relationship, there will be disagreements. Learn how to work through them; listen to the teacher, communicate your thoughts, and remember that there will be compromises for both of you. Think about the issues that are important to you and focus on those.

Finally, develop a relationship with the principal of the school. This is one person rarely mentioned as a team member, but he or she is required to be at IEP meetings. Principals have the ability to access district resources and bring to the team the bigger picture. Principals set the tone for the entire school and influence the attitude of the staff.

Working with education professionals will be both challenging and rewarding. The common goal should be to create the best education possible for your child. The spirit of IDEA provides the impetus to accomplish that goal. Mutual respect and appreciation will carry you through times of disagreement and provide the foundation on which you build new academic ventures.

Private Therapy

In addition to the services written in your child's IEP, another option you may want to consider is to have your child see a private therapist. A private therapist is not affiliated with the school district; he or she may be associated with a hospital or he or she may have his or her own practice. Therapies can include speech-language, physical, occupational, and social. You may take your child to the therapist's office or he or she may come to your home. He or she might even arrange to meet you in a public place such as a swimming pool or a fast food restaurant with a play area.

Other aspects about private therapy to consider include:

- You get to visit with the therapist every time your child is seen, and you can sit in on sessions with your child. This will help you learn how to carry over activities at home.
- Private therapy is usually more individualized. The therapist is focused on your child exclusively. You may also opt for group therapy in a private setting. This

allows your child to benefit from an individualized approach within a group delivery system.

- When you see a private therapist you pick the therapist. In school, therapists can change from year to year, requiring them to get to know your child anew each year. Consistency for children with fragile X syndrome brings a lot of benefits.

The other obvious side of private therapy is you pay for it. Private therapy can be very expensive, sometimes in the range of $100 per hour. Private therapy is funded under some insurance. Most private therapists will bill your insurance, but in some cases you will have to submit the claims. Insurance can be a huge hassle. Often, frequent reports from the therapists are required, usually every three to six months. And with many insurance companies, there is a limit to how much can be spent on therapy. For example, an insurance company may have a $2000 limit on physical therapy, and that may not even cover a year of therapy! If you want your child to have private therapy and you are not able to afford it there are sometimes grants available from local community organizations created to help families handle some of the issues around having a child with a disability. Your local office of The Arc or ACL may be able to provide you with information.

If private therapy seems to be an important alternative or is used in addition to the school program, it will be necessary to weigh the benefits against the time and effort it takes to get to the sessions. Time away from the home and other family members can create additional stress. Some families opt for private therapy when their child is young and then let the school district take over when he gets into school. Others start when their child is young and continue until he is well into his school years. Others are comfortable just using the school therapists. It is this choice that empowers you to do what you think is best for your child and your family.

:: Educational Issues for Older Children

Teaching Strategies

As your child enters middle school, other challenges will emerge. Typically developing peers at this age are more conscious of their appearance and social status; while conforming to a social norm, they become less tolerant of individual differences. Adolescents need this time to claim their own identity and self-image. As this process transpires, adolescents spend less time maintaining relationships established in the elementary grades and spend more time figuring out who they are by trying out new friends. Your middle school child with fragile X syndrome will encounter these characteristics in his classmates.

Fortunately for individuals with fragile X syndrome, their good sense of humor becomes a vehicle through which they can build friendships and acceptance. Unlike other children with disabilities, they are able to read non-verbal cues and are able to borrow language phrases from one experience for use in another social setting. For example, after overhearing peers at a football game cheer on the long pass with "Go for the Hail Mary pass" Timmy used the phrase appropriately when watching a game on television.

Academic and cognitive differences become more evident at this age. Table 5 on the next page offers strategies to use when teaching middle school children with fragile X syndrome.

Transition Plan

By the time children with fragile X syndrome reach the age of 14, school districts are required to begin to make plans for their transition to post-secondary education or employment. For children with high academic ability, the plan will support a traditional path for technical school or college preparation.

For children who require vocational training, their transition plan must emphasize community access, independent living skills, employment skills, and vocational placement. In preparing a vocational plan, you and your child may be interviewed to determine future goals related to independent living, recreational interests, and work preferences. Vocational testing can be used to determine the most appropriate work

:: TABLE 5.   TEACHING STRATEGIES

Social Acceptance	Strategies
Feeling rejected by typical peers	Develop more opportunities for one-to-one interaction
Unable to adequately relate socially	Utilize extended family members or older friends to encourage and support social engagement
Behavioral outbursts become more socially debilitating	Discourage participation in anxiety-provoking activities, large groups, gymnasiums, close proximity to other people

Language Differences	Strategies
Verbal interaction is difficult	Speech and language, social group therapy
Confused by verbal and social nuances	Utilize visual cues (photographs, videotapes or drawings) whenever possible to illustrate social nuances
Difficulty using verbal skills to express feelings	Process feelings later after negative feelings have subsided
Use third person "he" to talk through an incident.	This makes the discussion less threatening and indirect

Obsessive/Compulsive Tendencies	Strategies
Perseverative language about a perceived insult or emotional injury	Encourage conversation about the incident
Obsessional thinking of perceived emotional injury	Role play about how a similar incident could be handled the next time; example, "You could ask Jason to follow you and watch you."
Oversensitivity to an altercation or disagreement	Referral to a physician to assess efficacy of medication

environment for your child (sheltered, enclave, supported, competitive). Your child may be assessed by a vocational counselor or a high school teacher. A variety of job placements will be surveyed and tried out in order to determine the most viable and successful placement. Sometimes schools provide work-study experiences within the school community in order to teach entry-level employment skills before community work sites are used. For example, your child may get a training job working in the school cafeteria.

It is also important to include other community agencies in formulating a transition plan in order to better understand what is available in your community and to assist you in the transition from a school system into a community.

Vocational Training

Vocational training for people with fragile X syndrome is in its infancy. As educators gain knowledge about the best educational and behavioral strategies for children with fragile X syndrome, this information will be used to  design more effective vocational training programs. As children with fragile X syndrome mature, the school program may include more emphasis on teaching your child how to function in an adult environment. This would be one of the first steps in vocational training.

You will need to familiarize yourself with the community agencies responsible for adult services early. Your child may be wait-listed for adult services even at a young age. It is never too soon to pursue your options because of the limited availability. Private funding is available on a limited basis, but will vary in each community.

Some people with fragile X syndrome prefer job tasks that are outside and flexible, and which avoid working in close proximity to co-workers. Others prefer a social environment that includes other people.

The following is a general list of suggested work conditions to consider in planning your child's work experience:

- Use primarily gross motor skills
- Avoid confinement
- Provide opportunities to move about
- Avoid close proximity of other workers
- Avoid fine motor tasks and sequential ordering tasks
- Position work stations with back to wall and view of exit
- Use workgroup to help stay on task and to engage and sustain interest
- Provide a social component
- Provide lots of variety
- Provide structured breaks and predictable schedule

■■ Behavior

Behavioral Characteristics

Children with fragile X syndrome sometimes have behavior problems that can interfere with learning. You and your child's teachers and therapists should be aware of these behaviors and develop appropriate behavior management strategies. Table 6 is a compilation of behaviors often seen in children with fragile X syndrome.

Not all children have all the behaviors listed. As a matter of fact, as children pass through certain developmental levels, specific behaviors will emerge while others will disappear. As children with fragile X syndrome mature into adults, research shows that behavioral difficulties subside, resulting in decreased behavioral excesses, including aggression. Understanding the development of your child's behavior is critical to formulating a behavior management plan to improve those behaviors.

Behavior Management Plans

Because children with fragile X syndrome can have behavior that interferes with learning, it is important to develop and include a behavior management plan in their IEPs. Under IDEA, children cannot be denied an appropriate public education because they have behavior problems. This forces educators to carefully address behavior by understanding the function of it before developing an intervention.

Most behaviors, even disruptive behaviors, persist only if serving a purpose. For example, young children learn that when they cry, they get attention either by being fed, changed, or played with. That behavior persists as long as it gets the desired attention. When children learn to communicate their needs by other methods—such as speaking—the disruptive behavior usually stops. From their own experiences over a long period of time, children learn that their behavior leads to something,

∷ TABLE 6. COMMON BEHAVIORS IN CHILDREN WITH FRAGILE X SYNDROME	
Hyperactivity (ADHD)	Excessive motion, darting about, rushing, difficulty staying still
Impulsivity	Difficulty waiting until needs can be met; requiring immediate attention; making decisions quickly without forethought
Limited Attention Span and Concentration (ADD)	Difficulty sustaining attention, easily distracted, unable to focus and attend
Difficulty Tolerating Changes in Routine	Easily upset by changes in schedule, routine, people, or expectations
Ritualistic and Repetitive Behavior	Compulsive repetition of hand movements, behavioral rituals such as turning lights off and on, closing doors and drawers, and verbal repetition or perseveration
Social Anxiety or Shyness	Difficulty interacting with others upon request; avoids eye contact, handshakes, or other forms of social interaction
Aggression	Hitting or striking out at others, often directed toward the primary caregiver

called a consequence. Educational researchers and educators have also learned that often a particular behavior results from something that has just happened. For example, a child who begins to flap his hands may have just experienced noises or crowds that overstimulated him. From extensive study of both the causes and function of behavior for children with fragile X syndrome (and other children with disabilities), educators and therapists have learned effective methods to help change negative or disruptive behavior. Two of these methods are described below.

Antecedent-Behavior-Consequence (ABC)

The ABC model for behavior management uses the function of behavior to help children reduce inappropriate behavior. It works by studying each element of a specific behavior to understand what causes the behavior (antecedent), the behavior (behavior), and what happens after the behavior (consequence). For example, one day at school Casey is given a math worksheet to complete (antecedent). He refuses to do any work (behavior). The teacher says he can try again later, and Casey goes off to do his school job that he loves (consequence). Vary the antecedent: As part of his daily scheduled routine, Casey is given a math worksheet to complete that has been modified to his level. The teacher works through an example and explains she is there to help if anyone needs it (antecedent). When Casey is handed the worksheet he just looks at it. The teacher repeats, "Just let me know if you need help." Casey works through the paper, slowly, and finishes (behavior). Casey goes off to do his school job (consequence). Vary the consequence: Casey is given a math worksheet to complete (antecedent). He refuses to do any work (behavior). The teacher says, "When your paper is completed, then you can do your school job" (consequence). Casey sits down and completes his paper so he can do his school job.

Not allowing Casey to go to his school job until his work is completed is considered a natural consequence. Another natural consequence might be that he be denied recess until his work is completed. Although it is important to impose natural consequences it is not always possible. Sometimes a consequence has to be imposed within contrived circumstances.

The ABC model works best when the antecedent is addressed. This often changes the resulting behavior; for example, if the antecedent is eliminated, the behavioral episode usually will not follow. If after observing behavioral episodes over time you determine that your child acts out in the morning following a transition from his classroom to the PE class, you can focus on the transition instead of the behavior. You might want to transition him after or before the others have gone or assign him a special job to carry equipment or a note to the PE teacher before the others leave the room. Carefully isolating the specific cause of behavior allows parents and teachers to "change the rule" so that the behavior ceases to serve a purpose.

In using the ABC model, it is critical to define a behavior in simple terms so that all primary caretakers and educators agree on what constitutes an infraction. Implementation of the plan must be consistent because the more consistent it is, the sooner the behavior will be reduced or even eliminated.

After studying your child's behavior, a plan for modifying his behavior can be developed that both you and your child's teachers can use. The following is an example of a viable behavior management plan. You should always review any plan that teachers want to use. It may be your school district's policy to obtain written parent consent for any behavior program. In addition, a method of data collection is needed to determine how well the plan is working.

Behavior Plan Using the ABC Model

Behavior to Target: Wilson is being aggressive toward other students.
Baseline Data: three to four times per day, most often at 10:00 a.m., 12:30 p.m., & 2:30 p.m.

Antecedent: Behavior most often follows a transition from a gross motor activity (PE, recess) to a quieter activity such as seat work.
Behavior: The aggression observed is hitting a peer or throwing an object, three to four times per day, upon entering a quiet class-room environment.
Consequence: Told to stop, but with minimal effect.

Modify the Antecedent:
1. Wilson will be allowed to transition slowly in a quieter environment. He will help clean up the gym after PE and be allowed to pick up trash on the playground at the end of recess.

2. Wilson will then be allowed to engage in a calming activity such as deep breathing prior to entering the classroom.
3. Wilson will have access to a schedule that he can understand.
4. Wilson's classroom material will be modified before he gets to class.

The Behavior dictates the consequence.

Consequences:
1. Wilson will be rewarded for entering class and sitting without incident. Stickers will be used and over each weekly period Wilson will have the opportunity to choose an extra recess or a short end of day party for the whole class if enough stickers are earned.
2. If Wilson is aggressive, he will take a four-minute time out and then be redirected to the activity.

Maintenance:
The number of stickers gained at the end of each week will be reviewed. Plan will be re-evaluated weekly to determine whether it is working. Wilson will have the opportunity to have input on whether any of the antecedents need to be changed or modified.

Functional Analysis of Behavior

In this model of behavior management, a functional analysis of inappropriate behavior is conducted, and then a behavior plan is implemented. Initially the focus of this model is to reduce or eliminate the environmental conditions that may be affecting the behavior. Only then are efforts made to change the child's behavior.

A. Conduct a Functional Analysis of Behavior
   - A Functional Analysis of Behavior requires a trained staff member to observe a child for a designated period of time in the environment in which the inappropriate behavior occurs. The observer will determine the frequency, intensity, and precursors of the behavior. Precursors are behaviors, language, or an event observed right before the

targeted behavior occurs, and may include hand biting or flapping, verbal perseveration, or an event such as a fire drill. The observer will also survey any environmental conditions that may contribute to the behavior occurring and escalating and how the child may be using the behavior to get a need met even if it is to avoid the activity.

■ Take a baseline of the behavior. The baseline is the number of times that a particular behavior occurs prior to the behavior plan being implemented.

B. Assess environmental factors

■ Look at lighting, noise level and type, seating arrangement, past memory of any bad experiences, fear of not knowing what to expect, unknown changes to environment, large room size, no exit in sight, teacher's speaking style and mannerisms, number of other children in the room, amount of verbal instructions by the teacher.

■ Eliminate or change those factors that are the easiest and most realistic to remove.

C. Does the behavior continue?

■ If no, then behavioral intervention is complete.

■ If yes, then develop a behavior plan.

D. Behavior plan

■ Address the precursors. When the precursors occur, assign him a contrived errand to run to the office or lunchroom. The errand can incorporate a task that includes heavy work or input (carry books to the office, crate to lunchroom staff, push recycle bin to cafeteria). Ensure both the teacher and the child are prepared ahead of time.

■ Provide rewards for appropriate behavior.

E. When the behavior occurs

■ Break the behavioral cycle by utilizing remedies that redirect the child such as picture album, audio tape of favorite commercial, or a sensory integration activity.

■ Use natural consequences whenever possible.

- Discuss the situation with the child later to see if additional changes need to be made with the environment or with regards to expectations.
- Never scold, ostracize, or embarrass the student. Document in the behavior plan that the student has a disability. The student may be exempt from normal school policy related to suspension and expulsion due to his special education eligibility.

Behavior Plan Using a Functional Analysis of Behavior

Greg is in the third grade at Southern Hills Elementary. He refuses to do his math work even when natural consequences are imposed, for example, withholding recess.

Functional Analysis of Behavior:
- Greg was observed three consecutive days during math time. Math occurs right after lunch recess. Math class always began with a worksheet and everyone was expected to sit down and complete the sheet before formal instruction began.
- All three days, Greg was adamant about not doing his work. Two of the days he wadded up his paper and threw it on the floor and said, "This is too hard." One day he put his head down on his desk and refused to move. It appeared he did not like math and did not want to have anything to do with it.
- Observations prior to math class: Lunch recess was the activity prior to math and Greg seemed to come in with an "attitude" every day.
- Environmental conditions: Greg's desk was placed in the front of the class and the door was at the back of the class. There was a lot of noise activity while students were coming in from recess and Greg had to pass through all of that to get to his seat. His teacher assistant was late getting to class to help Greg transition two of the three days. There was no schedule of activities to follow the math class on any of the days. There was a substitute teacher one day.

Consider environmental factors and attempt to manipulate them before employing any behavioral intervention.

- Greg moved his seat to the back of the room away from most of the noise and activity.
- A daily schedule was written on the board and reviewed throughout the day.
- The class was reminded before they went to lunch that math was after lunch recess.
- Greg was given the opportunity to come in early from recess.
- The teacher assistant modified the math sheet prior to Greg seeing it and she was always on time to the classroom.
- Anytime there was going to be a substitute teacher, Greg was told about it the day before or the first thing in the morning.

Most often, the behavioral issue will resolve with proper attention to the antecedent, but if the behavior continues:

Develop a behavior plan:
- Greg was given an opportunity to choose the length and difficulty of his math work.
- When the teacher or the teacher assistant saw that Greg was having a hard time, one of them would ask Greg to carry some books to the office.
- Greg was rewarded for completing his math work with a choice of doing two activities that he enjoyed which were also acceptable to the teacher.

If the behavior persists:
- Greg does not have the opportunity to do any of the reward choice activities.
- Greg has to take the work home for homework.
- Greg is given the opportunity to discuss why he did not complete his work at school.

Effective behavior management is critical to your child's success and inclusion in school and the community. Your school district should be able to provide a behavioral psychologist to help develop an effective behavior management plan. You can also retain a private psychologist to help with behavior issues at home. Either way, there are professionals with experience to help you, your child, and your child's teachers.

▪▪ Conclusion

Education is the most important aspect of your child's development. Familiarize yourself with your state guidelines for services and get involved with the advocacy groups available to you and your child.

As soon as the diagnosis is made, your investigation should begin. Even though some aspects of development occur naturally over time, there are many therapeutic programs available that will enhance your child's development and ultimately improve his functioning level. If your child is diagnosed at an older age, it is *never* too late to pursue services that will maximize his functioning.

Some parents feel enormous guilt associated with passing on the gene that causes fragile X syndrome. This pain is often long suffering and may continue to surface at various stages of your child's development. You can use those feelings to motivate you to promote better educational programming by advocating for your child.

You are the ultimate expert about your child. You have a relationship with your child like no one else. It is important to trust your instincts in directing your child to maximize his potential. Your child will reap the benefits of your work and you will have given him the best gift a parent can give.

▪▪ References

Ayers, Jean. *Sensory Integration and the Child.* Los Angeles: Western Psychological Services, 1979.

Braden, Marcia L. *Curriculum Guide for Individuals with FXS.* Contact: 100 E. St. Vrain #200, Colorado Springs, CO 80903; (719) 633-3773; FAX (719) 633-9705, 1998.

Braden, Marcia L. *Fragile: Handle With Care, Understanding Fragile X Syndrome.* Contact: 100 E. St. Vrain #200, Colorado Springs, CO 80903; (719) 633-3773; FAX (719) 633-9705, 1997.

Braden, Marcia L. *Maximizing Learning Potential,* videotape. Contact: 100 E. St. Vrain #200, Colorado Springs, CO 80903; (719) 633-3773; FAX (719) 633-9705, 1997.

Braden, Marcia L. *The Logo Reading Program.* Contact: 100 E. St. Vrain #200, Colorado Springs, CO 80903; (719) 633-3773; FAX (719) 633-9705, 1989.

Chapman, Randy, Long, P., Williamson, C. *The Law and Education of Children With Disabilities.* Denver: The Legal Center for People with Disabilities and Older People, 1997. Contact: (303) 722-0300.

Colorado Department of Education, Early Childhood Initiatives. *From One Parent to Another.* Denver: 1999. Contact: (303) 866-6600, 1999.

Dykens, E.M., Hodapp, R.M. and Leckman, J.F. "Strengths and Weaknesses in the Intellectual Functioning of Males with Fragile X Syndrome," *American Journal of Medical Genetics* 28, no. 1 (1987): 13-15.

Hagerman, Randi, "Medical Intervention in Fragile X Syndrome," *National Fragile X Advocate* 1, no. 1 (1995): 1-4.

Hagerman, Randi J. "Physical and Behavioral Phenotype," in *Fragile X Syndrome: Diagnosis, Treatment and Research,* 2nd ed, edited by R. J. Hagerman and A. Cronister, 3-87. Baltimore: Johns Hopkins University Press, 1996.

Kaufman, A.S. and Kaufman, N.P. *Kaufman Assessment Battery for Children: Administration and Scoring Manual.* Circle Pines, MN: American Guidance Services, 1983.

Kemper, J.B., Hagerman, R.J., Ahmad, R.S., Mariner, R. "Cognitive Profiles and the Spectrum of Clinical Manifestation in Heterozygous Fra(X) Females," *American Journal of Medical Genetics* 23 (1986): 139-156.

Kemper, J.B., Hagerman, R.J., Altshul-Stark, D. "Cognitive Profiles of Boys with Fragile X Syndrome," *American Journal of Medical Genetics* 30, 1-2 (1988): 191-200.

Mazzocco, M.M., Hagerman, R.J., Pennington, B.F. "Problem Solving Limitations Among Cytogenetically Expressing Fragile X Syndrome Women," *American Journal of Medical Genetics* 43 (1992): 78-86.

National Information Center for Children and Youth with Disabilities (NICHCY), *The IDEA Amendments of 1997,* 1997. Contact: P.O. Box 1492, Washington, DC 20013; 1-800-695-0285.

Rogers-Connolly, T., Grebenc, R., Soper Hepp, E., Schrotberger, B., Wagner, A. "Understanding Special Education, Parents and Educators Planning Together." *Parents Encouraging Parents (PEP),* 1995. Colorado Department of Education, Denver; (303) 866-6600.

Rourke, B.P. "Syndrome of Nonverbal Learning Disabilities: The Final Common Pathway of White-Matter Disease/Dysfunction," *The Clinical Neuropsychologist* 1(1987): 109-234.

Rourke, B.P. "Socioemotional Disturbances of Learning Disabled Children," *Journal of Consulting and Clinical Psychology* 56 (1988): 801-810.

Sherman, S.L., Jacobs, P.A., Morton, N.E., Froster-Iskenius, U., Howard-Peebles, P.N., Nielsen, K.B., Partington, M.W., Sutherland, G.R., Turner, G., Watson, M. "Further Segregation Analysis of the Fragile X Syndrome with Special Reference to Transmitting Males," *Human Genetics* 69 (1985): 289-299.

Turner, G., Daniel, A., Frost, M. "X-Linked Mental Retardation, Macroorchidism, and the Xq27 Fragile Site," *Journal of Pediatrics* 96 (1980): 837-841.

■■ Parent Statements

Unfortunately the eligibility process requires that children have labels. This is a painful process for parents—no way around it until we begin to individualize all children, not just those with special needs.

The evaluation process was so painful.

Gary is seen once a year. The results of these tests are always depressing—but it helps to know what areas he most needs help in.

There was never a problem with the identification process or getting our sons to qualify for special education services.

I always enjoy having so many professionals care about my child.

I wonder if everything is going to get done on the IEP.

We've always made a priority of having good communication with the school staff.

I don't like IEP meetings; I wish I didn't have to educate myself on all of the laws, regulations, code, etc. It's certainly not something I set out to do. I wish there was a feeling of satisfaction when we finished too. I always kind of wonder what other parents are getting that I'm not.

We fully believe that the earlier our sons receive intervention, the better chances they have of adjusting to the world around them and learning how to live in it.

The program my son attends is good but the ratio of kids to teachers is too high. Gary requires a one-on-one system to concentrate. His class is too chaotic and distracting.

At three my son was transferred to an elementary school. We had to fight to get him into this school. The school that we were supposed to go to did not have a special education class, so we "kind of"' had our choice. The class that had a nurturing teacher's aide and a loving, but firm teacher who had been in special-ed for 12 years was our choice. Each year we try to fight for services (speech & occupational therapies) and to keep him in the same class at this particular elementary school. We had to help them understand how difficult transition is for Alex.

Every year you have to train a new group of people or at least a few. The good part is that you get better at it, the bad part is that you get tired of doing it.

My daughters have always qualified for summer school, but I always found it to be more like babysitting. The socialization was good though. Last summer I got tutors who were teachers to come in a couple of days a week to work directly with my children. That was really good!

My sons have never qualified for summer school. The school always gives some kind of line that they don't qualify.

On the one hand ESY appeals to me, but on the other, I think it's important for the boys to learn that there will not always be a routine. We enjoy doing things as a family, like camping, and this time away from school allows this.

My son has qualified for year-round school because of the concern that, over an entire summer vacation, he will have to readjust to school and his teachers from scratch. Summer school is really just for consistency, and not much for academics.

What we'd like to know regarding therapies: What are the most effective strategies, particularly in speech and language therapy, at this very early pre-speech phase in our children's lives? Is there any approach that will speed up speech production abilities?

Facilitating better communication is our number one need.

At one point we decided to move because there was no cohesive team of therapists (and little public funding) to deal with the developmental needs of our children.

While I would not advocate denying any child speech, occupational, or physical therapy, I have never been convinced that these specialties affected our sons' course of development in any significant way. And insofar as they separated children from their peers, created another set of people with whom to interact, and created another set of expectations which the boys felt they had to meet, they may have added to the general stress level.

A good therapist who helps teachers and parents find the right calming activities for a particular child is a treasure.

My son has speech therapy every other day.

An OT once told me that the amount of repetition needed to teach my child would be more than I could handle and that I should share some of the responsibility with her.

Therapies are good to get our kids going. Parents can learn a lot at this time too.

We truly believe that our children will not suffer from one missed opportunity, or even from one mediocre school year. They can be trusted to work at a level which they feel comfortable with encouragement from us. But they do not need to be pushed to excel, because the risk is that they will be pushed beyond the comfort zone which they can handle.

School is fabulous! The staff has a true commitment to inclusion and they are always trying to find ways to make every child as successful as they can be. Their efforts have paid off because our son flourishes there.

He attends a neighborhood public school and he's in a typical classroom setting. He has an aide for assistance as needed and that has a lot to do with his success.

The school district moved our son to a separate program and now we see the advantages and disadvantages of both inclusion and a self-contained classroom. I hate for my son to be in a "program" and would still opt for full inclusion, at least through elementary school.

The IEP is so important. Really think hard about what your child needs and make sure it gets written down.

The school issues seem to get harder every year.

Our son learns through a visual, hands-on, authentic approach. He needs verbal cues for direction and sometimes a calm, soothing voice of encouragement.

He has a hard time staying on task and he has difficulty with unstructured time. His conversational abilities are relatively weak which impedes good communication with his peers.

Teaching Gary through "real" activities is the key for him.

❧❀❧

Tony needs lots of movement regularly scheduled into his day.

❧❀❧

Whenever Patrick is "pulled out" of the regular education classroom, they take a peer with him.

❧❀❧

My son has a cooking class written into his IEP.

❧❀❧

My son has a "job" of delivering mail to teachers toward the end of the day. They are using it to teach numbers and reading.

❧❀❧

At the beginning of the year the teachers warn my son of upcoming fire drills. By the end of the year he knows what to do and how to deal acceptably with the sensory issues.

❧❀❧

Our son learns faster if you sing to him.

❧❀❧

Finding the "right" program is often a mixture of trial and error and dumb luck. In my experience, it is more dependent on finding the right teachers—teachers who are willing to experiment with a variety of ideas on my child's behalf. Without a skilled and open teacher, even the most carefully thought out program is likely to fizzle.

❧❀❧

Expect to give as well as take from your schools. I always volunteer, not only in the special education room, but also with all students and on school district committees. You will find many dedicated parents of typical students also volunteering their time on behalf of their children's education—and it always pays off in the long run if the administration sees you as a committed parent.

❧❀❧

Over the past 22 years, we have had the whole gamut of experiences with schools—from woeful inadequacy to a successfully integrated program with outstanding regular and special education teachers in a public high school. Among the lessons learned: it is worthwhile to cultivate experiences with typical age peers.

We have learned that our kids can weather experiences which we considered educationally disastrous, so that it doesn't hurt to lighten up when there is no way to change an imperfect placement.

We always look for a teacher who has experience with children with disabilities and who welcomes our child.

It seems to be the adults who have the hard time with inclusion, not the other children in the class. Guess it's what you grow up with.

I see Gary always receiving some therapy.

LEGAL RIGHTS
AND HURDLES

*James E. Kaplan and
Ralph J. Moore, Jr.*

■ Introduction

As the parent of a child with fragile X syndrome, it is important to understand the laws that apply to your child and you. There are laws that guarantee your child's rights to attend school and to live and work in the community; laws that can provide your child financial and medical assistance; and laws that govern your long-term planning for your child's future.

Knowing what your child is entitled to can help to ensure that your child receives the education, training, and special services he needs to reach his potential. You and your child will also be able to recognize illegal discrimination and assert his legal rights if necessary. Finally, if you understand how laws sometimes create problems for families of children with disabilities, you can avoid unwitting mistakes in planning for your child's future.

There are no federal laws that deal exclusively with fragile X syndrome. Rather, the rights of children with fragile X syndrome are found in the laws and regulations for children and adults with disabilities generally. In other words, the same laws that protect all persons with disabilities also protect your child. This chapter will familiarize you with these federal laws to enable you to exercise his rights effectively and fully.

It would be impossible to discuss here the law of every state or locality. Instead, this chapter reviews some of the most important legal concepts you need to know. For information about the particular laws in your area, contact the national office of The Arc (formerly the Association for Retarded Citizens) or the Association for Community Living (ACL) in Canada, your local or state affiliate of The Arc or ACL, or your state Parent Training and Information Center (PTIC). You should also consult with a lawyer familiar with disability law when you have questions or need specific advice.

▪▪ Your Child's Right to an Education

Until the middle of this century, children with disabilities were usually excluded from public schools. They were sent away to residential "schools," "homes," and institutions, or their parents banded together to provide private part-time programs. In the 1960s, federal, state, and local governments began to provide educational opportunities to children with disabilities; these opportunities have expanded and improved to this day.

Perhaps nothing has done more to improve educational opportunities for children with fragile X syndrome than the Individuals with Disabilities Education Act (IDEA). This law, originally enacted in 1975 and amended extensively in 1997, used to be called "The Education for All Handicapped Children Act of 1975" and was better known as "Public Law 94-142." IDEA has vastly improved educational opportunities for almost all children with disabilities. Administered by the U.S. Department of Education (DOE) and by each state, the law works on a carrot-and-stick basis.

Under IDEA, the federal government provides funds for the education of children with disabilities to each state that has a special education program that meets the standards contained in IDEA and regulations issued by DOE. To qualify for federal funds, a state must demonstrate that it is providing all children with disabilities a "free appropriate public education" (FAPE) in the "least restrictive environment" (LRE) that meets IDEA's standards. At a minimum, states that receive federal funds under IDEA must provide approved special educational services, opportunities for participation in the regular curriculum (inclusion), and a variety of procedural rights to children with disabilities and their parents. The lure of federal funds has been attractive enough to induce all states to provide special education for children with disabilities, including children with fragile X syndrome.

IDEA, however, has its limits. The law only establishes the minimum requirements in special education programs for states desiring to receive federal funds. In other words, the law does not require states to adopt an ideal educational program for your child with fragile X syndrome or a program that you feel is "the best." Because states have leeway under IDEA, differences exist from state to state in the programs or services available. For example, the student-teacher ratio in some states is higher than in others, and the quality and quantity of teaching materials also can vary widely.

States can create special education programs that are better than those required by IDEA, and some have. Check with the placement or intake officer of the special education department of your local school district to determine exactly what classes, programs, and services are available to your child. Parents, organizations, and advocacy groups continually push states and local school districts to exceed the federal requirements and provide the highest quality special education as early as possible. These groups need your support, and you need theirs.

What IDEA Provides

Since IDEA was passed in 1975, the law has been amended several times. Today IDEA consists of a large volume of laws and regulations. The Resource Guide at the end of this book tells you how to obtain copies of these laws and regulations from the U.S. Senate, House of Representatives, DOE, or national organizations. The summary below highlights the provisions most important for you and your child.

Coverage. IDEA is intended to make special education available to all children with disabilities, including children with mental retardation, learning disabilities, speech or language impairments, attention disorders, and multiple disabilities.

In most cases, a diagnosis of fragile X syndrome is enough to establish that IDEA applies to your child. Regardless of how your child's intellectual or physical impairments are labeled, he qualifies for services if his condition hinders learning.

Before your child is formally diagnosed or evaluated and "labeled" by your school district under IDEA, he may still be eligible for services under the law. Infants and toddlers under age three are eligible for early intervention services if they are found to be "at-risk of experiencing a substantial developmental delay" if services are not provided. And if your child is between ages three and nine, states may still, at their option, provide services if he is experiencing undiagnosed developmental delays.

"Free Appropriate Public Education." At the heart of IDEA is the requirement that children with disabilities receive a "free appropriate public education" in the "least restrictive environment." Children with fragile X syndrome are entitled to receive an education at public expense that takes into account their special learning needs and abilities and their right to go to school with their nondisabled peers. This section examines more precisely what each of the elements of "free appropriate public education" means. Following sections explain the term "least restrictive environment."

"Free" means that every part of your child's special education program must be provided at public expense, regardless of your ability to pay. This requirement is often satisfied by placement of your child in a public school, but the school district must pay the cost of all the necessary services your child will receive there. If no suitable public program is available, the school district must place your child in a private program and pay the full cost. Remember, IDEA does not provide for tuition payment for educational services for your child *not* agreed to by the school district or other governing agency (unless, as explained later in this chapter, the decision of your school district is overturned). As a result, if you place your child in a program that is not approved for your child by the school district, you risk having to bear the full cost of tuition.

It may be difficult for parents to accept that the "appropriate" education mandated by IDEA does not guarantee the best possible education that money can buy. It does, however, mandate an effective education: IDEA requires states receiving federal funds to achieve "educational success." They must establish measurable performance goals for children with disabilities that lead toward economic independence, community living, and employment as adults. Thus, IDEA attempts to hold school districts accountable for providing effective special education services. The nature and extent of services provided, however, typically depend on the nature and extent of the need. The law in this area is constantly evolving. Check with your local office of The Arc or ACL or your state PTIC for information about the current state of the law regarding what is considered an "appropriate" educational program.

Only you can assure that your child receives the most appropriate placement and services. Under IDEA, parents and educators are required to work together to design an individualized education program (IEP) for each child (IEPs are explained below). If you feel that a school district is not making the best placement for your child, you must demonstrate to school officials not only that your preferred placement is appropriate, but that the placement approved by the school district is not. The goal is to reach an agreement on the appropriate placement and services. If agreement cannot be reached, there are procedures for resolving disputes. These procedures are discussed later in the chapter.

"Special Education and Related Services." Under IDEA, an appropriate education consists of "special education and related services." "Special education" means instruction specifically designed to meet the unique needs of the child with disabilities, provided in a full range of settings, including regular education classrooms, separate classrooms, home instruction, or instruction in private schools, hospitals, or institutions. Regular education teachers, special education teachers, therapists, and other professionals—all provided by the school district at public expense—are responsible for delivering these educational services. In addition, supplementary aids and services can be provided to enable a student to participate in regular education classrooms.

"Related services" are defined as transportation and other developmental, corrective, and supportive services necessary to enable the child to benefit from special education. "Related services" are often a critical part of a special education program. Services provided by a trained speech or language therapist, occupational therapist, physical therapist, psychologist, social worker, school nurse, aide, or other qualified person may be required under IDEA as related services. Some services, however, are specifically excluded. Most important among these exclusions are medical services ordinarily provided by a physician or hospital. For example, immunizations cannot be provided as related services under IDEA.

Because speech and motor delays often result from fragile X syndrome, obtaining appropriate and adequate physical, occupational, and speech therapy as part of your child's special education program can be critical. Parents should demand that their child receive the related services he needs; these related services are your child's right under the law.

"Least Restrictive Environment." IDEA requires that children with disabilities must "to the maximum extent appropriate" be educated in the least restrictive environment. This requirement influences all decisions about your child under IDEA, and has over the years since IDEA's enactment become a major emphasis of the law. This result is due to the efforts of parents who have advocated for their children to be educated with their peers.

The least restrictive environment is the educational setting that permits your child to have the most contact possible at school with children who do *not* have disabilities as well as involvement in the general education curriculum. For example, your child should have the opportunity to learn the same subjects in the same classrooms as other children his age. Under IDEA, there is therefore a strong preference to integrate children with disabilities, including children with fragile X syndrome, in the schools and classes they would attend if they did not have a disability. IDEA is specifically intended at least in part to end the historical practice of isolating children with disabilities either in separate schools or out-of-the-way classrooms and is intended to open the doors of your neighborhood school to your child with fragile X syndrome. Once the door is open, IDEA requires your school to find ways to truly integrate your child into the typical educational life of the school while he receives the services and support he needs to succeed.

Some school officials might assert that your child with fragile X syndrome should be educated in a separate special setting. Most children with fragile X syndrome, however, can receive their instruction with typical peers, so long as proper in-classroom supports and therapy are provided. In some localities, all children with disabilities are educated in regular classrooms at all times.

Over the 25 years since IDEA was enacted, a wide range of placement options has developed from the time when children with disabilities were routinely segregated and isolated. IDEA supports many different types of educational placement. Many children spend all their time in regular classrooms with teachers or aides who can adapt the curriculum to their needs and help them with the regular education curriculum. Others spend most of their time in regular classrooms, but receive special education services in certain subjects in separate classrooms. Still others spend most of their time in separate classrooms, but have opportunities for inclusion in school activities such as assemblies, physical education, sports teams, music, and lunch and recess. The extent of your child's inclusion depends on a variety of factors and will be set forth in your child's IEP.

IDEA also recognizes that public schools may not be suitable for all educational and related services required for some children. In these cases, federal regulations allow for placement in private schools, or even residential settings, if the school district can demonstrate that this placement is required to meet the child's individual educational needs. When placement within the community's regular public schools is determined to be not appropriate, the law still requires that he be placed in the least restrictive educational environment suitable to his individual needs, which can include some participation in regular school classroom programs and activities. Even a student whose parents enroll him in a private school without school district approval or funding may still be eligible for some services such as speech therapy.

Neither your child's fragile X syndrome itself nor his developmental delay is a sufficient reason for a school district to refuse to provide opportunities for your child to learn with his typical peers. Some of the most important learning in school comes from a student's peers and from modeling typical behavior. Thus, in IEPs, the school district must explain how much each child with disabilities will or will not be included in regular education classes and why.

When Coverage Begins under IDEA. IDEA requires all states to begin special education services at the age of three. In addition, IDEA also includes a program of grants to states that create an approved program for early intervention services for infants with disabilities from birth until age three.

Some form of early intervention services under IDEA is available in each state. But there is wide variation in what services are provided, how and where those services are provided, and which agency provides them. You should check with your local school district, the state education agency, your local office of The Arc or ACL, or your state PTIC about the availability of early intervention services, which can include speech-language, physical, or occupational therapy to help infants and toddlers with fragile X syndrome to maximize their early development.

You may be charged, however, for some of the early intervention services your child receives. The law seeks to have insurance companies and Medicaid cover some of the costs.

Under IDEA, special education services must continue until children reach at least age 18. A state that offers education to all students until age 21, however, must do the same for students who receive special education services.

Length of School Year. Under IDEA, states must provide more than the traditional 180-day school year when the needs of a child indicate that year-round instruction is a necessary part of a "free appropriate public education." In most states, the decision to offer summer instruction depends on whether your child will "regress," or lose a substantial amount of the progress made during the school year without summer services; this is called "regression." If so, these services must be provided at public expense. Because some children with fragile X syndrome can regress without year-round services, parents should not hesitate to request year-round instruction, but you or school staff must be prepared to document your child's need for year-round services.

Identification and Evaluation. Because IDEA applies only to children with disabilities, your child with fragile X syndrome must be evaluated before he is eligible for special education. The law requires states to develop testing and evaluation procedures designed to identify and evaluate the needs and abilities of each child before he is placed in a special education program. All evaluation and re-evaluation procedures are required to take into account your input.

For parents of a child with fragile X syndrome, identification is somewhat simpler. School districts almost uniformly recognize that children with fragile X syndrome need some form of special education or related services. A medical diagnosis of fragile X syndrome should therefore be sufficient. Your challenge will not be convincing a school district that your child needs services, but rather obtaining the needed services as early as possible. Doctors, organizations, and—most importantly—other parents can be extremely helpful at these initial stages.

Do not be deterred from seeking services if your child's condition is not fully understood, diagnosed, or "labelled." If your child is an infant or toddler (ages birth to three), your state may provide early intervention services for him if he is considered "at risk" for experiencing developmental delays. In addition, if your child is between ages three and nine, IDEA specifies that states *may* provide services to children who are experiencing some form of developmental delay, but do not have a formal diagnosis of disability. States are not required, however, to allow the use of the "developmental delay" label to establish eligibility for special education services. They also can limit the age range that the "developmental delay" label may be used for; for instance, to children age three to six. Contact your state Board of Education to find out your city's, county's, or state's policy about using the "developmental delay" label.

"Individualized Education Program." IDEA recognizes that each child with a disability is unique. As a result, the law requires that your child's special education program be tailored to his individual needs. Based on your child's evaluation, a program specifically designed to address his developmental problems must be devised. This is called an "individualized education program" or, more commonly, an "IEP."

The IEP is a written report that describes:

1. your child's present level of development in all areas;
2. your child's developmental strengths and needs;
3. both the short-term and annual goals of the special education program;
4. the specific educational services that your child will receive;
5. the date services will start and their expected duration;
6. standards for determining whether the goals of the educational program are being met;
7. the extent to which your child will participate in regular educational programs;
8. the behavior intervention programs that will be used to enable your child to participate in regular education classrooms without impeding his or other students' learning; and
9. parent concerns

Under federal regulations, educational placements must be based on the IEP, not vice versa. That is, the services your child receives and the setting in which he receives them should be determined by your child's individual needs, not by the availability of existing programs. "One size fits all" is not permitted by IDEA.

A child's IEP is usually developed during a series of meetings among parents, teachers, and other school district representatives. Your child may be present at these meetings. School districts are required to establish committees to make these placement and program decisions. These committees are sometimes referred to as Child Study Teams, Pupil Evaluation Teams (PET), or Administrative Placement Committees.

Writing an IEP is ideally a cooperative effort, with parents, teachers, therapists, and school officials conferring on what goals are appropriate and how best to achieve them. Because of IDEA's emphasis on inclusion, regular education teachers are required to be on the IEP team. Preliminary drafts of the IEP are reviewed and revised in an attempt to develop a mutually acceptable educational program.

The importance of your role in this process cannot be over-emphasized. IDEA requires the IEP team to consider "the concerns of the parents for enhancing the education of their child." This means that your goals for your child's education must be taken into account in drafting your child's IEP.

You cannot always depend on teachers or school officials to recognize your child's unique needs. To obtain the full range of services,

you may need to demonstrate that withholding certain services would result in an education that would *not* be "appropriate." For example, if you believe that a program using augmentative communication methods is necessary for your child, you must demonstrate that failing to provide these services would not be appropriate for your child's specific needs. And if you want an academic-oriented program for your child, you must demonstrate that a program that emphasizes only vocational or functional skills is not appropriate given your child's skills, abilities, and needs.

IEPs should be very detailed. You and your child's teachers should set specific goals for every area of development, and specify how and when those goals will be reached. Although the thought of specific planning may seem intimidating at first, a detailed IEP enables you to closely monitor the education your child receives and to make sure he actually receives the services prescribed. In addition, the law requires that IEPs be reviewed and revised at least once a year, and more often if necessary, to ensure that your child's educational program continues to meet his changing needs. Parents can also request a meeting with school officials at any time.

Because your child has special needs, his IEP must be written with care to meet those needs. Unless you request specific services, they may be overlooked. You should make sure school officials recognize the unique needs of your child—the needs that make him different from children with other disabilities and even from other children with fragile X syndrome.

How can you prepare for the IEP process? First, explore available educational programs, including public, private, federal, state, county, and municipal programs. Observe classes at the school your child would attend if he did not have fragile X syndrome to see for yourself what different programs and placements have to offer. Local school districts and local organizations such as The Arc or ACL can provide you with information about programs in your community. Second, collect a complete set of developmental evaluations to share with school officials— obtain your own if you doubt the accuracy of the school district's evaluation. Third, give thought to appropriate short-term and long-term goals for your child. Finally, decide for yourself what placement, program, and services are necessary for your child, and request them. If you want your child educated in his neighborhood school, request the services necessary to support him in that setting, such as supplementary aids. If no program offers enough of what your child needs, you should request that an existing program be modified to better meet your child's needs. For example, if your child would benefit educationally from learning sign language or using an augmentative communication system, but no programs currently offer such instruction, you should request the service anyway.

To support placement in a particular type of program, you should collect "evidence" about your child's special needs. Then support your position that a particular type of placement is appropriate by presenting letters from physicians, psychologists, therapists (speech-language, physical, or occupational), teachers, developmental experts, or other professionals, as the case may be. This evidence may help persuade a school district that the requested placement or services are the appropriate choices for your child. A few other suggestions to assist you in the process are:

1. Do not attend IEP meetings alone—bring a spouse, lawyer, advocate, physician, teacher, or whomever you would like for support, including, of course, your child;

2. Keep close track of what everyone involved in your child's case—school district officials, psychologists, therapists, teachers, and doctors— says and does;
3. *Get everything in writing*; and
4. Be assertive and speak your mind. Children with unique developmental challenges need parents to be assertive and persuasive advocates during the IEP process. This does not mean that school officials are always adversaries, but does mean you are your child's most important advocate. You know him best.

"Individualized Family Service Plan." Parents of children from birth to age three use a plan that is different from the IEP used for older children. States receiving grants to provide early intervention services must draft an "individualized family service plan" (IFSP). This plan is similar to the IEP, but with an early intervention focus. Unlike an IEP, which focuses primarily on the needs of the child, an IFSP emphasizes services for the family. In other words, the law recognizes that families with young children with special needs often have special needs themselves. Consequently, IFSPs do not simply specify what services are provided for the child with fragile X syndrome. They also describe services that will be provided to: 1) help parents learn how to use daily activities to teach their child with fragile X syndrome, and 2) help siblings learn to cope with having a brother or sister with fragile X syndrome. The procedures and strategies for developing a useful IFSP are the same as described above for the IEP. IFSPs are reviewed every six months.

One important recent change to IDEA requires that early intervention services be provided to children and families to the "maximum extent appropriate" in the child's "natural environment." This requirement means that services should be provided at the child's home or a place familiar to the child rather than at a center. This reflects IDEA's strong preference for inclusion.

As your child approaches age three, IDEA requires a written plan for your child's transition into preschool services. This transition process should begin three to six months before your child turns age three. Parents, teachers, and a representative of your local school district are required to participate. The plan must contain the "steps to be taken to support the transition of the toddler with a disability to preschool or other appropriate services" to ensure "a smooth transition" into preschool services.

Disciplinary Procedures

When IDEA was amended extensively in 1997, Congress added provisions to govern how children with disabilities were to be disciplined in public schools. These provisions apply to situations in which a child would be suspended from school, and restrict school district actions, depending on the length of a suspension. In general, schools must continue to provide a free appropriate education in the least restrictive environment even if a child is suspended. Schools that have previously failed to address behavior problems with appropriate functional behavior intervention cannot then suspend a child for that behavior. If the school already has a behavior intervention plan, school personnel must meet to review and, if necessary, revise the plan. And if a long suspension of 10 days or more is considered (or if a series of shorter suspensions amounts to more than 10 days), the school must present its plan and its proposed interim placement to a neutral hearing officer for approval. The school must also demonstrate that the behavior was not a manifestation of the child's disability and that the IEP was appropriate for the child at the time. In addition, parents have the right to appeal all disciplinary actions under the procedures explained below. Parents should closely monitor how these new provisions are being implemented to make sure public school districts do not slip back to the past practice of using "discipline problems" to routinely exclude children with disabilities.

Resolution of Disputes under IDEA

IDEA establishes a variety of effective safeguards to protect your rights and the rights of your child. For instance, written notice is always required before any change can be made in your child's identification, evaluation, or educational placement. In addition, you are entitled to review all of your child's educational records at any time. Your school district is prohibited from making decisions without first consulting or notifying you. Further, your school district is required to inform you of your rights under IDEA at each step of the process.

Despite these safeguards, conflicts between parents and school officials can arise. When they do, it is usually best to resolve disputes over your child's educational or early intervention program *during* the IEP or IFSP process, before firm and inflexible positions have been formed. Although IDEA establishes dispute resolution procedures that are designed to be fair to parents, it is easier and far less costly to avoid disputes by reaching agreement, if possible, during the IEP or IFSP process or by informal discussions with appropriate officials. Accordingly, you should first try to accomplish your objectives by open and clear communication and by persuasion. If a dispute arises that simply cannot be resolved through discussion, further steps can and should be taken under IDEA and other laws to resolve that dispute.

First, IDEA allows you to file a formal complaint with your local school district about *any matter* "relating to the identification, evaluation, or educational placement of the child, or the provision of free appropriate public education to such child." This means that you can make a written complaint about virtually any problem with any part of your child's educational or early intervention program. This is a very broad right of appeal, one that parents have successfully used in the past to correct problems in their children's education programs.

The process of challenging a school district's decisions about your child's education can be started simply by sending a letter of complaint. This letter, which should explain the nature of the dispute and your desired outcome, typically is sent to the special education office of the school district. IDEA requires that you notify your local school district or your state education agency with specific information about your complaint. You have the absolute right to file a complaint—you need not ask the school district for permission. For information about starting complaints, you can contact your school district, your local office of The Arc or ACL, your state PTIC, local advocacy groups, or other parents.

After filing of a complaint, IDEA requires parents to consider mediation of their dispute. IDEA encourages parents and school districts to resolve disagreements without hearings and lawsuits, if possible. Under IDEA, school districts must seek to resolve complaints through voluntary mediation, a process of negotiation, discussion, and compromise. In mediation, you and school officials meet with a neutral third party and try to reach a mutually acceptable solution. Your school district must present you with the option of mediation, but you are not required to pursue that option. If you decline the school district's request to mediate, you may still be required to meet with a neutral party to discuss the benefits of mediation. Mediation, however, cannot be used to deny or delay your due process rights; it is simply a free, voluntary approach aimed at reducing the costs of resolving disputes and avoiding costly lawsuits.

The first step in the complaint process is usually an "impartial due process hearing" before a hearing examiner. This hearing, usually held locally, is your first opportunity to explain your complaint to an impartial person, who is required to listen to both sides and then to render a decision. At the hearing, you are entitled to be represented by a lawyer or lay advocate; present evidence; and examine, cross-examine, and compel witnesses to attend. Your child has a right to be present at the hearing as well. After the hearing, you have a right to receive a written record of the hearing and the hearing examiner's findings and conclusions.

Just as with the IEP and IFSP processes, you must present facts at a due process hearing that show that the school district's decisions about your child's educational program are wrong. To overturn the school district's decision, you must show that the disputed placement or program does not provide your child with the "free appropriate public education" in "the least restrictive environment" required by IDEA. Evidence in the form of letters, testimony, and expert evaluations is usually essential to a successful challenge.

Parents or school districts may appeal the decision of a hearing examiner. The appeal usually goes to the state's education agency or to a neutral panel. The state agency is required to make an independent decision upon a review of the record of the due process hearing and of any additional evidence presented. The state agency then issues a decision.

The right to appeal does not stop there. Parents or school officials can appeal beyond the state level by bringing a lawsuit under IDEA and other laws in a state or federal court. In this legal action, the court must determine whether there is a preponderance of the evidence (that is, whether it is more likely than not) that the school district's placement is proper for that child. The court must give weight to the expertise of the school officials responsible for providing your child's education, although you can and should also present your own expert evidence.

During all administrative and judicial proceedings, IDEA requires that your child remain in his current educational placement, unless you and your school district or the state education agency agree to a move or a hearing officer agrees to an interim change of placement for disciplinary reasons. As explained above, if you place your child in a different program without agreement, you risk having to bear the full cost of that program. If the school district eventually is found to have erred, it may be required to reimburse you for the expenses of the changed placement. Accordingly, you should never change programs without carefully considering the potential cost of that decision.

Attorneys' fees are another expense to consider. Parents who ultimately win their dispute with a school district may recover attorneys' fees at the court's discretion. Even if you prevail at the local or state level (without bringing a lawsuit), you likely are entitled to recover attorneys' fees. However, you may not recover attorneys' fees for a mediated settlement, and attorneys' fees are reduced if you fail to properly notify the school district or state education agency of your complaint. A word of caution: A court can also limit or refuse attorneys' fees if you reject an offer of settlement from the school district, and then do not obtain a better outcome.

As with any legal dispute, each phase—complaint, mediation, hearings, appeals, and court cases—can be expensive, time-consuming, and emotionally draining. As mentioned earlier, it is wise to try to resolve problems without filing a formal complaint or bringing suit. When informal means fail to resolve a problem, formal channels should be pursued. Your child's best interests must come first. IDEA grants important rights that you should not be bashful about asserting vigorously.

IDEA is a powerful tool in the hands of parents. It can be used to provide unparalleled educational opportunities to your child with fragile X syndrome. The Reading List at the end of this book includes several good guidebooks about IDEA and the special education system. The more you know about this vital law, the more you will be able to help your child realize his fullest potential.

■■ Programs and Services When Your Child Is an Adult

Many children with fragile X syndrome grow to live independently or semi-independently as adults. To achieve community living and employment skills, your child may need some special services. These services include employment, job-training, and residential or community-living programs. Regrettably, these services are often unavailable because very few federal laws require states to offer programs for adults with disabilities and few states offer these programs on their own. Those programs that exist usually are underfunded and have long waiting lists. As a result, many parents must provide the necessary support and supervision on their own for as long as possible. Thousands of children receive education and training that equip them to live independently and productively, only to be sent home when they finish schooling with nowhere to go and nothing to do. Although in recent years, more emphasis has been placed on community living and employment, much progress is needed.

Now is the time to work to change this sad reality. The unemployment rate for people with disabilities is appallingly high, especially for young adults. As waiting lists for training programs grow, your child may be deprived of needed services, and, consequently, of his independence. Programs sponsored by charities and private foundations are limited and most families do not have the resources to pay the full cost of providing employment and residential opportunities. The only other remedy is public funding. Just as parents banded together in the 1970s to demand enactment of IDEA, parents must band together now to persuade local, state, and federal officials to take the steps necessary to allow adults with disabilities to live in dignity. Parents of *children* with disabilities should not leave this job to parents of *adults* with disabilities; children become adults all too soon. One great way to become involved is to begin to work with groups like The Arc or ACL.

Vocational Training Programs

One educational program supported by federal funding is available to most adults with fragile X syndrome. Operating somewhat like IDEA, this federal law makes funds available to states to support vocational training and rehabilitation programs for qualified people with disabilities. As with IDEA, states that desire federal funds for this program must meet the standards established in the law. These laws set forth procedures—similar to those under IDEA— to review decisions affecting the services provided to an individual.

Adults must fulfill two requirements to qualify for job-training services: 1) they must have a physical or mental disability that constitutes a "substantial handicap to employment;" and 2) they must be expected to benefit from vocational services. In the past, some people with disabilities, including people with fragile X syndrome, were denied vocational training services because it was believed that they would never be able to meet the law's second requirement of eventual full-time or part-time employment. Now the law requires that services and training be provided to people even if what they achieve is "supported employment," which means employment in a setting with services such as a job coach or special training that allows an individual to work productively.

The state Departments of Vocational Rehabilitation, sometimes called "DVR" or "Voc Rehab," are charged with administering these laws. Adults who apply for Voc Rehab services are evaluated, and an "Individualized Plan for Employment " (IPE), similar to an IEP, is developed. The IPE sets forth the services needed to enable a person with a disability to work productively. The law requires that IPEs be developed in partnership between the individual and his vocational rehabilitation counselor so that the individual can make informed choices about his vocational training.

You should contact your state vocational rehabilitation department or your local office of The Arc or ACL for specific information on services available to your child when he is an adult. Despite limited federal and state budgets, some states, communities, and organizations offer their own programs, such as group homes, supported employment programs, social activity groups, continuing education, and life-skills classes. Other parents and community organizations likely will have information about these local programs.

∷ Developmentally Disabled Assistance and Bill of Rights Act

Under a federal law called the Developmentally Disabled Assistance and Bill of Rights Act, states can receive grants for a variety of programs. Important among them is a protection and advocacy (P&A) system. A P&A system advocates for the civil and legal rights of people with developmental disabilities. P&A offices have been leaders in representing institutionalized people seeking to improve their living conditions or to be placed in the community. In addition, P&A offices may be able to represent persons who cannot afford a lawyer for an IDEA due process hearing or a discrimination suit. Because some people with fragile X syndrome may not be able to protect or enforce their own rights, state P&A systems offer necessary protection. Contact the National Association of Protection and Advocacy Systems (in the Resource Guide) for more information.

∷ Anti-Discrimination Laws

In a perfect world, no one would be denied opportunities or otherwise discriminated against solely on the basis of disability, race, sex, or any other factor beyond his control. Unfortunately, our world remains imperfect, and the federal government has enacted several laws to ensure that children, adolescents, and adults with disabilities be given the right to live and work in the community to the fullest extent possible. This section reviews the highlights of the landmark Americans with Disabilities Act and the Rehabilitation Act of 1973, both of which prohibit discrimination against your child with fragile X syndrome and all people with disabilities.

The Americans with Disabilities Act

The Americans with Disabilities Act (ADA), enacted in 1990, prohibits discrimination against people with disabilities, including children and adults with fragile X syndrome. The law is based on and operates in the same way as other well-known federal laws that outlaw racial, religious, age, and sex discrimination. The ADA applies to most private employers, public and private services, public accommodations, businesses, and telecommunications.

Employment. The ADA states that no employer may discriminate against a qualified individual with a disability "in regard to job application procedures, the hiring or discharge of employees, employee compensation, advancement, job training, and other terms, conditions, and privileges of employment." In other words, private employers cannot discriminate against employees or prospective employees who have a disability. The law defines "qualified individual with a disability" as a person with a disability who, with or without reasonable accommodation, can perform the essential functions of a job. "Reasonable accommodation" means that employers must make an effort to remove obstacles from the job, the terms and conditions of employment, or the workplace that would prevent an otherwise qualified person from working because he has a disability. Accommodations can include job restructuring, schedule shuffling, modified training and personnel policies, and access to readers or interpreters. Failing to make reasonable accommodations in these respects is a violation of this law.

The law does not *require* employers to hire people with disabilities or to make accommodations if an "undue hardship" will result for the employer. Rather, employers may not refuse to employ qualified people with disabilities solely because of the existence of the disability. For example, if a person with fragile X syndrome applies for a job as an office assistant, the employer may not refuse to hire him if he is as qualified as or *more* qualified than other applicants to perform the job's duties and the employer's refusal was based on the applicant's fragile X syndrome. The employer is not required to hire qualified people with fragile X syndrome, but cannot refuse to hire a person who otherwise can perform the job because of his disability. The employer may not either inquire whether the applicant has a disability or fail to make some reasonable accommodation to enable a person with fragile X syndrome to work productively. The employment section of the ADA applies only to companies that employ 15 or more persons.

The ADA specifies procedures for people with disabilities who believe they have been the victim of employment discrimination. A person must file a complaint with the federal Equal Employment Opportunity Commission (EEOC), the agency responsible for resolving employment discrimination complaints. If the agency does not satisfactorily resolve the dispute, a lawsuit may be brought to prohibit further discrimination and to require affirmative action. The ADA allows an award of attorneys' fees to a person with a disability who wins a lawsuit. Your local office of The Arc or ACL may be able to provide basic information about how to challenge discriminatory employment practices, but a lawyer likely will be required.

Public Accommodations. One of the most stunning and potentially far-reaching provisions of the ADA is the prohibition of discrimination in public accommodations. Mirroring the approach of the civil rights laws of the 1960s, the ADA bans discrimination against people with disabilities virtually *everywhere,* including in hotels, inns, and motels; restaurants and bars; theaters, stadiums, concert halls, auditoriums, convention centers, and lecture halls; bakeries, grocery stores, gas stations, clothing stores, pharmacies, and other retail businesses; doctor or lawyer offices; airport and bus terminals; museums, libraries, galleries, parks, and zoos; nursery, elementary, secondary, undergraduate, and postgraduate schools; day care centers; homeless shelters; senior citizen centers; gymnasiums; spas; and bowling alleys. Virtually any place open to the public must also be open to people with disabilities, unless access is not physically or financially feasible. No longer can businesses exclude people with disabilities just because they are different. The excuse that people with disabilities are "not good for business" is now unlawful thanks to the ADA.

For example, a theater, restaurant, or museum cannot exclude people with fragile X syndrome from their facilities, cannot restrict their use to certain times or places, and cannot offer them only separate programs, unless to do otherwise would impose unreasonable cost on these facilities. The end result is that the new law does not merely prohibit active discrimination, but rather imposes a duty to open our society to all people with disabilities.

Like other civil rights laws, the ADA also requires integration. The law bans the insidious practice of "separate but equal" programs or facilities that offer separate services to people with disabilities, rather than access to programs offered to everyone else. The law prohibits the exclusion of people with disabilities on the grounds that there is a "special" program available just for them. For example, a recreation league (public or private) cannot uniformly exclude people with disabilities on the ground that a comparable separate league is offered.

People who are the victims of discrimination can file a lawsuit to prohibit further discrimination. And if the U.S. Department of Justice brings a lawsuit to halt a pattern and practice of discrimination, monetary damages and civil penalties may be imposed. Again, your local office of The Arc or ACL, as well as your state P&A office, will be able to provide information and assist in a discrimination complaint.

The ADA protects rights and opportunities for people with fragile X syndrome. By prohibiting discrimination and requiring reasonable accommodation, the ADA stands as a true Bill of Rights for people with all disabilities, including fragile X syndrome.

The Rehabilitation Act of 1973

Before the ADA was enacted, discrimination on the basis of disability was prohibited only in certain areas. Section 504 of the Rehabilitation Act of 1973 continues to prohibit discrimination against qualified people with disabilities in *federally funded programs.* The law provides that "No otherwise qualified individual with handicaps in the United States . . . shall, solely by reason of his handicap, be excluded from the participation in, be denied the benefits of, or be subjected to discrimination under any program or activity receiving federal financial assistance. . . ."

An "individual with handicaps" is any person who has a physical or mental impairment that substantially limits one or more of that person's "major life activities," which consist of "caring for one's self, performing manual tasks, walking, seeing, hearing, speaking, breathing, learning, and working." The U. S. Supreme Court has determined that an "otherwise qualified" handicapped individual is one who is "able to meet all of a program's requirements in spite of his handicap." Programs or activities that receive federal funds are required to make reasonable accommodation to permit the participation of qualified people with disabilities. The law covers programs like day care centers, schools, and jobs in programs receiving federal funds.

Section 504 has been used to enforce the right of children with disabilities to be integrated in their school district, to challenge placement decisions, and to assert the right to special education services for children who do not qualify for services under IDEA. Even if a child functions at a level that disqualifies him from services under IDEA, his right to services may be enforceable under Section 504. This may be important for parents of very high functioning children with fragile X syndrome who may somehow not qualify for services under IDEA. Every local education agency is required to have a Section 504 Coordinator to answer questions. As with other legal issues, you should consult a qualified lawyer to explore claims under Section 504. Section 504 permits the recovery of reasonable attorneys' fees if you prevail in your challenge.

Fair Housing Laws

Under federal fair housing laws, it is illegal to discriminate against a person with a "handicap" in the sale or rental of housing. "Handicap" as defined by federal law and regulations includes fragile X syndrome. Under these laws, landlords cannot refuse to rent to a person with fragile X syndrome or a family with a member with fragile X syndrome because of his disability. In addition, landlords may not isolate people with disabilities in one part of a building or deny them access to any common facilities available to other tenants. They must also make "reasonable" accommodations for all people with disabilities. This law is enforced by the federal Department of Housing and Urban Development (HUD) where discrimination complaints can be sent or filed by telephone or even over the Internet.

■■ Health Insurance

Often the mere fact of a child's disability can cause serious problems for families in finding and maintaining health insurance that covers the child. Unfortunately, in many states, insurance companies do not offer health or life insurance at a fair price, or sometimes at any price, to children or adults with fragile X syndrome. This practice results from the belief that these children and adults are likely to submit more insurance claims than others. Until they become adults, children who are covered from birth by their parents' insurance face fewer problems, but coverage depends on the particular terms of the insurance.

About half the states have laws against discrimination that prohibit insurance companies from denying coverage based on a disability like fragile X syndrome. The drawback to all of these laws, however, is that insurance companies are allowed to deny coverage based on "sound actuarial principles" or "reasonable anticipated experience." Insurers rely on these large loopholes to deny coverage. In short, the laws often are ineffective in protecting families of children with disabilities from insurance discrimination. Even the ADA does not prohibit these same "sound actuarial" practices that frequently result in denied coverage.

A few states have begun to lessen the health insurance burdens on families with children with disabilities. These states have passed insurance reform laws that prohibit exclusion of children with disabilities from coverage or prohibit exclusion of pre-existing conditions. Other states offer "shared risk" insurance plans, under which insurance coverage is offered to people who could not obtain coverage otherwise. The added cost is shared among all insurance companies (including HMOs) in the state. To be eligible, a person must show that he has been recently rejected for coverage or offered a policy with limited coverage. The cost of this insurance is usually higher and the benefits may be limited, but even limited coverage is usually better than no health insurance at all. Some state laws also cover people who have received premium increases of 50 percent or more. In addition, Medicare and Medicaid may be available to help with medical costs. Check with your state insurance commission or your local office of The Arc or ACL for information about health insurance programs in your area.

:: Planning for Your Child's Future: Estate Planning

Although some children with fragile X syndrome grow into independent adults, many can never manage completely on their own. This section is written for parents whose children may need publicly funded services or help in managing their funds when they are adults.

The possibility that your child may always be dependent can be overwhelming. To properly plan for your child's future, you need information in areas you may never have considered before. Questions that deeply trouble parents include: "What will happen to my child when I die? Where and with whom will he live? How will his financial needs be met? How can I be sure he receives services he needs to assure his safety, health, and quality of life?

Some parents of children with fragile X syndrome delay dealing with these issues, coping instead with the immediate demands of the present. Others begin to address the future when their child is quite young, adding to their insurance, beginning to set aside funds for their child, and sharing with family and friends their concerns about their child's future needs. Whatever the course, parents of children with fragile X syndrome need to understand certain serious planning issues that arise from their child's disabilities. Failure to take these issues into account when planning for the future can have dire consequences both for the child with disabilities and for other family members.

There are three central issues that families of children with fragile X syndrome need to consider in planning for the future. These are:

- possible cost-of-care liability;
- the complex rules governing government benefits; and
- the child's ability to handle his own affairs as an adult.

The disabilities of children with fragile X syndrome may affect planning in a number of other ways as well. For example, more life insurance may be needed, and the important choice of trustees and guardians may be more difficult. Issues about insurance coverage and financial management face most parents in one form or another. Cost-of-care liability, government benefits, and the inability to manage one's own affairs as an adult, however, present concerns that are unique to parents of children with disabilities.

▪▪ Cost-of-Care Liability

Many adults with fragile X syndrome receive residential services of some kind paid for in part by the state. Most states require the recipients of residential services to pay for the services if they have the funds to do so. Some states impose liability for daytime and vocational services as well. Called "cost-of-care liability," these requirements allow states to tap the funds of the person with disabilities to pay for the services the state provides. States can reach funds owned outright by a person with disabilities and funds set aside in improperly written trusts. A few states even impose liability on parents for the care of an adult with disabilities. This is an area parents need to look into early and carefully.

You should understand clearly that payments required to be made to satisfy cost-of-care liability do *not* benefit your child. Ordinarily they add nothing to the care and services your child will receive. Instead, the money is added to the general funds of the state to pay for roads, schools, public officials' salaries, and so on.

It is natural for you to want to pass your material resources on to your children by will or gift. In some cases, however, the unfortunate effect of leaving a portion of your estate to your child with fragile X syndrome may be the same as naming the state in your will—something few people do voluntarily, any more than they voluntarily pay more taxes than the law requires. Similarly, setting aside funds in your child's name, in a support trust, or in a Uniform Transfers to Minors Act (UTMA) account may be the same as giving money to the state—money that could better be used to meet the future needs of your child.

What can you do? The answer depends on your circumstances and the law of your state. Here are three basic strategies parents use:

First, strange as it may seem, in a few cases the best solution may be to disinherit your child with fragile X syndrome, leaving funds instead to siblings in the expectation that they will use these funds for their sibling's benefit, even though they will be under no *legal* obligation to do so. The absence of a legal obligation is crucial. It protects the funds from cost-of-care claims. The state will simply have no basis for claiming that the person with disabilities owns the funds. This strategy runs the risk, however, that the funds will not be used for your child with fragile X syndrome if the siblings: 1) choose not to use them that way; 2) suffer financial reversals or domestic problems of their own, exposing the funds to creditors or spouses; or 3) die without making arrangements to safeguard the funds.

A preferable method, more often, in states where the law is favorable is to leave funds intended for the benefit of your child with fragile X syndrome in what is called a "discretionary" special-needs trust. This kind of trust is created to supplement, rather than replace, money the state may spend on your child's care and support. The trustee of this kind of trust (the person in charge of the trust assets) has the power to use or not use the trust funds for any particular purpose as long as they are used for the benefit of the beneficiary—the child with fragile X syndrome. In many states, these discretionary trusts are not subject to cost-of-care claims because the trust does not impose any *legal* obligation on the trustee to spend funds for care and support. In contrast, "support" trusts, which *require* the trustee to use the funds for the care and support of the beneficiary with a disability, can be subjected to state cost-of-care claims.

Discretionary special needs trusts can be established during your lifetime or at your death under your will. As with all legal documents, the trust documents must be carefully written. It is generally wise, and in some states it is essential, to include provisions stating expressly that the trust is to be used to supplement rather than replace publicly funded services and benefits.

A third method to avoid cost-of-care claims is to create a trust, either during your lifetime or under your will, that affirmatively describes the kind of expenditures that are allowable for your child with fragile X syndrome in a way that leaves out care from state-funded programs. Like discretionary trusts, these trusts—sometimes called "luxury" trusts—are intended to supplement, rather than take the place of, public benefits. The state cannot reach these funds because the trust does not allow trust funds to be spent for care provided by state programs.

In determining what estate planning techniques to use, you should consult an attorney who is experienced in estate planning for parents of children with disabilities. Individualized estate planning is essential because each state's laws differ and because each family has unique circumstances.

‖ Government Benefits

People with disabilities may be eligible for any of a number of federal, state, and local benefit programs. These programs provide a wide variety of benefits and each has its own eligibility requirements. Some of these programs provide income while others provide specific benefits for persons with disabilities. The principal programs that provide income, apart from work programs, are SSI and SSDI, described below, but these are not the only programs of this kind; income is also provided for disabled survivors of federal employees and railroad employees, for example. Other programs, such as housing assistance, provide benefits that supplement income. Perhaps the most important benefit programs are those that pay for medical care—Medicare and Medicaid. These programs are also described below.

In planning for the future, it is useful to take these programs into account. For obvious reasons, it is important to avoid arrangements that will interfere with eligibility. A key point to know about eligibility is that some but not all of these programs are "means-tested." That is, the programs are available only to people without substantial financial means. SSI and Medicaid are means-tested, while SSDI and Medicare are not. Housing assistance is means-tested. If it may be important for your child with fragile X syndrome to qualify for one of these programs, funds should not be given to him directly, either now or under a will when you (or his grandparents) die. Instead, you should consider one or a combination of the three planning strategies described above to avoid cost-of-care liability: disinheritance; or more commonly, a discretionary special needs trust; or in some states, a luxury trust. In addition to avoiding cost-of-care liability, each of these strategies is intended to minimize interference with eligibility for the important means-tested benefit programs.

The principal features of four of the most important of these programs—SSI, SSDI, Medicaid, and Medicare—are described in more detail below.

SSI and SSDI

There are two basic federally funded programs that can provide additional income to people with fragile X syndrome who cannot earn enough to support themselves. The two programs are "Supplemental Security Income" (SSI) and "Social Security Disability Insurance" (SSDI). SSI pays monthly checks to children and adults with serious disabilities (along with senior citizens) who lack other income and resources. SSDI pays a monthly check to adults who are too disabled to work who have either acquired Social Security coverage based on their own past earnings, or whose disability began before age eighteen and who are the children of deceased or retired persons who earned Social Security coverage. Both SSI and SSDI are designed to provide a monthly income to people with disabilities who meet the programs' qualifications. Both program are administered by the Social Security Administration (SSA).

SSI. As of 2000, SSI pays eligible individuals $512 per month and eligible couples $769 per month. These amounts are reduced by other income of the recipient. If the recipient lives at home or is otherwise provided with food, clothing, and shelter by others, the benefit is generally reduced by about one-third.

To establish eligibility on the basis of disability, an individual must meet both a disability test and certain tests of financial need. To qualify as "disabled," an adult applicant's condition must be so disabling that he cannot engage in "substantial gainful activity." This means that he cannot perform any paid job, whether or not a suitable job can be found. The test of disability for minor children is different: whether the child's condition "results in marked and severe functional limitations." SSA regulations prescribe a set of tests and functional criteria for making these determinations. The criteria include:

1. Your child's cognitive ability, as measured by standardized IQ tests;
2. Your child's behavior patterns, including his ability to adapt to different environments; and
3. Your child's communication ability.

In making an eligibility determination SSA is required to consider all the factors that can affect your child's ability to work (or the equivalent criteria for children under age 18). Both the symptom (such as behavior) and its intensity are considered as part of a functional analysis. SSI's eligibility requirements do not end with the disability test. Eligibility is also based on financial need. To establish need, one must satisfy both a "resource" test and income tests. An applicant is ineligible if his assets ("resources") exceed $2,000 for an individual or $3,000 for a couple. The income of an SSI applicant or recipient also affects eligibility. The SSI rules allow a $20 "disregard" for monthly income of all kinds and an additional $65 "disregard" per month for earned income. Unearned income in excess of the $20 disregard reduces SSI benefits dollar for dollar. Earned income in excess of the disregards reduces SSI benefits $1 for every $2 earned, under a statutory work incentive program. In calculating an applicant's income, SSA also disregards certain impairment-related work expenses. In addition, under the PASS program (Plans for Achieving Self-Support), an SSI recipient can receive additional income or assets if they will be used to make it possible for the recipient to work in the future or to establish a business or occupation that will enable him to become gainfully employed.

In these determinations, SSA "deems" the resources and income of the parents of a child under age 18 who lives at home to be resources and income of the child. Thus, children with disabilities under age 18 who live with their parents are eligible only if their parents are very poor. When a child is 18, however, the attribution ("deeming") of parental resources and income to the child stops, and eligibility is determined on the basis of the child's own resources and income. Thus, many people with disabilities become eligible for SSI on their 18th birthday. To be eligible, however, they cannot have excess resources or income. If a child reaches his 18th birthday with more than $2,000 in assets in his own name, he will not be eligible for SSI unless and until he disposes of the excess assets.

Many people with fragile X syndrome work. Finding a job for a child with fragile X syndrome is a goal most parents strive hard to achieve. It is unfortunate that earning a salary can lead to a reduction or elimination of SSI benefits, because SSI is intended to provide income to people whose disabilities prevent them from working. Most significantly, in many states the loss of SSI may lead to a loss of medical coverage under Medicaid, discussed below. At this writing, Congress is considering additional work incentives to provide continued Medicare or Medicaid coverage for people who work their way out of SSI (or SSDI).

SSDI. People with disabilities may also qualify for SSDI—disability benefits under the Social Security program. The test for disability is the same as it is for SSI. People do not have to be poor to qualify for SSDI, unlike SSI, however; there are no financial eligibility requirements based on resources or unearned income, although earned income is severely limited. To be eligible, an applicant must qualify on the basis of his own work record for Social Security purposes, or he must be unmarried, have a disability that began before age 18, and be the child of a parent covered by Social Security who has retired or died.

As with SSI, your child's employment can cause serious problems. The work incentive program under SSI does not apply to people on SSDI, who lose eligibility if they earn more than $700 per month, because they are then deemed not to be disabled. This rule places an unfair burden on recipients of SSDI by forcing them to make a choice between work and financial security (and medical insurance). SSDI rules allow recipients to work for only a limited trial period without losing eligibility. Although most people with disabilities that are severe enough to meet the SSA tests become eligible for SSI at age 18, they may become eligible for SSDI on their parents' work record when their parents retire or die, thus subjecting them to the SSDI rules described above. However, if SSDI rules reduce benefits below SSI levels, SSI generally will make up the difference.

Medicare

Medicare is a federal health insurance program that helps pay for the medical expenses of people who qualify. People who are eligible for SSDI benefits, either on their own account or on a parent's account, will also be eligible for Medicare, starting at any age, after a waiting period. These persons will automatically receive Part A (hospital) coverage, and they can elect Part B (medical) coverage, for which they will pay a premium. If a person can also qualify for Medicaid, discussed below, Medicaid may pay the Medicare Part B premium. In some cases, children or adults with disabilities who would not otherwise be eligible for Medicare may qualify if a third party—parents, relatives, charities, or even state and local governments—pays into Medicare. Called "third party buy-in," this works very much like purchasing private health insurance. Check with your local SSA office for details.

Medicaid

Medicaid is also important to many people with fragile X syndrome. It pays for medical care for people who do not have private health insurance or Medicare and lack sufficient income to pay for medical care. It also provides certain benefits that are not covered by Medicare, including prescription drug coverage and financial aid for the purchase of wheelchairs. In many states, under so-called "Medicaid waivers," it pays for residential services for many people with disabilities.

Because Medicaid is funded by both federal and state governments, there are differences among states in the range of benefits offered. For example, some states provide "optional" services such as dental care, speech or language therapy, and occupational therapy. Consequently, parents must check with their state or local SSA office to make sure they are receiving the maximum range of Medicaid benefits available in their state.

Medicaid is funded partly by the states and partly by the federal government, and is administered by the states. In most states, if your child meets the eligibility criteria for SSI, he will qualify for Medicaid when he reaches age 18. Because eligibility is based on financial need, however, placing assets in the name of your child can disqualify her.

Other Medicaid Services. There are two important issues related to Medicaid that seriously affect the lives of people with fragile X syndrome:

1. Under current law, Medicaid pays for residential services for people with disabilities in large Medicaid-certified residential institutions, called "intermediate care facilities" (ICFs). Most people with disabilities such as fragile X syndrome are best served in the *community*, not in institutions, however. The Secretary of HHS has the authority to "waive" the ICF requirement, and current administrative practice is friendly to applications for these waivers. As a result, most states have received waivers allowing Medicaid funding of services in community-based facilities. The services that can be provided under this waiver include respite care, adaptive technologies, nutritional counseling, social services, homemaker services, and case management. Future adminis-

trative practice in this area could change, however, without a statutory mandate.

2. *Early and Periodic Screening, Diagnosis, and Treatment Program (EPSDT).* Under this Medicaid program, states provide periodic medical and developmental assessments of children under the age of 21 whose parents qualify for Medicaid, and provide the services—medical and otherwise—needed to treat any diagnosis. These services can include physical, occupational, and speech therapies, immunizations, assistive devices, and vision, dental, and medical treatment. Your state or county department of health services should have an EPSDT contact who can help you determine if your child is eligible for services under this program. Your county or state P&A office can also help you obtain EPSDT services.

It is important for you to become generally familiar with the complex rules governing SSI, SSDI, Medicare, and Medicaid. You can contact your local SSA office, or call their national toll-free number (800-772-1213). Again, we repeat the importance of avoiding a mistake that could disqualify your child from receiving needed benefits by implementing one of the basic strategies described in this chapter.

Children with Special Health Care Needs Program (HCP)

Under a program of grants administered by the Maternal and Child Health Bureau of the U.S. Department of Health and Human Services, states receive funds to pay for a wide variety of health-related services to children of low income families. Services can include evaluations, clinic visits, hospitalization, surgery, medications, physical, occupational, and speech therapy, dental care, and genetic testing, Each state sets its own financial eligibility requirements based on a family's annual income. Unlike Medicaid, however, your child's assets do not affect eligibility. States can select the conditions that will be covered. This list is generally very broad; children with fragile X syndrome should qualify for services if their parents are eligible financially. There is also variation among states in the age at which these services cease to be available; generally between age 18 and age 21. Each state has a coordinator for this program typically at the state departments of health or human services. Your local office of The Arc can help you locate the state coordinator.

Children's Health Insurance Program (CHIP)

In 1997, Congress enacted a new health insurance program, the Children's Health Insurance Program (CHIP), to provide free or low-cost health insurance to children whose parents' income is too high to qualify for Medicaid and too low to be able to afford private family insurance. In most states, uninsured children age 18 and under in families with an income of less than $32,900 qualify for coverage under CHIP. Most states currently participate in this program and offer a wide range of coverage for children, including checkups, immunizations, doctor visits, prescription drugs, and hospital care. Applications for coverage under the CHIP program can be obtained from state or local health and human services departments.

▪▪ Competence to Manage Financial Affairs

Even if your child with fragile X syndrome may never need state-funded residential care or government benefits, he may need help in arranging his financial affairs. Care must be exercised in deciding how to make assets available for your child. There are a wide variety of arrangements that can allow someone else to control the ways in which money is spent after you die. Of course, the choice of the best arrangements depends on many different considerations, such as your child's capacity to manage assets, his relation-ship with his siblings, your financial situation, and the availability of an appropriate trustee or financial manager. As an adult, your child will want to be consulted regarding decisions that affect him; you should arrange for that.

Choosing trustees and financial managers is harder for a person who will need assistance all his life than it is for a minor child who can take charge of his own affairs when he becomes an adult, because the trust or other arrangements must last so much longer after parents die. Consequently, particular consideration must be given to mechanisms for changing trustees after the original trustees can no longer serve. Each family is different. A knowledgeable lawyer can review the various alternatives and help you choose the one best suited to your family.

Need for Guardians

Parents frequently ask whether they should nominate themselves or others as guardians once their child with fragile X syndrome becomes an adult. A guardian is a person appointed by a court or by law to manage the legal and financial affairs of someone else. The appointment of a guardian costs money and may result in the curtailment of your child's rights—the right to marry, to have a checking account, to vote, and so on. Therefore, a guardian should be appointed only if and when needed. If one is not needed during your lifetime, it usually is sufficient to nominate guardians in your will.

Your child's fragile X syndrome is not by itself a sufficient reason to establish a guardianship, either when your child becomes an adult or at any other time. A guardian will be needed in certain situations, however. For example, guardianship may be necessary if your child inherits or acquires property that he lacks the capacity to manage. Also, a guardian may be required if a medical provider refuses to serve your child without authorization by a guardian. Occasionally it is necessary to appoint a guardian to gain access to important legal, medical, or educational records. Unless there is a specific need that can be solved by the appointment of a guardian, however, there is no reason to consider guardianship.

Life Insurance

Parents of children with fragile X syndrome should review their life insurance coverage. The most important use of life insurance is to meet financial needs that arise if the insured person dies. Many people who support dependents with their wages or salaries are underinsured. This problem is aggravated if hard-earned dollars are wasted on insurance that does not provide the amount or kind of protection that could and should be purchased. It is therefore essential for any person with dependents to understand basic facts about insurance.

The first question to consider is: Who should be insured? Life insurance deals with the *financial* risks of death. The principal financial risk of death in most families is that the death of the wage earner or earners will deprive dependents of support. Consequently, life insurance coverage should be considered primarily for the parent or parents on whose earning power the children depend, rather than on the lives of children or dependents.

The second question is whether your insurance is adequate to meet the financial needs that will arise if you die. A reputable insurance agent can help you determine whether your coverage is adequate. Consumer guides to insurance listed in the Reading List of this book can also help you calculate the amount of insurance you need.

The next question is: What kind of insurance policy should you buy? Insurance policies are of two basic types: term insurance, which provides "pure" insurance without any build-up of cash value or reserves, and other types (called "whole life," "universal life," and "variable life"), which, in addition to providing insurance, include a savings or investment factor. The latter kinds of insurance, sometimes called "permanent" insurance, are really a combined package of insurance and investment.

People with children who do not have disabilities try to assure that their children's education will be paid for if they die before their children finish school. Many people use life insurance to deal with this risk. When their children are grown and educated, this insurance need disappears. Term insurance is a relatively inexpensive way to deal with risks of this kind.

On the other hand, people with fragile X syndrome may need supplemental assistance throughout their lives. That need may not disappear completely during their parents' lifetimes. If the parents plan on using life insurance to help meet this need when they die, they must recognize, in deciding what kind of insurance to buy, that term insurance premiums rise sharply as they get older. Consequently, they should either adopt and stick to a savings and investment program to eventually replace the insurance, or consider purchasing whole life or universal life.

Whether you buy term insurance and maintain a separate savings and investment program, or instead buy one of the other kinds of policies that combine them, you should make sure that the insurance part of your program is adequate to meet your family's financial needs if you die. A sound financial plan will meet these needs and will satisfy savings and retirement objectives in a way that does not sacrifice adequate insurance coverage.

Finally, it is essential to coordinate your life insurance with the rest of your estate plan. This is done by designating the beneficiary—choosing who is to receive any insurance proceeds when you die. If you wish any or all of these proceeds to be used for your child's support, you may wish to designate a trustee under your will or the trustee of a separate life insurance trust as a beneficiary of your insurance. Upon your death, the trustee will receive the insurance proceeds and use them for the benefit of your child in accordance with the trust. If you do not name a trustee, but instead name the child with fragile X syndrome as a beneficiary, your child's share of the proceeds may be subject to cost-of-care claims, or may interfere with eligibility for government benefits, described earlier.

❖ A Guide to Estate Planning for Parents of Children with Fragile X Syndrome

More than most parents, the parents of a child with fragile X syndrome need to attend to estate planning. Because of concerns about cost-of-care liability, government benefits, and competency, it is vital that you make plans. Parents need to name the people who will care for their child with fragile X syndrome when they die. They need to review their insurance to be sure it is adequate to meet their child's special needs. They need to make sure their retirement plans will help meet their child's needs as an adult. They need to inform grandparents of cost-of-care liability, government benefits, and competency problems so that grandparents do not inadvertently waste resources that could otherwise benefit their grandchild. Most of all, parents need to make wills so that their hopes and plans are realized and the disastrous consequences of dying without a will are avoided.

Proper estate planning differs for each family. Every will must be tailored to individual needs. There are no formula wills, especially for parents of a child with fragile X syndrome. There are some common mistakes to avoid, however. Here is a list:

No Will. In most states, the children (including a child with a disability) of a married person who dies without a will are entitled to equal shares in a portion of the assets the parent owns at death. The entire estate of a single parent who dies without a will must be divided equally among the children. The result is that your child with fragile X syndrome will inherit property in his own name. His inheritance may become subject to cost-of-care claims and could jeopardize eligibility for government benefits. These and other problems can be avoided with a properly drafted will. Do not ever allow your state's laws to determine how your property will be divided upon your death. No parent of a child with fragile X syndrome should die without a will.

A Will Leaving Property Outright to the Child with Fragile X Syndrome. A will that leaves property to a child with fragile X syndrome in his own name is often just as bad as no will at all, because it may subject the inheritance to cost-of-care liability and may disqualify him for government benefits. Parents of children with fragile X syndrome do not just need any will, they need a will that meets their special needs.

A Will Creating a Support Trust for Your Child with Fragile X Syndrome. A will that creates a support trust (described above) presents much the same problem as a will that leaves property outright to a child with fragile X syndrome. The funds in these trusts may be subject to cost-of-care claims and jeopardize government benefits. A qualified lawyer experienced in these issues can help draft a will that avoids this problem.

Insurance and Retirement Plans Naming a Child with Fragile X Syndrome as a Beneficiary. Many parents own life insurance policies that name a child with fragile X syndrome as a beneficiary or contingent beneficiary, either alone or in common with siblings. The result is that insurance proceeds may go outright to your child with fragile X syndrome, creating cost-of-care liability and government benefits eligibility problems. Parents should designate the funds to pass either to someone else or to go into a properly drawn trust. The same is true of many retirement plan benefits.

Use of Joint Tenancy in Lieu of Wills. Spouses sometimes avoid making wills by placing all their property in joint tenancies with right of survivorship. When one of the spouses dies, the survivor automatically becomes the sole owner. Parents try to use joint tenancies instead of wills, relying on the surviving spouse to properly take care of all estate planning matters. This plan, however, fails completely if both parents die in the same disaster, if the surviving spouse becomes incapacitated, or if the surviving spouse neglects to make a proper will. The result is the same as if neither spouse made any will at all—the child with fragile X syndrome shares in the parents' estates. As explained above, this result may expose the assets to cost-of-care liability and give rise to problems with government benefits. Therefore, even when all property is held by spouses in joint tenancy, it is necessary that both spouses make wills.

Establishing UTMA Accounts for Your Child with Fragile X Syndrome. Over and over again well-meaning parents and grandparents open bank accounts for children with disabilities under the Uniform Transfers to Minors Act (UTMA). When the child reaches age 21, the account becomes the property of the child, and may therefore be subject to cost-of-care liability. Perhaps more important, most people with disabilities first become eligible for SSI and Medicaid at age 18, but the UTMA funds will have to be spent or financial eligibility for these programs will be lost, thus making the state and federal governments the indirect beneficiaries of funds the family has set aside. Parents and relatives of children with fragile X syndrome who are likely to need government-funded services or benefits should *never* set up UTMA accounts for their child with fragile X syndrome, nor should they open other bank accounts in the child's name.

Failing to Advise Grandparents and Relatives of the Need for Special Arrangements. Just as the parents of a child with fragile X syndrome need properly drafted wills or trusts, so do grandparents and other relatives who may leave (or give) property to the child. If these people are not aware of the special concerns—cost-of-care liability, government

benefits, and competency—their plans may go awry and their generosity may be wasted. Make sure anyone planning gifts to your child with fragile X syndrome understands what is at stake.

Children and adults with fragile X syndrome are entitled to lead full and rewarding lives. But many of them cannot do so without continuing financial support from their families. The *only* way to make sure your child has that support whenever he needs it is to plan for tomorrow today. Doing otherwise can rob him of the future he deserves.

∷ Conclusion

Parenthood always brings responsibilities. Substantial extra responsibilities confront parents of a child with fragile X syndrome. Understanding the pitfalls for the future and planning to avoid them will help you to meet the special responsibilities. In addition, knowing and asserting your child's rights can help guarantee that he will receive the education and government benefits to which he is entitled. Being a good advocate for your child requires more than knowledge. You must also be determined to use that knowledge effectively, and, when necessary, forcefully.

∷ Parent Statements

People with special needs have all the legal rights that anyone else has. It is good that we live in a country civilized enough to recognize that. For many with disabilities, it takes an extra effort and extra resources to provide appropriate education and appropriate services. But, in some ways, providing government entitlements discourages many individuals of good will from offering their gifts of companionship and friendship, which are far more valuable than any legal safeguards.

With all of the fight for money these days around schools it is a good thing we have IDEA.

I think the number of "programs" in our school district has doubled since IDEA was reauthorized.

IDEA or no IDEA, my child has a right to attend school just like every other kid.

Generally, our OT is covered, but speech therapy isn't. The insurance company requests OT progress reports every 6 months.

Our insurance won't cover anything except regular doctor visits. After diagnosis they stopped, saying they couldn't cover things that were "mental."

Thinking about all of the adult issues when William turns 21 is more than I can think about right now.

I will not plan very much for my child's future because he has yet to finish building it! I won't accept the ideas of group homes or entry level jobs as his lot in life because there's so much more out there for him.

In planning for the future, we have tried to be guided by what our sons envision for themselves, rather than being swayed by programs and services which may be available. In some cases this has meant passing by some opportunities for county services in order to honor our sons' personal choices.

We have tried to assure that each has a circle of supportive friends who will care about him and help him find creative ways to face life challenges.

We don't have a will yet. I know we need one though.

Wills scare the hell out of me, but I know my kids need me to face it like a grownup.

In general, I advocate looking to alternate systems before invoking legal remedies. If we are interested in having a good plan put into action by people who are heavily invested in making it work, we are wise to rely on methods other than court action to enforce our children's rights.

We used mediation once. It did not resolve anything.

ADVOCACY

Jamie Stephenson

■ Introduction

When I was asked to write this chapter, I was a bit confused about what was expected. How could I, a parent, write about advocacy? I was not a professional lobbyist or a motivational speaker. In fact, I had been just "flying by the seat of my pants" as an advocate. I had successfully advocated for my child and for the Fragile X Resource Center of Northern New England, which I founded, and for the regional parent support group I coordinate. This parent group meets at different hospitals in the Boston area and provides support, networking opportunities, and information for parents  from all six New England states. But I had no magic formula for achieving those successes. So what could I possibly put into this chapter?

I soon realized that the best parent-advocates follow their hearts, not a list of guidelines. They know what is right (especially for their own children) and have the energy to pursue it. *You* are the expert;

this chapter will present information and "food for thought" that you can use or disregard as you wish. I will also help you to identify the natural talent that you bring to your job as an advocate.

Advocacy is the act of speaking up on behalf of another person. Lawyers are referred to as advocates. Parents are referred to as advocates when they behave in a diplomatic, tactful, professional manner. They are referred to as hysterical and unreasonable when they do not. For example, during one special education team meeting I began to cry, demanding that my son's school cut the (obscenity) and give my son the aide he needed. I was having a bad day but the IEP team members didn't take it that way. Until that moment, the teachers and administrators treated me with quiet respect. Afterward, they approached me warily, afraid of another emotional outburst. I lost my credibility that day and it took months to regain it. I learned well the lesson, "It's not what you say, it's how you say it."

I have two children with fragile X syndrome and have been an active advocate in several different venues, but my career as an advocate began years before I ever heard of fragile X syndrome. It started over a simple matter of breastfeeding. Fifteen years ago I had decided to breastfeed my first child because my husband and I believed that infants do best on breast milk and we wanted our child to have a good start. When she was born, we stayed in the hospital for four days and were at the mercy of the newborn nursery schedule, not a situation that fosters breastfeeding. So I firmly stated to the nurses that I wanted my baby brought to me whenever she was awake, and I questioned them if she was kept in the nursery for more than two hours. In this simple way, I was advocating for my child when she was only hours old. The reason that I was able to do this was because I believed I was right and I did not care if the nurses liked me. I was not apologetic about my request even though I was in the vulnerable position as a hospital patient, but I was not rude either. I just politely asserted my rights.

As you can see from the above example, advocacy comes naturally to parents. It is almost instinctive to want your child to have the best of everything. But the wise parent knows that the "best" is not always what a child needs. Sometimes meeting your child's needs involves setting a reasonable bedtime so that he gets the sleep that he requires. Other times it involves convincing a school principal why your child needs to have a particular teacher, supplementary support aide, or related service in order to be successful. These two examples require very different skills. Sending a child to bed when he wants to stay up requires a firm attitude. Changing a principal's mind requires sophisticated interpersonal skills and some degree of mental fortitude on top of that firm attitude.

When a child with fragile X syndrome enters a family, the need for advocacy expands into unfamiliar territory. You may find yourself trying to get medical professionals to complete diagnostic tests in a timely fashion or trying to convince a team of five professional educators that your child needs to be placed in the regular classroom. Whatever the challenge, you as the parent will also be the best advocate for your child (note that in this chapter "parent" refers to any adult caregiver, including foster parents, adoptive parents, step-parents, grandparents, and adult siblings).

There will be times when you may think that your efforts have been unsuccessful. But your failures will teach you more than your successes will. Advocacy, like parenting, is not a science or an art, it is a craft. If today's piece of pottery doesn't come out perfectly, there will be a better one tomorrow as long as you do not quit. If today's team meeting turns into a disaster, you can be assured that you will have plenty of opportunity in future meetings to try again because team meetings are a permanent part of life with a child with fragile X syndrome.

You will most often advocate for your own child. You must assure that your child has the best possible educational services and support in the classroom. If your child is an adult, you must be sure that he is comfortable with his job, transportation, and living situation. In general, throughout your life you must constantly advocate for two things:

1. Any person (professional or paraprofessional) who has contact with your child must be qualified and knowledgeable about fragile X syndrome, and committed to caring; and

2. Your child's program must foster his abilities while addressing his needs.

The list is short, isn't it? When subdivided into the more detailed issues listed below, you can see how advocacy can expand to include venues ranging from IEP team meetings to the United States Congress. At any given time you will probably be advocating in one of these areas or thinking of doing so.

- *Early intervention services*—You might need to request home based services, for example.
- *School inclusion*—You may have to use all the charm and finesse you possess to convince the school staff that they can do it and that you are willing to help in any way you can.
- *An individualized education program (IEP)*— Not a standard cookie-cutter IEP. You might advocate for services that are not standard, like sensory integration therapy.
- *Related services*—A bus ride that is so traumatic that your child needs the entire morning to calm himself is not appropriate and you must insist on a change.
- *Inclusion in recreational activities*—In addition to convincing the organizers of the local town recreation program to allow your child to participate, you may have to play an active role beyond the average parent who only drops their child off and picks him up.
- *Appropriate adult services*—If your child can read and has mastered some mathematics, for example, you can advocate for a job placement that utilizes those skills.
- *Preservation of the human services system*—You may have to lobby your state legislature to prevent program cuts affecting people with developmental disabilities.
- *Preservation of federal laws mandating special education and adult services*—You can advocate to your representatives in Congress to protect federally mandated programs, like special education, social security, and Medicaid, that benefit people with developmental disabilities.

■ *Medical and educational research initiatives*—You may lobby Congress to add fragile X syndrome to the list of research priorities when funding the National Institutes of Health budget, for example.

This chapter discusses advocating for your child and explains how fragile X syndrome requires a special type of advocacy. It also offers some strategies used by successful parent-advocates, and outlines some skills that can help you be a better, less stressed advocate. Finally, it touches on the issue of group advocacy, an important part of the fragile X syndrome culture.

▪▪ Advocating for Your Child

A family who has just received a diagnosis of fragile X syndrome is entering a unique world. Sometimes families must also face that there are other family members who have symptoms but have not been diagnosed. In addition, the diagnosis doesn't affect only you and your child, but also the members of your extended family. If you have older relatives with fragile X syndrome, you probably have a lot of first-hand knowledge about living with the condition, but may not have a lot of knowledge about the genetic and neurological aspects. The parents of a child who is the only individual with fragile X syndrome in a family may through research learn a lot about the medical and scientific aspects but may not know anything about life with fragile X syndrome.

Ask Questions

After your child is diagnosed with fragile X syndrome, you will need to gather information about the condition in order to be a competent advocate. Acquiring knowledge—from genetics to medical issues to education—will be a lifelong pursuit.

Initially you should ask questions like "Is there any treatment? What are the effects on my other family members? How do I access services? Which agencies and organizations can help my family and me? How will this affect his future?" You may not understand all of the medical jargon about brain function and genetics, but no one really knows exactly how the brain works. And remember that your child is a unique individual and, like everyone else, his future depends on life experiences and environment as well as heredity.

Go beyond labels or basic information; ask for more detailed facts. A physical therapist may tell you your child has "low tone" but you remember the broken nose you received when your son threw his head back while you were holding him. How can someone with so much strength have low muscle tone? Ask the therapist to explain further or explain it a different way. Don't ever feel like your questions are bothersome or stupid. The professionals really do not know how much you understand and don't want to appear to be "talking down" to you. Give them a sense of what you understand. Become informed by asking questions.

Educating yourself about fragile X syndrome can help your child reach his maximum potential. Whatever your experience, remember that knowledge is power and you possess more knowledge about your child than anyone else. Your interest in fragile X syndrome is keen and will motivate you to seek information. Ask a lot of questions and expand your knowledge base. Your child will benefit from any new information you acquire. When my son entered preschool, special education programs in my area did not include vestibular stimulation (sensory integration) therapy. The specialists had not been trained in it, they did not have the proper equipment, and they believed it was not a valid therapy. I brought a lot of information to his special education team and eventually a program was set up which benefited my child and many others after him.

You are becoming informed about fragile X by reading this book. At the same time, you are learning about your role as an advocate by reading this chapter. Learn as much as you can and continue to stay informed as research brings more insight into fragile X syndrome. It is important to have a solid knowledge base when you begin to advocate for your child so that you can comfortably converse with professionals about the uniqueness of your child. You can help them see your child as a person rather than a "fragile X case study." In order to do this, you must know the current theories about fragile X syndrome and what the past (sometimes erroneous) theories were. When talking with a professional about your child, you must pay close attention to what he or she says about your child and about fragile X syndrome. There are hundreds of genetic conditions which cause developmental disability and you cannot expect every medical or educational professional to be an expert on fragile X syndrome. You can help fill in their information gaps.

An important source of information and advocacy is the National Fragile X Foundation which was founded in 1987. It has been a "cutting edge" resource for parents ever since. The Foundation sponsors conferences and research projects on fragile X syndrome and supports an international network of Resource Centers. The Foundation can put you in touch with the Resource Center in your area. The Resource Center may have a support group you can attend or help you start one. Some resource centers publish newsletters and mail out packets of up-to-date information about fragile X syndrome. The resource center in your area may even hold regular symposia on fragile X syndrome.

Several states also have their own fragile X syndrome associations. You can find out from the National Foundation or from your doctor if there is a fragile X syndrome association in your area which you can contact to find out what is going on in your region. See the Resource Guide at the end of the book.

You can also gather valuable information at fragile X syndrome or general disability conferences and workshops. There are conferences that focus on special education laws and there are workshops on estate planning to name just two. You might find that a conference on early childhood sponsored by your state department of education is a good place to learn about the latest theories and practices for teaching young children and what programs are available in your state. If your child is older, a workshop on supported employment and independent living might be the best place to collect information to help you plan his adulthood.

Of course, a conference that focuses solely on fragile X syndrome is the best place to get up-to-the-minute information specific to this condition. You may be able to find a fragile X syndrome conference in your local area. The low cost and limited travel can be a real plus. But there is nothing like the International Fragile X Conferences sponsored by the National Fragile X Foundation. The time and expense are well worth the sacrifice because you will get information on every aspect of life with fragile X syndrome from inheritance patterns to DNA technology to best educational practices and starting a support group. I strongly recommend attending the International Conference at least once.

Federal law also provides resources to help train you as an advocate. Each state has a federally funded Parent Training and Information Center (see Resource Guide) offering free workshops and courses for parents of children with disabilities. The training covers special education laws and regulations and parental rights in the special education process. The training will give you confidence and empower you to advocate for your child's educational needs. It will also help you to better understand your child's needs.

Armed with this war chest of information, you become the expert when advocating for your child. Remember to use your expertise wisely.

Create A Network

In addition to information, you need to develop a network of contacts—parents, teachers, attorneys, advocates, and organizations—to use as resources in your advocacy efforts. The National Fragile X Foundation and its Resource Centers are logical places to begin. Contacting the National Foundation and your regional Resource Center can put you in touch with people who are involved in fragile X syndrome and who have lots of experience with it. FRAXA Research Foundation is another useful national organization. FRAXA advocates and raises funds for research toward better understanding of fragile X syndrome.

Another national organization to contact is The Arc (formerly called the Association for Retarded Citizens or ARC). In Canada this organization is known as the Association for Community Living (ACL). Both have state (or provincial) or county offices. Your local Arc or ACL can give you information about parent training and support groups where you can meet other parents in your area who have children with special needs. They can also give you information about recreational activities for your child such as the Special Olympics, summer camps, after school activities for children with special needs, and regular recreation programs which include people with special needs. The Arc or ACL may also offer scholarships for parents to attend workshops and conferences. These scholarships are especially helpful to defray the cost of the big national conferences, which can be expensive. The Arc or ACL can also tell you about legislative efforts on behalf of people with disabilities.

There are several other useful groups. The Alliance of Genetic Support Groups (see Resource Guide) advocates for consumers in the genetic research community and the federal government. Parent-to-Parent Support and Information System is a grass roots organization that has become a major resource for individuals with disabilities and their families. The Alliance and Parent-to-Parent are very supportive of parent-advocates. The Alliance publishes a monthly newsletter, keeps a national directory of genetic support groups, holds a national conference every two years, and provides written materials on many diverse topics including health insurance, informed consent, starting a support group, and obtaining nonprofit status. Parent-to-Parent holds a conference every two years where families can network and learn what other parent-advocates are doing.

There are national, regional, and local conferences and symposia offered on fragile X syndrome and other disabilities. In addition to the informational sessions at a conference, there are numerous opportunities to network with professionals and other parents. By attending conferences and workshops and support group meetings, you will quickly expand your network to include parents and professionals in your local area, parents from other states, and some of the top fragile X syndrome researchers in the world.

∷ Advocating for Your Child

Your child's diagnosis of fragile X syndrome may overwhelm you at first. You might have a large body of medical literature to sift through and digest. Your extended family members may be in various stages of grief, denial, and acceptance. You may have a disturbing view of your child's future. And during all of this emotional and mental turmoil, you must continue tending to your child's daily needs.

Your child needs love from you and personal care, first and foremost. But parenting extends far beyond the basics of daily care, especially when your child has a disability. A child with fragile X syndrome usually needs extra attention, patience, and advocacy, even during the early years of preschool and elementary school.

Beginning with early intervention, you will find yourself constantly explaining your child's behavior and development to professionals and caretakers. In speaking for your child and his needs, you become his advocate. You must always treat the professionals as knowledgeable partners in your child's care, even though they may sometimes seem like complete chowderheads. They don't have the benefit of your years of experience with your child. Your job as a parent-advocate is to help them know your child better. Keeping a level head during the early years after diagnosis is almost impossible because

you are still grieving and need to shed a lot of tears and let out a lot of anger. But you should always try to be calm when meeting with your child's professional team. You will probably have to train yourself to do it. Through trial and error you will learn what topics are your "hot buttons" during team meetings so prepare to redirect the discussion or try to avoid those topics altogether.

As you become an experienced advocate for your child, you will probably expend less energy controlling your emotions and more time crafting an educational plan to meet your child's needs. You can (and should) keep yourself abreast of the current research on fragile X syndrome so you can educate your child's professional team. Educational strategies for students with fragile X syndrome have changed and continue to evolve as more research emerges. For example, a decade ago behavior management included restraints and lemon juice spray, two things that can exacerbate behavior issues in people with fragile X syndrome. Research focused specifically on the origins of challenging behavior suggests that a quiet, gentle, noninvasive, preventative approach to behavior management is a better alternative. You might need to provide copies of the current research on fragile X syndrome to professionals who are not up to date on behavior management.

Your advocacy will continue into your child's IEP process, and you may have to guide IEP team members to the goals and objectives specifically tailored to your child's needs. For example, eye contact is a standard IEP goal although research long ago proved that individuals with fragile X syndrome attend better when allowed to look away from a speaker. Sometimes a teacher will discover this independently; usually you will have to advocate to remove the "eye contact objective" from your child's IEP. But don't expect the professionals to take your word all the time. You should bring a folder containing current research papers supporting your position to share with the team.

Be prepared to be flexible. Compromise is very difficult for a parent who knows exactly what his child needs. But, like learning to control your emotions, knowing how to compromise is a necessary skill to use at a meeting. You should have high expectations for your child's program, but realize that we live in an imperfect world. For example, if you believe your child can benefit from daily sensory integration therapy but the team recommends only two sessions per week, you might be able to get a third session added but probably won't be able to convince the team to recommend five sessions each week. You will have to decide when to compromise and when to continue to negotiate.

Finally, parent-advocates will often volunteer in the school. Teachers and other school personnel notice which parents are giving extra time to the school. When you volunteer you send the message that you care about quality education and are willing to commit your time to see it happen. In public schools, volunteer opportunities abound and range from daily classroom work to an occasional baking assignment. You don't have to be PTA president but you do have to do *something*. You can attend planning meetings, run classroom parties, build sets for the school play, make phone calls, or just send in a bottle of juice for a classroom party. Educators will appreciate anything you do, and will respect your position concerning the effort the school should be making to educate your child.

When your child enters the adult service system, you can use the advocacy skills you develop during his school years. You will first need to educate yourself about the human services system, its goals and programs. Next you will have to educate a new group of professionals—including caseworkers, direct care providers, and social workers—about your child and about fragile X syndrome. You will have learned to control your emotions (which might be more difficult than you expect) and you will be ready to advocate for your child's adult life, which extends much longer than the 12 to 19 years of public school. Also you might find volunteer opportunities at the agency serving your child. Fundraising is an important activity in adult services. You may need to be more active in your adult child's life but in a different way.

▚ Public Advocacy

You may decide to engage in advocacy in a wider arena that will not only benefit your own child but other children as well. Many parents have participated in public advocacy with great success. The special education laws, which entitle our children to a free and appropriate education, were enacted because of the efforts of many dedicated parent-advocates who saw that their children could learn and benefit from an education. This seems so obvious nowadays, but our children's right to an education like everyone else had to be fought for and won; parents led this fight. Parent advocacy also led to other important changes in the lives of people with disabilities. For example, the closing of New Hampshire's institution where people with mental retardation were warehoused (and institutions in many other states) was prompted by parents who were appalled by the conditions there and filed a lawsuit against the state. In another case, one family's efforts to take their daughter home from the hospital even though she could not breathe without a respirator led to the change in Medicaid regulations to allow Medicaid coverage outside the hospital for a seriously ill child regardless of family income. The work of many of the local support groups for fragile X syndrome (even the National Fragile X Foundation itself) is made possible by parent volunteers who advocate for assistance from public and private funding sources. There are many opportunities to be a public advocate and your time and energy will be well spent in any of them.

Here is a list of issues parents have advocated for and which might be issues on which you may want or need to focus:

- Change school district policies (e.g., classroom aides) to facilitate inclusion
- Creative state funding schemes for adult services
- Home-based early intervention programs
- Federal funding for fragile X syndrome research
- Community-based services

- Community inclusion supports
- Preserving and enhancing federal and state special education laws and regulations

Your Own Backyard

If your child is in public school, begin by connecting with a special education support group. These groups are usually customized to the issues at hand locally. Parents in my school district started a group when their children entered high school. The group held coffees for administrators and staff in order to pass on information on inclusion and curriculum adaptation. They also met with each other to share information and support each other. If there is one already in place, for example Children and Adults with Attention Deficit Hyperactivity Disorder (C.H.A.D.D.), join it and contribute to its efforts on behalf of children with special education needs. You can help shape the group's agenda by attending meetings to offer your input and volunteering to do some work for the group. When you decide to advocate for a change in policy to benefit your child, you will have the support of the group.

You may decide to advocate for disability rights in general. There are support groups that address those issues in most states. Sometimes you may find a group that is for parents of children with fragile X syndrome, but you should be willing to join forces with advocates in other disability areas. You may find five people who are willing and able to work to improve the lives of people with fragile X syndrome, but you will find 50 people who will advocate for better housing for all adults with disabilities. There is strength in numbers and the more people you have, the more attention you will get.

Starting A Local Advocacy Group

If there are no groups in your area, or the groups you find do not meet your needs, you can start a group yourself. If you think that you can't organize a group, think again. Have you ever hosted a dinner party, or a PTA committee, or a fundraising event for a club, or a kid's birthday party? If you have done anything with a goal and steps to reach that goal, you have the skills to organize a group.

- *Goals.* First you need to choose goals for your group around fragile X syndrome. Some goals are short term, like bringing families together. Other goals are long term such as increasing awareness of fragile X syndrome in your area.

A goal can be very tangible such as changing your school district's policy of sending all special education students to a separate school, or it can be as intangible as improving communication among families. After the initial goals are achieved, your group can shape its future goals based on the ideas and needs of the members.

■ **Membership.** Once your group has goals, you will identify potential members and contact them. If your goals are focused on fragile X syndrome, you will probably begin by contacting a genetics center in your area or the public health department to send information about the group to fragile X syndrome families. Don't expect the medical office to give you their mailing list, but they may be willing to mail something out for you. Also, place an announcement in a big city newspaper announcing the formation of your group. If you are having a meeting, be sure to include that information in your notice. If your goals are related to special education, your group will include other disability areas in addition to fragile X syndrome. Placing a notice in local disability organization newsletters, such as The Arc or ACL, will help spread the word about your group.

To contact potential members for a special education advocacy group you can request time at a school PTA meeting or talk with the principal of the school about putting a notice in the school newsletter. Because of confidentiality laws, the school cannot give you the names of children with educational disabilities, so don't even ask.

■ **Activities.** You will need appropriate activities for the group to participate in while working toward its goals. For example, a picnic for families to meet each other and share information will help parents connect. If the goal is to lobby for better services for children with special needs, you will need a meeting to plan how and who to lobby. Both of these examples are good activities to begin a group. The idea is to create opportunities for bonding among the members so that the group will be strong.

■ **Delegate Tasks.** Once you have at least one other person who is committed to the group (sometimes that person is your spouse), begin to share the job load. One person can handle the publicity and the other can research possible meeting places. When the group is large, jobs can be separated into parts. For example, for publicity one person can send a notice to the newspapers while another person contacts the regional medical center to send a notice to clients. It is important that everyone in the group feels like he is making a contribution; even a small job will make someone feel connected to the group.

- **Follow Up.** You should have a plan for continuing the group. Another project, or a second event, or a workshop, or even a picnic to celebrate the achievement of goals will give meaning to the group and help it continue and move into new territory.

∷ Advocating Beyond Your Backyard

Your advocacy group may become strong and active enough to move into a wider arena. Or your child's needs may require broader advocacy on a statewide or national level because of the specific change you want to make. Or you may decide to become an individual public advocate for disability rights or for fragile X syndrome. There are numerous opportunities for you as a parent and consumer to become involved in public advocacy.

In 1993, a national study of family participation in shaping state public health programs and policies found that parents were members on 98 percent of the state advisory committees and task forces, and involved in 90 percent of the Federal Block Grant processes.[1] Many federal and state programs require consumer (parents, families, and individuals with disabilities and special needs) participation on policy-making committees. State policy makers readily acknowledge the value of the consumer input.

Several years ago, I met a very interesting mother at a conference. She was raising eight children, six of whom were adopted and had disabilities. We had a wonderful conversation and shared a lot. A few months later, she asked me to come with her to a meeting of

[1] "Families in Program and Policy", CAPP National Parent Resource Center (1993)

the New England Regional Genetics Group (NERGG), a federal genetics public health committee. I was asked to represent the consumers in my state on the NERGG steering committee. It was an unfamiliar role for me, but I strongly believed that the medical and

public health professionals on the committee needed to hear from the families who receive genetic services. So I accepted the position on NERGG which meant that I had an equal vote on any policy decisions. I have found that the professionals on the committee are very receptive to my thoughts and ideas. Many times I have presented the family perspective on an issue and discovered that the professionals were surprised by it and learned something from it. I feel satisfied to know that I bring something unique to that committee. It is very rewarding.

You can also lobby public officials to address your goals. If you decide to do so, you need to find out which public official has the power to make your goal a reality. If your goal is to change a special education policy, begin with your local school board or other elected official who has control of the public schools, such as your city or county superintendent of education. If you want to change the laws governing the insurance industry (for example, pre-existing condition exclusions) you must lobby your state legislature or state insurance commissioner because insurance is regulated by the states. If you want to preserve the Americans with Disabilities Act, you will have to make an appeal to your senators and congressmen. Even if you do not plan to lobby any of these public officials right now, find out who they are and become knowledgeable about their voting records. You must keep yourself informed. You may want to make periodic contact with your elected officials just to let them know you and your group are there. You can serve as an information source because you are knowledgeable about disability issues and fragile X syndrome. State and federal legislators have a lot of contact with corporate organizations and professional lobbyists but do not get many calls or letters from constituents. So, be sure to make that contact.

I became involved in an effort within my state to enact a law which would protect citizens from discrimination based on genetic traits. I worked with several legislators and a national genetic watchdog group. We formulated a bill that was introduced and discussed at a legislative committee hearing. My job was to tell the committee members the story of how my family was unable to get health insurance because of my children's diagnosis of fragile X syndrome. I was nervous and rather intimidated, but determined to support this legislation.

Several people were there representing the insurance industry and they looked very professional. But I told my story and distributed copies of my statement to the committee members. My testimony was well received and the committee thanked me. The bill was not approved by that committee, but we tried again the following year. The bill eventually passed and became part of New Hampshire law.

Another time, a group of parents and advocates for persons with developmental disabilities came together to lobby the New Hampshire legislature for a statewide family support program. People held strategy meetings in their homes, set up phone chains to alert families when a vote was eminent, arranged transportation for families to state house hearings, and celebrated their successes. They also documented their efforts in a professionally produced video for other family advocate groups to use as a training tool.

Fragile X syndrome parent groups have advocated for family issues for many years. The earliest efforts resulted in breaking down the medical professional code of confidentially. Parents who were desperate to talk with other parents convinced doctors to match them up. Support groups formed, and networks grew. Eventually, connecting a newly diagnosed family with an experienced supporting parent became part of best practices in genetic diagnosis. Also, family advocates have lobbied Congress for increased funding for fragile X syndrome research and have raised hundreds of thousands of dollars themselves for research.

■■ Conclusion

Do you remember Dorothy in the Wizard of Oz? Her goal was to get home to Kansas and she went to lots of different people and places to get someone to take her back. In the end she found out that she always had the power to get home—the ruby slippers on her feet. You can reach your goal because you have the power and no one can take it from you. Let me know how you are doing. Good luck!

■■ Parent Statements

Advocacy is promoting and ensuring fair (not necessarily equal) treatment for your child and working with problems or challenges in a creative, collaborative way.

In general, I like to think of advocacy as "speaking in consort with" our children. It takes great strength in conviction to move from "speaking on behalf of" our children to joining voices with them.

I went to training sessions on special education laws and parents' rights. After that, I felt more confident at meetings because I had knowledge of the system.

Patrick will learn in time to advocate for himself but at this time, he's not fully able to defend or protect his rights, so we as parents have the responsibility to do it for him.

We advocate because, when we add our voice to that of others, it is more likely to be heard and responded to.

Every parent should be their child's advocate at certain points in time. I have found it uniquely important with a child with special needs because I want to model for everyone that my child is important,

capable, and lovable and that he deserves their respect. If I work for my child's best interests, others may follow my lead.

Non-emotional assertiveness, that's the ticket.

When you advocate for your child it often helps other children too, especially if you share your strategy with other parents.

My pediatrician has always acknowledged that I know more about fragile X syndrome than she does. She always treats me with great respect. Whenever she sees an article about fragile X syndrome in one of her professional journals, she sends me a copy.

I attended a small conference recently. One of the speakers was a mother who had two children with fragile X syndrome. She was so positive and confident. I felt better after listening to her. I realized that fragile X syndrome was not the end of the world.

Three years after my son's diagnosis, I discovered that I was pregnant again. By that time, I had learned everything there was to know about fragile X syndrome and had been in constant contact with researchers in New York and Colorado. When I went to a new doctor for a prenatal visit, he pulled an aged textbook off the shelf in his office and proceeded to read me the paragraph on fragile X syndrome. What an insult! I ran away from him as fast as my minivan could travel.

There was one medical professional that I used to take my son to who apologized all the time for not offering me prenatal testing when I was pregnant. She doesn't realize that I am happy to have him and it hurts me to know that her attitude about him is so negative. Like she thinks he should not have been born.

Tony has a fear of moving surfaces and the scale at the doctor's office was always a problem for him. But the doctor would say, "He looks like he weighs enough," and let it go at that.

I always felt like a school child when meeting with the principal at my son's school. I would enter the room with great resolve and then feel so intimidated by the principal that my fortitude would dissolve.

My first IEP meeting was confusing and I was overwhelmed. At the end they gave me a paper to sign saying that I agreed with the plan. What a nightmare! I hadn't really understood a thing they said and I was so afraid that I would "agree" to the wrong plan and my son would suffer. Now, after seven years of IEP Team meetings, I know a lot more and feel very relaxed and focused when I go in the room.

When embarking on negotiations, start with the assumption that everyone is on the side of providing good services (even if you suspect otherwise). Give people the opportunity to work with you rather than against you by sharing your plans and dreams with them, by making an effort to under-stand the constraints placed upon them and helping them find a way to deal with those constraints, by being willing to pitch in and do your share (and more) of the work which needs to be done, and by never failing to recognize the good work which others perform. You can avoid a lot of pain, wasted time, money, and energy by cooperating rather than confronting.

I ask myself how much impact this particular decision will have on the overall curriculum or therapy regime. I also have to decide if my request is feasible, if I trust the person who I am dealing with and whether I feel I could live with a compromise. Asking trusted friends or associates for advice is helpful too.

Whenever we have a meeting scheduled for my son's team, I can't sleep the night before and, sometimes, not the night after either. It seems like his whole future depends on that one hour. It is incredibly stressful.

One of my favorite professionals is my son's preschool teacher. She hasn't had him in class for five years now but I still call just to talk, especially if it has been a bad week.

❦

All parents advocate one way or another for their children; they do so to assure that teachers serve them properly, that school districts provide appropriate programs, that their children have whatever advantages that the parents think are valuable, that others recognize their children's good qualities, and that specific problems get solved. Parents of children with special needs are no different from others in this respect.

❦

My son used to gag and vomit a lot when he was little. One time I was in a conversation with several parents and one genetics professional. I told them about how my son threw up during his sister's birthday party and it landed neatly in a bowl of M&Ms. Everyone, except the genetics person, burst out laughing. He just looked confused. I felt sorry for him.

❦

I started a support group in my area. It helped us to all get connected. We met a few times and then we had to stop it because everyone had so much other stuff to do.

❦

I go to support groups meetings occasionally to keep up contacts but I just don't have the time to go on a regular basis.

❦

I think it is especially important for families that are newly diagnosed to have a group available. It seems that these families ask for and participate in them. Once they reach a state of "reality/realism" the needs can change.

❦

I think as the boys get older I will want to join a group just to hear what our options are at that time.

❦

I have never grown totally tired of meetings on fragile X. Because we have two boys that are affected, I think the fragile X thing surrounds us daily. We feel more of an obligation to participate in stuff. It's always a pleasure to meet other families too.

When all else fails, a legal battle might be necessary. But recognize that the person who was to be helped is particularly vulnerable in any legal fracas. The outcome might turn out to be that people will serve your child out of obligation rather than out of a regard for his humanity.

The best advocacy happens when you can get people to share your (or your child's) vision of the future and then invent a way to get there. People tend to think of advocacy as confrontation. But confrontation stifles creativity. And in an era of shrinking governmental resources, creativity is needed to design living situations that allow our children to enjoy the pleasures of interdependence, to be valued members of the community, and to share their special gifts with others.

In looking for advocacy groups to join, I prefer people who are focused on working together with school districts to make IDEA succeed, and not just a group focused on suing.

At parent meetings, there are often people who are still adjusting to their child's diagnosis, and channeling their anger into advocacy. I try to be patient and let them process their emotions, but I need more— parents who are closer to my stage of life and my level of adjustment.

Our state is prosperous, but ranks near the bottom on funding education for children with disabilities. Prisons, bridges, and roads get plenty of funds, but not kids like mine. It may require a lawsuit against our state for its failure to equitably fund education. I feel a little out of my league, but I am willing to do what is necessary to achieve fairness.

At one meeting it came up that we should go to the state and ask for more money for special education. My comment was that we should first analyze how we currently spend our money, see if that is most effective, and decide where we go from there.

Sometimes at meetings I find that I am more of a listener. I need to have a good knowledge base before I can question or challenge current practices.

GLOSSARY

ABC's of Behavior Management: One technique of discipline for inappropriate behavior; includes *A*—Antecedent: what goes on before the behavior; *B*—Behavior: what happens as a result of *A;* and *C*—Consequence: what happens as a result of *B. See also* Applied Behavior Analysis.

Absence Seizure: A type of seizure that involves staring and eye blinking. Formerly known as petit mal seizure.

Abstract Concepts and Abstract Reasoning: Information that is not concrete or practical, and cannot be experienced directly through the senses such as touch. *See also* Concrete Concepts.

Academic Skills: Traditional educational subjects such as reading, writing, and arithmetic. *See also* Functional Behaviors and Skills.

Acetaminophen: Non-aspirin pain reliever.

ADA: *See* the Americans with Disabilities Act.

Adaptive Skills: *See* Self-Help Skills.

ADD: *See* Attention Deficit Disorder.

Adderall™: One of the trade names for *dextroamphetamine.*

Adenine: One of four *nucleotide bases* that make up *deoxyribonucleic acid (DNA).*

ADHD: *See* Attention Deficit and Hyperactivity Disorder.

Advocacy: Speaking or writing in support of someone or something.

Akathisia: Involuntary restless muscle movements.

Amblyopia: A condition in which the brain turns off or suppresses the vision from a weak eye. Also known as a lazy eye.

American Association on Mental Retardation (AAMR): The oldest and largest interdisciplinary organization of professionals involved in *mental retardation.*

American Sign Language (ASL): A method of communicating through the use of hand signs.

Americans with Disabilities Act (ADA): A federal law that prohibits discrimination against people with disabilities in employment, public accommodations, and access to public facilities.

Amino Acid: Building blocks for proteins, composed of four *nucleotide bases*.

Amniocentesis: A prenatal genetic testing procedure during which a very thin needle is inserted through a woman's stomach skin and into the uterus, using an *ultrasound scan* of the fetus, to obtain amniotic fluid which contains cells from the fetus, usually performed at 16 to 18 weeks of pregnancy.

Amphetamine: A central nervous system stimulant.

Annual Goal: An element of the *IEP* that sets desired outcomes. Progress toward these goals is discussed at the *annual review* meeting.

Annual Review: The yearly review of the *IEP.*

Antecedent: *See* ABC's of Behavior Management.

Antibiotics: Medicines prescribed to treat bacterial infections in the body, such as ear infections.

Anticipated Regression: *See* Regression.

Anticonvulsants: Medications prescribed to reduce the frequency or severity of seizures.

Antihypertensive: Medications prescribed to treat high blood pressure and symptoms such as *hyperactivity*.

Antipsychotics: Medications prescribed to control mental illnesses and symptoms such as aggressive behavior.

Applied Behavior Analysis (ABA): A highly structured approach to teaching that involves systematically studying what happens before a behavior ("antecedent") and what happens after a behavior ("consequence") in order to understand why a behavior does or does not occur. *See also* ABC's of Behavior Management; Behavior Management Plan.

Arched Palate: A high mouth roof. A feature sometimes seen in children with *fragile X syndrome*.

Articulation: The ability to speak distinctly.

ASL: *See* American Sign Language.

Assessment: Identification of a child's developmental and educational strengths and needs, when there is concern that a child may have a developmental delay in one or more areas. Also known as an evaluation or developmental evaluation.

Assessment of Support: A new method to categorize *mental retardation* that relies less on *IQ scores* and more on determining the level of support a person needs to get along in his environment, consisting of four levels: intermittent: does not require constant support, but may need short-term support for special times such as finding a job; limited: requires some supports consistently, such as handling finances and maintaining job skills; extensive: needs daily support in some aspects of living, such as job support and nutrition; and pervasive: requires constant, intensive support for all aspects of life. *See also* Mental Retardation.

Assistive Technology: A device that improves the ability of a person to function, such as the use of a talking device.

Associative Learning: A style of learning in which information can be recalled if it is related to a bigger whole.

Astigmatism: Blurred vision caused by irregularities in the shape of the cornea.

"At Risk of Experiencing a Developmental Delay": Under *IDEA,* the term used to provide services for infants and toddlers until age 3 who have not received a specific diagnosis.

Attention Deficit Disorder (ADD): *See* ADHD. The symptoms for this condition do not include *hyperactivity.*

Attention Deficit Hyperactivity Disorder (ADHD): A condition diagnosed in children characterized by the following symptoms: distractibility, restlessness, short *attention span, impulsivity,* and *hyperactivity.*

Attention Span: The length of time an individual is able to hold his or her concentration; some children with *fragile X syndrome* have short attention spans. *See also* Attention Deficit Disorder; Attention Deficit Hyperactive Disorder.

Audiologist: Health care professional trained to evaluate the quantity and quality of hearing of an individual.

Auditory Distraction: Any noise that prevents an individual from maintaining focus. *See also* Auditory Stimulation.

Auditory Learner: One who learns through listening to information. *See also* Visual Learner.

Auditory Memory: The ability to remember what has been heard.

Auditory Perception: To become aware of sound.

Auditory Processing: How people deal with the sounds in the environment.

Auditory Stimulation: Any sound that stimulates the nervous system.

Augmentative Communication: Methods of communication that do not include speech, such as signing and picture boards.

Autistic-Like Behaviors: Behaviors that include verbal *perseveration,* poor eye contact, and limited social awareness, sometimes seen in children with *fragile X syndrome.*

Aversion: Strong avoidance of a *stimulus* perceived as unpleasant.

Batelle Developmental Inventory: A standardized test used to measure a child's general developmental skills.

Bayley Scales of Infant Development: A developmental test that assesses fine motor skills for children 30 months and under.

Behavior: In the *ABC's of Behavior Management,* what happens as a result of an *antecedent. See also* ABC's of Behavior Management.

Behavioral Outburst: *See* Outburst.

Behavior Management Plan: A plan designed to modify behavior. These plans address existing behavior, goals, support, and intervention.

Benzodiazepine: A class of medication sometimes prescribed to treat anxiety. Valium™ (*diazepam*) is in this class of medication.

Bypass Strategies: Educational strategies used to "get around" a developmental weakness. For example, a person with poor fine motor skills who has difficulty writing may learn to type on a computer.

Carbamazepine: Medication prescribed to control seizures. Also known as Tegretol™.

Cardiologist: A medical doctor who specializes in the functioning of the heart and the treatment of heart disorders.

Carrier: *See* Fragile X Carrier.

Case Manager: A person who coordinates services for individuals with disabilities. Also known as a *service coordinator.*

Catapres™: The trade name for *clonidine.*

CGG Repeat: The number of times the sequence of *Cytosine-Guanine-Guanine* repeats on the X chromosome.

Characteristics of Service and Accommodations: The part of the *IEP* that states the educational and related services your child needs in order to accomplish his goals and objectives and the adjustments the school will make to enable him to succeed.

Child Find: A program under *IDEA* for identifying children with disabilities and referring them for *special education and related services,* ages 3 through 21.

Chorionic Villus Sampling (CVS): A prenatal procedure that is usually performed at 10 to 12 weeks of pregnancy during which a small amount of tissue is withdrawn from the placenta through a tube inserted through the vagina into the uterus. The tissue is commonly used for genetic testing.

Chromosome: The rod-shaped structures that contain the genetic material.

Chromosome Analysis or Test: A genetic test that examines a person's *chromosomes,* usually a blood test. Used in the past to diagnose *fragile X syndrome,* but *FMR1 DNA Analysis* is now used. *See also* FMR1 DNA Analysis.

Chronological Age: The age of an individual determined by date of birth. *See also* Developmental Age.

Class Size: The number of children in a class.

Cleft Palate: A fissure in the roof of the mouth that occurs very early in fetal development.

Clonidine: An *antihypertensive* medication sometimes prescribed to treat *ADHD.* Also known as Catapres™.

Club Foot: A malformation of the foot noted at birth that appears misshapen or twisted.

Cluttered Speech: Speaking fast and at an erratic rhythm, resulting in words getting crammed together, making speech harder to understand.

Cognitive Skills: The ability to understand concepts, pay attention, remember, reason, and solve problems.

Complaint: *See* Formal Complaint.

Complex Partial Seizure: A type of seizure during which there is a change in consciousness and sometimes unusual behaviors such as automation-like movements. Formerly known as temporal lobe seizure.

Compression: A technique used by physical therapists that involves bringing the bones of a joint together. Also known as joint compression.

Concrete Concepts: Events or activities that can be perceived by the senses. *See also* Abstract Concepts.

Congenital: Present at birth.

Connective Tissue: The material that holds our bodies together, such as cartilage, ligaments, tendons, and skin. Many children with fragile X syndrome have loose connective tissue.

Consequence: In the *ABCs of Behavior Management,* what happens as a result of *Behavior. See also* ABC's of Behavior Management.

Consumer: A person who purchases or receives services or materials.

Cost-of-Care Liability: Costs for state-provided services, such as residential services, for which the state requires recipients to pay if he or she has the funds to do so.

Crossed Eyes: *See* Strabismus; Esotropia.

Cupped Ears: A bowing that occurs at the top of the ear because the fold near the top of the ear is often not well-developed.

Curvature of the Spine: *See* Scoliosis.

CVS: *See* Chorionic Villus Sampling.

Cylert™: The trade name for *pemoline.*

Cytogenetic Analysis: *See* Chromosome Analysis or Test and FMR1 DNA Analysis.

Cytogenetics: The study of *chromosomes, genes,* and *heredity.*

Cytosine: One of four *nucleotide bases* that makes up *deoxyribonucleic acid (DNA).*

DD: *See* Developmental Disability.

Deletion: In *genetics,* a missing *gene* or a missing section of a gene. *See also* CGG Repeat.

Deoxyribonucleic Acid (DNA): The chemical basis of *genes.* DNA has a structure resembling a twisted ladder; the rungs of this ladder carry the genetic code involving four *nucleotide bases*: *adenine, thymine, guanine, and cytosine.*

Deoxyribonucleic Acid (DNA) Analysis: *See* FMR1 DNA Analysis.

Depakote™: The trade name for *valproic acid.*

Department of Social Services: A federally funded, state administered agency that provides public assistance—money, food, or shelter—to people who qualify. Also known as welfare.

Department of Vocational Rehabilitation (DVR): A state agency responsible for administering *vocational training* programs.

Depth Perception: Ability to judge depth and other three-dimensional relationships visually.

Development: The natural process of growth that occurs as people mature from infancy through childhood, adolescence, and into adulthood, acquiring increasingly complex skills.

Developmental Age: The term sometimes used to describe the equivalent *chronological age* level at which a child functions.

Developmental Delay: The situation when a child is not acquiring skills at the same rate as other children.

Developmental Disability (DD): When the acquisition of *cognitive skills* is delayed; distinguished from a physical disability.

Developmental Evaluation: *See* Assessment.

Developmentally Disabled Assistance and Bill of Rights Act: A federal law that sets forth some basic rights of people with disabilities, and a national system of legal and advocacy offices to protect the rights of people of disabilities.

Developmental Milestone: Basic skills which mark developmental progress and underlie future *development,* such as a child learning to walk before he learns to climb stairs. The age at which milestones are achieved are used to measure *development.*

Dexedrine™: One of the trade names for *dextroamphetamine.*

Dextroamphetamine: A *stimulant medication* that is sometimes prescribed to treat *ADHD. See* Dexedrine™ and Adderall™.

Diazepam: Medication sometimes prescribed to treat anxiety. Also known as Valium™.

Direct DNA Analysis: *See* FMR1 DNA Analysis.

Direct Language: Being literal in one's expression or in reacting to what others say.

Disability: A term used to describe a delay in physical or cognitive *development.* Also known as *special needs.* The older term *handicapped* is also sometimes used.

Discretionary Special Needs Trust: Created to supplement, rather than replace, money the state may spend on your child's care and support. A method of avoiding *cost-of-care liability.*

Dislocation: *See* Joint Dislocation.

DNA: *See* Deoxyribonucleic Acid.

DNA Linkage Testing: *See* Fragile X Linkage Analysis.

Due Process Hearing: *See* Impartial Due Process Hearing.

Dysfluency: Speaking with hesitations, repeated syllables, or prolonged sounds so that speech is not smooth. Also known as stuttering or stammering.

Dyspraxia: Difficulty planning a sequence of motor (muscle) movements such as touching each finger in sequence or writing or speaking. *See also* Motor Planning.

Early Intervention: Term generally used for developmental or educational services provided to children birth to age three.

ECG: *See* Electrocardiogram.

Echolalia: The repetition word-for-word of what is heard. For example, when a question is repeated back instead of being answered.

Education for All Handicapped Children Act (Public Law 94-142): *See* Individuals with Disabilities Education Act (IDEA).

EEG: *See* Electroencephalogram.

EEOC: *See* Equal Employment Opportunity Commission.

EKG: *See* Electrocardiogram.

Electrocardiogram (EKG or ECG): A machine that records the heart's electrical impulses, used to diagnose cardiac defects and problems.

Electroencephalogram (EEG): A machine that records the brain's electrical impulses, used to diagnose conditions such as seizures.

Eligibility: Under *IDEA,* the criteria that must be met in order for children to receive *special education and related services.*

Endocarditis: An infection of the inner lining of the heart.

ENT: The abbreviation for an ears, nose, and throat specialist.

Equal Employment Opportunity Commission (EEOC): The federal agency responsible for resolving employment discrimination complaints and enforcing anti-discrimination laws such as *The Americans with Disabilities Act.*

Eskalith™: The trade name for *lithium carbonate.*

Esotropia: A condition in which an eye(s) turns inward. Also known as a crossed eye(s). *See also* Exotropia; Strabismus.

Estate Planning: Financial planning for a child or adult's future when his or her parents are deceased.

Eustachian Tubes: The tubes that run from the middle ear to the back of the throat that drain the fluid that can accumulate in the middle ear.

Evaluation: *See* Assessment.

Executive Function: Cognitive processing during which some information must be held in short-term memory in order to complete a task; a task that requires both a set of instructions and a sequence. This type of processing is difficult for some children with *fragile X syndrome.*

Exotropia: A condition in which an eye(s) turns outward. *See also* Esotropia.

Expressive Language: The ability to communicate thoughts, ideas, and feelings with words and gestures.

Extended School Year (ESY): Services provided by the school district during part of the summer months.

Extraneous Noise: Background or a passing noise such as a garbage truck that most people filter out.

Eye Contact: Looking into the eyes of the person to whom one is speaking.

Family Tree: A diagram that allows a genetic counselor to see how the fragile X mutation may have been passed down in a family and to specifically identify relatives at risk. Also known as a pedigree.

Farsightedness: A condition in which distant objects can be seen clearly, but nearby objects are blurred. Also known as hyperopia.

Fine Motor Skills: Movements that use the small muscles, such as the hands and fingers. Grasping, buttoning, drawing, writing, and opening the lid of a jar are examples of fine motor skills. Also known as hand skills.

Flat Feet: A condition in which there is little to no arch in the foot. Also known as Pes Planus.

Fluency: In language, speaking smoothly.

Fluoxetine: Medication prescribed to treat aggressive behaviors, improve depression, and decrease obsessive-compulsive behaviors. This medication can reduce anxiety and improve mood. Also known as Prozac™.

Fluvoxamine: Medication prescribed to treat aggressive behavior, improve depression, and decrease obsessive-compulsive behavior. Also known as Luvox™.

FMR1 DNA Analysis: A test that examines a person's *FMR1 gene* by using specialized laboratory techniques called *southern blot analysis* and *polymerase chain reaction (PCR)*. This testing can determine the size of *CGG repeats*. Also known as *Direct DNA Analysis*.

FMR1Gene: *See* Fragile X Mental Retardation 1 Gene.

FMR1 Protein: The protein produced by the *FMR1 gene* that is believed to be critical for intellectual development.

Focal Motor Seizure: *See* Simple Partial Seizure.

Folic Acid: Part of the vitamin B complex that is sometimes used to treat *ADHD*.

Food Texture: How food feels, to hands, fingers, tongue, and mouth.

Formal Complaint: A parental right under *IDEA* to object to any aspect of their child's *special education and related services*.

Fragile X Carrier: Both males and females who do not show any obvious symptoms of *fragile X syndrome* but have one *FMR1 gene* that has been altered. Carrier males have a *premutation* whereas carrier females can have either a *premutation* or a *full mutation*.

Fragile X Chromosome: The X chromosome that contains the fragile X gene.

Fragile X Linkage Analysis: An older test, used in the past, that examined a person's DNA; it was sometimes able to predict whether or not a person was a *fragile X carrier*.

Fragile X Mental Retardation 1 (FMR1) Gene: The name of the gene at the *fragile X site.*

Fragile X Site: The location on the *chromosome* of the fragile X gene.

Fragile X Syndrome: A condition that is caused by a mutation in genetic information on the *X chromosome.* Often causes delays in *development.*

FRAXA: A national organization that provides information and supports research on *fragile X syndrome. See* Resource Guide for more information, address, and phone number.

"Free Appropriate Public Education" (FAPE): The central right under *IDEA,* to which every child with a disability is entitled. The education is provided at public expense and must be appropriate based on the child's developmental strengths and needs.

Full Mutation: When the number of *CGG repeats* at the FMR1 site exceeds 200 repetitions, causes *fragile X syndrome.*

Functional Behaviors and Skills: Behaviors that are required for independence such as cooking, cleaning, shopping, and using transportation. *See also* Self-Help Skills; Academic Skills.

Gastroesophageal Reflux: A condition in which the sphincter at the top of the stomach relaxes, allowing stomach contents to flow back up through the esophagus and sometimes into the mouth. Also known as reflux.

Gaze Aversion: Avoidance of eye contact.

Gene: The basic unit of heredity, located at specific points on *chromosomes*, made up of *DNA* and protein.

Generalizing Skills: The ability to transfer a skill learned in one setting (e.g., the classroom) to other settings (e.g., home); includes both *functional* and *academic* skills.

Gene Therapy: A current area of research where unaltered genes are injected into the body to compensate for an altered gene. *See also* Protein Replacement.

Genetic: Inherited.

Genetic Counselor: A health care professional with a Master's degree in human genetics or genetic counseling who interprets complex family histories, assesses genetic risk, and discusses available options, including family planning.

Geneticist: Physicians or doctoral level scientists who study genetics; may also provide genetic counseling services.

Global Developmental Delays: Delays in all areas of development rather than just one or two.

Grand Mal Seizure: *See* Tonic-Clonic Seizure.

Gravitational Insecurities: Fear or avoidance of activities that require the feet to be off the ground, such as being placed on a counter or riding on an escalator.

Grieving Process: Refers to the emotional process that many people experience after a serious loss; stages usually include denial, anger, bargaining, depression, and acceptance.

Gross Motor: Movements such as walking, running, and throwing a ball that use the large muscles of the body, such as the arms and legs.

Guanine: One of four *nucleotide bases* that make up *deoxyribonucleic acid (DNA)*.

Guardian: A person appointed by law to manage the legal and financial affairs of someone else.

Hallucal Crease: A single crease in the middle of the ball of the foot, sometimes seen in children with *fragile X syndrome*.

Hand Flapping and Hand Biting: Behavior sometimes seen in children with *fragile X syndrome* when they are excited or angry. They may do this to try to calm themselves or to give their brain one clear stimulus to focus on when they are overwhelmed.

Handicapped: Older term referring to people with *disabilities*.

Hand Skills: *See* Fine Motor Skills.

Heart Murmur: A sound that can be heard through a stethoscope when the heart is not working properly. One type, sometimes seen in children with *fragile X syndrome*, is *mitral valve prolapse*.

Hereditary: Transmission of characteristics such as eye, hair, and skin color and certain conditions such as *fragile X syndrome* from parent to child.

Hernia: A condition in which an organ protrudes through a tear in the surrounding tissue. *See also* Inguinal Hernia.

Hyperactivity: Behavior that includes frequent movement, flitting from one activity to another, or having difficulty remaining seated.

Hyperextensible: Unusual flexibility in a joint, allowing a limb to extend beyond the normal range of motion. Also referred to as hyperflexible.

Hyperopia: *See* Farsightedness.

Hypervigilance: An intense interest that consumes a child's entire attention.

Hypotonia: Low muscle tone, sometimes seen in the torso of children with *fragile X syndrome*.

Ibuprofen: A medication used for pain relief which also has anti-inflammatory qualities, such as Motrin™ or Advil™.

IDEA: *See* Individuals with Disabilities Education Act.

IEP: *See* Individualized Education Program.

IFSP: *See* Individualized Family Service Plan.

Imipramine: A medication that is sometimes prescribed to treat *ADHD*. Also known as Tofranil™.

Imitation Skills: The ability to repeat what is seen or heard.

Impartial Due Process Hearing: The first step in an appeal process under *IDEA* where parents have the opportunity to explain their complaint concerning their child's special education to an impartial person, who is required to listen to both sides and then render a decision.

Impulsivity: Behavior or speech without thought.

Inclusion: Educating all children, including children with disabilities, together in the same schools and classrooms. Placing children with disabilities in the same schools and classrooms they would attend if they did not have disabilities, with the supports and services necessary for them to succeed.

Individualized Education Program (IEP): A written plan that specifies the *special education and related services* for a child with a *disability* who has been evaluated and determined to be eligible under *IDEA*, for children ages three to 21.

Individualized Family Service Plan (IFSP): A written plan that specifies the services for eligible children and their families under *IDEA*, for children birth to age three.

Individualized Habilitation Plan (IHP): *See* Individualized Plan for Employment (IPE).

Individualized Plan for Employment (IPE): A written plan that specifies the vocational training services for adults who qualify for services under the Department of Vocational Rehabilitation. Sets forth the services needed to enable a person with a disability to work productively. Also known as an Individualized Habilitation Plan (IHP) and Individualized Written Rehabilitation Plan.

Individualized Written Rehabilitation Plan (IWRP): *See* Individualized Plan for Employment (IPE).

Individuals with Disabilities Education Act (IDEA): A federal law originally passed in 1975 and subsequently amended that requires states to provide a free appropriate public education in the least restrictive environment for children with disabilities ages birth to 21.

Inguinal Hernia: A hernia that occurs in the groin area.

Inherited: Traits, such as eye and hair color or certain conditions such as *fragile X syndrome*, passed genetically from one generation to another. Also known as genetic. *See also* Hereditary.

Inherited Mental Retardation: Intellectual impairment that is inherited or passed genetically from one generation to another. *See also* Mental Retardation.

Initial Evaluation: The assessment a child receives in order to qualify for *special education and related services* under *IDEA*.

Initial Staffing: The first meeting when an *IEP* is developed under *IDEA*.

Integration: When children with disabilities are taught with peers in the same classroom. *See also* Inclusion.

Intelligence Quotient (IQ): A numerical measurement of intellectual capacity that compares a child's chronological age to his or her "mental age," as shown on *standardized tests*.

Interdisciplinary Team: In education, a group of professionals from various areas of expertise (e.g., *OT, PT, Speech, Social Worker*) who evaluate children and usually prepare a report of developmental strengths and needs. These professionals may also work with children when their services are included in an *IEP. See also* Multidisciplinary Team.

In Vitro: Eggs which are fertilized outside a woman's body.

IQ Score: *See* Intelligence Quotient.

IWRP: The abbreviation for Individualized Written Rehabilitation Plan.

Joint Compression: *See* Compression.

Joint Dislocation: When a body joint slips out of appropriate alignment.

Kaufman Assessment Battery for Children (KABC): A *standardized test* used to *assess* cognitive ability in children from age 2 ½ to 12 ½ years.

Label: The name or names given to specific *developmental delays* in children with disabilities.

Language: Communication using words, gestures, and signs. *See also* Expressive Language, Receptive Language, and Sign Language.

Lazy Eye: *See* Amblyopia.

LD: *See* Learning Disability.

LEA: *See* Local Education Agency.

Learning Disability (LD): A condition that makes learning in one or more areas, such as math, reading, language, and writing, more difficult.

Least Restrictive Environment (LRE): An important requirement of *IDEA* that children with disabilities be educated, to the maximum extent possible, with children who do not have disabilities, as well as involved in the general curriculum.

Lithium Carbonate: A medication prescribed to help reduce violent and aggressive behavior. Also known as Eskalith™.

Local Education Agency (LEA): The local agency, or school district, that provides public education.

Loose Connective Tissue: Connective tissue that is overly flexible or relaxed. *See also* Connective Tissue.

Low Muscle Tone: Decreased muscle tone. *See also* Hypotonia.

LRE: *See* Least Restrictive Environment.

Luvox™: The trade name for *fluvoxamine.*

Luxury Trusts: A trust that is designed to only supplement, rather than take the place of, state benefits, in order to avoid *cost-of-care liability.*

Macro-orchidism: Large testicles; a more common feature of males who have *fragile X syndrome,* often seen at puberty.

Mainstreaming: When children with disabilities are included for parts of the regular school day with students who do not have disabilities. *See also* Inclusion.

Malocclusion: When the upper and lower teeth do not meet properly when the jaw is closed.

Mean Length of Utterance (MLU): The average number of words in an uttered sentence, used to measure *expressive language* ability.

Mediation: Parents and school officials meet with a neutral third party and try to reach a mutually acceptable resolution of a *formal complaint.*

Medicaid: A federal program that pays for medical care for people who do not have private health insurance or *Medicare* and lack sufficient income to pay for medical care.

Medicare: A federal health insurance program that helps pay for the medical expenses of people who qualify.

Mellaril™: The trade name for *thioridazine.*

Mental Retardation: The term used by some doctors and teachers to describe people who score in the lowest three percentiles on *IQ tests.* There are four levels of mental retardation: Mild—IQ between 50 and 69; Moderate—IQ between 35 and 50; Severe—IQ between 20 and 35; Profound—IQ of 20 and below. A newer system uses the level of support a person needs to get along in his environment: Intermittent—does not require constant support; Limited—requires some supports consistently; Extensive—needs daily support; Pervasive—requires constant support. *See also* Assessment of Support.

Metacognition: Knowing how to approach solving a problem.

Methylation: The process by which a gene's function is turned off. In people with *fragile X syndrome,* the condition associated with a *full mutation* in which the *FMR1 gene* is turned off and cannot perform its function.

Methylphenidate: A drug that stimulates the central nervous system. It is sometimes prescribed to treat *ADHD.* Also known as Ritalin™.

Middle Ear Infection: *See* Otitis Media.

Milestone: *See* Developmental Milestone.

Mitral Regurgitation: A condition in which the *mitral valve* allows blood to flow back into the left atrium when the heart muscle contracts. This can lead to excess strain on the left ventricle.

Mitral Valve: Valve that allows blood to flow from the left atrium of the heart to the left ventricle; controls the direction of blood flow in the heart.

Mitral Valve Prolapse: A condition in which the *mitral valve* bows up when the left ventricle contracts, causing a *heart murmur* or clicking sound.

Modelling: When behavior is demonstrated for another to imitate.

Mosaicism: Variation among cells in genetic composition. In *fragile X syndrome,* the existence of a *full mutation* in some cells and a *premutation* in other cells.

Motor Planning: The ability to take in information, decide what needs to be done, and then perform a physical task, such as kicking or catching a ball.

Motor Tic: Involuntary movements of the muscles that generally affect the face, arms, or legs.

MR: *See* Mental Retardation.

Mullen Scales of Early Learning: A comprehensive assessment of cognitive, language, and motor abilities in children birth to 68 months.

Multidisciplinary Team: *See* Interdisciplinary Team.

Multihandicapped: *See* Multiple Disabilities.

Multiple Disabilities: The existence of more than one developmental delay in a child, such as motor, cognitive, speech.

Murmur: *See* Heart Murmur.

Mutation: Change in genetic material or genes, such as the DNA material (CGG repeats) on the *FMR1 gene.*

Myopia: *See* Nearsightedness.

National Fragile X Foundation: A national organization that provides information on *fragile X syndrome. See* Resource Guide for more information, address, and phone number.

Natural Environment: The location where a child typically lives, such as home or a place familiar to the child rather than a center or school; *IDEA* mandates that *early intervention* services be provided in this environment.

NDT Certified: Therapists who have had extensive training in *neurodevelopmental therapy,* an approach to integrating the various sensory and motor systems.

Nearsightedness: A condition in which vision of nearby objects is clear, but distant objects are blurred. Also called myopia.

Neurodevelopmental Therapy (NDT): An approach to *sensory integration* therapy.

Neurologist: A medical doctor who specializes in the function of the brain and the nervous system.

Noncategorical Placement: The term used for children who qualify for special education services but who do not have a specific diagnosis or *label.*

Nonpenetrant Male: A male who carries the *premutation* form of the fragile X gene, but who is not affected cognitively. Also known as a *fragile X carrier* or a *transmitting male.*

Nucleotide Bases: The four chemicals that make up *DNA: adenine, cytosine, guanine,* and *thymine.*

Nystagmus: A condition that causes constant jerking of the eyes from side to side.

Objective: In an *IEP,* the specific steps toward meeting an *annual goal.*

Obsessive-Compulsive Disorder: Behavior characterized by compelling thoughts or impulsive urges and shown through repetition of certain activities.

Occupational Therapist (OT): A professional who provides *occupational therapy.*

Occupational Therapy (OT): Treatment designed to develop and improve fine motor, self-help, and cognitive skills.

Olfactory: The sense of smell.

Ophthalmologist: A medical doctor who specializes in the treatment of the eye.

Optic Cortex: The area of the brain that perceives visual stimuli.

Optician: One who prepares and fits eyeglasses.

Optometrist: A non-medical professional who specialize in the treatment of vision. Optometrists examine the eyes, prescribe lenses, and provide vision therapy, but cannot perform surgery or prescribe medication.

Oral Motor Planning: The ability to coordinate the sound-making movements of the mouth and tongue to produce speech.

Oral Stimulation: Activities such as rubbing the gums or lips in order to reduce *oral tactile defensiveness.*

Oral Tactile Defensiveness: Being overly sensitive or having an *aversion* to touch in the mouth area.

Orthodontist: A medical doctor who deals with dental crowding and correcting bite.

Orthopedist: A medical doctor who specializes in treating bone and joint conditions. Also known as an orthopedic doctor.

Orthotics: Plastic shoe inserts that provide additional support for the feet.

OT: *See* Occupational Therapy; Occupational Therapist.

Otitis Media: Middle ear infection; it can be caused by a buildup of fluid that normally drains through the *eustachian tubes.*

Otolaryngologist: An ENT doctor.

Otoscope: An instrument used by doctors to examine the ear canal.

Outburst: A tantrum during which the child's behavior may appear to be "out of control." Also referred to as a behavioral outburst.

Palate: The roof of the mouth.

Palmar Crease: *See* Simian Crease.

Palmar Grasp: To grab an object using the four fingers pressed against the palm of the hand.

Para-educator: *See* Paraprofessional.

Parallel Play: Children playing side-by-side independently rather than with each other.

Parallel Speech: When a child's experiences are described for him or her as they occur; for example, "You are eating an apple."

Paraprofessional: A support aide or assistant in the classroom. Also known as a para-educator.

Parent Training and Information Center (PTIC): Organizations mandated under *IDEA,* based in most states, that provide information to families about special education issues, rights, and laws. *See* the National Information Center for Children and Youth with Disabilities in the Resource Guide to obtain a list of each state's PTIC.

Paroxetine: Medication prescribed to reduce seratonin levels in the body, sometimes prescribed to treat aggressive behaviors because it reduces anxiety and improves mood. Also known as Paxil™.

Part B: The section of *IDEA* that pertains to children age 3 through 21.

Part C: The section of *IDEA* that pertains to children birth to age three.

Paxil™: The trade name for *paroxetine.*

PCR: *See* Polymerase Chain Reaction.

PDD: *See* Pervasive Developmental Disorder.

Peabody Picture Vocabulary Test-Revised: A *standardized test* that is used to evaluate the language ability in people two and a half years and older.

Pectus Excavatum: An indentation in the center of the chest, the result of the way the bones come together, sometimes seen in people with *fragile X syndrome.*

Pediatrician: Medical doctor specializing in the treatment of children.

Pedigree: *See* Family Tree.

Pemoline: A stimulant medication sometimes prescribed to treat *ADHD.* Also known as Cylert™.

Periodontal Disease: Disease of the gums.

Periodontist: Medical doctor who specializes in the treatment of periodontal disease.

Perseveration: Excessive repetition of activities, motion, or words.

Pervasive Developmental Disorder (PDD): A range of conditions that include autism and can include symptoms such as verbal *perseveration,* poor eye contact, limited social awareness, and the need for sameness.

Pervasive Lack of Relatedness: A condition in which a person has difficulty relating to others.

Pes Planus: *See* Flat Feet.

Petit Mal Seizure: *See* Absence Seizure.

PE Tubes: *See* Pressure Equalizing Tubes.

Phonetics: The particular sounds that make up a spoken language. *See* Whole Language.

Physical Therapist (PT): Professional who provides *physical therapy.*

Physical Therapy (PT): Treatment designed to develop and improve gross motor skills.

Pincer Grasp: Using the thumb and the index finger to grasp a small object.

Polymerase Chain Reaction (PCR): A molecular laboratory technique used to rapidly amplify *DNA*; sometimes used as part of *FMR1 DNA Analysis.*

Poor Eye Contact: Not being able to maintain eye contact for any period of time. Also referred to as *gaze aversion* and an *aversion* to eye contact.

Poor Topic Maintenance: Jumping from one topic to another in conversation. Also referred to as *tangential speech.*

Poor Word Retrieval: Trouble finding the right word or words to respond to a question.

Precursors: Behaviors, language, or events observed right before a behavioral episode occurs, and may include hand biting or flapping, verbal perseveration, or an event such as a fire drill.

Preimplantation Diagnosis: A procedure that involves *DNA* testing of in vitro fertilized embryos prior to implantation.

Premature Ovarian Failure: A condition, sometimes seen in female carriers, in which estrogen levels drop at an earlier age than usual and menopause begins, often before the age of 40.

Premutation: For *fragile X syndrome,* the term referring to CGG repetitions of between 50 and 200.

Prenatal Diagnosis: *Genetic* testing (such as for *fragile X syndrome*) in a baby before it is born.

Preschool: Educational or daycare services provided to children between the ages of three and five, before kindergarten.

Present Level of Development or Functioning: A child's current status on developmental scales; a required element of an *IEP.*

Pressure Equalizing (PE) Tubes: Tubes, which look like tiny plastic rivets and are usually inserted into the eardrum under anesthesia by an ear, nose, and throat doctor, that allow fluid to drain from the ear when it becomes infected.

Prominent Ears: Ears that are larger or that stand out away from the head more than usual.

Pronated Ankles: Ankles that turn inward.

Proprioceptive System: The body's ability to sense its position in the environment. Receptors in the muscles, tendons, and joints that are linked to the nervous system and transmit information, so that the brain is aware of the location of the body and limbs.

Protection and Advocacy (P&A) System: A nationwide program of state and local offices to advocate for the civil and legal rights of people with developmental disabilities.

Protein Replacement: An area of research focusing on the function of the *FMR1 protein* and ways in which to introduce to the bodies of people with an insufficient amount of the protein, such as people with *fragile X syndrome;* this includes stimulating the body's production of the FMR1 protein. *See also* Gene Therapy.

Prozac™: The trade name for *fluoxetine.*

Psychiatrist: A medical doctor who specializes in diagnosing and treating mental illnesses.

Psychologist: Professional who specializes in understanding human behavior; they can help a family with behavior management for their child.

PT: *See* Physical Therapist.

PTIC: *See* Parent Training and Information Center.

Ptosis: A condition in which the upper eyelid droops.

Pulmonary: Related to the lungs.

Reasonable Accommodation: A requirement of the *ADA* that employers must make an effort to remove obstacles from the job that would prevent an otherwise qualified person from working because he or she has a disability.

Receptive Language: The ability to understand the words and associated gestures of spoken language. *See* Expressive Language.

Reciprocal Movement: The alternating movement of the arms and legs as in walking or crawling.

REEL: Receptive-Expressive Emergent Language Scale, a screening tool used to assess verbal skills in young children.

Reflux: *See* Gastroesophageal Reflux.

Regression: The loss of learned skills by lack of use or practice. In determining whether a child qualifies for *Extended School Year,* the amount of regression likely during school breaks will be assessed.

Rehabilitation Act of 1973: Section 504 of this federal law prohibits discrimination against qualified people with disabilities in programs receiving funds from the federal government.

Related Services: Services to supplement special education under *IDEA;* they include transportation and services provided by a *Speech Language Therapist,* an *OT,* a *PT,* a *psychologist,* or a *social worker.*

Repetitive Behavior: *See* Perseveration.

Repetitive Speech: *See* Perseveration.

Resource Specialist/Resource Teacher: *See* Special Education Teacher.

Respite Care: Care for an individual with a disability that is provided by a skilled adult to give family or caregivers a break; this can range from a few hours per week to an overnight.

Risperdal™: The trade name for *risperidone.*

Risperidone: An antipsychotic medication sometimes prescribed for aggressive behavior. Also known as Risperdal™.

Ritalin™: The trade name for *methylphenidate.*

SBE Prophylaxis: *See* Subacute Bacterial Endocarditis Prophylaxis.

Scatter Skills: When some developmental skills are delayed while some are in the average to above average range.

Scoliosis: A curvature of the spine.

Screening: The process to identify children who may have a *developmental delay.* A child may be recommended for an *assessment* as a result of a screening.

Section 504: *See* Rehabilitation Act of 1973.

Segregation: The exclusion of children with disabilities from regular classrooms with their peers; confining children with disabilities to separate classrooms, separate teachers, and separate education.

Seizure: Involuntary movements, behaviors or changes in consciousness triggered by abnormal electrical discharges in the brain that lead in some cases to unconsciousness.

Self-Help Skills: Skills that enable a person to take care of him- or herself; they include the ability to feed, dress, clean, and toilet oneself. Also referred to as adaptive skills.

Self-Stimulation: Providing stimulation to oneself; hand-flapping and rocking are self-stimulating behaviors.

Sensorimotor Development & Sensorimotor Skills: The ability to perceive, integrate, and process sensory and motor information from the environment and to respond appropriately. Also called sensory integration.

Sensory Integration: *See* Sensorimotor Development & Sensorimotor Skills.

Sequential Processing: Learning a skill, processing information, or performing a task in an ordered, step-by-step way.

Sertraline: Medication sometimes prescribed to treat aggressive behaviors because it reduces anxiety and improves mood. Also known as Zoloft™.

Service Coordinator: The person responsible for overseeing the services provided to a child with a disability and his family. Also known as a *case manager.*

Sex Chromosomes: The pair of chromosomes that determines gender.

Side Effect: An unintended result of or reaction to a medication; varies from medication to medication and from person to person.

Sign Language: Use of hands and facial expression to communicate.

Simian Crease: A single crease instead of a double crease on the upper part of the palm, usually extending all the way from one side of the palm to the other. Sometimes seen in children with *fragile X syndrome*.

Simple Partial Seizure: A type of seizure during which only one part of the body shows stiffening or jerking; the child is usually awake and alert during this seizure. Formerly known as *focal motor seizure*.

Simultaneous Processing: Using the entirety of a *stimulus* to gain understanding. For example, an individual with *fragile X syndrome* is more likely to identify a missing part from a whole image than to identify a whole image from its independent parts.

Single Palmar Crease: *See* Simian Crease.

Slow Release (SR) Tablet: A type of medication that is released into the body over a period of time rather than all at once.

Social Anxiety: Being anxious in social situations. *See also* Social Avoidance.

Social Avoidance: The desire to stay away from social interactions and situations. *See also* Social Anxiety.

Social Security Administration (SSA): The federal agency that administers both *SSI* and *SSDI*.

Social Security Disability Insurance (SSDI): A federal program that pays monthly checks to qualified adults who are too disabled to work who either acquired Social Security coverage based on their own past earnings, or whose disability began before age 18 and who are the children of deceased or retired persons who earned Social Security coverage. Administered by the *Social Security Administration*.

Social Skills: The ability to function in groups, from making friends to gauging how another feels to obeying society's moral rules.

Social Worker: A professional who helps another with social skills.

Sonogram: *See* Ultrasound Scan.

Sonography: *See* Ultrasound Scan.

Southern Blot Analysis: A molecular laboratory technique often used as part of *FMR1 DNA Analysis*.

Special Education and Related Services: Under *IDEA*, instruction specifically designed to meet the unique needs of a child with disabilities provided in a full range of settings; along with *related services*.

Special Education Teacher: A teacher primarily responsible for providing or overseeing *special education and related services* to children with *disabilities* or who assists a regular education teacher in providing them.

Special Needs: *See* Disability.

Speech and Language Pathologist (SLP): A professional who works to improve language development and speech.

Speech Delay: When speech and language development does not progress in a typical manner.

Speech Therapist: *See* Speech and Language Pathologist.

Speech Therapy: Treatment designed to improve language and speech development.

Sphincter: A ring-like muscle at the top of the stomach that closes to prevent food from moving into the esophagus; malfunctions in some children with *fragile X syndrome,* resulting in *gastroesophageal reflux.*

SSDI: *See* Social Security Disability Insurance.

SSI: *See* Supplemental Security Income.

Staffing: An *IEP* meeting.

Staffing Team: The participants at an IEP meeting, including parents.

Stammering: *See* Dysfluency.

Standardized Test: A test used to *assess* a child's *development* that compares one child's performance with the performance of many other children.

Stanford-Binet Intelligence Scale: A *standardized test* used to assess the intellectual ability of people age two and up.

Stiffening: A reaction seen in children with *fragile X syndrome* who are upset, frustrated, or angry; the whole body tenses or just hands tense up in a fisting movement.

Stimulant Medications: Medications that stimulate the parts of the brain that control concentration.

Stimulus: An object, event, emotion, or sensation that human senses pick up that can arouse the nervous system.

Stuttering: *See* Dysfluency.

Strabismus: A condition in which the eyes are crossed; results in eyes that do not work in a coordinated way.

Subacute Bacterial Endocarditis (SBE) Prophylaxis: An *antibiotic* taken to prevent infection resulting from a dental procedure in persons who have *mitral valve prolapse* or other heart defects. *See also* Endocarditis.

Supplemental Security Income (SSI): A federal program that pays monthly checks to qualified children and adults with serious disabilities (along with senior citizens) who lack other income and resources. Administered by the *Social Security Administration.*

Supported Employment: Employment in a setting with services such as a job coach or special training that enables an individual with disabilities to work productively.

"Support" Trust: A trust that is designed so the funds are used for the general care and support of the beneficiary with a disability; can be subjected to state *cost-of-care liability.*

Sydney Line: *See* Simian Crease.

Syntax: In language, proper sentence structure.

Tactile: Relating to touch.

Tactile Defensiveness: Being overly sensitive or having an aversion to touch.

Tangential Speech: *See* Poor Topic Maintenance.

Tardive Dyskinesia: A condition that causes facial movements such as sucking or lip smacking, grimacing, or a fixed upward gaze, together with unusual body movements; can be a *side effect* of some medications.

Tegretol™: The trade name for *carbamazepine.*

Temporal Lobe Seizure: *See* Complex Partial Seizure.

Thioridazine: An *antipsychotic* medication prescribed for aggressive behavior in adults; can also decrease delusions, paranoia, and hallucinations, which can also be associated with aggression. Also known as Mellaril™.

Thymine: One of four *nucleotide bases* that make up *deoxyribonucleic acid (DNA).*

Tofranil™: The trade name for *imipramine.*

Tonic-Clonic Seizure: A type of seizure that usually involves jerking and stiffening of the arms and legs. Formerly know as grand mal seizure.

Transition Plan: Required under *IDEA* for children at age three who are moving from early intervention services into preschool, and at age f14 for those moving from school to work.

Transmitting Male: A male who carries the *premutation* form of the *fragile X gene,* usually not affected cognitively. Also known as a *fragile X carrier* or *nonpenetrant male.*

Triad: Refers to the three specific differences in appearance that tend to occur most often in males with *fragile X syndrome:* 1) a long face, 2) prominent or long ears, and 3) larger-than-average testicles *(macro-orchidism).*

Triennial Evaluation & Triennial Review: Under *IDEA,* a review of the IEP that takes place every three years that includes re-evaluation for continued eligibility.

Trust: A legal instrument that sets aside property to be administered by someone for the benefit of others.

Ultrasound Scan: Use of high frequency sound waves to produce a picture of a fetus in the uterus. Also known as a sonogram.

Valium™: The trade name for *diazepam.*

Valproic Acid: *Anticonvulsant* medication prescribed for the treatment of seizures. Also known as Depakote™.

Vestibular System: A part of the sensory system that enables the body to regulate balance and maintain equilibrium.

Vineland Adaptive Behavior Scales: A *standardized test* that assesses communication, daily living, socialization, fine motor, and gross motor skills in children from birth to two and a half years of age.

Vision Therapist: A professional who works with children to improve the function and coordination of their eyes and vision.

Visual Clutter: Having so much to look at that it is difficult to know what is important and what is not.

Visual Distractions: Any visual *stimulus* that does not allow an individual to stay focused, such as a crowd of people or a group of pictures. *See also* Visual Stimulation.

Visual Learner: A child who learns best by being presented with information that can be seen.

Visual Memory: The ability to remember what has been shown or seen.

Visual-Motor Processing: Using both visual and motor skills to perform tasks such as putting a peg in a pegboard.

Visual Perception: To become aware of visual stimuli.

Visual Processing: How the brain and central nervous system process visual stimuli.

Visual Stimulation: An excessive amount of visual stimuli at one time, such as crowded areas.

Visual Tracking: The ability to watch an object move across one's field of vision from left to right to read.

Vocational Training: Job training services.

Wechsler Preschool and Primary Scale of Intelligence-Revised: A *standardized test* used to *assess* cognitive ability in children from age two to six-and-a-half years.

Welfare: *See* Department of Social Services.

Whole Language: An educational approach that is based on the idea that children learn to read and write by being exposed to the printed word. Children are taught to guess at words by looking at pictures, memorize frequently used words, and predict words they think will come next. Inventive spelling is allowed. For example, children are asked to write words using the sounds of the word—"clock" might be spelled "clk".

Whole Word: A reading and writing educational approach where a child learns to read an entire word, rather than using phonics to sound out letters. It is emphasized for longer words with configurations that children can easily recognize, for example, "refrigerator." Also referred to as a sight word.

X Chromosome: The sex chromosome that is present in both males and females. Females have two X chromosomes and males have one.

XX: Female sex chromosomes.

XY: Male sex chromosomes.

Y Chromosome: The sex chromosome that is present only in males.

Zoloft™: The trade name for *sertraline.*

Zygote: The cell that results when a sperm fertilizes an egg. All of the genetic information is contained within this cell.

READING LIST

▦ Chapter 1

Batshaw, Mark L., M.D. **Children with Disabilities.** 4th ed. Baltimore: Paul H. Brookes, 1997.
This parent-friendly reference book contains information on a variety of disabilities including fragile X syndrome.

Dillworth, Wendy, ed. **Fragile X—A to Z: A Guide for Families.** West Newbury, MA: FRAXA Research Foundation, 1997.
Practical tips for parents by parents of children who have fragile X syndrome for areas from "A to Z."

Finucane, Brenda, Allyn McConkie-Rosell, and Amy Cronister. **Fragile X Syndrome: A Handbook for Families and Professionals.** Elwyn, PA: Elwyn, Inc., 1993. Contact: National Fragile X Foundation; 1-800-688-8765.
A 24-page introductory guide for families, teachers, and childcare providers.

Hagerman, Randi Jenssen, M.D. and Amy Cronister. **Fragile X Syndrome: Diagnosis, Treatment, and Research.** 2nd ed. Baltimore: The Johns Hopkins University Press, 1996.
Comprehensive information from diagnosis and research to treatment and intervention.

Haller, Mary Cathryn and Paul D. Nolting. **Learning Disabilities 101: A Primer for Parents.** Highland City, FL: Rainbow Books, 1999.
Good introduction for parents who have just had a child identified as learning disabled (LD). The book defines the basic terms,

gives ideas on working with professionals, and helps parents figure out their options.

Powers, Michael. **Children with Autism: A Parents' Guide.** 2nd ed. Bethesda, MD: Woodbine House, 2000.
Completely revised and updated, this book discusses current diagnostic criteria, family life, education, and advocacy, and includes the latest information on Applied Behavior Analysis.

Richard, Gail and Debra Reichart Hoge. **The Source for Syndromes.** East Moline, IL: Linguisystems, 1999.
Describes various disabilities including fragile X syndrome; includes information on behavioral and speech-language characteristics along with suggested goals for a young child.

Schopmeyer, Betty B. and Fonda Lowe. **The Fragile X Child.** San Diego: Singular Publishing Group, 1992.
Written by therapists for therapists, the book provides information that is somewhat technical in nature about occupational therapy and speech and language therapy.

Sweeney, Wilma. **The Special-Needs Reading List.** Bethesda, MD: Woodbine House, 1998.
A guide to publications, organizations, and web sites for parents seeking information on a wide variety of disability issues, including fragile X syndrome, daily care, family life, education, legal rights, advocacy, and technology.

∷ Chapter 2

Gill, Barbara. **Changed by a Child: Companion Notes for Parents of a Child with a Disability.** New York: Doubleday Books, 1997.
Written by a mother of a child with Down syndrome, this collection of essays will inspire parents who have a child with any disability.

Kephart, Beth. **A Slant of Sun: One Child's Courage.** New York: W.W. Norton & Company, 1998.
A beautifully written personal account by a mother about her son who has been identified with "pervasive developmental disorder not otherwise specified."

Kushner, Harold S. **When Bad Things Happen to Good People.** New York: Avon Books, 1994.
A rabbi writes about his son who died in his early teens of a rare condition called progeria; helpful to parents faced with unexpected news.

Marsh, Jayne D.B. **From the Heart: On Being the Mother of a Child with Special Needs.** Bethesda, MD: Woodbine House, 1995.
Nine mothers reflect on family life with a child who has a disability.

Meyer, Donald J. **Uncommon Fathers: Reflections on Raising a Child with a Disability.** Bethesda, MD: Woodbine House, 1995.
A collection of essays written by fathers who have children with disabilities; a heart-warming and wonderful perspective.

Simons, Robin. **After the Tears: Parents Talk About Raising a Child with a Disability.** Orlando: Harcourt Brace, 1987.
Describes some of the emotions you may feel after getting a diagnosis for your child; helps you to see that whatever you are feeling is okay.

:: Chapter 3

Ilse, Sherokee. **Precious Lives Painful Choices: A Prenatal Decision-Making Guide.** Long Lake, MN: Wintergreen Press, 1993.
An objective look at the options and resources in deciding whether to continue a pregnancy.

:: Chapter 4

Koplewicz, Harold S. **It's Nobody's Fault: New Hope and Help for Difficult Children and Their Parents.** New York: Times Books/Random House, 1997.
This book describes that challenging behavior can, in some cases, be the result of chemical differences in the brain rather than a parenting style.

Lynn, George. **Survival Strategies for Parenting Your ADD Child: Dealing With Obsessions, Compulsions, Depression, Explosive Behavior, and Rage.** Grass Valley, CA: Underwood Books, 1996.
Provides stress management techniques and strategies for dealing with challenging behavior and low self-esteem in children with ADD.

Tranfaglia, Michael, M.D. **A Medication Guide for Fragile X Syndrome.** West Newbury, MA: FRAXA Research Foundation, 1997.
A comprehensive guide to the medications most-often prescribed for children with fragile X syndrome.

Wilens, Timothy E., M.D. **Straight Talk about Psychiatric Medications for Kids.** New York: The Guilford Press, 1999.
While it is not written specifically about fragile X syndrome, this parent-friendly book contains a wealth of information about medications that may be prescribed for your child.

▪▪ Chapter 5

Baker, Bruce L. and Alan J. Brightman. **Steps to Independence: Teaching Everyday Skills to Children with Special Needs.** 3rd ed. Baltimore: Paul H. Brookes, 1997.
A practical guide to teaching daily living skills such as dressing, toilet training, and chores to children with developmental disabilities. There is also a section on managing behavior issues at home.

Dinkmeyer, Don, Gary D. McKay, and James S. Dinkmeyer. **The Parent's Handbook: Systematic Training for Effective Parenting.** Circle Pines, MN: American Guidance Service, 1997.
A book filled with practical approaches to parenting in a positive way; valuable for raising any child. There are also books specifically for teens and one for children under the age of six.

Greene, Ross W. **The Explosive Child: A New Approach for Understanding and Parenting Easily Frustrated, "Chronically Inflexible" Children.** New York: HarperCollins, 1998.
While not specifically for children with fragile X syndrome, the book presents strategies for parenting children with challenging behavior, from understanding the "meltdown" to ideas for avoiding and eliminating them. There is a lot of information to digest, but the author provides several chapter summaries.

Miller, Nancy B. **Nobody's Perfect: Living & Growing with Children Who Have Special Needs.** Baltimore: Paul H. Brookes, 1994.
A book that offers support that there are many right ways to raise a child with a disability and includes a section on relationships.

Wheeler, Maria. **Toilet Training for Individuals with Autism & Related Disorders: A Comprehensive Guide for Parents & Teachers.** Arlington, TX: Future Horizons, 1998.

Offers many ideas to help your child be successful in this area; over 200 tips and more than 40 case examples.

∷ Chapter 6

Carlson, Richard. **Don't Sweat the Small Stuff with Your Family.** New York: Hyperion, 1998.

A book filled with short chapters that provide ideas about simplifying various aspects of family life, including "letting go" of the small things that can really bug you.

Davis, Martha, et al. **The Relaxation and Stress Reduction Workbook.** 4th ed. Oakland, CA: New Harbinger Publications, 1998.

Describes stress reduction methods such as breathing exercises, visualization, time management, biofeedback, and hypnosis.

Exceptional Parent Magazine. 555 Kinderkamack Road, Oradell, NJ 07649; Contact: 877-372-7368. http://www.eparent.com/.

A monthly magazine that provides information and ideas for parents and families of children with disabilities and the professionals who work with them.

Greenspan, Stanley, M.D. and Serena Wieder. **The Child with Special Needs: Encouraging Intellectual and Emotional Growth.** New York: Perseus Press, 1998.

Includes methods for parents to use in increasing communication and social skills at home.

Greenstein, Doreen. **Backyards and Butterflies: Ways to Include Children with Disabilities in Outdoor Activities.** Cambridge, MA: Brookline Books, 1997.

Loaded with ideas on making the outside world fun and successful for everyone, from gardening to going on a picnic.

Hamaguchi, Patricia M. **Childhood Speech, Language & Listening Problems: What Every Parent Should Know.** New York: John Wiley & Sons, 1995.

Different types of speech, language, and listening problems are described, as well as information on diagnosis and treatment; includes ideas on improving communication at home.

Meyer, Donald. **Living with a Brother or Sister with Special Needs: A Book for Sibs.** 2nd ed. Seattle: University of Washington Press, 1996.
A compassionate book for children eight years and up that explains the most common disabilities, and validates the emotions and concerns that siblings of children with disabilities often have, along with strategies for working through those emotions.

Meyer, Donald. **Views from Our Shoes.** Bethesda, MD: Woodbine House, 1997.
Fifty children share their thoughts about a brother or sister with a disability; appropriate for children in the third through seventh grade.

Stengle, Linda J. **Laying Community Foundations for Your Child with a Disability: How to Establish Relationships That Will Support Your Child after You're Gone.** Bethesda, MD: Woodbine House, 1996.
A book that includes checklists and tables that help parents plan for their child's future in the community.

▪▪ Chapter 7

Ames, Louise Bates, Frances L. Ilg, and Carol Chase Haber. **Your One-Year-Old: The Fun-Loving, Fussy 12-To 24-Month-Old.** New York: Doubleday, 1995.
Describes the typical development seen in a child of this age. This book is actually the first in a series of books; there is one for each year through age nine and another for 10- to 14-year–old children.

Hanson, Marci J., and Susan Harris. **Teaching the Young Child with Motor Delays: A Guide for Parents and Professionals.** Austin, TX: Pro-Ed, 1986.
Step-by-step instructions for teaching children important developmental skills, as well as information about how motor development affects development in other areas.

Newman, Sarah. **Small Steps Forward: Using Games and Activities to Help Your Pre-School Child with Special Needs.** London, England: Jessica Kingsley Publishers, 1999.

Provides parents and caregivers of children with developmental delays ideas to encourage their child's development in six areas: cognitive, linguistic, physical, sensory, social, and emotional skills. There are many activities that your child will enjoy in the early elementary years as well.

Schwartz, Sue and Joan E. Heller Miller. **The New Language of Toys: Teaching Communication Skills to Children with Special Needs.** 2nd ed. Bethesda, MD: Woodbine House, 1996.

Develop communication skills in an entertaining way using toys and games; store-bought and homemade toys are described.

Segal, Marilyn and Wendy Masi. **Your Child at Play: Birth to One Year: Discovering the Senses and Learning About the World (Your Child at Play Series).** New York: New Market Press, 1998.

Describes the typical development seen in children along with simple inexpensive ways to play with your child; great for first-time parents. This is the first in a series of books. The other books are about: one-to-two-, two-to-three-, three-to-five-, and five-to-eight-year-old children.

White, Burton L. **The New First Three Years of Life.** 20th ed. New York: Fireside, 1995.

Describes month-by-month childhood development that is based on research and stresses loving but firm parenting. He gives ideas on how to talk to, play with, and nurture your child; he discusses the abilities and limitations of developmental phases; and he has recommendations for toys.

∷ Chapter 8

Beckman, Paula J. and Gayle Beckman Boyes. **Deciphering the System: A Guide for Families of Young Children with Disabilities.** Cambridge, MA: Brookline Books, 1994.

A guide to early intervention and preschool special education, including explanations of assessment tools frequently used. A new edition is due out in 2000.

Block, Martin E. **A Teacher's Guide to Including Students with Disabilities in Regular Physical Education.** Baltimore: Paul H. Brookes, 1995.

Practical strategies for inclusion and suggestions for adapting specific sports activities are provided; also includes examples of goals and objectives for IEPs.

Braden, Marcia L. **Fragile: Handle With Care, Understanding Fragile X Syndrome.** 1997. Contact: 100 E. St. Vrain #200, Colorado Springs, CO 80903; 719-633-3773.

Discusses the various developmental stages of fragile X syndrome, and includes information on schools and legal issues.

Briggs, Freda. **Developing Personal Safety Skills in Children with Disabilities.** Baltimore: Paul H. Brookes, 1995.

Covers the "why's" and "how's" of teaching personal safety skills to children with disabilities.

Coleman, Jeanine G. **The Early Intervention Dictionary: A Multidisciplinary Guide to Terminology.** 2nd ed. Bethesda, MD: Woodbine House, 1999.

Every term you are likely to hear from medical professionals, therapists, educators, and psychologists is explained in this book.

Klauber, Julie and Avery Klauber. **Inclusion & Parent Advocacy: A Resource Guide.** Centereach, NY: Disability Resources, 1996. (Order from Disability Resources, 4 Glatter Lane, Centereach, NY 11720. 516-585-0290).

A resource guide that describes books, pamphlets, videos, curriculum kits, and other sources of inexpensive information about inclusive education programs.

Kranowitz, Carol Stock. **The Out-Of-Sync Child: Recognizing and Coping With Sensory Integration Dysfunction.** New York: Perigee, 1998.

Thorough discussion of sensory integration with strategies to use at home and at school; many examples are provided to illustrate different points.

Mannix, Darlene. **Life Skills Activities for Special Children.** West Nyack, NY: Center for Applied Research in Education, 1991.

Activities designed for teachers with students in the upper elementary grades, but also useful at home.

Mannix, Darlene. **Social Skills Activities for Special Children.** Upper Saddle River, NJ: Prentice-Hall, 1993.

A manual designed for teachers that includes lesson plans for teaching social skills to children in the upper elementary grades and older, also useful at home.

Pearpoint, Jack. **From Behind the Piano: The Building of Judith Snow's Unique Circle of Friends.** Toronto, Ontario: Inclusion Press International, 1990.

A story that brings new meaning to the word "friends."

Smith, Corinne and Lisa Strick. **Learning Disabilities A to Z.** New York: Simon & Schuster, 1999.

A wide range of issues from getting the diagnosis, to planning an IEP, to developing strategies for classroom success are covered.

Spiridigliozzi, Gail et al. **Educating Boys with Fragile X Syndrome.** Durham, NC: Child Developmental Unit, Duke University Medical Center, 1994. Contact: National Fragile X Foundation; 800-688-8765.

Full of practical ideas for teaching boys *and girls*; useable by parents, teachers, and therapists.

Turnbull, Ann P. and H.R. Turnbull. **Families, Professionals, and Exceptionality: A Special Partnership.** 3rd ed. Upper Saddle River, NJ: Prentice-Hall, 1997.

Ideas that are highlighted with personal stories bring out the concepts to creating this partnership.

Weber, Jayne Dixon. **Transitioning "Special" Children Into Elementary School.** 1994. Contact: 1270 Judson Drive, Boulder, CO 80303; 303-494-2740.

A quick read filled with ideas on getting your child started in kindergarten, and covers the emotional aspects that often accompany that change.

Wehmeyer, Michael L., Martin Agran, and Carolyn Hughes. **Teaching Self-Determination to Students with Disabilities.** Baltimore: Paul H. Brookes, 1998.
A textbook for special education teachers that is overwhelming at first glance, but filled with a variety of ideas and "programs" that have been used successfully with children.

Wilson, Phil, Tracy Stackhouse, Rebecca O'Connor, Sarah Scharfenaker, and Randi Hagerman, M.D. **Issues and Strategies for Educating Children with Fragile X Syndrome: A Monograph.** San Francisco: National Fragile X Foundation; 800-688-8765, 1994.
Designed to accompany the video *Educational Issues and Strategies,* this book provides information on medical issues, OT, SLP, and educational strategies.

⠿ Chapter 9

Anderson, Winifred, Stephen Chitwood, and Deidre Hayden. **Negotiating the Special Education Maze: A Guide for Parents and Teachers.** 3rd ed. Bethesda, MD: Woodbine House, 1997.
A guide that explains the system and how to obtain an appropriate education for a child with disabilities.

Baldwin, Ben. **The Complete Book of Insurance: The Consumer's Guide to Insuring Your Life, Health, Property, and Income.** Chicago, IL: Irwin Professional Publishing, 1996.
Written to help parents make informed decisions about buying insurance; covers all of the types of insurance and selecting an agent.

Bateman, Barbara D. and Mary Anne Linden. **Better IEPs: How to Develop Legally Correct and Educationally Useful Programs.** 3rd ed. Longmont, CO: Sopris West, 1992.
Provides ideas and examples on writing IEPs that are truly *individualized*; presents a three-step process for developing the IEP; and includes the IDEA amendments of 1997.

Chapman, Randy. **The New Handbook for Special Education Rights.** Denver: The Legal Center for People with Disabilities and Older People,

2000. Contact: 455 Sherman Street, Suite 130, Denver, CO 80203-4403; 303-722-0300; 800-288-1376.

Written for parents and advocates, this book explains the Individuals with Disabilities Education Act (IDEA) and Section 504 of the Rehabilitation Act of 1973, including the changes that came out in March 1999.

Detlefs, Dale and Robert J. Myers. **2000 Mercer Guide to Social Security and Medicare (Mercer Guide to Social Security and Medicare, 2000).** William M. Mercer, Inc., 2000.

These two critical and complex subjects are presented in a way that makes them easy to understand. This book describes your rights and benefits under these programs.

Goldberg, Daniel and Marge Goldberg. **The Americans with Disabilities Act: A Guide for People with Disabilities, Their Families, and Advocates.** Minneapolis: Pacer Center, 1994.

Explains all aspects of ADA: employment, public services, public accommodations, and telecommunications.

Jehle, Faustin F. **The Complete & Easy Guide to Social Security, Health Care Rights & Government Benefits.** Boca Raton, FL: Emerson-Adams Press, 1998.

A 14th edition that contains information on a variety of topics including: Social Security, Medicare, Medicaid, HMOs, Supplemental Security Income, and disability insurance.

Knowlen, Barbara Bradford. **How to Kick Ass and Win: A Consumer's Guide to Getting Services and Equipment from the State Vocational Rehabilitation Agency by Using the Appeals Process.** 3rd ed. 1999. Contact: Barrier Breakers, 4239 Camp Road, Oriskany Falls, NY 13425; 315-821-2460.

Written by a self-advocate, this guide gives how-to information, as well as the actual forms that were used in her own experiences in "working" with the VR agency.

Russell, L. Mark. **Planning for the Future: Providing a Meaningful Life for a Child with a Disability after Your Death.** Evanston, IL: American Publishing Co., 1995.

A practical guide to developing a comprehensive estate plan; may have to be back-ordered.

Schlachter, Gail and R. David Weber, eds. **Financial Aid for the Disabled and Their Families: 1998-2000.** San Carlos, CA: Reference Service Press, 1998.

Provides information about federal aid for families who have a child with a disability, as well as sources of scholarships, fellowships, and grants in aid.

Siegel, Lawrence and Marcia Stewart. **The Complete IEP Guide: How to Advocate for Your Special Ed. Child.** Berkeley, CA: Nolo Press, 1999.

A comprehensive guide that outlines the components of the IEP, how to develop a good program for a child, and how to resolve differences with school districts.

Wilson, Reg and the Merritt editors. **How to Insure Your Life: A Step by Step Guide to Buying the Coverage You Need at Prices You Can Afford.** Santa Monica, CA: Merritt Publishing, 1996.

Practical advice on getting the best life insurance coverage for the money. It gives you the information you need to make smart decisions, everything from why you need it, to how much you need, to describing the different types of life insurance.

:: Chapter 10

Alberti, Robert and Michael Emmons. **Your Perfect Right: A Guide to Assertive Living.** San Luis Obispo, CA: Impact Publishers, 1995.

A general book designed to empower its readers by helping them understand their rights to be assertive and teaching effective strategies from asking for what you want, to saying no, to managing anger.

Charlton, James I. **Nothing About Us Without Us: Disability Oppression and Empowerment.** Berkeley, CA: University of California Press, 1998.

A book sure to encourage the disability rights movement. The author interviews activists from ten countries and gives a global view of the oppression of people who have disabilities and the movement to counteract it. It convinces you that people with disabilities know what they want and they want to control their own lives.

Des Jardins, Charlotte. **How to Get Services by Being Assertive.** 2nd ed. Chicago: Family Resource Center on Disabilities, 1993.

This guide describes your child's legal rights to an education and how to get the services he or she needs.

Des Jardins, Charlotte. **How to Organize an Effective Parent/Advocacy Group and Move Bureaucracies.** 2nd ed. Chicago: Family Resource Center on Disabilities, 1993.

Instructions on starting a parent/advocacy group along with ideas on how to keep the group active.

Miller, Nancy B. and Catherine C. Sammons. **Everybody's Different: Understanding and Changing Our Reactions to Disabilities.** Baltimore: Paul H. Brookes, 1999.

The authors discuss disability differences and help you to gain a better understanding of your own reactions to people who have disabilities. There are activities and ideas on interacting with people who have disabilities, the goal being a greater appreciation of all people.

:: Videos

Educational Strategies and Issues for Children with Fragile X Syndrome. San Francisco: National Fragile X Foundation, 1994. Contact: 800-688-8765.

Features the inclusion of children with fragile X syndrome in regular education classrooms. Three boys are followed: a kindergartner, a fifth grader, and a freshman in high school. 60 minutes.

Fragile X Syndrome: Inclusion from a Mother's Perspective. San Francisco: National Fragile X Foundation, 1997. Contact: 800-688-8765.

A mother talks to her son's class about fragile X syndrome. 45 minutes.

Fragile X Syndrome "Vocations." San Francisco: National Fragile X Foundation, 1997. Contact: 800-688-8765.

In this 15 minute video, family members, neighbors, co-workers, and supervisors are interviewed to give an insight into employing an adult with fragile X syndrome.

:: Cassettes

Fragile X Syndrome: Medical and Educational Approaches to Intervention. Boulder, CO: Belle Curve Records, 2000.
Discusses ideas for developing educational programs.

Making Sense of Sensory Integration (Audio Cassette & Booklet). Boulder, CO: Belle Curve Records, 1998.
Information and checklists that explain sensory integrative functions that both parents and professionals will find useful.

Kranowitz, Carol and Stacey Szklut. **Teachers Ask About Sensory Integration** (Audio Cassette & Booklet). Boulder, CO: Belle Curve Records, 1999.
Carol Stock Kranowitz interviews occupational therapist Stacey Szklut about how to teach children who have difficulty with sensory integration. The included booklet contains classroom checklists, idea sheets, and sensory profiles.

Lande, Aubrey, Lois Hickman, and Bob Wiz. **Songames for Sensory Integration** (Audio Cassette & Booklet). Boulder, CO: Belle Curve Records, 1999.
Songs and activities that invite movement and dance, some for particular activities such as waking up and transitioning.

:: Books for Children

Baker, Pamela. **My First Book of Sign.** Washington, DC: Gallaudet University Press, 1986.
Sign descriptions for 150 common words are shown.

Beatty, Monica Driscoll. **Blueberry Eyes.** Santa Fe, NM: Health Press, 1996.
An illustrated story for children aged three to eight about a little girl who has strabismus and wears a patch, and has eye muscle surgery to correct it.

Derby, Janice. **Are You My Friend?** Scottdale, PA: Herald Press, 1993.
Each of us can do something well, and each of us has a hard time with something. The message: we are all more alike than we are different.

O'Connor, Rebecca. **Boys with Fragile X Syndrome.** San Francisco: National Fragile X Foundation, 1995. Contact: 800-688-8765.

A children's book written to help educate siblings, friends, and educators about the characteristics of fragile X syndrome.

Steiger, Charles. **My Brother has Fragile X Syndrome.** San Francisco: National Fragile X Foundation, 1998. Contact: 800-688-8765.

The author writes about his older brother who has fragile X syndrome.

Thompson, Mary. **My Brother, Matthew.** Bethesda, MD: Woodbine House, 1992.

A young child talks about his younger brother who has a disability; gives a wonderful insight into children.

Westridge Young Writers Workshop. **Kids Explore the Gifts of Children with Special Needs.** Topeka, KS: Econo-Clad Books, 1999.

Students at elementary levels get to know other students who have disabilities, and then write about their experiences.

Wheeler, Cindy. **Simple Signs.** Topeka, KS: Econo-Clad Books, 1999.

Simple American Sign Language (ASL) signs that preschoolers will love, like dog, cat, happy, and sleep. There is also a second book called **More Simple Signs** that includes additional words that young children might use.

∷ Publisher's Phone Numbers and Websites

Addison-Wesley Longman, Inc.
781-944-3700   http://www.awl.com/

American Guidance Services (AGS)
800-328-2560   http://www.agsnet.com/

Avon Books
212-261-6800   http://www.avonbooks.com/

Belle Curve Records, Inc.
888-357-5867   http://www.bellecurve.com/

Paul H. Brookes Publishing
800-638-3775   http://www.pbrookes.com/

Brookline Books
800-666-BOOK http://www.brooklinebooks.com/

The Center for Applied Research in Education
See Prentice-Hall Direct
800-947-7700 http://www.phdirect.com/

Doubleday
800-323-9872 http://www.randomhouse.com/

Family Resource Center on Disabilities
312-939-3513
http://ameritech.net/users/frcdptiil/index.html/

FRAXA Research Foundation
978-462-1866 http://www.fraxa.org/

David Fulton Publishers
44-0-171-405-5606 http://www.fultonbooks.co.uk/

Econo-Clad books
800-255-3502 http://www.econoclad.com/

Emerson-Adams Press
561-391-0964 http://www.emerson-adamspress.com/

Fireside
See Simon & Schuster
212-698-7007 http://www.simonsays.com/

Future Horizons, Inc.
800-489-0727 http://www.futurehorizons-autism.com/

Gallaudet University Press
202-651-5488 http://gupress.gallaudet.edu/

Guilford Press
800-365-7006 http://www.guilford.com/

Harcourt Brace Co.
800-225-5425 http://www.hbschool.com/

HarperCollins
212-207-7000 http://www.harpercollins.com/

Health Press
505-474-0303 http://www.healthpress.com/

Herald Press
724-887-8500   http://www.mph.org/

Impact Publishers
805-466-5917   http://www.impactpublishers.com/

Inclusion Press International
416-658-5363   http://www.inclusionpress.com/

Johns Hopkins University Press
410-516-6900   http://www.press.jhu.edu/press/books/

Jessica Kingsley Publishers
215-625-8900   http://www.jkp.com/

The Legal Center for People with Disabilities and Older People
800-288-1376; 303-722-0300   http://www.thelegalcenter.org/

Linguisystems, Inc.
800-776-4332   http://www.linguisystems.com/

Merritt Publishing
800-638-7597   http://www.ecs.com/hosting/merritt

National Fragile X Foundation
800-688-8765   http://www.fragilex.org/

New Harbinger Publications
800-748-6273   http://www.newharbinger.com/

Nolo Press
800-728-3555   http://www.nolo.com/

PACER Center
612-827-2966   http://www.pacer.org/

Penguin Books
800-788-6262   http://www.penguinputnam.com/

Perigee
800-788-6262   http://www.penguinputnam.com/

Prentice-Hall
800-643-5506   http://www.prenticehall.com/

Prentice-Hall Direct
800-947-7700   http://www.phdirect.com/

Pro-Ed
800-897-3202   http://www.proedinc.com/

Random House
800-733-3000   http://www.randomhouse.com/

Reference Service Press
916-939-9620   http://www.rspfunding.com/

Simon & Schuster
212-698-7007   http://www.simonsays.com/

Singular Publishing Group
800-521-8545   http://www.singpub.com/

Times Books/Random House
800-733-3000   http://www.randomhouse.com/

Underwood Books
No phone calls   http://www.underwoodbooks.com/

University of California Press
510-642-4247   http://www-ucpress.berkeley.edu/

University of Washington Press
800-441-4115   http://www.press.uchicago.edu.com/

Viking Children's Books
800-788-6262   http://www.penguinputnam.com/

John Wiley & Sons
800-225-5945   http://www.wiley.com/

Woodbine House
800-843-7323   http://www.woodbinehouse.com/

W.W. Norton & Company
800-233-4830   http://www.wwnorton.com/

▚ Book Websites

Amazon.com
http://www.amazon.com/

Barnes & Noble.com
http://www.barnesandnoble.com/

Borders.com
http://www.borders.com/

Special Needs Project
"Good Books about Disabilities"
324 State Street
Santa Barbara, CA 93101
800-333-6867; 805-962-5087
http://www.specialneeds.com/

RESOURCE GUIDE

The Resource Guide contains the following information:
- Organizations specific to fragile X syndrome.
- Other national sources of information that cover a variety of topics pertaining to disabilities.
- Sources of equipment and supplies for hard-to-find toys and therapy equipment.
- Websites that contain information on a variety of disability topics.
- Suggested curriculum for children with fragile X syndrome.

For further information about any of these organizations, call, write, or visit their web page and request a copy of their newsletter, catalog, or other publications.

▓ Organizations Specific to Fragile X Syndrome

FRAXA Research Foundation
45 Pleasant Street
Newburyport, MA 01950
978-462-1866; 978-463-9985 (fax)
E-mail: kclapp@fraxa.org
Web: http://www.fraxa.org/
A national nonprofit organization that funds research aimed at finding a treatment or cure for fragile X syndrome. FRAXA was founded in 1994 by three parents of children with fragile X syndrome and has funded over $2.5 million in research grants and fellowships at universities around the world. Publishes a quarterly newsletter, *FRAXA Update*.

National Fragile X Foundation
P.O. Box 190488
San Francisco, CA 94119
800-688-8765; 510-763-6030
510-763-6223 (fax)
E-mail: natlfx@sprintmail.com
Web: http://www.nfxf.org/ or http://www.fragilex.org
Their mission is to promote education and research of fragile X syndrome, and disseminate information and new findings. The Foundation holds a bi-annual conference that is an opportunity to share and exchange the latest information and research into fragile X syndrome. Publishes a newsletter, *The Foundation Quarterly*.

FRAXA—U.S. Chapters
To find the Chapter closest to you, contact FRAXA. As this book went to press, chapters were located in the following states; some states have more than one chapter: Alaska, California, Florida, Georgia, Hawaii, Illinois, Indiana, Kentucky, Massachusetts, Michigan, Missouri, Montana, Nebraska, New York, North Carolina, Ohio, Oregon, Pennsylvania, South Carolina, Texas, Washington, Washington, DC.

FRAXA's International Chapters
England, Israel, Germany, Spain

National Fragile X Syndrome Foundation's Regional Support Groups—U.S.
To find the Support Group closest to you, contact The National Fragile X Foundation. As this book went to press, Support Groups were located in the following states; some states have more than one group: Arizona, California, Colorado, Connecticut, Illinois, Kentucky, Maryland, Massachusetts, Michigan, Missouri, Montana, Nevada, New Jersey, New Mexico, New York, Ohio, Oregon, Washington.

National Fragile X Syndrome Foundation's Regional Support Groups—Outside the U.S.
Australia, Canada.

Fragile X Organizations Around the World
The following countries have organizations that make information available in many languages: Argentina, Australia, Canada,

Germany, Conquer Fragile X (funds research in Israel), Italy, Spain, Uruguay. Contact FRAXA for the latest information on these countries.

▪▪ Other National Sources of Information

The organizations, companies, and other resources listed below offer a variety of information and services that can be helpful to families of children with fragile X syndrome. Also, many of their websites have links to other sites that may be of interest to you.

American Academy of Ophthalmology
P.O. Box 7424
San Francisco, CA 94120-7424
415-561-8500; 415-561-8533 (fax)
Web: http://www.eyenet.org/
Provides information on finding an ophthalmologist and has brochures and fact sheets on strabismus and amblyopia.

American Association of University Affiliated Programs (AAUAP)
8630 Fenton Street, Suite 410
Silver Spring, MD 20910
301-588-8252; 301-588-2842 (fax)
Web: http://www.aauap.org/
UAPs are found in every state. Each is affiliated with a major research university and offers clinical services and technical assistance in the community for children with developmental disabilities. AAUAP can help you find the university-affiliated program closest to you.

American Occupational Therapy Association
4720 Montgomery Lane
P.O. Box 31220
Bethesda, MD 20824-1220
301-652-2682; 301-652-7711 (fax)
Web: http://www.aota.org/
This is the professional association for occupational therapists. The organization distributes publications about occupational therapy and can refer you to an OT in your area.

American Optometric Association
243 N. Lindbergh Blvd.
St. Louis, MO 63141
314-991-4100; 314-991-4101 (fax)
Web: http://www.aoanet.org/
  Provides general information on keeping your eyes healthy, with specific information on certain issues such as crossed eyes (strabismus).

American Physical Therapy Association
1111 N. Fairfax Street
Alexandria, VA 22314
703-684-2782
Web: http://www.apta.org/
  This is the professional organization for physical therapists and provides the latest physical therapy news along with PT product information.

American Speech-Language-Hearing Association (ASHA)
10801 Rockville Pike
Rockville, MD 20852
800-498-2071; 877-541-5035 (fax)
Web: http://www.asha.org/
  The professional association for speech-language pathologists; has information on speech and language therapy and audiologists in your area, as well as brochures on various speech and language issues and development.

The Arc of the United States
1010 Wayne Avenue, Suite 650
Silver Spring, MD 20910
301-565-3842; 301-565-5342 (fax)
Web: http://www.thearc.org/
  Formerly known as the Association for Retarded Citizens, this is an organization of and for people with mental retardation and their families and advocates. The site has fact sheets and a publications catalog on many aspects of developmental delays. There is information on the chapter nearest you.

Autism Society of America
7910 Woodmont Avenue, Suite 300
Bethesda, MD 20814-3015
301-657-0881; 800-3-AUTISM; 301-657-0869 (fax)
Web: http://www.autism-society.org/
    This organization provides information, supports research, and advocates for services for people with autism. Publishes the newsletter, *The Advocate.*

Canadian Association for Community Living (CACL)
Kinsmen Building, York University
4700 Keele Street
North York, Ontario M3J 1P3 Canada
416-661-9611; 416-661-5701 (fax)
Web: http://www.cacl.ca/
    Similar to The Arc in the U.S., the CACL is dedicated to ensuring that people with disabilities are welcomed into their communities. They advocate for people with disabilities, support over 400 local associations across Canada, and publish information on various activities and issues related to people with disabilities.

CH.A.D.D. (Children and Adults with Attention Deficit Disorder)
8181 Professional Place, Suite 201
Landover, MD 20785
800-233-4050; 301-306-7090 (fax)
Web: http://www.chadd.org/
    CH.A.D.D. works to improve the lives of families and individuals with ADD through support, education, and advocacy. Their website offers a variety of publications and has several links to other sites from government to health issues.

Children's Defense Fund (CDF)
25 E Street NW
Washington, DC 20001
800-CDF-1200
202-628-8787
Web: http://www.childrensdefense.org/
    An organization that works to improve the lives of children, especially poor and minority children and those with disabilities. The site has several publications and links to other sites.

Council for Exceptional Children

1920 Association Drive
Reston, VA 20191-1589
888-CEC-SPED; 703-620-3660 (local); 703-264-9494 (fax)
Web: http://www.cec.sped.org/
  This is the professional association for special education teachers, administrators, and related service providers interested in the needs of children who have disabilities or are gifted. Their catalog offers a variety of materials on education-related topics.

DO-IT

University of Washington
Box 354842
Seattle, WA 98195-4842
206-685-DOIT (3648)
888-972-DOIT (3648) in Washington, outside Seattle
206-221-4171 (fax)
509-328-9331 — voice/TTY, Spokane office
Web: http://www.washington.edu/doit/
  DO-IT (Disabilities, Opportunities, Internetworking, and Technology) strives to increase the number of individuals with disabilities in challenging academic programs, through training programs, publications, and resources.

Federation for Children with Special Needs

1135 Tremont Street, Suite 420
Boston, MA 02120
617-236-7210; 800-331-0688 (in MA)
617-572-2094 (fax)
Web: http://www.fcsn.org/
  The Parent Training and Information Center for Massachusetts that has resources and information available for families who have a child with a disability.

Genetic Alliance

4301 Connecticut Avenue, NW, #404
Washington, DC 20008-2304
202-966-5557; 202-966-8553 (fax)

800-336-GENE (helpline only)
Web: http://medhlp.netusa.net/agsg/agsg1164.htm/
Formerly The Alliance of Genetic Support Groups, Inc., this is a national coalition for people who have or who are at risk for genetic conditions; large number of links to sites concerning disabilities.

Internal Revenue Service (IRS)
"Disability" and "Information for Persons with Disabilities"
800-829-3676
Web: http://www.irs.ustreas.gov/search/
Describes forms that can be used for tax assistance and tax deductions by persons with disabilities.

Learning Disabilities Association of America (LDA)
4156 Library Road
Pittsburgh, PA 15234-1349
412-341-1515; 412-344-0224 (fax)
Web: http://www.ldanatl.org/
The LDA has over 600 local chapter dedicated to supporting individuals with learning disabilities. The national office offers a wide range of publications and resources.

Learning Disabilities Association of Canada
323 Chapel Street, Suite 200
Ottawa, Ontario K1N 7Z2 Canada
613-238-5721; 613-235-5391 (fax)
Web: http://educ.queensu.ca/~lda
This nonprofit organization supports local chapters, provides information, and advocates for people with learning disabilities in Canada.

March of Dimes Birth Defects Foundation
1275 Mamaroneck Avenue
White Plains, NY 10605
888-MODIMES (663-4637)
Web: http://www.modimes.org/
Their mission is to improve the health of babies by reducing birth defects, reducing infant mortality, reducing the number of low birth weight babies, and increasing the number of women who get prenatal care.

National Association of Protection and Advocacy Systems
900 Second Street, NE, Suite 211
Washington, DC 20002
202-408-9514; 202-408-9520 (fax)
Web: http://www.protectionandadvocacy.com/
 An advocacy office that provides help on such issues as IDEA disputes and discrimination complaints; provides locations of local P&A offices.

National Center for Latinos with Disabilities
1921 South Blue Island Avenue
Chicago, IL 60608
800-532-3393; 312-666-3393; 312-666-1787 (fax)
Web: http://homepage.interaccess.com/~ncld/
 Organization focuses on the empowerment of Latinos with disabilities and their families through advocacy, training, and information.

National Council on Independent Living
1916 Wilson Blvd., Suite 209
Arlington, VA 22201
703-525-3406; 703-525-3409 (fax)
Web: http://www.paraquad.org/networks.html
 A source of information on affordable and accessible housing for people with disabilities.

National Early Childhood Technical Assistance System (NECTAS)
137 East Franklin Street, Suite 500
Chapel Hill, NC 27514-3628
919-966-8426; 919-966-7463 (fax)
Web: http://www.nectas.unc.edu/
 Provides technical assistance to states on a variety of issues related to disability, has publications and lots of links to other sites and information.

National Easter Seal Society
230 W. Monroe, Suite 1800
Chicago, IL 60606
800-221-6827; 312-726-1494 (fax)
Web: http://www.easter-seals.org/

The National Easter Seal Society helps families of children with disabilities through local affiliates with services such as screenings, therapies, public education, and advocacy.

National Information Center for Children and Youth with Disabilities (NICHCY)
P.O. Box 1492
Washington, DC 20013-1492
800-695-0285; 202-884-8200 (voice/TDD)
Web: http://www.nichcy.org/
The national information and referral center that provides information on disabilities and related issues for families, educators, and other professionals. NICHCY offers personal responses to specific questions, publications (many can be taken right off the internet), referrals to other organizations, information searches of their databases and library, and some materials are also available in Spanish. Especially useful are NICHCY's "State Sheets," which list a wide variety of resources and support as well as organizations in each state.

National Rehabilitation Information Center (NARIC)
1010 Wayne Avenue, Suite 800
Silver Spring, MD 20910
800-346-2742; 301-562-2400; 301-562-2401 (fax)
Web: http://www.naric.com/
A collection of federally funded research projects related to disability and rehabilitation available online or hard copy, and they offer personal responses to questions.

National Transition Alliance for Youth with Disabilities (NTA)
Transition Research Institute
University of Illinois
113 Children's Research Center
51 Gerty Drive
Champaign, IL 61820
217-333-2325
Web: http://www.dssc.org/nta/html/index_2.htm
Works to improve the transition process and results of youth with disabilities; individual state information is provided.

Office of the Americans with Disabilities Act
Civil Rights Division
U.S. Dept. of Justice
Disability Rights Section
P.O. Box 66738
Washington, DC 20035-6738
202-307-1198
ADA Information Line: 800-514-0301
Web: http://www.usdoj.gov/crt/ada/publicat.htm
    The federal agency that distributes information and answers questions from the public about the Americans with Disabilities Act. Information can be obtained on the web site, sent by fax, or by U.S. mail.

PACER Center
4826 Chicago Avenue South
Minneapolis, MN 55417-1098
612 -827-2966; 612-827-7770 (TTY); 800-53-PACER (In MN)
Web: http://www.pacer.org/
    An organization that offers publications, training, and technical assistance to improve the lives of children and youths with disabilities both regionally and nationally.

Senate Document Room
Hart Building
Washington, DC 20515
202-228-2815 (fax)
    Obtain a copy of any federal bill or law, including IDEA or the ADA, by contacting this office. Requests must be submitted by fax, by mail, or in person (but not by phone).

Sibling Information Network
University of Connecticut
A.J. Pappanikou Center
249 Glenbrook Road, U-64
Storrs, CT 06269-2064
203-344-7500
Web: http://www.parentsoup.com/library/organizations/bdfa009.html
or http://medhlp.netusa.net/agsg/agsg1164.htm
    This organization for siblings of people with disabilities publishes a quarterly newsletter with information on resources and family issues.

Sibling Support Project
Children's Hospital and Medical Center
PO Box 5371, CL-09
Seattle, WA 98105
206-368-4911; 206-368-4816 (fax)
Web: http://www.seattlechildrens.org/departmt/sibsupp/default.htm
A national program dedicated to the brothers and sisters of people
with disabilities; they offer peer workshops for siblings of children
with disabilities, publications, and access to local groups.

Special Olympics
1325 G Street, NW, Suite 500
Washington, DC 20005
202-628-3630; 202-824-0200 (fax)
Web: http://www.specialolympics.org/
A nonprofit organization of sports competition for people with
disabilities; information on sites worldwide can be found here.

TASH
29 W. Susquehanna Avenue, Suite 210
Baltimore, MD 21204
410-828-8274; 410-828-6706 (fax)
Web: http://www.tash.org/
TASH is an international organization that advocates for the inclusion of people with disabilities in all aspects of life; publishes a
journal and a newsletter.

Technical Assistance Alliance for Parent Projects
Alliance Coordinating Office:
PACER Center
4826 Chicago Avenue South
Minneapolis, MN 55417-1098
888-248-0822; 612-827-2966; 612-827-3065 (fax)
Web: http://www.taalliance.org/
Provides technical assistance for establishing, developing, and
coordinating parent training and information programs.

United Cerebral Palsy Associations
1660 L St., NW, Suite 700

Washington, DC 20036
800-872-5827; 202-776-0414 (fax)
Web: http://www.ucpa.org/
    A national organization that works for the inclusion of people with disabilities. Publishes a bimonthly newsletter called *Washington Watch* that reports on legislation and court rulings that affect people with disabilities. The site also has a large resource base.

:: Sources of Equipment & Supplies

This section provides only a representative sampling of the many companies in the United States and Canada that offer adaptive equipment, toys, and clothing. To locate additional sources, check *The Exceptional Parent Magazine,* which includes advertisements for all kinds of special toys, equipment, and educational products.

Abilitations
Sportime International
1 Sportime Way
Atlanta, GA 30340
800-850-8602; 800-845-1535 (fax)
Web: http://www2.abilitations.com/index.shtml/
    Catalog contains equipment for movement, positioning, sensorimotor activities, exercise, and aquatics.

ABLEDATA
Macro International
8401 Colesville Road, Suite 200
Silver Spring, MD 20910
800-227-0216; 301-608-8958 (fax)
Web: http://www.abledata.com/
    ABLEDATA is a database containing information on assistive technology and rehabilitation equipment. Search the database free of charge from the web site or pay a small fee to have a search performed. There are also low-cost information packets on selected subjects.

Dragonfly Toy Company
291 Yale Avenue
Winnipeg, Manitoba R3M 0L4 Canada

800-308-2208; 204-453-2320 (fax)
Web: http://www.dftoys.com/
    Dragonfly specializes in toys, books, and other products for children with disabilities.

Enabling Devices
Toys for Special Children
385 Warburton Avenue
Hastings, NY 10706
800-832-8697; 914-478-7030 (fax)
Web: http://www.enablingdevices.com/
    Offers a wide variety of learning and assistive devices for people with disabilities, including adaptive toys and augmentative communication devices.

Flaghouse, Inc.
601 Flaghouse Drive
Hasbrouck Heights, NJ 07604-3116
800-793-7900; 800-793-7922 (fax)
Web: http://www.flaghouse.com/
    Offers four catalogues: physical education, special populations, furniture, and rehabilitation.

Flaghouse Canada, Inc.
235 Yorkland Blvd., Suite 300
North York, Ontario M2J 4Y8
800-265-6900; 800-265-6922 (fax)
    See description above.

HDIS (Home Delivery Incontinent Supplies Co.)
9385 Dielman Industrial Drive
St. Louis, MO 63132
800-269-4663; 314-997-0047 (fax)
Web: http://www.coast-resources.com/
    HDIS carries a full line of incontinence products that will fit children of any size.

Kapable Kids
P.O. Box 250

Bohemia, NY 11716
800-356-1564; 516-563-7179 (fax)
Web: http://www.kapablekids.com/
Catalog with learning materials and products for inclusion, early intervention, and special needs.

Kaplan

P.O. Box 609
1310 Lewisville-Clemmons Road
Lewisville, NC 27023-0609
800-334-2014; 800-452-7526 (fax)
Web: http://www.kaplanco.com/
Sells most educational materials a teacher would need; has four catalogues, one of which is for exceptional children and it contains products for developing communication and gross and fine motor skills.

North Coast Medical

18305 Sutter Blvd.
Morgan Hill, CA 95037-2845
800-235-7054; 877-213-9300 (fax)
Web: http://www.ncmedical.com
Sells adaptive equipment to make everyday tasks easier.

Pocket Full of Therapy

P.O. Box 174
Morganville, NJ 07751
800-PFOT-124; 732-441-0404 (fax)
Web: http://pfot.com/
This site offers a variety of therapy products and toys for developing the areas that OTs usually work on, such as fine motor, motor planning, and tactile/proprioception.

■■ Websites

The Fragile X Listserv

FRAXA started the listserv in 1995 to serve the entire fragile X community. The listserv provides an opportunity to exchange information with people from around the world about fragile X syndrome. Emory University sponsors the listserv. *How to join:* Send e-mail to

LISTSERV@LISTSERV.CC.EMORY.EDU with the following command in the body of your e-mail message: SUBSCRIBE FRAGILEX-L; *How to leave (unsubscribe):* Send e-mail to: LISTSERV@LISTSERV.CC.EMORY.EDU with the following command in the body of your e-mail message: SIGNOFF FRAGILEX-L; *Helpful Note:* This is an active discussion group, and if you find that too many messages are filling your inbox, you can choose the DIGEST option. The DIGEST sends you one batch message each day, with all individual listserv messages included. When you subscribe, you will receive an e-mail message with instructions on how to get the DIGEST.

Americans with Disabilities Act Document Center
Web: http://janweb.icdi.wvu.edu/kinder/index.htm
Provides online full-text copies of ADA Statute, Regulations, ADAAG (Americans with Disabilities Act Accessibility Guidelines), Federally Reviewed Tech Sheets, and Other Assistance Documents

The Beach Center on Families and Disability of Kansas
Web: http://www.lsi.ukans.edu/beach/
Online source of information about various disability issues.

BehaveNet®, Inc.
Web: http://www.behavenet.com/
Provides information and links to resources on a wide range of behavioral conditions and issues.

Children's Software Review
Web: http://www.childrenssoftware.com/
Publishes a magazine and offers online reviews of children's software; comprehensive catalogue and publisher directories.

The Disability Resource
Web: http://www.disabilityresource.com/
Online bookstore specializing in books and videos on disabilities; over 300 titles.

Disability Resources, Inc.
Web: http://www.disabilityresources.org
Provides extensive list and database of online information sources.

Disability Training
Web: http://www.disabilitytraining.org/
Information on training and education to help build supportive communities in Iowa; the information is also available to people who do not live in Iowa.

Educational On-Line Resource Organizations Directory (EROD)
Department of Education
Web: http://www.ed.gov/EdRes/index.html
Contains organizations that provide information and assistance on a broad range of education-related topics.

Educational Resources Information Center (ERIC)
Web: http://www.accesseric.org/resources/pocket/what.html
ERIC is a database with nearly 1 million abstracts of documents and journal articles on education research and practice. You can search the database online and you call for assistance for searches.

Exceptional Parent Magazine
Web: http://www.eparent.com/
The magazine's online resource that has information and ideas for families of children with disabilities.

Family & Advocates Partnership for Education
Web: http://www.fape.org/
Provides copies of IDEA and regulations.

The Family Village
Web: http://familyvillage.wisc.edu/
Resources and information for persons with disabilities and their families.

A Heartbreaking Choice Website
Web: http://erichad.com/ahc/
This site offers support to parents who choose to "interrupt" their pregnancies after a prenatal diagnosis.

Kid Info
Web: http://www.kidinfo.com/

Site designed to be used by kids, teachers, and parents; has homework help, reference resources, online stories and games, teacher resources, and parenting tips.

Kidsclick!
Web: http://sunsite.berkeley.edu/kidsclick/
Touted as a web search site for kids, it is also very useful for parents.

Med Help International
Web: http://medhlp.netusa.net/
Contains information about various disabilities including fragile X syndrome.

National Association of Protection and Advocacy Systems
Web: http://www.protectionandadvocacy.com/
Provides protection of the rights of persons with disabilities; an organization is based in each state.

National Health Information Center
Web: http://nhic-nt.health.org/
Offers a database of organizations and reports of health information that can be searched online.

National Parent to Parent Support and Information System
Web: http://www.nppsis.org/
Links families who have children with disabilities nationwide, provides parents with access to health care information, and can help parents find their local Parent to Parent Organization.

Parents Magazine
Web: http://www.parents.com/
Parents Magazine online resource of general parenting information.

Special Child
Web: http://www.specialchild.com
An online magazine for parents of children with disabilities.

Special Education Resources on the Internet (SERI)
Web: http://www.hood.edu/seri/serihome.htm

Information that may be useful to those in special education can be accessed at this site.

Wrightslaw
Web: http://www.wrightslaw.com/
Has the latest information on advocacy for children with disabilities and access to special education law.

Yahooligans!
Web: http://www.yahooligans.com/
A directory of internet sites for children; also has parents' and teachers' guides.

▪▪ Educational Materials & Software

The following companies publish, sell, or review educational materials or software. Only partial listings of products are included. See the website or request a catalog for a complete listing of the latest products.

Addison-Wesley Longman
One Jacob Way
Reading, MA 01867-3999
781-944-3700; 781-944-9338 (fax)
Web: http://www.awl.com/
Educational publisher of books and learning programs in the major disciplines at all grade levels.

American Guidance Service
4201 Woodland Road
Circle Pines, MN 55014
800-328-2560; 612-786-4343; 800-471-8457 (fax); 612-786-9077 (fax)
Web: http://www.agsnet.com/
Publishes assessments, textbooks, and other educational materials for students with a range of abilities; has curriculum on reading, writing, math, science, and early learning.

Apple Peelings
4298 Shirley Lane
Salt Lake City, UT 84124
800-284-5497; 801-277-4098; 801-277-2420 (fax)

Web: http://www.applepeelings.com/
Materials for the classroom for reading, writing, math, vocabulary, and social studies.

Attainment Company
P.O. Box 930160
Verona, WI 53593-0160
800-327-4269
Web: http://www.attainmentcompany.com/
Software includes: Math Time, Basic Coins, Dollars and Cents, Ready, Set, Read!, Looking For Words, IEP Success Program, Working It Out Together, and Nobody's Perfect. Life Skill programs include: Personal Success, Keeping House, Looking Good, Shopping Smart, Plan Your Day, and Select A Meal. Video: Disability Issues series.

Compu-Teach
PMB 137
16541 Redmond Way, Suite C
Redmond WA 98052
800-448-3224; 425-885-0517; 425-883-9169 (fax)
Web: http://www.compu-teach.com/
Software includes: See The USA, Math & Reading Bonus Pack, Joshua's Reading Machine, and Once Upon A Time series.

Don Johnston Incorporated
26799 W. Commerce Drive
Volo, IL 60073
800-999-4660
Web: http://www.donjohnston.com/
Software includes: Programs for writing, reading, word study, math, creative expression, and for single switch users. Hardware: Includes switches, overlays, boards, screens, and mouse controls.

Edmark Corporation
P.O. Box 97021
Redmond, WA 98073-9721
800-691-2986; 425-556-8430 (fax)
Web: http://www.edmark.com/
Software: Mighty Math Series, Thinkin' Things Series, Words Around Me (reading), Early Learning House Series that includes Millie's

Math House, Bailey's Book House, Sammy's Science House, Trudy's Time and Place House. Hardware: Touch Window, Visual Voice Tools, TouchFree Switch.

Educational Design
800-221-9372; 212-675-6922 (fax)
Web: http://www.educationaldesign.com/
Publishes teaching materials for all ages and abilities.

Educational Resources
Customer Support
1550 Executive Drive
P. O. Box 1900
Elgin, IL 60193-1900
(800) 860-7004
Web: http://www.edresources.com/
Comprehensive software list and ordering capability; also has early childhood classroom materials.

Golden Books
50 Commerce Drive
Trumbull, CT 06611
800-543-0954; 800-825-8235 (fax)
Web: http://www.goldenbooks.com/
In additional to their traditional read-aloud books, there is the *Road to Reading*, the *Road to Writing*, and *Step Ahead Books*.

Humongous Entertainment
P.O. Box 3383
Redmond, WA 98052
800-499-8386; 425-424-3975 (fax)
Web: http://www.humongous.com/
Software includes: Big Thinkers Kindergarten and First Grade, Freddi Fish ™, Blue's Clues, Let's Explore the Airport, Let's Explore the Farm, and Let's Explore the Jungle.

Innovative Learning Concepts
6760 Corporate Drive
Colorado Springs, CO 80919
888-TOUCHMATH (888-868-2462); 719-593-2446 (fax)

Web: http://www.touchmath.com
Multi-sensory approach to learning math skills.

IntelliTools
55 Leveroni Court, Suite 9
Novato, CA 94949
800-899-6687; 415-382-5959; 415-382-5950 (fax)
Web: http://www.intellitools.com/
    Software Includes: Exploring Patterns, Exploring Patterns Activity Book , MathPad, Animal Habitats, Hungry Shark and Friends, Hands-On Concepts Story Kits, Number Concepts 1. Programs for switch users: SwitchIt! Suite, SwitchIt! Arcade Adventure, SwitchIt! Early Math with Spider and Friends. Hardware: Access Pac, IntelliKeys, Overlay Maker, IntelliTalk, IntelliPics, ClickIt!, Keyguards.

Knowledge Adventure
800-242-4546
Web: http://www.knowledgeadventure.com/
    Software: Series that include Jump Start, Blaster Learning, Plan Zone!, Fun and Learning Games, and Language Arts.

Lakeshore Learning Materials
800-421-5354; 310-537-8600; 310-537-5403 (fax)
Web: http://www.lakeshorelearning.com/
    Educational materials in three catalogues: Infant to kindergarten, grades 1-2-3, middle to high school; only some of the materials in the catalogue are shown on the web site. Can purchase online, or store locations are shown.

The Learning Company (TLC)
Web: http://www.learningcompany.com/
    Reviews software from the following TLC companies: Broderbund, Creative Wonders, Compton's TLC, Mindscape, and SkillsBank. The products are sold through Mattel Interactive Family.

Learning Resources
380 N. Fairway Drive
Vernon Hills, IL 60061
800-333-8281; 847-573-8425 (fax)
Web: http://www.learningresources.com/

Variety of educational materials for phonics and language, math, science, and early learning are described; there is a catalogue.

Logo Reading System
Marcia Braden, Ph.D.
100 E. St. Vrain #200
Colorado Springs, CO 80906
719-633-3773
Method of teaching reading that uses logos seen on a regular basis.

Mattel Interactive Family
800-395-0277 (order); 800-358-9144 (customer service)
Web: http://www.shopmattel.com/
Software: Arthur, Carmen Sandiego, Clue Finders™, Dr. Seuss, Little Bear™, Madeline™, Reader Rabbit ®, Sesame Street ®. *See also* The Learning Company.

PEP—Parents, Educators, Publishers
Web: http://www.microweb.com/pepsite/Software/publishers.html
List of educational software publishers that provides direct links to their sites.

Prentice-Hall Direct
P.O. Box 11075
Des Moines, IA 50336
800-947-7700
Web: http://www.phdirect.com/
Online source of teacher resources: curriculum and classroom activities, from early childhood to high school, including special education; can also be used at home.

PRO-ED, Inc.
8700 Shoal Creek Blvd
Austin, TX 78757
800-897-3202; 512-451-3246; 512-451-8542 (fax)
Web: http://www.proedinc.com/
Publishes, produces, and sells books and materials on psychology; special education; and speech, language, and hearing for parents and professionals.

SRA/McGraw-Hill
A Division of the McGraw-Hill Companies
1221 Avenue of the Americas
New York, New York 10020
888-SRA-4543; 912-228-1982 (fax)
Web: http://www.sra4kids.com/teacher/reading/index.html
    Publishes educational curriculum for teachers in the major subjects for all grade levels and abilities.

Sunburst Communications
A Houghton Mifflin Company
101 Castleton Street
Pleasantville, NY 10570
800-321-7511 (software); 800-431-1934 (video); 914-747-3310; 914-747-4109 (fax)
Web: http://sunburstdirect.sunburst.com/
    Software includes: A to Zap!, Type to Learn™, Reading Who? Reading You!, Write On!™, Awesome Animated Monster Maker™, Safari Search, and Everything Weather.

Superkids Educational Software Review
Web: http://www.superkids.com/
    Reviews educational software and provides direct links to retailers who sell the product.

Walt Disney Computer Software
Web: http://www.disneystore.com/. Search for "CD/ROM"
    Software for many of the Disney characters.

CONTRIBUTORS

Marcia L. Braden, Ph.D., is a licensed psychologist and special education consultant practicing in Colorado Springs, Colorado. She received her Ph.D. in Educational Psychology after completing her Dissertation Publication, *A Screening Instrument for FRA-X Males* in 1991. Through the years she has worked with hundreds of children and adolescents with fragile X syndrome. Dr. Braden has published numerous articles related to educational and behavioral management strategies. She is a contributing author to the book, *Fragile X Syndrome: Diagnosis, Treatment, and Research* (Johns Hopkins University Press, 1996), and the author of *Fragile: Handle With Care Understanding Fragile X Syndrome* (1996). Dr. Braden created the Logo Reading System, and she has produced several videotapes related to issues associated with fragile X syndrome. She has lectured nationally and internationally about fragile X syndrome, autism, and related disabilities.

Mary Jane Clark, is the mother of a daughter, Elizabeth, and son, David, whose diagnosis of fragile X syndrome in 1989, led to the broadcast of the first, hour-long, network television news program about the syndrome. Ms. Clark, a writer and producer at CBS News in New York, is also the author of several, well-received and reviewed media-thrillers, including *Do You Want To Know A Secret?* (St. Martin's Press, 1998) in which a character with fragile X syndrome holds the key to solving the story's mystery. Published in English, French, German, Dutch, and Japanese, Clark hopes that, through her writing, more people around the world will learn about fragile X syndrome. She serves on the Board of Directors of The FRAXA Research Foundation, which funds critical research into fragile X syndrome.

Amy Cronister, M.S., is a board certified genetic counselor and the Manager of Clinical Services for Genzyme Genetics in Scottsdale, Arizona. Ms. Cronister first became interested in fragile X syndrome when she worked as a cytogenetic technologist in the early 1980s. Since that time, she has been actively involved with educating families and health care professionals about the condition. Under the directorship of Dr. Randi Hagerman, she coordinated a statewide community outreach program in Colorado designed to help identify and assist individuals with fragile X syndrome. She has served on the Board of Directors of the National Fragile X Foundation and as a member of the Foundation's International Clinical and Scientific Advisory Board. Ms. Cronister has lectured and published widely on the genetic counseling aspects of fragile X syndrome and is co-editor and contributor of the book, *Fragile X Syndrome: Diagnosis, Treatment and Research* (Johns Hopkins University Press, 1996).

Brenda Finucane, M.S., is the Director of Genetic services at Elwyn, Inc., a private, nonprofit organization near Philadelphia, Pennsylvania which provides a variety of residential and day services for people with developmental disabilities. Among its many clients are over 80 children and adults diagnosed with fragile X syndrome. Ms. Finucane is a member of the International Clinical and Scientific Advisory Board of the National Fragile X Foundation.

Dr. Randi Jenssen Hagerman, M.D., is Professor of Pediatrics at the University of Colorado Health Sciences Center. She is Co-Section Head of the Section of Developmental and Behavioral Pediatrics, and she is also the Director of the Fragile X Treatment and Research Center at the Child Development Unit at The Children's Hospital. Although she sees all children with developmental disabilities, she has spent over 20 years in clinical work and research into fragile X syndrome. She helped to establish the National Fragile X Foundation in 1984 and presently is on the Board of Directors of the foundation, and is also the Chairman of the Scientific and Clinical Advisory Committee for the National Fragile X Foundation. She lectures nationally and internationally regarding fragile X syndrome and has written three books on this subject.

James E. Kaplan and Ralph J. Moore, Jr., are both active in the area of the legal rights of children with disabilities. They are the co-authors of the "Legal Rights and Hurdles" chapters in Woodbine House's parents' guides to children with mental retardation, epilepsy, autism, Down syndrome, and cerebral palsy. Mr. Moore, a partner in the law firm of Shea & Gardner in Washington, DC, is the author *of Handbook on Estate Planning for Families of Developmentally Disabled Persons in Maryland, the District of Columbia, and Virginia* (Md. DD Council, 3rd edition, 1989). Mr. Kaplan is Of Counsel in the law firm of Jensen, Baird, Gardner & Henry in Portland, Maine.

Ave Lachiewicz, M.D., attended medical school at the University of Minnesota in Minneapolis. She completed a residency in pediatrics at Albert Einstein affiliated programs in New York City and a fellowship in Child Development at the Center for Development and Learning in Chapel Hill, North Carolina. She presently works at Duke University Medical Center in Durham, North Carolina. She runs clinics for children and adults with fragile X syndrome, attention-deficit/hyperactivity disorder, and developmental disabilities.

Penny L. Mirrett, Ph.D., is a researcher at the Frank Porter Graham Child Development Center, University of North Carolina-Chapel Hill. Prior to joining the ongoing studies in 1996 that are part of the *Carolina Fragile X Project,* Dr. Mirrett was involved in research, assessment, and intervention for children with fragile X syndrome and their families at Duke University Medical Center. Her primary research interests include early speech and language development, craniofacial disorders, genotype-phenotype correlations, and early detection and intervention for children with developmental disabilities.

David York Moore, MRCGP (UK), Family Physician, is a fifth generation family doctor. He qualified from the London Hospital Medical College in 1976. He has been a general practitioner in Barnstaple in the West of England since 1983. He is married with three children, the youngest of whom has fragile X syndrome. He has been on the committee of the Fragile X Society (UK), and was their Research Officer for two years.

Jamie Stephenson, is a staff writer on The New Hampshire Challenge, a statewide quarterly newspaper for families who have members with disabilities, and Director of the Fragile X Resource Center of Northern New England. She received her B.A. and M.A. from Boston University. She has served on the New Hampshire Family Support State Advisory Council, the New Hampshire Pre-School Task Force, the New Hampshire Interagency Coordinating Council, and the Board of Directors of the New Hampshire Congress of Teachers and Parents. She is a member of the New Hampshire Safe and Drug Free Schools Committee and the New England Regional Genetics Group Board of Directors where she serves as chairman of the Finance Committee. She is mother to four beautiful children, two of whom have fragile X syndrome.

INDEX

Antecedent-Behavior-
Consequence (ABC), 138,
139, 140, 292-94
Antibiotics, 95, 100, 128
Anticonvulsants, 104-105
Anti-discrimination laws, 325-29.
  See also Individuals with
  Disabilities Education Act
  (IDEA)
Antipsychotic medication, 111
Anxiety, 22, 38, 291
  cognition and, 214-15
  communication and, 219, 278
  depression and, 112
  environment and, 268-69
  testing and, 250
Appeal, legal, 320-21
Appearance, 8, 11-15
Appetite, 105, 108, 109
Apprehension, 36
Arc, The, 53, 114, 148, 167,
  286, 308, 354-55
Arch supports, 98
Articulation, 110, 218.
  See also Speech
Assessment. *See* Testing
Assistive technology, 223
Association for Community
  Living (ACL), 53, 114, 148,
  167, 286, 308, 354-55
Associative learning, 265
Astigmatism, 13
At-risk, 245, 314-15
Attention, 106, 200
Attention Deficit Hyperactivity
  Disorder (ADHD), 106-
  110, 136, 141, 214-15,
  232-33, 291
Attention span, 10, 17, 18, 22,
  109, 291
Attitude, 161-63
Attractiveness, 15
Audiological exam, 96

Auditory memory, 210
Auditory perception, 213-14
Auditory processing, 17, 18,
  19-20, 107, 213-14, 224
Augmentative communication,
  217, 279
Aunts, 57-59
Autism, 23, 130, 232-33
Avoidance behavior, 215
Babysitters, 148
Balance, 20, 163-65, 182-83,
  201-202, 228-29
Baselines, 295
Batelle Developmental
  Inventory, 215-16
Bathing, 128-29
Bayley Scales of Infant
  Development, 215-16
Baylor Medical School, 28
Bedtime, 129
Bed wetting, 109
Behavior, 20-24, 105-106, 232-
  34, 290-98. *See also* Autism
  ADHD, 106-111
  aggression, 105, 111-12, 291
  agitation, 111
  anxiety, 112
  avoidance, 215
  crying, 134-35
  escape, 215, 233-34
  hypervigilance, 23
  obsessive-compulsive, 111,
    112
  redirecting, 237-38
  shyness, 291
  tantrums, 21, 190-91, 233,
    237-38
Behavioral characteristics, 7.
  See also Behavior
Behavioral management, 107,
  137-41, 290-98
Bell, 28
Beneficiaries, 342

Benefits, government, 333-39.
See also Americans with
Disabilities Act (ADA);
Individuals with Disabili-
ties Education Act (IDEA)
Benzodiazepines, 112
Betrayal, 37
Birth to three, 244-46
"Bite" problems, 13
Blood pressure, 108, 111
Blood tests, 77-78
Blurred vision, 101
Bones, 12
Boredom, 233
Bowel movements, 97, 126-27,
231-32
Bracing, 99
Brain, 14
Brazelton, T. Berry, 227-28
Breaks, 53-55, 145-49
Budget, 173
Busing, 132
Bypass strategies, 214
Caffeine, 215
Calming techniques, 105-106
Carbamazepine, 105, 111
Cardiac arrhythmias, 110
Cardiologist, 100
Carlson, Richard, 174
Carriers, 7, 9, 17, 28, 58-59,
75-77
female, 72, 74
genetic counseling and, 82
male, 73
testing, 77-78
Case manager, 116-17
Case management, 281
Catapres™, 109-110
Catheter, 80
Causes, 8-9
Cells, 7-8, 68-69, 80
Cerebellum, 19
Cervix, 80

Change in routine, 122-23
Characteristics, 10-11, 68
cognitive, 15-18
communication, 24
physical, 8, 11-15, 19-20, 95
Checklist, 25-26
Chest, 15
Children's Health Insurance
Program (CHIP), 339
Children and Adults with
Attention Deficit/
Hyperactivity Disorder
(C.H.A.D.D.), 359
Children with Special Health
Care Needs Program
(HCP), 338-39
Child Study Teams, 315-16
Chin, 14
Choices, 123, 124, 167-68,
230-31
Chores, 161, 167-68
Chorionic Villus Sampling, 79-80
Chromosomes, 7-10, 69
Chromosome testing, 77
Classroom size, 268, 276
Cleft palate, 13, 98
Clonidine, 109-110, 111
Closure, 264
Clothes, 230
Club foot, 14
Cluttering, 222
Cognition, 7-9, 15-18, 252
development and, 200-201,
205, 209-217
genetics and, 71-76
testing, 211-12, 215-16,
234-35, 263, 282
College, 287
Communication, 16-24, 125,
252, 334
accommodations and, 270,
284-85
behavior and, 134-39, 233-34

ABOUT THE EDITOR

Jayne Dixon Weber is the mother of two children: a daughter, Cassie, 9, and a son, Ian, 12, who was diagnosed with fragile X syndrome 10 years ago. Ms. Weber authored the book *Transitioning "Special" Children Into Elementary School* (1994), in which she describes her experience of transitioning Ian into a regular education kindergarten class. For the last five years she has been a Parent Resource Consultant at the University of Colorado-Boulder. In that role she travels throughout the state of Colorado and gives workshops on improving the transition process for children from birth through the early elementary years. She is an advocate in her community and continually strives to improve services for all children who have disabilities.